Computer and Information Science

Computer and Information Science

**Edited by
Fiona Hobbs**

www.willfordpress.com

Published by Willford Press,
118-35 Queens Blvd., Suite 400,
Forest Hills, NY 11375, USA

ISBN: 978-1-68285-377-1

Cataloging-in-Publication Data

Computer and information science / edited by Fiona Hobbs.
   p. cm.
Includes bibliographical references and index.
ISBN 978-1-68285-377-1
1. Computer science. 2. Information science. 3. Information technology. I. Hobbs, Fiona.
QA76 .C66 2017
004--dc23

For information on all Willford Press publications
visit our website at www.willfordpress.com

Printed in the United States of America.

Contents

Preface...VII

Chapter 1   **Cross-Entropy-Based Energy-Efficient Radio Resource Management in HetNets with Coordinated Multiple Points**..................................1
Jia Yu, Shinsuke Konaka, Masatake Akutagawa and Qinyu Zhang

Chapter 2   **An Approach to the Classification of Cutting Vibration on Machine Tools**...18
Jeng-Fung Chen, Shih-Kuei Lo and Quang Hung Do

Chapter 3   **Ultra-Reliable Link Adaptation for Downlink MISO Transmission in 5G Cellular Networks** 28
Udesh Oruthota, Furqan Ahmed and Olav Tirkkonen

Chapter 4   **Closed-Loop Feedback Computation Model of Dynamical Reputation Based on the Local Trust Evaluation in Business-to-Consumer E-Commerce**...46
Bo Tian, Jingti Han and Kecheng Liu

Chapter 5   **Geospatially Constrained Workflow Modeling and Implementation**......................67
Feng Zhang and Yuetong Xu

Chapter 6   **A Specification-Based IDS for Detecting Attacks on RPL-Based Network Topology**..79
Anhtuan Le, Jonathan Loo, Kok Keong Chai and Mahdi Aiash

Chapter 7   **On-Body Smartphone Localization with an Accelerometer**.......................98
Kaori Fujinami

Chapter 8   **Nearest Neighbor Search in the Metric Space of a Complex Network for Community Detection**..121
Suman Saha and Satya P. Ghrera

Chapter 9   **Efficient Dynamic Integrity Verification for Big Data Supporting users Revocability**...137
Xinpeng Zhang, Chunxiang Xu, Xiaojun Zhang, Taizong Gu, Zhi Geng and Guoping Liu

Chapter 10   **Feature Engineering for Recognizing Adverse Drug Reactions from Twitter Posts**...153
Hong-Jie Dai, Musa Touray, Jitendra Jonnagaddala and Shabbir Syed-Abdul

Chapter 11   **A Comparative Study on Weighted Central Moment and its Application in 2D Shape Retrieval**..173
Xin Shu, Qianni Zhang, Jinlong Shi and Yunsong Qi

Chapter 12   **A Framework for Measuring Security as a System Property in Cyberphysical Systems**..185
Janusz Zalewski, Ingrid A. Buckley, Bogdan Czejdo, Steven Drager, Andrew J. Kornecki and Nary Subramanian

Permissions

List of Contributors

Index

Preface

This book has been a concerted effort by a group of academicians, researchers and scientists, who have contributed their research works for the realization of the book. This book has materialized in the wake of emerging advancements and innovations in this field. Therefore, the need of the hour was to compile all the required researches and disseminate the knowledge to a broad spectrum of people comprising of students, researchers and specialists of the field.

This book on computer and information science deals with the use of high-speed computing technologies for the storage, retrieval and manipulation of information. Data engineers create and maintain conceptual data warehouses that can perform specific functions with the data stored by an organization. Functions for ensuring data quality are validation, sorting, summarization, aggregation, analysis and classification of computer data. This book elucidates the concepts and innovative models around prospective developments with respect to computer and information science. It presents researches and studies performed by experts across the globe. This book is an essential guide for both academicians and those who wish to pursue this discipline further.

At the end of the preface, I would like to thank the authors for their brilliant chapters and the publisher for guiding us all-through the making of the book till its final stage. Also, I would like to thank my family for providing the support and encouragement throughout my academic career and research projects.

Editor

Cross-Entropy-Based Energy-Efficient Radio Resource Management in HetNets with Coordinated Multiple Points

Jia Yu [1,2], Shinsuke Konaka [1], Masatake Akutagawa [1] and Qinyu Zhang [2,*]

[1]   Graduate School of Advanced Technology and Science, Tokushima University, Tokushima 770-8501, Japan; yujia_hitsz@hotmail.com (J.Y.); konaka@ee.tokushima-u.ac.jp (S.K.); makutaga@ee.tokushima-u.ac.jp (M.A.)
[2]   Communication Engineering Research Center (CERC), Shenzhen Graduate School, Harbin Institute of Technology, Shenzhen 518055, China
*   Correspondence: zqy@hit.edu.cn

Academic Editor: Willy Susilo

Abstract: Energy efficiency and spectrum efficiency are the most important issues for future mobile systems. Heterogeneous networks (HetNets) with coordinated multiple points (CoMP) are wildly approved as a promising solution to meet increasing demands of mobile data traffic and to reduce energy consumptions. However, hyper-dense deployments and complex coordination mechanisms introduce several challenges in radio resource management (RRM) of mobile communication systems. To address this issue, we present an RRM approach for CoMP-based HetNets, which aims to maximize weighted energy efficiency while guaranteeing the data rate of each transmission. The proposed RRM approach is based on a cross-entropy (CE) optimization method that is an effective and low-complexity heuristic algorithm. Furthermore, we also give the implementations of the proposed RRM approach in centralized and decentralized mode, respectively. At last, extensive simulations are conducted to validate the effectiveness of the proposed schemes.

Keywords: cross-entropy (CE) method; heterogeneous network (HetNet); coordinated multipoint (CoMP); energy efficiency (EE)

1. Introduction

Heterogeneous networks (HetNets) [1,2] are proposed in long-term evolution-advanced (LTE-A) systems by the 3rd Generation Partnership Project (3GPP) to not only meet the rapidly increasing demands of mobile data traffic, but also to reduce the huge energy consumptions caused by data transmissions. A HetNet is a hierarchical network where low-power access points (APs, also named small cell sites [3,4]) are included in a macro-cell, in order to provide highly qualified services. Typical small cell sites include pico, femto, relay and so forth. Femto [5] is mainly for indoor transmissions, while pico [6] is used outdoors in a crowded place, such as a university. Relay [7] is usually built in a remote area far from the macro-cell site (named the Evolved Node B, or eNodeB, in LTE-A HetNet) to extend the coverage of the macro-cell. Figure 1 presents a simple example of a HetNet.

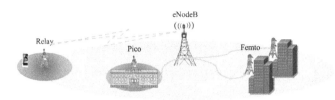

Figure 1. Illustration of a HetNet.

Although HetNets are widely considered as the main trend in the development of mobile communication systems [3], several challenges should be dealt with before implementation in the real world. One of the major challenges is severe intercell interference aggravated by the dense deployment, which crucially affects the performance of HetNets. As a promising measurement to deal with intercell interference, coordinated multiple point (CoMP) [8] techniques are considered to be helpful for HetNets. The basic idea of CoMP techniques is to coordinate coordinated neighboring cells, so that intercell interference can be reduced to a large extent. According to the different ways to cooperate, CoMP techniques are classified into two categories, coordinated scheduling/coordinated beamforming (CS/CB) and joint processing (JP) [9]. CS/CB CoMP makes neighboring cells jointly pre-code according to global channel state information (CSI) to avoid potential interference, while JP CoMP allows neighboring cells to jointly process signals intended for a specific user in the overlapping area. Joint transmission (JT) is a typical JP CoMP technique that requests of cooperating cells to transmit the same data packets to a user independently and simultaneously. In this paper, we take JT CoMP as an example to discuss the performance of CoMP-based HetNet, and the study can also be extended to other CoMP techniques.

To fulfill the requirements of the future mobile networks, CoMP-based HetNets need to provide qualified services as much as possible while maintaining acceptable energy consumption. According to report [10], energy consumption caused by information and communications technology (ICT) has contributed up to 5% of the world-wild power supply at present. To avoid the further increase of energy consumption, mobile networks are required to significantly improve the utility efficiency of power resources. Radio resource management (RRM), which adaptively allocates radio resources, such as frequency and power, according to CSIs, is beneficial for CoMP-based HetNets to enhance the energy efficiency.

In this paper, we focus on RRM in a CoMP-based HetNet for the purpose of improving the energy efficiency while guaranteeing high data rates, as well as user fairness. An optimization problem aiming at maximizing weighted energy efficiency is formulated, where the weights are employed for maintaining the fairness of users's data rates. Several crucial constraints in practice are taken into consideration in the formulated problem. Besides the limitation on total power at each transmitter, backhaul links, which connect small cells to the eNodeB for exchanging data and control information, are considered to have restricted capacity. Additionally, the lowest data rate of each transmission is defined, in order to guarantee the quality of transmissions and avoid wasting of energy. Since the formulated problem is unsolvable mixed integer programming (MIP), we separate the whole problem into a scheduling subproblem under the assumption of equal power allocation and a power allocation subproblem with known scheduling results. We first proposed a centralized scheduling algorithm based on cross-entropy (CE) and a corresponding power allocation algorithm. Since centralized algorithms involve numerous calculations, the time delay could be intolerable in a large-scale network. An alternative method to decrease the time delay is to conduct resource allocation in a decentralized way, where calculations are distributed to small cells. For this reason, we also propose modified algorithms that can be used in a decentralized mode.

The rest of this paper is organized as follows. In Section 2, we present the considered system model. Then, the mathematical formulation of the discussed problem is described in Section 3. Section 4 proposes a centralized strategy of resource allocation, which includes a CE-based scheduling algorithm and a power allocation algorithm. Section 5 modifies the proposed algorithms, so that they can be utilized in a decentralized system. Simulation results and relevant analysis are shown in Section 6. At last, we conclude our work in Section 7.

2. System Model

For the sake of simplicity, each independent transmitter, including the macro-cell site and micro-cell sites, is hereby designated as a transmit point (TP) in this paper. We consider a downlink system in a CoMP-based HetNet with M TPs and K user elements (UEs), as shown in Figure 2. N_T and N_R represent the number of antennas on each TP and each UE, respectively. A control unit (CU) is assumed to be located at the center of the network, which is responsible for managing data information, as well as collecting all CSI in this network. TPs are connected to the CU by backhaul links, whereby control information and data packets are delivered to TPs from the CU. Since JT CoMP is employed in our work, there are a large number of data packets that need to be transmitted via backhaul links.

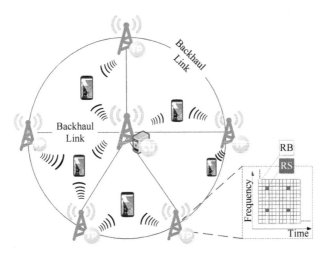

Figure 2. System model.

The unit of the radio resource in both time and frequency dimensions is referred to as the resource block (RB). As defined in the LTE standard, an RB consists of 12 consecutive subcarriers for a duration of a transmit time interval (TTI) [12]. In this paper, we assume all TPs share the same spectrum bandwidth, which is divided into N_{RB} RBs in total. Major notations used in this paper are listed in Table 1. Several other important assumptions are considered in our work: channel fading is considered to be quasi-static, so that channel coefficients remain constant per TTI; perfect CSI acknowledgment is assumed at both receivers and transmitters; TPs are synchronized in terms of time, frequency and phase, which is reasonable in the considered system thanks to backhaul connections.

Table 1. Major notations. TP, transmit point; UE, user element; RB, resource block.

Name	Meaning	Name	Meaning
N / K	number of TPs/UEs	$\mathcal{U}_m$	set of UEs that attaching to TP m
N_T / N_R	number of antennas at a TP/UE	R_k^n	data rate of UE k on RB n
$\mathcal{M}$	set of all of the TPs	$\bar{R}_k$	accumulated average data rate of UE k
$\mathcal{M}_k$	CoMP set of UE k	p_m^n	transmit power used at TP m on RB n
$\beta_{m,k}^n$	index implying the scheduling result	N_{RB}	number of RBs

2.1. CoMP Set Selection

Ideally, a UE can achieve the optimal data rate if all TPs cooperatively transmit to it. However, the corresponding power consumption and computational complexity are unaffordable. An alternative is to select a CoMP set for the UE according to channel conditions. TPs in the CoMP set can provide the UE a favorable data rate at a much lower cost.

A UE-specific selection of the CoMP set includes three steps:

1. TPs broadcast reference signals (RSs) periodically.
2. A UE hears the channels and measures them according to the strength of the received RSs. Based on the measurements and a given selection rule, the UE can decide its own CoMP set.
3. The UE acknowledges its decision to the CU.

Denote $\mathcal{M}_k$ as the CoMP set of UE k and $\mathcal{M}$ as the set including all TPs in the network. UE k decides its $\mathcal{M}_k$ following the rule below:

$$
\begin{cases}
m \in \mathcal{M}_k & m = \arg_{\mathcal{M}} RS \text{ (the strongest) or} \\
& RS \text{ (the strongest)} - RS \text{ (TP } m) \leq \Delta \\
m \notin \mathcal{M}_k & \text{otherwise}
\end{cases}
\tag{1}
$$

where RS indicates the strength of the reference signal and Δ is a threshold in dB. UE k distinguishes the strongest RS in the first place and adds the corresponding TP to the CoMP set $\mathcal{M}_k$. Other TPs will be added to $\mathcal{M}_k$ only if the strengths of their RSs are no less than (RS(the strongest) $- \Delta$) dB. As suggested in LTE releases, a rational Δ is in the range of $5 - 6$ dB [11].

In the case where $\mathcal{M}_k$ includes only 'the strongest TP', UE k is referred to as a non-CoMP UE in this paper, since no cooperation occurs during downlink transmissions towards it. On the contrary, UE k' is referred to as a CoMP UE if its CoMP set $\mathcal{M}_{k'}$ includes more than one TPs. A CoMP UE is possibly is located at an overlapping area of neighboring cells where intercell interference seriously damages transmissions. To combat interference, TPs in $\mathcal{M}_{k'}$ are asked to conduct JT CoMP transmissions to UE k' for strengthening transmit signals and reducing inter-cell interference.

2.2. Dynamic JT CoMP Transmission

JT CoMP allows TPs in UE's CoMP set to simultaneously transmit the desired data signal to it. Owing to the spatial separation of the transmit antennas, multiple versions of the desired signal will be received by the UE, which generates extra spatial diversity gain and strengthens the signal. According to information theory [18], the obtained data rate of a JT CoMP transmission to UE k on RB n is given as:

$$
R_k^n = b \log \left(1 + \frac{\sum\limits_{m \in \mathcal{M}_k} \left\| \mathbf{H}_{m,k}^2 \mathbf{w}_m^n \right\|^2 p_m^n}{\sum\limits_{m' \in \mathcal{M} \setminus \mathcal{M}_k} \left\| \mathbf{H}_{m',k}^n \mathbf{w}_{m'}^2 \right\|^2 p_{m'}^n + \sigma^2} \right)
\tag{2}
$$

where $\mathbf{H}_{m,k}^n$ is an $N_R \times N_T$ channel matrix between TP m and UE k on the n-th RB. $\mathcal{M} \setminus \mathcal{M}_k$ is the complementary of $\mathcal{M}_k$ in $\mathcal{M}$, which includes all of the interfering TPs. $\mathbf{w}_m^n$ is the precoding vector with dimensions of $N_T \times 1$, which maps data stream s_m^n onto the transmit antennas of TP m, and $(\mathbf{w}_m^n)^H \mathbf{w}_m^n = 1$, $E\|s_m^n\| = 1, \forall m, n$. p_m^n is the power used by TP m for transmitting on RB n, and $\mathbf{n}_k^n \sim \mathcal{CN}(\mathbf{0}, \sigma^2 \mathbf{I}_{N_R})$ is the corresponding complex Gaussian noise vector. b represents the bandwidth of an RB, which is standardized to be 180 kHz in LTE-A systems [12].

Equation (2) implies a static coordinated strategy where TPs in $\mathcal{M}_k$ are all required to serve UE k all of the time. However, static strategies are not always optimal due to the time variation of wireless channels. To further improve the network performance, we use a dynamic JT CoMP strategy where a subset of each $\mathcal{M}_k$ rather than $\mathcal{M}_k$ is adaptively determined to perform JT CoMP transmission. Define a scheduling index $\beta_{m,k}^n \in \{0, 1\}$ to indicate scheduling results, where $\beta_{m,k}^n = 1$ means that TP

m is chosen to transmit to UE k on the n-th RB. Then, the data rate of a dynamic JT transmission can be given as:

$$R_k^n = b \log \left(1 + \frac{\sum\limits_{m=1}^{M} \beta_{m,k}^n \left\| \mathbf{H}_{m,k}^2 \mathbf{w}_m^n \right\|^2 p_m^n}{\sum\limits_{m'=1}^{M} \left(1 - \beta_{m',k}^n\right) \left\| \mathbf{H}_{m',k}^n \mathbf{w}_{m'}^2 \right\|^2 p_{m'}^n + \sigma^2} \right) \tag{3}$$

where $\sum_{m=1}^{M} \beta_{m,k}^n \geq 1$.

3. Problem Formulation

In this work, we consider a practical RRM problem in terms of both spectrum and power in a CoMP-based HetNet modeled in the last section. To improve the synthesis performance, the objective involves data rates, power consumption and fairness among UEs at the same time.

The optimal data rate of the network can be achieved if resources are allocated to UEs with better channel conditions, regardless of those in "poor" condition. A side-effect of this scheme is unfavorable fairness of UEs' data rates. In order to enhance the fairness, we introduce the concept of proportional fairness into the objective of the RRM problem. As in [13], we weighted UE's data rate by its average data rate determined by:

$$\bar{R}_k = \alpha \bar{R}_k^{\text{before}} + (1 - \alpha) R_k \tag{4}$$

where $0 < \alpha < 1$ is the forgetting factor. The introduced weights bring UEs with worse channel conditions more of a possibility to occupy resources and, therefore, increase the UEs' data rates. The fairness of UEs' data rates in the network will be improved in this way. To quantify the degree of this fairness, [14] introduces a fairness factor, defined as:

$$F = \left(\sum_{k=1}^{K} R_k \right)^2 \bigg/ K \sum_{k=1}^{K} R_k^2 . \tag{5}$$

Additionally, for the purpose of conserving energy, energy efficiency should be thoughtfully considered. The energy efficiency is defined by the ratio of the obtained data rate to the total power consumed correspondingly. Combining with proportional fairness principle, the objective of the RRM problem is formulated as,

$$\max_{\beta_{m,k}^n, p_m^n} \sum_{k=1}^{K} \sum_{n=1}^{N_{\text{RB}}} \frac{R_k^n}{\bar{R}_k} \bigg/ \sum_{m=1}^{M} \sum_{n=1}^{N_{\text{RB}}} \sum_{k=1}^{K} \beta_{m,k}^n p_m^n \tag{6}$$

Equation (6) can be considered to maximize the weighted energy efficiency of the network.

In a practical network, system performance is restricted by several factors. In addition to limited transmit power at each TP, the finite capacity of backhaul links defines the upper limit of throughput achieved by a TP during a TTI. Furthermore, to guarantee the quality of transmissions, we impose a threshold to the data rate of each transmission. In summary, the RRM problem of the considered system can be formulated as:

$$\max_{\beta_{m,k}^n, p_m^n} \sum_{k=1}^{K} \sum_{n=1}^{N_{RB}} \frac{R_k^n}{\bar{R}_k} \Big/ \sum_{m=1}^{M} \sum_{n=1}^{N_{RB}} \sum_{k=1}^{K} \beta_{m,k}^n p_m^n$$

$$\text{s.t. C1: } 0 \leq p_m^n \leq S, \forall m, n$$

$$\text{C2: } \beta_{m,k}^n \in \{0, 1\}, \sum_{k=1}^{K} \beta_{m,k}^n \leq 1, \ \forall m, n, k \tag{7}$$

$$\text{C3: } \sum_{n=1}^{N_{RB}} \sum_{k=1}^{K} \beta_{m,k}^n R_k^n \leq C_m, \forall m$$

$$\text{C4: } R_k^n \geq R_{\text{thres}}, \forall k, n$$

In Equation (7), C1 shows the power constraint at each transmission where S is the largest transmit power allowed by the system; C2 ensures each index $\beta_{m,k}^n$ to be a bit number, so that a TP can serve no more than one UE on each RB; C3 demonstrates the constrained throughput of a TP caused by the limited capacity of backhaul connections to the CU, where C_m represents the capacity of the backhaul link connecting TP m and the CU; and C4 guarantees the data rate of each ongoing transmission, where R_{thres} is the given threshold of the data rate.

4. Centralized Algorithm

Since the problem in Equation (7) is NP-hard, it is unpractical to achieve the optimal solution. An alternative method is to consider the problem as a combination of a scheduling problem under the consumption of equal power allocation and a power allocation problem with a given scheduling result. In this way, an approximated solution of the problem can be obtained in polynomial time.

In the rest of this section, we propose a heuristic algorithm based on CE for RB scheduling with equal transmit power at the first place. Then, a Karush-Kuhn-Tucker-method to solve the power allocation problem is presented. The algorithm involving both RB scheduling and power allocation proposed in this section is centralized, which means that the resource allocation is operated at the CU with global CSI. The centralized algorithm is capable of achieving a favorable system performance, but it requires significant computational effort of the CU. In the next section, we also propose a decentralized algorithm of resource allocation with lower complexity and delay of computation, which leads to decreased performance unavoidably.

4.1. CE-Based Scheduling Algorithm

The objective of the considered RB scheduling problem becomes:

$$\max_{\beta_{m,k}^n, p_m^n} \sum_{k=1}^{K} \sum_{n=1}^{N_{RB}} \frac{R_k^n}{\bar{R}_k} \Big/ \sum_{m=1}^{M} \sum_{n=1}^{N_{RB}} \sum_{k=1}^{K} \beta_{m,k}^n S \tag{8}$$

where S is the fixed transmit power. The objective is constrained by C2, C3 and C4 in Equation (7). We first propose a CE-based algorithm to solve the RB scheduling problem described above.

The CE method is a typical heuristic algorithm to estimate the probabilities of rare events in complex stochastic networks [15] and to deal with linear programming. The basic idea of the CE method is to generate sufficient samples under a given strategy and then update the generating strategy according to samples. After iteratively repeating this procedure, generated samples will converge to the optimal solution. The proposed CE-based scheduling algorithm follows three major stages, including initialization, iteration and a complementary stage to close unfavorable transmissions, as shown in Figure 3.

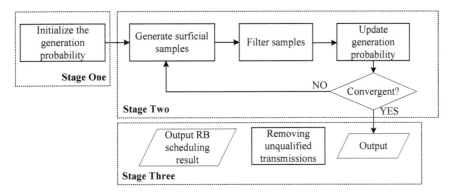

Figure 3. The major principle of the CE method.

4.1.1. Initialization

Let $\mathbf{X}^m = [x^m_{(1)}, ..., x^m_{(n)}, ..., x^m_{(N_{RB})}]$ ($x^m_{(n)} \in [0, \mathcal{U}_m]$) denote a sample generated according to a given probability, which presents a possible scheduling result of TP m. $x^m_{(n)} = 0$ means that no transmission is scheduled on RB n of TP m. Otherwise, $x^m_{(n)}$ is the ID of the scheduled UE. In the CE method, the scheduling problem is regarded as a stochastic procedure. The distribution of $x^m_{(n)}$ is denoted by $\mathbf{q}^{m,n} = [q^{m,n}_0, q^{m,n}_1, ..., q^{m,n}_u, ..., q^{m,n}_{|\mathcal{U}_m|}]$, where $q^{m,n}_u = \mathbb{P}\{x^m_{(n)} = u\}$, $u \in [0, \mathcal{U}_m]$. Obviously, $q^{m,n}_u$ has the attributes of $0 \leq q^{m,n}_u \leq 1$ ($\forall u, m, n$) and $\sum_{u \in [0, \mathcal{U}_m]} q^{m,n}_u = 1$ ($\forall m, n$).

For the sake of accelerating convergence, we design the initial probability distribution according to estimated data rates. We first defined $\mathbb{P}\{x^m_{(n)} = 0\} = \text{Pr}_0$ where Pr_0 is a given value. This probability gives an opportunity to TP m for scheduling no transmission on RB n. For each $u \in \mathcal{U}_m$, the data rate R^n_u is estimated based on the fixed JT CoMP transmission, as given by (2), at the initialization stage. As suggested by C4 in (7), the transmission is considered to be unqualified if $R^n_u < R_{thres}$. To save energy, the proposed algorithm sets the corresponding probability to be zero, *i.e.*, $q^{m,n}_u = 0$. For the rest of the optional UEs, the probability is defined as $q^{m,n}_u = (R^n_u / R^m_{tot}) \times (1 - \text{Pr}_0)$, where R_{tot} indicates the sum data rate of all possible qualified transmissions, defined as:

$$R^m_{tot} = \sum_{\substack{k \in \mathcal{U}_m, \\ R^n_k \geq R_{thres}}} R^n_k \qquad (9)$$

Summarily, the initial distribution of $x^m_{(n)}$ is:

$$q^{m,n}_u = \begin{cases} \text{Pr}_0, & u = 0 \\ (1 - \text{Pr}_0) \times R^n_u / R^m_{tot}, & u \in \mathcal{U}_m, \text{and } R^n_u \geq R_{thres} \\ 0, & u \in \mathcal{U}_m, \text{and } R^n_u < R_{thres} \end{cases} \qquad (10)$$

4.1.2. Iteration

Each iteration of the proposed algorithm includes three steps. First, the algorithm generates adequate samples according to a given strategy. Then, it is necessary to exclude those samples that do not satisfy the constraints and to select "good" samples for the next stage. At last, the probability distribution needs to be updated according to the selected samples, so that "better" samples will be generated in the next iteration. After sufficient iterations, the algorithm gradually approaches the optimal solution.

Let N_{SAM} denote the number of samples generated in each iteration for each TP and $\mathbf{X}^m_1$, $\cdots, \mathbf{X}^m_i, \cdots, \mathbf{X}^m_{N_{SAM}}$ denote the corresponding samples, where $\mathbf{X}^m_i = [x^m_{i(1)}, \cdots, x^m_{i(n)}, \cdots, x^m_{i(N_{RB})}]$. Each sample can map into a scheduling index set $\{\beta_{m,k}^n, \forall k, n\}$, and leads to a weighted energy efficiency of TP m given as:

$$f_m\left(\mathbf{X}_i^m\right) = \sum_{n=1}^{N_{RB}} \frac{R_{x_{i(n)}^m}^n}{\overline{R}_{x_{i(n)}^m}} \Bigg/ \sum_{n=1,x_i^m(n)\neq 0}^{N_{RB}} S \tag{11}$$

where $\sum_{n=1,x_i^m(n)\neq 0}^{N_{RB}} S$ represents the total power consumption at TP m according to sample $\mathbf{X}_i^m$. The sum data rate of TP m can be estimated as $R_m\left(\mathbf{X}_i^m\right) = \sum_{n=1}^{N_{RB}} R_{x_{i(n)}^n}^n$.

A qualified sample should satisfy two requirements. First, the sum data rate R_m cannot exceed the backhaul capacity of TP m. Therefore, those samples lead to overlarge sum data rates, i.e., $R_m\left(\mathbf{X}_i^m\right) > C_m$, will be removed. Second, the value of $f_m\left(\mathbf{X}_i^m\right)$ should be high enough. Samples whose weighted energy efficiency $f_m\left(\mathbf{X}_i^m\right) < f_{thres}^{(t)}$ will also be removed, where $f_{thres}^{(t)}$ is a threshold that increases after each iteration until it converges. Consequently, N_{IM} ($N_{IM} \leq N_{SAM}$) qualified samples are left for updating the generation probability. Without loss of generality, qualified samples are denoted as $\mathbf{X}_j^m$ ($1 \leq j \leq N_{IM}$).

At the last stage of an iteration, probability distributions are updated on the basis of qualified samples in order to generate better samples in the next iteration. The updated possibility $\mathbb{P}\{x_{(n)}^m = u\}$ is:

$$q_u^{m,n} = N\left(x_{j(n)}^m = u\right) / N_{IM} \tag{12}$$

where $N\left(x_{j(n)}^m = u\right)$ represents the number of times that UE u appears in N_{IM} samples on the n-th RB.

The proposed iteration algorithm is summarized as Algorithm 1.

Algorithm 1 Iteration in the CE-based scheduling algorithm.

1: $f_{max} = f_{max\_pre} = 0$; $counter = 1$;
2: **while** $counter \leq N_{SAM}$ **do**
3:    Generate samples $\mathbf{X}^m$ according to the distribution $\mathbf{q}^{m,n}$.
4:    Calculate utility function of $\mathbf{X}_i^m$, i.e., $f\left(\mathbf{X}_i^m\right)$, according to (11).
5:    Calculate the sum data rate of $\mathbf{X}^m$, i.e., $R_m\left(\mathbf{X}^m\right) = \sum_{k\in\mathcal{U}_m} R_k^n$.
6:    **if** $f\left(\mathbf{X}^m\right) < f_{thres}^{(t)}$ **then**
7:        **CONTINUE;**
8:    **end if**
9:    **if** $R_m\left(\mathbf{X}^m\right) > C_m$ **then**
10:        **CONTINUE;**
11:    **end if**
12:    $\mathbf{X}_{counter}^m = \mathbf{X}^m$
13:    $counter = counter + 1$
14: **end while**
15: **for** $i = 1$ to N_{SAM} **do**
16:    Calculate $f\left(\mathbf{X}_i^m\right)$ according to (11).
17: **end for**
18: Sort samples in a descending order in terms of $f\left(\mathbf{X}_i^m\right)$. Denote the consequence by $\hat{\mathbf{X}}_1^m, \hat{\mathbf{X}}_2^m, \cdot, \hat{\mathbf{X}}_{SAM}^m$
19: Calculate $N_{IM} = \lceil(1-\rho)N_{SAM}\rceil$, and let $f_{thres}^{(t+1)} = f\left(\hat{\mathbf{X}}_{N_{IM}^m}\right)$
20: **if** $f\left(\hat{\mathbf{X}}_1^m\right) > f_{max}$ **then**
21:    $\mathbf{X}_{out}^m = \hat{\mathbf{X}}_1^m$, $f_{max\_pre} = f_{max}$, $f_{max} = f\left(\hat{\mathbf{X}}_1^m\right)$
22: **end if**
23: Update $\mathbf{q}^{m,n}$ according to (12)
24: Map $\mathbf{X}_{out}^m$ into $\beta_{m,k}^n$, and recalculate R_k^n according to (3)

4.1.3. Removing Unqualified Transmissions

The algorithm proposed above cannot ensure that the data rate of each transmission is as high as the given threshold R_{thres}. Since we put our purpose on improving energy efficiency, it is reasonable to close those transmissions that are estimated to be unqualified.

Algorithm 2 summaries the entire RB scheduling algorithm proposed above.

Algorithm 2 Centralized RB scheduling algorithm.

1: Calculate R_k^n according to Equation (2).
2: Initialize probability distribution $\mathbf{q}^m (m = 1, \cdots, M)$ according to Equation (10).
3: **for** $t = 1 : t_{\max}$ **do**
4:     **for** $m = 1 : M$ **do**
5:         Process **Algorithm 1, and output** $\mathbf{X}_{\text{out}}^m, (m = 1, \cdots, M)$
6:     **end for**
7:     Map obtained $\mathbf{X}_{\text{out}}^m$ into $\{\beta_{m,k}^n\}$.
8:     Update R_k^n according to Equation (3), and obtain $\{\beta_{m,k}^n\}$.
9:     **if** All of the elements in $\mathbf{q}^m (m = 1, \cdot, \cdot, \cdot, M)$ converge **then**
10:         Output $\mathbf{X}_{\text{out}}$
11:         **BREAK**
12:     **end if**
13: **end for**
14: Map obtained $\mathbf{X}_{\text{out}}^m$ into $\{\beta_{m,k}^n\}$.
15: **for** $n = 1 : N_{\text{RB}}$ **do**
16:     **for** $u = 1 : K$ **do**
17:         **if** $R_k^n < R_{\text{thres}}$ **then**
18:             Let the corresponding $\beta_{m,u}^n = 0$.
19:         **end if**
20:     **end for**
21: **end for**

4.2. Power Allocation Algorithm

With the obtained RB scheduling result, the power allocation problem can be given as:

$$\max_{\beta_{m,k}^n, p_m^n} \sum_{k=1}^{K} \sum_{n=1}^{N_{\text{RB}}} \frac{R_k^n}{\overline{R}_k} \bigg/ \sum_{m=1}^{M} \sum_{n=1}^{N_{\text{RB}}} \sum_{k=1}^{K} \beta_{m,k}^n p_m^n$$

$$\text{s.t. C1: } 0 \leq p_m^n \leq S, \forall m, n \tag{13}$$

$$\text{C3: } \sum_{n=1}^{N_{\text{RB}}} \sum_{k=1}^{K} \beta_{m,k}^n R_k^n \leq C_m, \forall m$$

$$\text{C4: } R_k^n \geq R_{\text{thres}}, \forall k, n$$

The objective function in (13) is a well-known non-convex function for which the optimal solution does not exist. In this work, we use an analytical method on the base of the KKT-condition to approach a local optimal solution of power allocation.

A solution of Equation (13) can be achieved by solving its dual function in terms of backhaul and data rate constraints given as:

$$\max_{p_m^n} \sum_{n=1}^{N_{\text{RB}}} \left(\sum_{k=1}^{K} \frac{R_k^n}{\overline{R}_k} \bigg/ \sum_{m=1}^{M} p_m^n \right) - \sum_{m=1}^{M} \lambda_m \left(\sum_{n=1}^{N_{\text{RB}}} \sum_{k=1}^{K} \beta_{m,k}^n R_k^n - C_m \right) + \sum_{n=1}^{N_{\text{RB}}} \sum_{k=1}^{K} \mu_{n,k} \left(R_k^n - R_{\text{thres}} \right) \tag{14}$$

$$\text{s.t. } 0 \leq p_m^n \leq S, \forall m, n$$

where $\{\lambda_m, \forall m\}$ and $\{\mu_{n,k}, \forall n,k\}$ are non-negative Lagrangian multipliers. However, the dual function given above is still hard to solve, since it involves too many variables (MN_{RB} variables and Lagrangian multipliers). To further simplify the problem, we intend to decompose Equation (14) into independent subproblems with fewer variables.

Let $\beta_m = \sum_{n=1}^{N_{\mathrm{RB}}} \sum_{k=1}^{K} \beta_{m,k}^n$. $\beta_m = 0$ indicate the situation where no transmission is scheduled for TP m. This is unreasonable in the high-loading network we considered. Thus, we suppose that $\beta_m \neq 0$; then C_m can be rewritten as:

$$C_m = \sum_{n=1}^{N_{\mathrm{RB}}} \sum_{k=1}^{K} \beta_{m,k}^n \frac{C_m}{\sum_{n=1}^{N_{\mathrm{RB}}} \sum_{k=1}^{K} \beta_{m,k}^n} = \sum_{n=1}^{N_{\mathrm{RB}}} \sum_{k=1}^{K} \beta_{m,k}^n \frac{C_m}{\beta_m} \tag{15}$$

After substituting (15) into (14), the problem can be decomposed into N_{RB} independent subproblems, where each subproblem is given as:

$$\max_{p_m^n} \quad \sum_{k=1}^{K} \frac{R_k^n}{\overline{R}_k} \Big/ \sum_{m=1}^{M} p_m^n - \sum_{k=1}^{K} \sum_{m=1}^{M} \lambda_m \beta_{m,k}^n \left(R_k^n - \frac{C_m}{\beta_m} \right) + \sum_{k=1}^{K} \mu_{n,k} \left(R_k^n - R_{\mathrm{thres}} \right) \tag{16}$$

$$\text{s.t. } 0 \leq p_m^n \leq S, \forall m$$

Each subproblem in Equation (16) involves M variables with Lagrangian multipliers only and can be solved independently on each RB. The computational complexity is significantly cut in this way. In the rest of this subsection, we propose an iterative method to address each subproblem.

Let $f_n(p_m^n, \lambda_m, \mu_{n,k})$ denote the objective function of Equation (16). Take the first order derivative in terms of p_m^n, and make it equal to zero; then, a possible value of power allocation, denoted by $\hat{p}_m^n$, can be obtained as follows,

$$\hat{p}_m^n = \left\{ \frac{\left(\frac{1}{\overline{R}_{k^*} \cdot p_{tot}^n} - \sum_{m=1}^{M} \lambda_m \cdot \beta_{m,k^*}^n + \mu_{n,k^*} \right) \cdot b \sum_{m \in \mathcal{M}} \beta_{m,k^*}^n \|\mathbf{H}_{m,k^*}^n \mathbf{w}_m^n\|^2}{\frac{1}{(p_{tot}^n)^2} \cdot \sum_{k=1}^{K} \frac{R_k^n}{\overline{R}_k} - \sum_{k=1;k \neq k^*}^{K} \left(\frac{1}{\overline{R}_k \cdot p_{tot}^n} - \sum_{m=1}^{M} \lambda_m \cdot \beta_{m,k}^n + \mu_{n,k} \right) \cdot \frac{\partial R_k^n}{\partial p_m^n}} - A_m^n \right\} \times \frac{1}{\|\mathbf{H}_{m,k^*}^n \mathbf{w}_m^n\|^2} \tag{17}$$

where $p_{tot}^n = \sum_{m=1}^{M} p_m^n$ and k^* is the UE scheduled on RB n of TP m, i.e., $\beta_{m,k^*}^n = 1$. The derivative $\partial R_k^n / \partial p_m^n$ and A_m^n are given by:

$$\frac{\partial R_k^n}{\partial p_m^n} = -\frac{b(\gamma_k^n)^2}{1 + \gamma_k^n} \frac{\left\| \mathbf{H}_{m,k}^n \mathbf{w}_m^n \right\|^2}{\sum_{m' \in \mathcal{M}} \beta_{m',k}^n \left\| \mathbf{H}_{m',k}^n \mathbf{w}_{m'}^n \right\|^2 p_{m'}^n}, \forall k \neq k^* \tag{18}$$

and:

$$A_m^n = \sum_{m' \in \mathcal{M} \setminus \{m\}} \|\mathbf{H}_{m',k^*}^n \mathbf{w}_{m'}^n\|^2 p_{m'}^2 + \sigma^2 \tag{19}$$

respectively.

The obtained $\hat{p}_m^n$ above may not be in the range of $[0, S]$. Therefore, the real power allocation needs to be adjusted following the rule given by:

$$p_m^{n(t)} = \max \{ \min \{ \hat{p}_m^n, S \}, 0 \} \tag{20}$$

where t indicates the times of the iteration.

Lagrangian multipliers can be updated in each iteration by the sub-gradient method [16] as follows,

$$\lambda_m^{(t+1)} = \max\left\{\lambda_m^{(t)} - v_\lambda^{(t)}\left(\sum_{n=1}^{N_{\mathrm{RB}}}\sum_{k=1}^{K}\beta_{m,k}^n R_k^n - C_m\right), 0\right\}$$

$$\mu_{n,k}^{(t+1)} = \max\left\{\mu_{n,k}^{(t)} - v_\mu^{(t)}\left(R_{\mathrm{thres}} - R_k^n\right), 0\right\} \tag{21}$$

where $v_\lambda^{(t)}$ and $v_\mu^{(t)}$ are the step sizes used in the current iteration for updating λ_m and $\mu_{n,k}$.

5. Decentralized Algorithm

The centralized strategy of resource allocation proposed above is processed on the CU with the global CSI at the beginning of each TTI. It is possible that the time delay caused by processing is too long to guarantee the effectiveness of a large-scale system involving numerous TPs and UEs. An alternative method for shortening the time delay is a decentralized strategy that distributes calculations to each TP instead of the CU. Under a decentralized strategy, global CSIs are shared between TPs at the first place. Then, the resource allocation is processed at each TP independently and simultaneously, according to the known CSIs and a given strategy. In this way, the time delay of processing can be significantly decreased, even in a large-scale network. However, due to the lack of knowledge about the scheduling results of other TPs, the accuracy of the decentralized one is unavoidably worse than the centralized one.

In this section, we propose a decentralized strategy with the similar CE-based scheduling and KKT-based power allocation to the centralized proposed above. Simulation results presented in Section 6 will prove that the decline of system performance under the proposed decentralized strategy is acceptable.

5.1. Decentralized RB Scheduling Algorithm

A decentralized RB scheduling algorithm based on the CE method is proposed in this subsection. The same as the centralized one proposed in Subsection 4.1, the decentralized scheduling algorithm initializes the probability distribution $\mathbf{q}^m$ at the first place. Then, the iteration procedure is processed to obtain RB scheduling results. It should be noticed that the decentralized strategy cannot accurately estimate data rates of ongoing transmissions due to the lack of information about the scheduling results of other TPs. Therefore, the decentralized scheduling algorithm deletes the procedure of removing unqualified transmissions (as described in Section 4.1.3). In the simulation, we consider unqualified transmissions as failures, which waste energy and contribute nothing to the data rates of the system. Algorithm 3 summarizes the decentralized RB scheduling based on the CE method.

Algorithm 3 Decentralized RB scheduling algorithm.

1: Calculate R_k^n according to Equation (2).
2: Initialize probability distribution $\mathbf{q}^m (m = 1, \cdots, M)$ according to Equation (10).
3: **for** $t = 1 : t_{\max}$ **do**
4:    Process Algorithm 1, and output $\mathbf{X}_{\mathrm{out}}^m, (m = 1, \cdots, M)$
5:    **if** All of the elements in $\mathbf{q}^m = [q^{m,n}, \forall n]$ converge **then**
6:        Output $\mathbf{X}_{\mathrm{out}}$
7:        **BREAK**
8:    **end if**
9: **end for**
10: Map the obtained $\mathbf{X}_{\mathrm{out}}^m$ into $\{\beta_{m,k}^n\}$.

5.2. Power Allocation Algorithm

In this subsection, we modify the power allocation algorithm proposed in Subsection 4.2 to be decentralized, so that it can be processed at each TP independently and simultaneously. The individual power allocation problem of each TP is given by:

$$\max \quad \sum_{k=1}^{K}\sum_{n=1}^{N_{RB}}\beta_{m,k}^n\frac{R_k^n}{\bar{R}_k}\Big/\sum_{k=1}^{K}\sum_{n=1}^{N_{RB}}\beta_{m,k}^n p_m^n$$

$$\text{s.t. } C1: \ 0 \le p_m^n \le S, \ \forall n$$

$$C3: \ \sum_{n=1}^{N_{RB}}\sum_{k=1}^{K}\beta_{m,k}^n R_k^n \le C_m$$

$$C4: \ R_k^n \ge R_{\text{thres}}, \forall n, k \in \mathcal{U}_m$$

(22)

As in Subsection 4.2, we constitute and solve the dual function of Equation (22), instead of solving it directly. The dual function in terms of constraints C3 and C4 is given as:

$$\max_{p_m^n} \ \sum_{n=1}^{N_{RB}}\left(\sum_{k=1}^{K}\beta_{m,k}^n\frac{R_k^n}{\bar{R}_k}\Big/\sum_{k=1}^{K}\beta_{m,k}^n p_m^n\right) - \lambda_m\left(\sum_{n=1}^{N_{RB}}\sum_{k=1}^{K}\beta_{m,k}^n R_k^n - C_m\right)$$

$$+ \sum_{n=1}^{N_{RB}}\sum_{k=1}^{K}\mu_{n,k}\beta_{m,k}^n\left(R_k^n - R_{\text{thres}}\right)$$

$$\text{s.t. } \ 0 \le p_m^n \le S, \ \forall n$$

(23)

Substituting Equation (15) into Equation (23), we can decompose the power allocation problem into N_{RB} independent subproblems. Let $f_{m,n}$ denote the objective of the subproblem on RB n of TP m, which is given as:

$$f_{m,n} = \sum_{k=1}^{K}\beta_{m,k}^n\frac{R_k^n}{\bar{R}_k}\Big/\sum_{k=1}^{K}\beta_{m,k}^n p_m^n - \sum_{k=1}^{K}\lambda_m\beta_{m,k}^n\left(R_k^n - \frac{C_m}{\beta_m}\right) + \sum_{k=1}^{K}\mu_{n,k}\beta_{m,k}^n\left(R_k^n - R_{\text{thres}}\right)$$

(24)

$\sum_{k=1}^{K}\beta_{m,k}^n = 0$ means that TP m does not schedule any transmissions on RB n. In this case, power allocation is not required, *i.e.*, $p_m^n = 0$. In the case where $\sum_{k=1}^{K}\beta_{m,k}^n = 1$, transmit power p_m^n can be obtained by an iterative method proposed in the rest of this subsection.

Let k^* denote the UE of TP m scheduled on RB n (*i.e.*, $\sum_{k=1}^{K}\beta_{m,k}^n = \beta_{m,k^*}^n = 1$). Taking the first order derivative of $f_{m,n}$ with respect to p_m^n, we obtain:

$$\frac{\partial f_{m,n}}{\partial p_m^n} = \left(\frac{1}{\bar{R}_{k^*}p_m^n} - \lambda_m + \mu_{n,k^*}\right)\frac{\partial R_{k^*}^n}{\partial p_m^n} - \frac{R_{k^*}^n}{\bar{R}_{k^*}\left(p_m^n\right)^2}$$

(25)

where:

$$\frac{\partial R_{k^*}^n}{p_m^n} = \frac{b\sum\limits_{m\in\mathcal{M}}\beta_{m,k^*}^n\left\|\mathbf{H}_{m,k^*}^n\mathbf{w}_m^n\right\|^2}{\left\|\mathbf{H}_{m,k^*}^n\mathbf{w}_m^n\right\|^2 p_m^n + \sum\limits_{m'\in\mathcal{M}\setminus\{m\}}\left\|\mathbf{H}_{m',k^*}^n\mathbf{w}_{m'}^n\right\|^2 p_{m'}^n + \sigma^2}$$

(26)

Let $\partial f_n / \partial p_m^n = 0$. An expression of p_m^n in the t-th iteration can be obtained by solving the equation, which is given as:

$$p_m^{n(t)} = \sqrt{\frac{R_{k^*}^n}{\bar{R}_{k^*}^n}} \times \sqrt{\frac{\left\| \mathbf{H}_{m,k^*}^n \mathbf{w}_m^n \right\|^2 p_m^{n(t)} + \sum_{\substack{m' \in \mathcal{M} \\ m' \neq m}} \left\| \mathbf{H}_{m',k^*}^n \mathbf{w}_{m'}^n \right\|^2 p_{m'}^{n(t)} + \sigma^2}{b \left\| \mathbf{H}_{m,k^*}^n \mathbf{w}_m^n \right\|^2 \left(\frac{1}{\bar{R}_{k^*} p_m^{n(t)}} - (\lambda_m - \mu_{n,k^*}) \right)}} \tag{27}$$

where multipliers λ_m and μ_{n,k^*} should be updated according to Equation (21). A suboptimal p_m^n can be approached after sufficient iterations.

6. Simulation Results

We consider a HetNet downlink system with 37 TPs, where only 19 TPs of these conduct actual communications to UEs, and the others wrap them around to produce virtual interference. The radius of each small cell is 250 m, since a dense deployment is considered. The system includes 100 RBs, each of which is under a bandwidth of 180 kHz. Therefore, the overall bandwidth of the system is 18 MHz. Additionally, 2×2 MIMO links are created using the space channel model (SCM) [17]. Each simulation lasts 20 TTIs, where a TTI is 1 ms. Important parameters used in the simulation are listed in Table 2.

Table 2. Parameters in the simulation.

Parameters	Value
Layout of cells	37 hexagon cells; wrap-around used
Radius of cells	250 m
Central frequency	2 GHz
N_{RB}, number of RBs	100
S_m, limit of transmit power	20 Watt
$N_T \times N_R$	2×2
number of TTI / TTI	20 /1 ms
α	0.1
Channel model	SCM (path loss + shadowing + MIMO fading)
Minimal distance (TP and UE)	35 m
Height of transmit/receive antenna	35 m/1.5 m
Penetration loss	20 dB
Traffic model	full buffer
Speed of UE	10 m/s

The simulation is carried out to prove the proposed algorithms effectiveness. A greedy algorithm, named max capacity, is also simulated as a benchmark. The max capacity algorithm tends to allocate resources to UEs with good channel conditions, in order to reach the optimal throughput of the network. In this way, UEs with worse channel conditions may no chance to communicate. Therefore, the fairness of the max capacity algorithm is unfavorable. Figures 4 and 5 compare the performances of the max capacity algorithm to that of the proposed one.

Figure 4 demonstrates the average throughput per TP and fairness factor (as defined by Equation (5)) of the system under different resource allocation algorithms, when the transmit power of each TP is 20 Watts. It is obvious that max capacity algorithm achieves an outstanding throughput and a much worse fairness factor than the proposed one. The future mobile communication system targets to provide not only high throughput of the network, but also quality service to every UE. Therefore, the max capacity is no longer appropriate. The proposed algorithms have much better fairness factors. More importantly, as shown in Figure 5, the proposed centralized algorithm can also achieve an energy efficiency as good as that of max capacity.

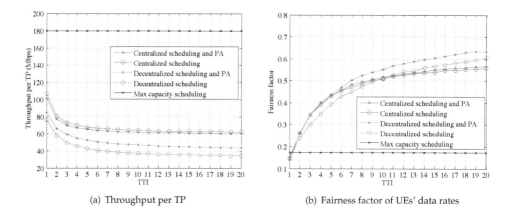

(a) Throughput per TP   (b) Fairness factor of UEs' data rates

Figure 4. System performances under different resource allocation algorithms (20 Watts, infinite C_m, $R_{thres} = 180$ kbps).

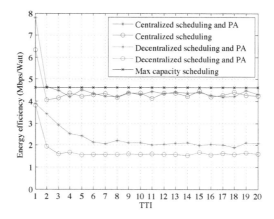

Figure 5. Energy efficiencies under different resource allocation algorithms (20 Watts, infinite C_m, $R_{thres} = 180$ kbps).

Results in Figures 4 and 5 also compare the performance of the centralized algorithm proposed in Section 4 and that of the decentralized algorithm in Section 5. The results show that both energy efficiency and throughput are decreased when the decentralized algorithm is used.

Figure 6 shows the system performances of the proposed algorithms when the transmit power of each TP is 40 Watts. Comparing the results to Figures 4 and 5, it can be seen that the energy efficiency of the centralized algorithm significantly decreases when the transmit power of each TP is up to 40 Watts, while the throughput does not increase. This proves that high-level transmit power is not appropriate in a dense network. Additionally, the results demonstrate that the decentralized algorithm is more robust, since both energy efficiency and throughput are changed a little when different transmit powers are used.

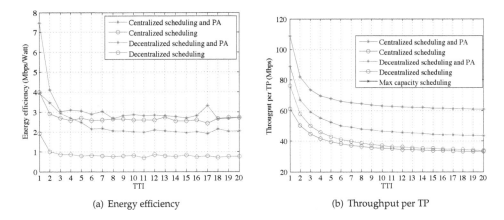

(a) Energy efficiency

(b) Throughput per TP

Figure 6. System performance under different strategies (40 Watts, infinite C_m, $R_{\text{thres}} = 180$ kbps).

Simulations are also conducted under infinite, 100-Mbps and 80-Mbps backhaul limits, respectively, with a fixed R_{thres} of 360 kbps, to clearly illustrate the effect on system performance caused by backhaul constraints. Restricted backhaul capacity leads to a low throughput per TP, as shown in Figure 7a, since fewer transmissions are scheduled in this case. However, the tendency is different in terms of energy efficiency. Figure 7b shows that the energy efficiencies of the proposed algorithms under different backhaul limits are almost the same. This is explained by the fact that the power consumed by transmissions is also reduced when backhaul capacity is restricted.

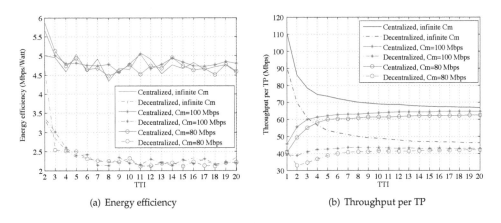

(a) Energy efficiency

(b) Throughput per TP

Figure 7. System performance under different backhaul capacity (20 Watts, $R_{\text{thres}} = 360$ kbps).

At last, we conduct simulations when R_{thres} is 180 kbps, 360 kbps and 540 kbps, respectively, with the fixed backhaul capacity of 100 Mbps. This shows that the throughput of our proposals grows as the increase in R_{thres}, as shown in Figure 8a. This is because more resources are assigned to the UEs with better channel conditions, which are possible to achieve for quality transmissions. Figure 8b illustrates that the value of R_{thres} hardly affects the energy efficiency of the system. Since those transmissions estimated to be inferior to the given R_{thres} are closed, no (or little) power is wasted. Therefore, that energy efficiency of the system can be maintained at a high level.

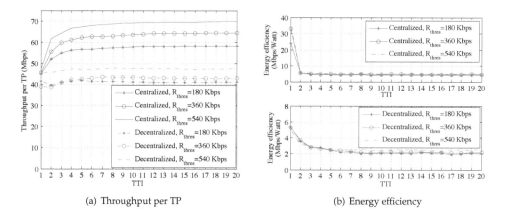

(a) Throughput per TP   (b) Energy efficiency

Figure 8. System performance under different R_{thres} (20 Watts, $C_m = 100Mbps$).

7. Conclusions

In this paper, we have studied a constrained RRM problem aiming at improving energy efficiency in a CoMP-based HetNet. To solve the problem, we first propose a CE-based RB scheduling algorithm under the assumption of equal power allocation. Then, a KKT-based algorithm for power allocation is presented. The proposed algorithms are considered to be used in a centralized way at the first place. Since the centralized strategy for RRM takes a long time delay in large-scale networks, we modified the proposed one in order to adapt to a decentralized system in order to shorten the time delay for processing. Simulation results compare performances of both the centralized and the decentralized and discuss the influence on system performance caused by the considered constraints.

Acknowledgments: We acknowledge Yonsuke Kinouchi, Takahiro Emote and Ye Wang for useful comments for this work and the modification of this paper.

Author Contributions: Jia Yu was responsible for the conception of the paper and the main writing. Shinsuke Konaka, Masatake Akutagawa and Qinyu Zhang were all responsible for the concept of the paper, supervising the work and reviewing.

Conflicts of Interest: The authors declare no conflict of interest.

References

1.   Damnjanovic, A.; Montojo, J.; Wei, Y.; Ji, T.; Lou, T.; Vajapeyam, M.; Yoo, T.; Song, O.; Malladi, D. A survey on 3GPP heterogeneous networks. *Wirel. Commun.* **2011**, *3*, 10–21.
2.   Zhang, N.; Cheng, N.; Gamage, A.; Zheng, K.; Mark, J.W.; Shen, X. Cloud Assisted HetNets Toward 5G Wireless Networks. *IEEE Commun.* **2015**, *53*, 59–65.
3.   Bottai, C.; Cicconetti, C.; Morelli, A.; Resellini, M.; Vitale, C. Energy-efficient user association in extremely dense small cell networks. In Proceedings of the 2014 European Conference on Networks and Communications (EuCNC), Bologna, Italy, 23–26 June 2014; pp. 1–5.
4.   Hoydis, J.; Kobayashi, M.; Debbah, M. Green Small-Cell Networks. *Veh. Technol. Mag.* **2011**, *1*, 37–43.
5.   Rangan, S. Femto-macro cellular interference control with subband scheduling and interference cancelation. In Proceedings of the 2010 IEEE GLOBECOM Workshops (GC Wkshps), Miami, FL, USA, 6–10 December 2010; pp. 695–700.
6.   Wang, Y.; Pedersen, K.-I. Performance analysis of enhanced inter-cell interference coordination in LTE-Advanced heterogeneous networks. In Proceedings of the 2012 IEEE 75th Vehicular Technology Conference (VTC Spring), Yokohama, Japan, 6–9 May 2012; pp. 1–5.
7.   Peng, M.; Liu, Y.; Wei, D.; Wang, W.; Chen, H. Hierarchical cooperative relay based heterogeneous networks. *Wirel. Commun.* **2011**, *3*, 48–56.

8. Irmer, R.; Droste, H.; Marsch, P.; Grieger, M.; Fettweis, G.; Brueck, S.; Mayer, H.-P.; Thiele, L.; Jungnickel, V. Coordinated multipoint: Concepts, performance, and field trial results. *IEEE Commun. Mag.* **2011**, *2*, 102–111.

9. LG Electronics. CoMP configurations and UE/eNB behaviors in LTE-Advanced; R1-090213. In Proceedings of the 3GPP TSG RAN WG1 Meeting, Ljubljana, Slovenia, 12–17 January 2009.

10. Tombaz, S.; Vastberg, A.; Zander, J. Energy-and-cost-efficient ultra-high-capacity wireless access. *Wirel. Commun.* **2011**, *5*, 18–24.

11. Maattanen, H.; Hamalainen, K.; Venalaiene, J.; Schober, K.; Enescu, M.; Valkama, M. System-level performance of LTE-Advanced with joint transmission and dynamic point selection schemes. *EURSIP J. Adv. Signal Process.* **2012**, *247*, 1–18.

12. Introduction to Downlink Physical Layer Design. In *LTE, The UMTS Long Term Evolution—from Theory to Practice*, 2nd ed.; Sesia, S., Toufik, I., Baker, M., Eds.; Wiley: West Sussex, United Kingdom, 2009; pp. 135–137.

13. Yu, W.; Kwon, T.; Shin, C. Multicell coordination via joint scheduling, beamforming and power spectrum adaptation. *IEEE Trans. Wirel. Commun.* **2013**, *7*, 1–14.

14. Shen, Z.; Andrews, J.-G.; Evans, B.-L. Adaptive resource allocation in multiuser ofdm systems with proportional rate constraints. *IEEE Trans. Wirel. Commun.* **2005**, *6*, 2726–2737.

15. Rubinstein, R.-Y. Optimization of computer simulation models with rare events. *Eur. J. Oper. Res.* **1997**, *1*, 89–112.

16. Palomar, D.; Chiang, M. A tutorial on decomposition methods for network utility maximization. *IEEE J. Select. Areas Commun.* **2006**, *8*, 1439–1451.

17. Salo, J.; Galdo, G.-D.; Salmi, J.; Kyosti, P.; Milojevic, M.; Laselva, D.; Schneider, C. MATLAB implementation of the 3GPP spatial channel model. Available online: http://read.pudn.com/downloads86/sourcecode/app/331591/scm_11-01-2005.pdf (accessed on 28 January 2016).

18. Shannon, C.E. A mathematical theory of communication. *Bell Syst. Tech. J.* **1948**, *27*, 379–423.

2

An Approach to the Classification of Cutting Vibration on Machine Tools

Jeng-Fung Chen [1,†], Shih-Kuei Lo [1,†] and Quang Hung Do [2,*]

[1] Department of Industrial Engineering and Systems Management, Feng Chia University, Taichung 40724, Taiwan; jfchen@fcu.edu.tw (J.-F.C.); p0256809@fcu.edu.tw (S.-K.L.)

[2] Department of Electrical and Electronic Engineering, Faculty of Information Technology, University of Transport Technology, Hanoi 100000, Vietnam

[*] Correspondence: hungdq@utt.edu.vn or quanghung2110@gmail.com

[†] These authors contributed equally to this work.

Academic Editor: Willy Susilo

Abstract: Predictions of cutting vibrations are necessary for improving the operational efficiency, product quality, and safety in the machining process, since the vibration is the main factor for resulting in machine faults. "Cutting vibration" may be caused by setting incorrect parameters before machining is commenced and may affect the precision of the machined work piece. This raises the need to have an effective model that can be used to predict cutting vibrations. In this study, an artificial neural network (ANN) model to forecast and classify the cutting vibration of the intelligent machine tool is presented. The factors that may cause cutting vibrations is firstly identified and a dataset for the research purpose is constructed. Then, the applicability of the model is illustrated. Based on the results in the comparative analysis, the artificial neural network approach performed better than the others. Because the vibration can be forecasted and classified, the product quality can be managed. This work may help new workers to avoid operating machine tools incorrectly, and hence can decrease manufacturing costs. It is expected that this study can enhance the performance of machine tools in metalworking sectors.

Keywords: vibration; artificial neural network; decision tree; support vector machine; naive Bayes classifier

1. Introduction

Machine tools play important roles in the metalworking sectors. Machine tools vibrate more or less when in operation. Excessive vibration may cause operational inefficiency, product-quality problems, and increase the cost of manufacturing. Therefore, predictions of cutting vibrations are important for reducing machine downtime and work piece failure costs. In the past, predictions of cutting vibrations were based on practical considerations, previous experience and common sense. Therefore, successful predictions of vibrations required staff with a considerable degree of knowledge and experience. Although data collection may be carried out by trained personnel, data processing and an assessment of the state of the machine tools are the tasks of engineers who have knowledge in various areas (design of machine tools, mathematics, dynamic processing, and signal processing, *etc.*) and who are able to apply this knowledge in this context. Since machine tools have become more complex and technologically sophisticated, traditional prediction methods have fallen behind. Research in the field of advanced machine tools control mainly focuses on modeling [1], detection [2,3], and the classification and planning aspect of the disturbance [4]. Not much research or commercial systems tackle the prediction of the cutting vibration before operation is commenced. In this paper, a classification model based on an artificial neural network (ANN) approach is presented to predict the level of a cutting vibration. It focuses on the prediction of the cutting vibrations before work is commenced. As is known, especially in the aerospace industry, the raw material cost is very expensive. This study can help new workers to avoid manufacturing defective work pieces and thus can reduce the cost of manufacturing.

This rest of this paper is organized into seven sections. A review of the literature is presented in Section 2. Previous classification approaches are described in Section 3. The artificial neural network (ANN) architecture is illustrated in Section 4. An application of the presented ANN classifier is shown in Section 5. Section 6 is devoted to experimental results and discussion. Finally, Section 7 presents the conclusions.

2. Literature Review

The literature review includes the skills of monitoring machining processes, vibrations of machine tools, and the past research related to the vibrations of machine tools.

2.1. Skills of Monitoring Machining Processes

In recent years, the monitoring of machining processes has been recognized as being one of the key revolutionary technologies. There are several reasons behind this need. One is the factory automation, especially the ever-increasing popularity of computer-aided technologies such as CAD/CAM and FMS. Other than this, there has been a dramatic demand for more sophisticated and precise parts, which in turn has resulted in the increasing requirement of more intelligent machine tools.

Intelligent machine tools require the use of various sensors and a decision-making process based on the information obtained by the sensors. The research in monitoring machining process include: (1) the use of multiple sensors to sense machining states; (2) the extraction of features sensitive to machining conditions; and (3) the development of a pattern classifier capable of correctly classifying the state of cutting processes [5]. Of all the various applications for machine intelligence, the monitoring of tool wear, breakage, and chatter have been the most important monitoring subjects in the machine tool industry [6–10]. For the research of using neural networks to monitoring machining process, unsupervised neural networks have often been used to monitor tool breakage [11], and supervised neural networks have often been used to monitor tool wear [12–14]. Several noticeable studies are as follows: In a work by Leone et al., regression analysis and artificial neural network paradigms were used to predict the tool wear development [10]. The data were collected from turning of Inconel 718 aircraft engine components. The results showed that the accuracy of the artificial neural network prediction is better than the regression analysis, especially when a limited number of data is unknown. Nakai et al. [8] estimated diamond tool wear during the grinding of advanced ceramics using neural networks. Acoustic emission and cutting power signals were acquired during the tests, and data were obtained from these signals. The results showed that the models successfully estimated tool wear. D'Addona et al. [9] employed the neural network model to estimate the optimal tool life utilization in turning of aircraft engine products. The results indicate that the model can provide a step increase in productivity while preserving the surface integrity of the machined parts.

2.2. Vibrations of Machine Tools

The vibrations that occur in the machining processes ordinarily fall into three types [15]: (1) free vibrations; (2) forced vibrations; and (3) self-excited vibrations (chatter). Free vibrations occur when a mechanical system is set off with an initial input and then allowed to vibrate freely.

Forced vibrations may be because of one or more of the following causes:

(1)   Out-of-balance rotating or reciprocating machine components. This is due to the fact that the mechanisms transfer energy in uniformly timed impulses to faulty gears, belts, balls, and roller bearings.

(2)   Vibrations transmitted from other machines through foundations.

(3)   Vibrations caused by chip formation. When a discontinuous type of chip is formed, the recurring fractures of the metal in the shear plane ahead of the tool produce periodic variations. Similarly, in the case of machining operations that produce a continuous chip with a built-up edge, there is a variation in the force on the cutting tool. Yet another source of forced variation may be caused by the formation of chips of varying thickness obtained. The frequency of these periodic variations depends upon the frequency of discontinuity in the chip of the built-up edge, or the number of teeth in the milling cutting.

Of the three types of vibrations, the self-excited type is ordinarily the most severe. Self-excited vibrations are mainly caused by the dynamic instability of the cutting. The theory of chatter is complex, and a large number of parameters are involved in the chatter phenomena. The self-excited vibrations will be discussed in Section 5.2.

2.3. Past Research Related to the Vibrations of Machine Tools

Choudhury et al. [16] developed a system for on-line vibration control on a turning lathe. A correlation was established between cutting parameters (speed, feed…) and the control of vibrations during machining. Ema and Marui [17] presented a theoretical analysis on chatter vibration in drilling and its suppression. The stability of chatter vibration, occurring in drills for deep-hole machining, was investigated theoretically. After conducting the experiment, they found that, if the logarithmic decrement of the drills becomes greater than some value by the application of an impact damper, the chatter vibration can be suppressed completely.

Quintana et al. [18] studied the chatter vibration issue and classified the existing methods developed to ensure the stable cutting of those using out-of-process or in-process, as well as those modifying system behavior passively or actively. Out-of-process strategies focused on predicting, estimating and identifying the SLD through machining process modeling and analytical-experimental methods. In-process strategies focused on identifying or recognizing chatter through the use of several sensor technologies, process monitoring and signal treatment. Passive strategies focused on the use of passive elements, devices, methodologies or techniques that change or modify the system behavior and improve its performance against chatter. Active strategies focused on the use of elements, strategies, devices or actuators that actively modify the system behavior so as to suppress chatter as soon as it occurs. In this study, an ANN classifier is used to classify vibration classes.

3. Previous Classification Approaches

In order to demonstrate the effectiveness of the presented ANN classifier, the performance of the ANN classifier is compared with three commonly used classifiers, namely the decision tree classifier, the support vector machine classifier, and the Naive Bayes classifier. These three classifiers are described as follows.

3.1. Decision Tree

A decision tree (DT) is a hierarchical structure consisting of decision rules that recursively divide independent inputs into homogenous classes. The purpose of constructing a DT is to identify the set of decision rules that can be employed to predict outcomes from a set of input variables. A DT is called a regression tree if the target variables are continuous. If the target variables are discrete, it is called a classification tree [19]. Although the computational complexity of a decision tree may be high, it can be used to identify the most important input variables in a dataset.

3.2. Support Vector Machine (SVM)

A support vector machine (SVM) is a supervised learning method based on the statistical learning theory [20]. SVM has been successfully applied to a number of classification applications. By using the training data, SVM can map the input space into a high-dimensional feature space. In the feature space, the optimal hyper plane can be searched by maximizing the margins or distances of class boundaries. The training points closest to the optimal hyper plane are called support vectors. After the decision surface is obtained, it can be applied to classify the new data.

Consider a training dataset of (x_i, y_i), with $i = 1, \ldots, m$. The optimal separating hyper plane can be represented as [20]:

$$g(x) = sign \left(\sum_{i=1}^{m} y_i \alpha_i K (x_i, x_j) + b \right) \tag{1}$$

where $K (x_i, x_j)$ is a kernel function, α_i is a Lagrange multiplier, and b is the offset of the hyper plane from the origin. Equation (1) is subject to $0 \leqslant \alpha_i \leqslant C$ and $\Sigma \alpha_i y_i = 0$, where C is the penalty. Only those training points lying close to the support vectors have nonzero α_i. However, in real-world problems, there is noise in the data. Hence, there may be no linear separation in the feature space. Therefore, the optimal hyper plane can be represented as:

$$y_i(w.x_i+b) \geqslant 1 - \xi_i, \; \xi_i \geqslant 0 \tag{2}$$

where w is the weight vector that measures the orientation of the hyper plane in the feature space and ξ_i is the ith positive slack variable that measures the amount of violation.

3.3. Naive Bayes Classifier

The naive Bayes classifier is based on Bayes' theorem and the idea that the probability of a given data point belongs to a particular class [21]. Assume that there are n training samples (x_i, y_i), where $x_i = (x_{i1}, x_{i2}, \ldots, x_{im})$ and y_i are two m-dimensional vectors. For a new sample x_{test} to predict its class by using Bayes' theorem, then:

$$y_{test} = \arg \max_{y} P(y \,|\, x_{test}) = \arg \max_{y} \frac{P(x_{test} \,|\, y)P(y)}{P(x_{test})} \tag{3}$$

The above equation requires the estimation of distribution $P(x \,|\, y)$, since the estimation of distribution $P(x \,|\, y)$ is impossible in some cases. Hence, the Naive Bayes classifier makes a strong independent assumption on this probability distribution by the following equation [21]:

$$P(x \,|\, y) = \prod_{i=1}^{m} P(x_i \,|\, y) \tag{4}$$

This means that the individual components of x are conditionally independent with respect to y, and the classification can then proceed by estimating m one-dimensional distributions $P(x_j \,|\, y)$.

4. Artificial Neural Network (ANN) Architecture

In this study, an artificial neural network is implemented and the back propagation algorithm is applied for classification. Generally, the procedure of classification by using ANN consists of three steps: (1) data pre-processing, training, and testing; (2) the features from the data pre-processing step are fed to the ANN and a classifier is generated through the ANN; and (3) the testing data is used to verify the efficiency of the classifier.

4.1. The Feed-Forward Neural Network

The ANN is inspired by biological neural networks such as the brain. ANNs can represent complex relationships between inputs and outputs and can find patterns in data. ANNs have the notable ability to derive meaning from complicated or imprecise data and can be used to extract patterns and detect trends that are too complicated to be recognized by either humans or traditional computing techniques. This means that neural networks have the ability to identify and respond to patterns that are similar but not identical to the ones with which they have been trained. The ANN has become one of the most important data mining techniques and can be used for both supervised and unsupervised learning. In fact, feed-forward neural networks (FNNs) are the most popular neural networks in practical applications. For a given set of data, a multi-layered FNN can provide a good non-linear relationship. Studies have shown that an FNN, even with only one hidden layer, can approximate any continuous function [22,23]. Therefore, it is the most commonly used technique for classifying nonlinearly separable patterns and approximating functions.

Feed-forward neural networks often have one or more hidden layers (Figure 1). Multiple layers of neurons with non-linear transfer functions allow the network to learn non-linear and linear relationships between input and output vectors. The linear output functions let the network produce values inside the range −1 to 1 (Figure 2). On the other hand, if the outputs of network are restricted to the values between 0 and 1, then the output layer should use a log-sigmoid transfer function.

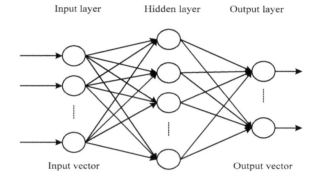

Figure 1. A feed-forward neural network with one hidden layer.

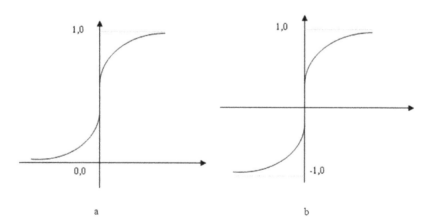

Figure 2. (a) A sigmoid function; (b) A hyperbolic tangent function.

Before training a feed-forward network, the weight and biases must be initialized. Once the network weights and biases have been initialized, the network is ready for training. Random numbers around zero are used to initialize weights and biases in the network. The training process requires a set of proper inputs and targets as outputs. During training, the weights and biases of the network are iteratively adjusted to minimize the network performance function. There are several training algorithms for feed-forward networks. All these algorithms use the gradient of the performance function to determine how to adjust the weights to minimize the performance. The gradient is determined using a technique called back propagation, which involves performing computational backwards through the network.

4.2. Back-PropagationAlgorithm

Back propagation was created by generalizing the Widrow-Hoff learning rule [24] to a multiple layer network and a non-linear differentiable transfer function. Input vectors and corresponding target vectors are used to train a network until it can approximate a function, associate input vectors with specific output vectors, or classify input vectors in an appropriate way as defined in this study. A sigmoid layer and a linear output layer are capable of approximating any function with a finite number of discontinuities. The back propagation algorithm consists of two paths: the forward path and backward path. The forward path includes creating a feed-forward network, initializing weight, simulation and training the network. The network weights and biases are updated in the backward path. The training process is as follows:

Step 1: Design the structure of FNN and set input parameters of the network.

Step 2: Set learning rate η and momentum rate α.

Step 3: Initialize the connection weights W_{ji}, W_{ki} and bias weights θ_j, θ_k to random values.

Step 4: Set stopping criteria.

Step 5: Start training by applying input patterns one at a time and propagate through the layers to calculate total error.

Step 6: Back-propagate error through output and hidden layers and update biases and weights.

Step 7: Back-propagate error through hidden and input layers and update biases and weights.

Step 8: Repeat step 5 to step 8 until stopping criteria are reached.

5. An Application of the Presented ANN Classifier

In this section, an application of the proposed ANN model to the prediction of the vibration class of a CNC milling machine is demonstrated. In order to simplify the experiment, only plane-surface machining is considered. Furthermore, it is assumed that both the machine tool and the cutting tool are in good condition, that the cutting tool (an end mill cutter, S45C) is suitable for cutting the work piece (made of cast iron), that the work piece is properly held (only up milling is considered), and that no cutting fluid is used. (Note that without the above assumptions, the dataset would contain an enormous amount of data).During the experiment, a vibration analyzer, VA12, was used to measure the vibration. The vibration analyzer can measure vibrations based on the acceleration, velocity, and displacement. In this study, the vibration was measured according to the velocity. The dataset was collected by an expert working with a machine tool factory in Taiwan. The data collection steps include (1) putting a set of input parameters into the NC panel; (2) using the vibration analysis instrument (VA-12) to measure the data of velocity; and (3) measuring the classification of vibration class according to the velocity.

The vibration classes are divided into three classes (based on the machine tool industry in Taiwan): (1) the velocity below G2.5 (2.5 mm/s) is good (no vibration, class 3); (2) the velocity between G2.5 to G6.3 is acceptable (light vibration, class 2); and (3) the velocity over G6.3 is not good (vibration, class 1). The dataset consists of 360 cases and the 10-fold cross validation method was used for the validation of the developed model. The dataset was divided into two groups: The first group (containing 60% of the data) was used for training the model and the second group (containing 40% of the data) was employed for testing the model. The dataset belongs to the Manford Machine Company in Taiwan and can be requested by contacting the corresponding author by email.

5.1. CNC MillingMachine

Computer numerical control (CNC) milling machines, featuring high speed, high accuracy, and high productivity, have been used for machining parts in many industrial fields. In general, CNC milling machines are grouped by the number of axes they can operate. X- and Y-axes designate horizontal movement of the work piece (forward-and-back and side-to-side on a flat plane), and Z-axis represents the vertical movement. The structure of milling machines includes two sectors: one consisting of the base, saddle, table, head stock and column (Figure 3), and the other consisting of the spindle, magazine, NC panel, cover, and so on (Figure 4).

Figure 3. The cast parts of a milling machine.

Figure 4. The accessory parts of a milling machine.

5.2. The Dynamic Behavior of Machine Tools

As mentioned in Section 2.2, machine tools can encounter free vibrations, forced vibrations and self-excited vibrations (chatter) during operating. Free vibrations and forced vibrations are less destructive compared to chatter. Chatter is induced and maintained by forces generated from the cutting process [25]. For example, increasing spindle speeds may result in the onset of chatter. Chatter can create large cutting forces and thus may accelerate tool wear and even cause tool failure, resulting in vibrations of the machine tools. In order to analyze chatter's dynamic behavior of machine tools, the rigidity and stability are two important characteristics that need to be taken into account.

The conditions of rigidity and stability of the machine tools can cause vibrations during machining processes. The rigidity or stability changes resulted from several phenomena including (1) chip thickness variation; (2) penetration rate variation; and (3) cutting speed variation. Each of these phenomena, in turn, is caused by several input parameters during operations (see Figure 5). For example, the chip thickness variation is affected by (a) the number of teeth (n), (b) the diameter of the cutter (d_e) or the radial tool engagement (a_e), and (c) the depth of cut/axial depth of cut (a_p). The penetration rate variation is affected by (a) the feed per tooth (f_z) and (b) the feed speed (v_f). The cutting speed variation is affected by (a) cutting speed (v_c) and (b) revolutions per minute (n-rpm).

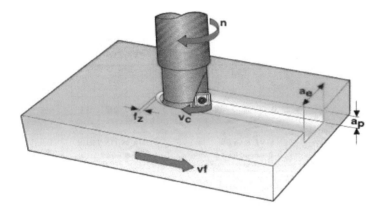

Figure 5. An example of a milling process.

5.3. Identifying Input and Output Variables

Based on the discussion in Section 5.2 and on a literature review, seven input variables that may affect the vibrations of machine tools during machining were identified. These input variables are (1) the number of teeth (n); (2) the diameter of the cutter (d_e) or the radial tool engagement (a_e); (3) the depth of cut/axial depth of cut (a_p); (4) the feed per tooth (f_z); (5) the feed speed (v_f); (6) the cutting speed (v_c); and (7) the revolutions per minute (n-rpm).

The final step of all classification approaches is to assign each data an appropriate output (class label). According to the description at the top of Section 5, the class labels were defined as 1, 2, and 3 for Vibration, Light Vibration, and No Vibration, respectively.

6. Results

The models were coded and implemented in the Matlab environment (Matlab R2013b). In the experiment, a 10-fold cross validation method was employed to avoid over-fitting. In the process, the training dataset was divided into 10 subsets. Each classifying combination was trained 10 times. Each time, one of the 10 subsets served as the validation set and the remaining subsets were treated as the training sets. The classifying combination having the highest accuracy on the validation set (based on averaging over 10 runs) was selected.

Different neural network architectures with different numbers of hidden layers and neurons were investigated. The Levenberg-Marquardt algorithm [26] was used to train the neural networks. The performance was measured using mean squared error, and the network architecture with the highest efficiency was selected. The selected architecture consisted of a single hidden layer with 9 neurons. After training and validating, the ANN classifier was tested using the testing dataset. The efficiency of the classifier was determined by comparing the predicted and actual class labels for the testing dataset. The results show that the overall accuracy of the ANN classifier was 90.27%.

To assess the performance of the ANN, the results obtained by the ANN classifier were compared with those obtained by other classification approaches. The 10-fold cross validation method was also used to select the classifier combinations. The prediction accuracy of the SVM classifier for the testing dataset came out to be 55.56%. For the naive Bayes classifier, the prediction accuracy was 71.53%. The classification and regression tree (CART) algorithm was used for constructing the decision tree model. The obtained accuracy for the decision tree classifier was 76.39%. The performance of these approaches for the classification of vibration classes are summarized in Figure 6, together with confusion matrices. When these results are compared with those obtained by the ANN model, it can be seen that the ANN classifier outperformed the SVM, naive Bayes, and DT classifiers .Based on these results, it is concluded that the ANN model is capable of effectively classifying the vibration conditions.

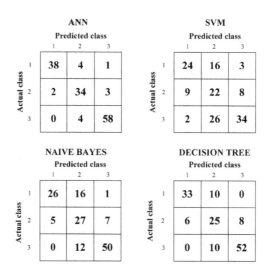

Figure 6. Confusion matrices obtained by different classification approaches.

7. Conclusions

By classifying vibration conditions into different classes, factories are able to provide better managing services. Thus, a classifier that can correctly classify cutting vibration is a necessity for any machine tool factory. Although there are various classifiers, however, increasing the classification accuracy is still a subject of great importance. In this study, an ANN model to classify the vibration conditions is proposed. The classification accuracy of the model was evaluated by comparing it with other well-known classifiers, including SVM, Naive Bayes, and DT classifiers. The obtained results demonstrated that the ANN model outperformed the others. It is hoped that this study may be used as a reference for different machining processes to predict cutting vibrations. It is also expected that this study can make a significant contribution to the machine tool industry.

Acknowledgments: This research was funded by the National Science Council of Taiwan under Grant No. MOST 103-2221-E-035-052.

Author Contributions: Jeng-Fung Chen conceived of the work. Quang Hung Do conducted the literature review. All of the authors developed the research design and implemented the research. The final manuscript has been approved by all authors.

Conflicts of Interest: The authors declare no conflict of interest.

References

1. Zhu, J.; Ni, J.; Shih, A.J. Robust machine tool thermal error modeling through thermal Mode concept. *J. Manuf. Sci. Eng.* **2008**, *130*. [CrossRef]
2. Whalley, R.; Abdul-Ameer, A.; Ebrahimi, M.; El-Shalabi, S. Adaptive machine tool system regulation. *Control Theory Appl. IET* **2009**, *3*, 33–48. [CrossRef]

3. Altintas, Y. Research on metal cutting, machine tool vibrations and control. *J. Jpn. Soc. Precis. Eng.* **2011**, *77*, 470–471.
4. Kruth, J.-P.; Van Ginderachter, T.; Tanaya, P.I.; Valckenaers, P. The use of finite state machines for task-based machine tool control. *Comput. Ind.* **2001**, *46*, 247–258. [CrossRef]
5. Cho, D.W.; Leeb, S.J.; Chu, C.N. The state of machining process monitoring research in Korea. *Int. J. Mach. Tools Manuf.* **1999**, *39*, 1697–1715. [CrossRef]
6. Meredith, D. Practical tool condition monitoring. *Manuf. Eng.* **1998**, *120*, 34–39.
7. Westkämper, E.; Westerbusch, R. The Diagnosis and monitoring system DIAMANT. *Product. Eng.* **1993**, *1*, 131–134.
8. Nakai, M.E.; Aguiar, P.R.; Junior, H.G.; Bianchi, E.C.; Spatti, D.H.; D'Addona, D.M. Evaluation of Neural Models Applied to the Estimation of Tool Wear in the Grinding of Advanced Ceramics. *Expert Syst. Appl.* **2015**, *42*, 7026–7035. [CrossRef]
9. D'Addona, D.; Segreto, T.; Simeone, A.; Teti, R. ANN Tool Wear Modelling in the Machining of Nickel Superalloy Industrial Products. *CIRP J. Manuf. Sci. Technol.* **2011**, *4*, 33–37. [CrossRef]
10. Leone, C.; D'Addona, D.; Teti, R. Tool Wear Modelling through Regression Analysis and Intelligent Methods for Nickel Base Alloy Machining. *CIRP J. Manuf. Sci. Technol.* **2011**, *11*, 327–331. [CrossRef]
11. Ko, T.J.; Jung, M.Y. On-line monitoring of tool breakage in face milling using a self-organized neural network. *J. Manuf. Syst.* **1995**, *14*, 80–90. [CrossRef]
12. Ko, T.J.; Dong, W.C. Cutting state monitoring in milling by a neural network. *Int. J. Mach. Tools Manuf.* **1994**, *34*, 695–676. [CrossRef]
13. Ko, T.J.; Dong, W.C. Adaptive Optimization of Face Milling Operations Using Neural Networks. *J. Manuf. Sci. Eng.* **1998**, *120*, 443–451. [CrossRef]
14. Ko, T.J.; Dong, W.C. Adaptive modelling of the milling process and application of a neural network for tool wear monitoring. *Int. J. Adv. Manuf. Technol.* **1996**, *12*, 5–13. [CrossRef]
15. Siddhpura, M.; Paurobally, R. Experimental investigation of chatter vibration in facing and turning process. *Int. J. Mech. Aerosp. Ind. Mechatron. Manuf. Eng.* **2013**, *7*, 84–89.
16. Choudhury, S.K.; Goudimenko, N.N.; Kudinov, V.A. On-Line control of machine tool vibration in turning. *Int. J.Mach. Tools Manuf.* **1997**, *37*, 801–811. [CrossRef]
17. Ema, S.; Marui, E. Theoretical analysis on chatter vibration in drilling and its suppression. *J. Mater. Process. Technol.* **2003**, *138*, 572–578. [CrossRef]
18. Quintana, G.; Garcia-Romeu, M.L.; Ciurana, J. Surface roughness monitoring application based on artificial neural networks for ball-end milling operations. *J. Intell. Manuf.* **2011**, *22*, 607–617. [CrossRef]
19. Debeljak, M.; Dzeroski, S. *Decision Trees in Ecological Modelling in Modelling Complex Ecological Dynamics*; Springer: Berlin/Heidelberg, Germany, 2001.
20. Sharma, A.; Kumar, R.; Varadwaj, P.K.; Ahmad, A.; Ashraf, G.M. A comparative study of support vector machine, artificial neural network and Bayesian classifier for mutagenicity prediction. *Interdiscip. Sci. Comput. Life Sci.* **2011**, *3*, 232–239. [CrossRef] [PubMed]
21. Bahler, D.; Stone, B.; Wellington, C.; Bristol, D.W. Symbolic, neural, and Bayesian machine learning models for predicting carcinogenicity of chemical compounds. *J. Chem. Inf. Model.* **2000**, *40*, 906–914. [CrossRef]
22. Hornik, K.; Stinchombe, M.; White, H. Universal Approximation of an unknown Mapping and its Derivatives Using Multilayer Feed-forward Networks. *Neural Netw.* **1990**, *3*, 551–560. [CrossRef]
23. Cybenko, G. Approximation by superposition of a sigmoid function. *Math. Control Signals Syst.* **1989**, *2*, 303–314. [CrossRef]
24. Abdi, H.; Valentin, D.; Edelman, B.; O'Toole, A.J. A Widrow-Hoff Learning Rule for a Generalization of the Linear Auto-associator. *J. Math. Psychol.* **1996**, *40*, 175–182. [CrossRef]
25. Siddhpura, M.; Paurobally, R. A review of chatter vibration research in turning. *Int. J. Mach. Tools Manuf.* **2012**, *61*, 27–47. [CrossRef]
26. More, J.J. The Levenberg-Marquardt algorithm: Implementation and theory. *Lect. Notes Math.* **2006**, *630*, 105–116.

Ultra-Reliable Link Adaptation for Downlink MISO Transmission in 5G Cellular Networks

Udesh Oruthota *,†, Furqan Ahmed † and Olav Tirkkonen †

Department of Communications & Networking, Aalto University, P.O. Box 13000 FI-00076 AALTO, Espoo, Finland; furqan.ahmed@aalto.fi (F.A.); olav.tirkkonen@aalto.fi (O.T.)
* Correspondence: udesh.oruthota@aalto.fi (U.O.)
† These authors contributed equally to this work.

Academic Editors: Mikael Skoglund, Lars K. Rasmussen and Tobias Oechtering

Abstract: This paper addresses robust link adaptation for a precoded downlink multiple input single output (MISO) system, for guaranteeing ultra-reliable (99.999%) transmissions to mobile users served by a small cell network (e.g. slowly moving machines in a factory). Effects of inaccurate channel state information (CSI) caused by user mobility and varying precoders in neighboring cells are mitigated. Both of these impairments translate to changes of received signal-to-noise plus interference ratios (SINRs), leading to CSI mispredictions and potentially erroneous transmissions. Knowing the statistics of the propagation channels and the precoder variation, backoff values can be selected to guarantee robust link adaptation. Combining this with information on the current channel state, transmissions can be adapted to have a desired reliability. Theoretical analysis accompanied by simulation results show that the proposed approach is suitable for attaining 5G ultra-reliability targets in realistic settings.

Keywords: 5G; link adaptation; mobility; precoder; SINR variability; ultra-reliable communication

1. Introduction

The evolution of mobile communication systems has culminated in the dawn of a 5G vision, which envisages providing services, both human and machine centric, with diverse quality of service (QoS) requirements and applications [1]. In order to address these challenges, a number of targets have been identified for 5G, to be achieved in 2020 time-frame. The foremost is enhancing existing mobile data volume by a factor of $1000\times$, which is to be attained by addition of new spectrum, enhancement of spectral efficiency of existing systems, greater number of antennas, and smaller cells. In contrast, new and significantly more challenging targets stem from the application of various wireless technologies to machine-centric domains such as machine type communications (MTC) or machine to machine communications. It comprises of two main paradigms—massive MTC and mission-critical MTC. In massive MTC, the idea is to connect a large number of machines such as sensors, actuators, and other devices to a common platform, paving the way for Internet of Things. Most of these machines will likely be low-cost, requiring low-data volumes and energy consumption, but long deployment periods. On the other hand, mission critical MTC scenarios are usually characterized by very low latency, high reliability, and high availability. This has led to an emergence of new use cases, which often consist of very stringent requirements in terms of latency, reliability, and availability — collectively referred to as ultra-reliable communications (URC) in 5G systems. URC is primarily envisioned to be applied at short time-scales, where it has a multitude of applications such as vehicle-to-vehicle communication and smart grid control. A target envisioned for URC in 5G is 99.999% reliability with 2 ms latency [2]. This presents novel challenges at multiple levels, and requires complete rethinking of system design approaches. URC networks differ from conventional mobile broadband systems, in that the focus is not on the peak and median performance, but on the situation of lower 0.00001 percentile of users. URC network design is essentially based on the analysis of worst case scenarios, and the preventive measures one can take to avert them.

The concept of reliability pertaining to 5G systems can be defined in many ways, depending on the use case at hand. In order to develop a systematic framework inclusive of all use cases, ultra-reliability can essentially be understood as a network property that constitutes three dimensions [3,4]: availability, reliability, and latency. The network is unavailable when it is undergoing an unscheduled downtime. The main factors that impact availability include hardware/software faults, human errors, natural disasters, depletion of network resources due to overloading, *etc.* On the other hand, latency is an end-to-end network design issue, and its enhancement may require changes in architecture and procedures at different layers. It can be improved by reducing delays emanating from propagation, processing, large packet sizes, and queuing. Finally, reliability can be considered as the probability of successful transmission across a wireless link, given that the system is available, and is able to meet the minimum latency requirements.

A multitude of factors contribute to reliability at a network level. In particular, mobility related changes in the channels of users and existence of multiple nodes in the network competing for the same resources, may lead to a significant increase in problem complexity. Accordingly, impairments such as interference, inaccuracy in channel state information (CSI), and link adaptation errors cause loss in reliability. These issues can be addressed via an efficient management of network radio resources across multiple degrees of freedom (e.g., time, space, frequency). For instance, in [5], resource allocation is considered to mitigate interference, and guarantee a network-wide target data rate to the users. It is worth noting that high availability and reliability, as well as low latency are needed to ensure URC, but the relative significance of these may vary across use cases.

In this work, we address link adaptation from an URC perspective. In adaptive modulation and coding (AMC) protocols, the transmission rate is selected based on a channel quality indicator (CQI), which is a part of the CSI measured by the intended receiver, and fed back to the transmitter. However, if the channel undergoes fading, the measured CSI becomes outdated due to the unavoidable feedback and processing delays. The channels at the time instant of transmission, can thus differ substantially from the measured channels. With outdated CSI, the outage performance is severely degraded, and the channel capacity is affected [6,7]. In addition to mobility induced variations in the channels, the use of radio resources in interfering cells may also change between the measurement and the transmission instants. For example, changes in precoding may change the interference [8]. In order to ensure that a transmission is received within the tight latency window required by URC, robust link adaptation is needed. Consequently, transmissions can be received with very high reliability.

1.1. Related Work

General aspects of reliability and availability for communication networks have been studied in a number of works. The problem formulation, proposed methods and algorithms are often network specific. In particular, reliable routing and data delivery protocols have been studied quite extensively for mobile *ad hoc* networks [9], and wireless sensor networks [10].

In the context of 5G networking, the concept of ultra-reliability is, however, different in terms of scope, motivation, and requirements. From a 5G perspective, the area is in its infancy, and existing works mostly discuss ideas at a conceptual level, and propose different use cases which may benefit from ultra-reliability [1]. A detailed exposition is given in [2], which proposes a reliable service composition framework for guaranteeing a high level of reliability—the probability that a certain amount of data is transmitted in the given time frame. Identified sources of unreliability include resource depletion and interference. In [11], an availability indicator parameter is introduced as a key enabler for ultra-reliability in 5G, where availability is defined in terms of absence or presence of link reliability at the time of transmission.

In cellular packet data systems, hybrid automatic repeat requests (HARQ) are utilized in conjunction with AMC to enable robustness [12,13]. A certain probability of retransmissions is desirable, when maximizing the system throughput with a given reliability target, see e.g., [14,15]. In order to achieve near-optimal performance, open-loop link adaptation is a viable option [16], where the AMC thresholds are tuned to keep a desirable retransmission probability. However, when targeting high reliability with strict latency required by URC, one cannot solely rely on HARQ. To make intelligent link adaptation decisions, it is beneficial to know the statistics of the channel, or the signal-to-interference-plus-noise ratio (SINR), of the realized transmission conditioned on the measured SINR. Next, by selecting a suitable backoff, a suitable modulation and coding scheme can be chosen, which support a target outage probability. An example of such SINR-statistics aware link adaptation related to interferer precoding variation can be found in [17].

1.2. Contributions

In this paper, the idea is to enable robust link adaptation, so that user data rates can be supported with the desired reliability. In order to decode transmissions successfully within delay constraints, a transmission rate has to be selected such that a codeword can be decoded with high reliability. Without loss of generality, we focus on achieving a reliability target of 99.999%, and leave out the availability considerations.

We investigate SINR variations caused by the mobility related changes in the wanted and interfering channels, as well as interferer precoders. It is assumed that the channels are Rayleigh fading with Jakes' Doppler spectrum [18], and single stream precoding from N_T transmit antennas is used. Link adaptation is based on perfect knowledge of the instantaneous channel state at the time of measurement, channel statistics, and the correlation between measured and realized channels. Using this information we devise robust link adaptation, which can support URC targets. A transmission rate is selected so that the channel capacity at the time of transmission supports the selected rate with high probability. We find that fading of the link between transmitter and receiver, even with moderate mobility, dominates over fading of interference, and interference variability. Moreover, knowledge of channel and interference statistics, as well as the instantaneous channel and interference realization, is invaluable for robust link adaptation for URC.

1.3. Notation and Organization

Vectors are represented using boldface lower-case letters. The conjugate transpose is represented by $(.)^H$, and $|.|$ denotes the absolute value. A probability density function (PDF) for random variable (RV)x is represented by $f_X(x)$ and the corresponding cumulative distribution (CDF) is $F_X(x)$. Probability of a given event θ is denoted by $P(\theta)$. The non-central chi square distribution with non-central parameter δ and degree of freedom (DoF) n is denoted by $\chi^2(x; n; \delta)$. The subscripts 0 and τ denote the variables at measurement phase and at a given transmission realization after $t = \tau$ ms from measurement, respectively.

The rest of the paper is organized as follows: Section 2 discusses the system model. Section 3 introduces the sources of SINR variability and the related statistical distributions. User mobility and changes in other-cell precoding are discussed. Backoff selection for robust link adaptation is considered. Finally, conclusions are drawn in Section 4.

2. System Model

A downlink multi-cell system is considered, where a number of base stations are deployed to serve mobile terminals (users). The association of users to base stations is fixed and known *a priori*, so that each user is served by a unique base station. The total bandwidth is shared by all cells in a universal frequency reuse manner, and the intra-cell resource allocation is orthogonal. Each base station has N_T transmit antennas, and users have a single receive antenna. The multiple transmit antennas at base stations are used for single-stream beamforming towards their respective users.

2.1. SINR Estimation

Link adaptation is based on the measurement performed by the intended receiver at a time $t = 0$. Known pilot symbols z_k are transmitted with at least N_T orthogonal precoding vectors $\mathbf{w}_k \in \mathbb{C}^{N_T \times 1}$, for $k = 1, \ldots, N_T$. We assume that all of these transmissions happen essentially simultaneously. With J transmissions from known interferers, the signal received at the user of interest at $t = 0$ for pilot transmission k

$$y_{0,k} = \mathbf{h}_0 \mathbf{w}_{0,k} z_k + \sum_{j=1}^{J} \mathbf{h}_{0,j} \mathbf{v}_{0,j} x_j + n \tag{1}$$

where $\mathbf{h}_0 \in \mathbb{C}^{1 \times N_T}$ is the channel gain vector for the desired transmission, $\mathbf{h}_{0,j}$ are the interfering channel vectors from transmitter j to the user of interest, and $\mathbf{v}_{0,j} \in \mathbb{C}^{N_T \times 1}$ are the precoders applied by the interfering transmitters, all at the time of measurement $t = 0$, on the time-frequency resource used for pilot transmission k. Here, x_j are the transmit symbols on jth transmission. All transmitted symbols are assumed to be of unit average energy, and all precoding vectors are assumed unit norm. As a concrete channel model we consider independent and identically distributed (i.i.d.) Rayleigh fading. The elements in the channel vectors $\mathbf{h}_0$ and $\mathbf{h}_{0,j}$ are assumed to be drawn from independent complex Gaussian processes with zero mean and variance S_{ave} and $I_{\text{ave},j}$, respectively. These variances carry information of the path losses of the signals. The channel realizations developed under fading processes after the measurement are drawn from the same distribution as the channels at a given measurement instance, and are conditioned on the measurement results. Additive White Gaussian Noise (AWGN) with variance N_0 is denoted by n. This variable may also model interference from other than the J known sources, which is assumed Gaussian.

We assume multiple orthogonal pilot transmissions of the form Equation (1) extending over multiple transmissions within a coherence time and bandwidth of the channels. This enables the receiver to reliably estimate the channel $\mathbf{h}_0$. Canceling the transmissions of the known pilot signals over the estimated channels from signals of Equation (1), interference plus noise powers can be estimated, and accordingly SINRs. Finally, we assume that the receiver knows the pilot signals of the J known interferers as well. In a communication frame at measurement time $t = 0$, there would thus be received signals of the type Equation (1) for the pilots of the J known interferers, making it possible to separate the contributions of the interferers to interference plus noise power at the time of measurement. Collecting statistics over longer periods, it is possible to estimate characteristics of the statistical distributions of the channels. Here, we assume these statistics are perfectly known. Collecting such statistics would be possible in environments where the channels remain wide sense stationary for extended periods of time, e.g., in factory environments [19].

For a forthcoming transmission to the user of interest, a precoder $\mathbf{v}_0$ is selected, either based on the measurements at time $t = 0$, or by some other means. If the transmitter selects the precoder, it is informed to the user. As a result, we have an estimated SINR

$$\gamma_0 = \frac{|\mathbf{h}_0 \mathbf{v}_0|^2}{\sum_{j=1}^{J} |\mathbf{h}_{0,j} \mathbf{v}_{0,j}|^2 + N_0} \tag{2}$$

for a forthcoming transmission. If the precoder is selected based on the user channel only, a typical choice would be to take $\mathbf{v}_0$ to be a normalized version of $\mathbf{h}_0^H$, or a quantized version thereof. Otherwise it may be, e.g., a common precoder which is used to serve all users in the cell in order to stabilize inter-cell interference. The J interfering transmissions are assumed to be independent.

This channel model extends readily to a situation where the interferer is a higher rank transmission. As rank-1 interference is the worst [17], we concentrate on it in the following discussion.

2.2. SINR Realized at Time of Transmission

The measured SINR γ_0 is used in link adaptation to choose an applicable transmission rate. For this, the measurement result is fed back by the receiver to the transmitter. There are delays in feedback, and in processing at the measuring end, and the transmitter. Accordingly, when the channel is used for a data transmission, both the propagation channel carrying the wanted signal component, and the channels of the interferers have changed. In addition, the precoders used in the interfering base stations may be changed according to their scheduling decisions. Accordingly, the SINR experienced by the realized transmission differs from γ_0.

The received signal for a data transmission at a transmission instance which is delayed τ seconds from the measurement is

$$y_\tau = \mathbf{h}_\tau \mathbf{v}_\tau x + \sum_{j=1}^{J} \mathbf{h}_{\tau,j} \mathbf{v}_{\tau,j} x_j + n \tag{3}$$

where $\mathbf{h}_\tau$ and $\mathbf{h}_{\tau,j}$ are the realized channel coefficients for the desired transmission and the interferers between the intended transmitters and the receiver, respectively, at time τ. The corresponding transmitted symbols are denoted by x and x_j. The precoders $\mathbf{v}_{\tau,j}$ applied on the interferers may be the same as the ones during the measurement, or they may be changed according to scheduling decisions. Therefore, the precoder $\mathbf{v}_\tau$ may either be $\mathbf{v}_0$, or a precoder selected on the basis of scheduling decisions. We assume that the precoder of the wanted signal transmission remains the same as the precoder used at SINR estimation.

We assume that $\mathbf{h}_\tau$ is a random vector drawn from the same distribution as $\mathbf{h}_0$. These two channels are correlated for short delays τ. The effect of channel dispersion due to Doppler shift can be modeled by [20]

$$\mathbf{h}_\tau = \rho \mathbf{h}_0 + \sqrt{1 - \rho^2} \tilde{\mathbf{h}} . \tag{4}$$

The estimation error $\tilde{\mathbf{h}}$ is an independent sample drawn from the same complex channel distribution as $\mathbf{h}_0$ and $\mathbf{h}_\tau$. Assuming Jakes' model, the normalized auto-correlation coefficient of a Rayleigh faded channel with constant velocity motion is $\rho = J_0(2\pi f_{D,max} \tau)$ [18]. The maximum Doppler shift is $f_{D,max} = 2\frac{v}{c}f$, and v, c and f are the velocity of the user, velocity of light, and the carrier frequency, respectively. Here, $J_0(\cdot)$ is a zeroth-order Bessel function of the first kind, and delay τ is measured in seconds. We remark that effects of imperfect channel estimation lead to a correlation model of the same form as Equation (4), see [21]. In that case, the correlation ρ would depend, not on τ, but on SINR, and the channel estimation algorithm. Accordingly, our model extends to imperfect channel estimation as well, with an appropriate interpretation of ρ.

2.3. Robust Link Adaptation

We assume a family of AMC schemes, consisting of a virtually continuous set of possible rates r for packet transmissions. When transmitted in a block fading channel with SINR γ, a packet error probability (PEP) function $P_e(r, \gamma)$ characterizes this family. This function is monotonously growing in r, and monotonously decreasing in γ. When blocks are sufficiently short such an AMC scheme may be coupled with a retransmission protocol which is able to operate within the target URC latency, see [22]. Based on the measured γ_0, and knowledge of channel statistics, we construct a probability density $f(\gamma_\tau | \gamma_0)$. When rate r is used, the expected probability of packet error is $\bar{P}_e(r) = \int P_e(r, \gamma) f(\gamma | \gamma_0) d\gamma$. If we could use infinitely long codewords, $P_e(r, \gamma)$ would be a step function at a threshold value $\gamma_t(r)$.

When targeting an outage probability P_{out}, maximizing r with infinitely long codewords would lead to the outage capacity. URC frame lengths are foreseen to be shorter than in LTE.

We are interested in indoors factory settings, however, where coherence bandwidths of tens of MHz are reported [19]. Accordingly, codewords may be of sizeable length in scenarios of interest. When extending to short packets, outage capacity may be an inaccurate performance metric [23]. Knowing the accurate $P_e(r, \gamma)$ and $f(\gamma|\gamma_0)$ would allow finding the maximum r with the given outage probability. Here, for simplicity, we assume step function $P_e(r, \gamma)$, so that maximizing the rate given P_{out}, can be achieved by first finding a threshold SINR γ_t so that $\int_0^{\gamma_t} f(\gamma|\gamma_0)d\gamma = P_{out}$, and then finding the r which guarantees error free transmission at this γ_t. Accordingly, one can compute a backoff $b = \gamma_0/\gamma_t$ related to the link adaptation based on γ_0. Then one can guarantee that irrespective of the SINR variability, the transmission can be reliably received with a very high probability. We consider URC outage probability $P_{out} = 10^{-5}$, i.e., 99.999% reliability.

3. Sources of SINR Variability

There are a number of sources of SINR/interference variability that can jeopardize reliability in a wireless/cellular network. These include the following:

1. Variations in wanted signal channel between time of measurement and time of transmission
2. Interference variability caused by the changes in channels of interferers
3. Interference variability caused by radio resource management (RRM) in interfering cells (Changing multi-antenna transmissions, channel activity, power control, uplink user scheduling)

We consider all of these, separately as well as their joint effect. SINR/interference variations caused by RRM may be stabilized by applying persistent RRM strategies. For example, downlink precoded multi-antenna transmissions, where the precoders are not user specific but frequency resource specific and optimized for a population of users, may be considered. As a result, the SINR misprediction of the third kind partially vanishes. Not much can be done to remove the variability of the first and second kind, however, if the user and/or the channel is mobile. To mitigate the impairments caused by these sources of SINR variability, we consider robust link adaptation where the SINR statistics of the realized transmission conditioned on the measured SINR are known.

3.1. Changes in Wanted Signal Power

The time selectivity of the desired channel induces SINR variability at the receiver, and is discussed next. For this, we first assume that the interference experienced by the user of interest remains static until the transmission is realized. The distribution of the signal power $S = |\mathbf{h}_\tau \mathbf{v}_0|^2$ is thus of interest. From Equation (4) we find

$$S = \left| \rho \mathbf{h}_0 \mathbf{v}_0 + \sqrt{1 - \rho^2} \tilde{\mathbf{h}} \mathbf{v}_0 \right|^2 . \tag{5}$$

Then, for a given channel measurement $\mathbf{h}_0$ and the precoder $\mathbf{v}_0$, S can be modeled as a magnitude of a sum of two squared independent Gaussian RVs with equal variance $\alpha = (1 - \rho^2)\frac{S_{ave}}{2}$, and means $\mu_\Re = \rho \Re\{\mathbf{h}_0\mathbf{v}_0\}$ and $\mu_\Im = \rho \Im\{\mathbf{h}_0\mathbf{v}_0\}$. Note that the probability distribution of the inner product of a channel vector $\mathbf{h}$ with i.i.d. Gaussian elements and an arbitrary unitary vector $\mathbf{v}$, is equal to the distribution of an element of the channel vector $\mathbf{h}$. Therefore, the PDF of the signal power $f_S(s)$ can be characterized by a non-central chi-square distribution with two DoF, and non-centrality $\delta = (\mu_\Re^2 + \mu_\Im^2)/\alpha = \frac{2\rho^2}{(1-\rho^2)}\frac{S_0}{S_{ave}}$. Here, $S_0 = |\mathbf{h}_0\mathbf{v}_0|^2$ is the measured signal power and S_{ave} is the average signal power at measurement. Note the underlying assumption that both S_0 and S_{ave} are known, along with the signal statistics. This means that the current fading state of the signal is precisely known. The PDF of the signal power is given by

$$f_S(s \mid \mathbf{h}_0, \mathbf{v}_0, S_{ave}) = \frac{1}{2\alpha}\text{Exp}\left\{ -\frac{s/\alpha + \delta}{2} \right\} I_0\left(\sqrt{\frac{\delta s}{\alpha}} \right) \tag{6}$$

where $I_0(\cdot)$ is the modified Bessel function of the first kind. The corresponding CDF is given by $F_S(s \mid \mathbf{h}_0, \mathbf{v}_0, S_{\text{ave}}) = 1 - Q_1(\sqrt{\delta}, \sqrt{s/\alpha})$, where $Q_M(a, b)$ is the Marcum-Q function, here with $M = 1$ [24]. The SINR variability caused by changing desired transmission signal power can be visualized from the CDF. The realized SINR is $\gamma_\tau = \frac{S}{I_0 + N_0}$, where $I_0 = \sum_{j=1}^{J} |\mathbf{h}_{0,j}\mathbf{v}_{0,j}|^2$ is the measured interference power which is considered fixed for the given transmission realization. Now, the outage probability becomes $\mathrm{P}(\gamma_\tau < \gamma_t)$. The URC outage probability target is achieved at a SINR threshold γ_t, and the required backoff to enable robust link adaptation is $b = \frac{\gamma_0}{\gamma_t}$. The outage probability can be further simplified to

$$\mathrm{P}\left(\frac{S}{I_0 + N_0} < \gamma_t\right) = F_X\left(\gamma_t(I_0 + N_0)\right)$$

$$= 1 - Q_1\left(\sqrt{\frac{2\rho^2}{(1 - \rho^2)} \frac{S_0}{S_{\text{ave}}}}, \sqrt{\frac{2}{(1 - \rho^2)b} \frac{S_0}{S_{\text{ave}}}}\right). \qquad (7)$$

We consider a delay between measurement and transmission of $\tau = 1$ ms, in accordance with the URC latency targets. For a carrier frequency $f = 3.6$ GHz, user velocities $v \approx 8, 7$, and 5 km/h would lead to auto-correlation coefficients $\rho \approx 0.97, 0.98$ and 0.99, respectively. Figure 1 demonstrates how the time selectivity of a channel affects the realized transmission, for three different situations. In the first, the channel of the desired transmission during the measurement is faded ($S_0/S_{\text{ave}} = -10$ dB), in the second it is slightly faded ($S_0/S_{\text{ave}} = -3$ dB), whereas in the third it is not faded ($S_0/S_{\text{ave}} = 0$ dB). In a faded state, when the measured signal power of the desired transmission is 10 times smaller than the average, the distribution of the realized signal power is wide, and the probability of dropping into deeper fade increases for the transmission instant at time $t = \tau$. Hence, the required backoff is significantly larger when the channel (at the time of measurement) is faded, when compared to the situation where it is on an average level (i.e., $S_0/S_{\text{ave}} = 0$ dB).

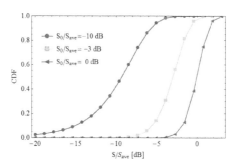

Figure 1. Cumulative distribution of the desired signal power for $\rho = 0.98$, and for three different values of S_0/S_{ave}. Relative realized signal powers S/S_{ave} dB are on the x-axis.

Note that the auto-correlation coefficient statistically characterizes the level of correlation between the measured and realized channels. When the channel (at a given channel instant) is in faded state, and $\rho \approx 1$, the probability of getting to a deeper fade is significant. Figure 2, in left half, shows how the required backoff b (in dB) varies with relative measured signal power $\frac{S_0}{S_{\text{ave}}}$ for three different channel auto-correlation coefficients $\rho = \{0.97, 0.98, 0.99\}$. If the measured transmission power is of the same order as the average transmission power, i.e., when the measured channel is in a typical fading state, the required backoff is relatively small. However, when the measured signal is in a fade, extreme backoffs are required to provide ultra-reliability. This is a consequence of the Rayleigh fading statistics used here, where arbitrarily deep fades have finite probability.

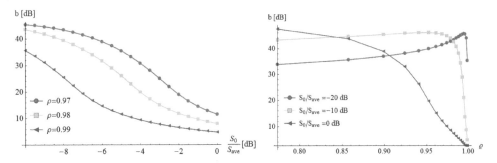

Figure 2. Backoff required for URC link adaptation against wanted signal variation. **Left:** Backoff *vs.* S_0/S_{ave} for three different ρ values; **Right:** Backoff *vs.* ρ for three different S_0/S_{ave} values.

The right half of Figure 2 shows the backoff as a function of ρ. With zero correlation, the wanted signal power at outage is $S_{out}/S_{ave} = -50$ dB, and the backoff is thus directly S_0/S_{out}. Here, S_{out} represents the instantaneous signal power S at URC outage. When the measured channel was in a typical fading state, with $S_0/S_{ave} = 0$ dB, the backoff is $b = 50$ dB at $\rho = 0$, shrinking monotonously to $b = 0$ dB at $\rho = 1$. For smaller S_0/S_{ave}, *i.e.*, when the measured channel was faded, the backoff first grows with increasing ρ. This is a consequence of the increase in correlation, which makes it more likely that the signal remains in a faded state, and goes into deeper fading. However, after a threshold, the backoff starts shrinking, going to $b = 0$ at $\rho = 1$. For example, for $S_0/S_{ave} = -20$ dB, the backoff at $\rho = 0$ would be $b = 30$ dB, from where it grows to a value of $b \approx 46$ dB at $\rho = 0.995$, before shrinking to zero.

3.2. Changes in Interfering Channels

In addition to changes in the wanted signal, mobility also causes changes in the interfering signals. To obtain the statistics of the SINR, the distribution of total interference power is essential. We consider the interference experienced at the receiver of interest, produced by J independent interference sources. Here, we assume that there is no change in the interference precoder from the time of measurement to the time of transmission. The realized interference power then is

$$I_\tau = \sum_{j=1}^{J} |\mathbf{h}_{\tau,j}\mathbf{v}_{0,j}|^2 \qquad (8)$$

where the realized channel $\mathbf{h}_{\tau,j}$ follows the autocorrelation model Equation (4). Note that the transmission power level is assumed to be absorbed in the channels. Then the total interference power can be represented as a linear combination of magnitude squared of J mutually independent complex Gaussian RVs with non-zero mean and unit variance, $I_\tau = \sum_{j=1}^{J} \alpha_j |X_j|^2$ where $\alpha_j = (1 - \rho^2) \frac{I_{ave,j}}{2}$.

The RV X_j is again characterized by complex Gaussian distribution with mean $\frac{\rho}{\sqrt{1-\rho^2}}\sqrt{\frac{2I_{0,j}}{I_{ave,j}}}$ where $I_{0,j} = |\mathbf{h}_{0,j}\mathbf{v}_{0,j}|^2$. The real and imaginary components of RV X_j are Gaussian with unit variance and mean $\mu_\Re = \frac{\rho}{\sqrt{1-\rho^2}}\frac{\Re\{\mathbf{h}_{0,j}\mathbf{v}_{0,j}\}}{\sqrt{I_{ave,j}/2}}$ and $\mu_\Im = \frac{\rho}{\sqrt{1-\rho^2}}\frac{\Im\{\mathbf{h}_{j,0}\mathbf{v}_{j,0}\}}{\sqrt{I_{ave,j}/2}}$, respectively. Hence, $|X_j|^2$ can be modeled as a non-central chi square distribution with two degrees of freedom, and non-centrality $\delta_j = \mu_\Re^2 + \mu_\Im^2$. In the subsequent analysis, we treat this as the sum of two real RVs. Without loss of generality, we can consider these two to have mean $\sqrt{\delta_j/2}$, not $\mu_\Re$ and $\mu_\Im$, *i.e.*, we distribute the mean evenly across the real and imaginary components of X_j. This is done for ease of notation and analysis, and is precise due to the underlying circular symmetry.

To characterize the distribution of total interference, we use an expansion discussed in [25]. The probability density function of $\sum_{i=1}^{n} \alpha_i (Z_i + \delta_i)^2$ where $Z_1, Z_2, ..., Z_n$ are mutually independent standard normal random variables given by

$$f_n(\alpha, \delta, y) = \sum_{k=0}^{\infty} a_k \beta^{-1} \chi^2 \left(\frac{y}{\beta}; n + 2k; \Delta \right) \tag{9}$$

where $\chi^2(y/\beta; n + 2k; \Delta)$ is a non-central chi-square distribution, with $n + 2k$ DoF and non-centrality parameter $\Delta = \sum_{i=1}^{n} \delta_i^2$. The parameter $\beta > 0$ can be chosen at will, to guarantee convergence. Applying Equation (9) to the distribution of the total interference, the PDF can be expressed as

$$f_I(i_\tau) = \sum_{n=0}^{\infty} a_n \beta^{-1} \chi^2 \left(\frac{i_\tau}{\beta}; 2(J + n), \Delta \right). \tag{10}$$

Here, the non-centrality is $\Delta = \sum_{j=1}^{J} \frac{2\rho^2}{(1-\rho^2)} \frac{I_{0,j}}{I_{\text{ave},j}}$, where $I_{0,j} = |\mathbf{h}_{0,j} \mathbf{v}_{0,j}|^2$ is the measured interference power of the jth interferer, and the average interference power of interferer j is $I_{\text{ave},j}$. The multiplicative coefficients a_n can be derived from a recurrence formula in [26], and $\beta > 0$ can be appropriately selected for fast convergence. In Appendix A, it is argued that a choice guaranteeing convergence is

$$\beta = \frac{2\alpha_{\max} \alpha_{\min}}{\alpha_{\max} + \alpha_{\min}} \tag{11}$$

where α_{min} and α_{max} are the minimum and maximum values of $\{\alpha_i\}_1^J$.

In practice, some of the interference signals may be relatively small when compared to some others ($I_{0,j}/\max\{I_{0,j}\} < 0.1$). This may lead to extremely slow convergence of the series Equation (10), even with an optimal selection of β. For details, see Appendix A. To ensure numerical stability, some weak interferers may be approximated. A Gaussian approximation of the interference power distribution is not optimal. For URC operation, we are especially interested in the tail of the total interference distribution, which a Gaussian approximation would not capture. Instead, the large fluctuations of the distribution in (10) can be treated with a moment matching non-central chi-square approximation. The interference powers of some of the weak interferers is added to the strongest interferer, and moment matching is applied to obtain an equivalent distribution model [27].

For the total realized interference in Equation (8), the kth cumulant is

$$\kappa_k = 2^{k-1}(k - 1)! \left[\sum_{j=1}^{J} \alpha_j^k + k \sum_{j=1}^{J} \alpha_j^k \delta_j \right]. \tag{12}$$

A non-central chi-square approximation can be derived such that the first two cumulants, the mean κ_1 and the variance κ_2 equal the corresponding statistics of the total realized interference power. The non-centrality parameter and the DoF of the chi-square approximation $\chi^2(x; \tilde{J}; \tilde{\Delta})$ can be directly obtained as $\tilde{J} = 2\kappa_1 - \kappa_2/2$ and $\tilde{\Delta} = \kappa_2/2 - \kappa_1$. To achieve more accuracy at the tail of the distribution, the first four cumulants may be considered. The parameters $\tilde{\Delta}$ and $\tilde{J}$ are determined so that the skewness (κ_3) of the actual distribution and the approximation are equal and the difference between the kurtoses (κ_4) of two distributions is minimized [27]. If $s_1^2 > s_2$, the approximation is characterized by $\tilde{\Delta} = s_1 a^3 - a^2$ and $\tilde{J} = a^2 - 2\tilde{\Delta}$, with $a = 1/(s_1 - \sqrt{s_1^2 - s_2})$. Else, if $s_1^2 \leq s_2$, $\tilde{\Delta} = 0$ and $\tilde{J} = a^2$ with $a = 1/s_1$. Here, $s_1 = \kappa_3/\kappa_2^{3/2}$ and $s_2 = \kappa_4/3\kappa_2^2$. The method proposed in [27] shows much smaller approximation errors for the model used in Equation (10), compared to Pearson's method [28].

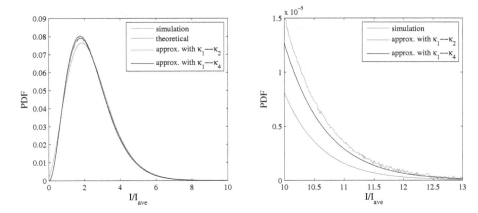

Figure 3. Interference power distributions for $J = 3$ independent interferers. The average interference powers are $I_{ave,1} = I_{ave,2} = I_{ave,3} = I_{ave}/3$. The instantaneous interference powers at the time of measurement are $I_{0,1} = 3/2I_{0,2} = 3I_{0,3} = I_{ave}/2$, so that the total measured interference power is $I_0 = I_{ave}$. **Left:** Theoretical Equation (10), simulation and moment matching approaches, where one moment matched non-central χ^2 distribution approximates the sum distribution; **Right:** Tail distribution with moment matching approaches.

Figure 3 shows the probability distribution of the total interference power, and its moment matching chi-square approximation. The figure on the left side depicts the theoretical probability density of (10) for $J = 3$ independent interference sources together with a simulated Monte Carlo realization of the distribution, and the moment matching approximations. The figure on the right side zooms in to the tail of the distribution with very large interferences. The approximation with the first four cumulants is especially good for the tail of the distribution. It is tight to the improbable very high interferences, that are of interest when addressing URC.

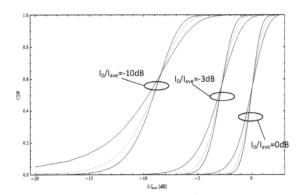

Figure 4. Realized interference distributions for three different I_0/I_{ave} dB, *vs.* realized interference powers I/I_{ave}. Interference contribution from $J = 1, 2, 3$ independent sources. The distribution with $J = 1$ in red is widest and with $J = 3$ in blue most narrow for all values of I_0/I_{ave}.

Figure 4 shows CDFs of realized total interference powers when there are $J = 1, 2, 3$ independent interferers. The measured total interference $I_0 = \sum_j I_{0,j}$ is set to $0, -3, -10$ dB, as compared to the average total interference $I_{ave} = \sum_j I_{ave,j}$. We assume that the average interference power is the same for all the individual interferers. When there are $J = 2$ interferers, the measured interference power of the first interferer is assumed to be $2/3$ of the total interference, whereas the second interferer is measured to contribute $1/3$ of the total. For $J = 3$ interferers, the ratios of the measured interference powers is assumed to be $1/2, 1/3, 1/6$. Note that here, just as in the case of the wanted signal, we assume that we know both the measured power and the average power, independently for all the J interferers. The number of interferers has a great impact on backoff selection. The distribution becomes wider with a decreasing number of interferers.

We proceed by considering the SINR variability caused by interference channel variability only. It is assumed that the measured signal power of the desired transmission, and the precoders of both the desired channel and interferers remain same from the time of measurement to the time τ of transmission. Then, the outage probability with backoff $b = \gamma_0/\gamma_t$ becomes

$$P\left(\gamma_\tau < \gamma_t\right) = 1 - F_I\left(b(I_0 + N_0) - N_0\right) \tag{13}$$

where $I_0 = \sum_{j=1}^{J} I_{0,j}$ is the total measured interference power, and the CDF of the total interference power is obtained from Equation (10) as

$$F_I(i) = \sum_{n=1}^{\infty} a_n \left(1 - Q_{J+n}\left(\sqrt{\Delta}, \sqrt{\frac{i}{\beta}}\right)\right). \tag{14}$$

For URC, the required backoff can be evaluated at $F_I(i) = 0.99999$ point.

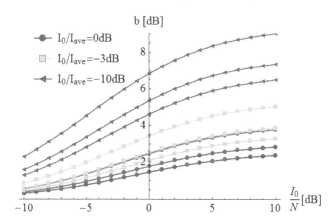

Figure 5. Required backoff for three different I_0/I_{ave}. Three curves per I_0/I_{ave} represents $J = 1, 2, 3$. The backoff for $J = 1$ is always largest and for $J = 3$ smallest for a given I_0/I_{ave}.

The required URC backoff for three values of the total measured-to-average-interference ratio I_0/I_{ave} is reported in Figure 5, for different values of I_0/N_0. For each value of I_0/I_{ave}, there are three curves, corresponding to $J = 1, 2, 3$. The relative power for $J = 2, 3$ are shown in Figure 4. When there are more interferers, the backoff is systematically smaller for the same total average interference I_0. The figure emphasizes that the backoff required due to interference variability is large when the interferers at the time of measurement are in a fade, *i.e.*, when I_0/I_{ave} is small. In these cases, it is likely that the interference will be larger at the time τ of the realized transmission. It should be noted that here, the wanted signal does not vary at all.

3.3. Changes in Precoders of Interferers

The precoders used in interfering base stations may not be the same as the ones used when the channel is measured. This may cause changes in the measured interference power, causing CSI mispredictions and SINR variability [8]. This effect is particularly strong in multiple input single output (MISO) channels. We assume that the precoder of the desired transmission is selected based on the wanted channel $\mathbf{h}_i$, and the precoders of J interfering base stations are selected according to the wanted channels of the intended receivers of the interfering transmissions. The precoders $\mathbf{v}_{j,\tau}$ used at the interfering base stations depend on the scheduled receivers in the interfering cells. We assume that these are uniformly selected from the space of all MISO precoders. If there is no mobility, the received SINR for the desired transmission is

$$\gamma_\tau = \frac{\lambda_0}{\sum_{j=1}^J \lambda_j |\mathbf{v}_j^H \mathbf{v}_{\tau,j}|^2 + N_0}. \tag{15}$$

Here, $\lambda_0 = ||\mathbf{h}_0||^2$ is the wanted signal power. The powers of interfering channels are λ_j correspond to the interfering channels $\mathbf{h}_{\tau,j} = \mathbf{h}_{0,j}$ in Equation (3), and $\mathbf{v}_j = h_j/\sqrt{\lambda_j}$ are the normalized interfering channels. We assume that the receiver is able to measure the average interference. The measured SINR is thus $\gamma_0 = \frac{\lambda_0}{I_0+N_0}$, where $I_0 = \mathrm{E}_{\mathbf{v}_{\tau,j}}\{\sum_{j=1}^J \lambda_j |\mathbf{v}_j^H \mathbf{v}_{\tau,j}|^2\}$. For a given channel vector distributed on a complex sphere with radius $\lambda_j = ||\mathbf{h}_{0,j}||^2$, the cumulative distribution of an inner product of the channel vector and a unitary precoder $\mathbf{v}_{\tau,j}$, $Z_j = \lambda_j |\mathbf{v}_j^H \mathbf{v}_{\tau,j}|^2$ can be obtained from [29]

$$F_Z(z_j) = 1 - \left(1 - \frac{z_j}{\lambda_j}\right)^{N_T-1}. \tag{16}$$

The corresponding PDF is then $f_Z(z_j) = \left(\frac{N_T-1}{\lambda_j}\right)\left(1 - \frac{z_j}{\lambda_j}\right)^{N_T-2}$. Hence, the PDF of the total interference power $Y = \sum_{j=1}^J Z_j$ induced from J independent interferes can be written as

$$f_Y(y) = \left(\frac{N_T-1}{\lambda_1}\right)\left(1 - \frac{z}{\lambda_1}\right)^{N_T-2} * \ldots * \left(\frac{N_T-1}{\lambda_J}\right)\left(1 - \frac{z}{\lambda_J}\right)^{N_T-2} \tag{17}$$

where $*$ is the convolution operation. Hence, the total interference power is distributed over $[0 \ \sum_j \lambda_j]$. This is a convolution of functions with compact support. Accordingly, for J interferers, the CDF is generically divided into 2^J disjoint regions with different functional form. The boundaries of the regions depend on the relative interference powers, see e.g. [30]. As an example of interference variation due to changes of precoders in neighboring cells, we consider a system with $J = 3, 2$, or 1 interferers. The eigenvalues of the interferers are $\lambda_1 = \lambda_2 = \lambda_3 = 1$ for $J = 3$, $\lambda_1 = 2$ and $\lambda_2 = 1$ for $J = 2$, and $\lambda_1 = 3$ for $J = 1$. We consider four different numbers of transmit antennas at the interferers, $N_T \in \{2, 5, 10, 100\}$. Figure 6 shows the PDF and CDF of the interference at the time of transmission, when the interferers select precoders randomly. For clarity of the figures, $N_T = 100$ is omitted. For $N_T = 2$, the 10^{-5} point of the complementary CDF of interference is virtually indistinguishable from the worst case interference. With increasing N_T, worst case precoders become increasingly unlikely — typical interfering signals are almost orthogonal to the wanted signal channel.

The observation that the distribution of the interference I becomes narrower with increasing N_T does not mean that it is easier to predict URC channel quality. Here, we have assumed that the channel quality estimated at the time of measurement is given by the interference power *averaged* over possible precoders. It turns out that the average is reduced more than the interference at outage, when N_T grows. To see this, the CDF of the realized interference is plotted in units of I_{ave} in the left half of Figure 7. For clarity, the distributions are plotted only for the $J = 3$ case. For $N_T = 2$, the distribution extends to $I/I_{\text{ave}} = 2$. The average interference is half of the realized. This distribution becomes broader with increasing N_T. The required backoff is plotted in the right half of the figure. The required backoff is $b = \frac{I_t/N_0+1}{I_0/N_0+1}$, where I_t the interference at the URC target. The required backoff grows with N_T. For $N_T = 2$, the backoff is virtually the same irrespectively of J. As the 0.99999 point of the CDF is close to the maximum interference, $I_t \approx 2I_{\text{ave}}$ in this case, and the backoff in an interference limited network when $I_0/N_0 \to \infty$ would be $b \approx 3$ dB.

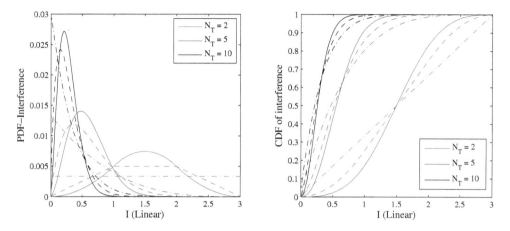

Figure 6. Effect of interferer precoder variation in multiantenna system. **Left:** PDF of realized interference power due to precoder variation for $J = 3$ interferers; **Right:** CDF of realized interference power. Dash-dot line-$J = 1$, dashed line-$J = 2$ and solid line-$J = 3$.

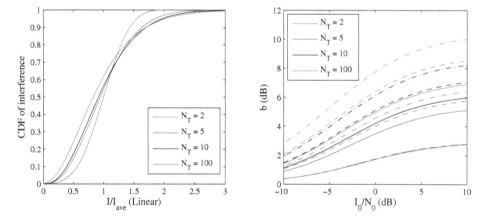

Figure 7. Effect of interferer precoder variation in multi-antenna system. **Left:** CDF of realized interference powers, relative to average interference, $J = 3$ interferers; **Right:** Backoff. Dash-dot line-$J = 1$, dashed line-$J = 2$ and solid line-$J = 3$.

3.4. Combined Effect

To understand the effect of wanted signal and interference variability, one has to combine these into one. The realized SINR Equation (2) can be modeled by $\gamma_\tau = \frac{S}{I+N_0}$ where S and I are RVs representing the power of the wanted signal and the interference, respectively. Then, the outage probability $P(\gamma_\tau \le \gamma_t)$ for SINR with combined wanted signal and interference variability is

$$P(\gamma_\tau < \gamma_t) = \int_0^\infty F_S(\gamma_t(y + N_0)) f_I(i) di. \tag{18}$$

The closed form expression for the outage probability can be derived after some mathematical manipulations. It is given by

$$P(\gamma_\tau < \gamma_t) = 1 - \frac{e^{-\left(\frac{\Delta}{2} + \frac{\gamma_t N_0}{2\alpha}\right)}}{2^{p+2q+m+J+n}} \sum_{n=0}^\infty \sum_{p=0}^\infty \sum_{q=0}^\infty \frac{a_n \Delta^q}{\alpha^p \beta^{q+J+n}} \frac{N_0^{p+q+J+n}}{(p!)^2 q!} \left(p! - p\Gamma\left(p, \frac{\delta}{2}\right)\right) U(a, b, \bar{z}) \tag{19}$$

where $U(a, b, \bar{z})$ is a confluent hypergeometric function (A confluent hypergeometric function is defined as $U(a, b, z) = \frac{1}{\Gamma(a)} \int_0^\infty e^{-zt} t^{a-1}(1+t)^{b-a-1}$, $\Re\{a\} > 0$). with $a = q + J + n$, $b = p + a + 1$, and $\bar{z} = \left(\frac{\gamma_t}{2\alpha} + \frac{1}{2\beta} \right) N_0$. Here, $\Gamma(a, b)$ is the incomplete Gamma function. Based on this, a suitable backoff can be numerically evaluated. For the detailed derivation, refer Appendix B. The required backoffs due to mobility for $J = 3$ and $\rho = 0.98$ in four different scenarios are reported in Table 1. The backoffs in the case that only the wanted signal is fading and in the case that only interference is fading are compared to the backoff for the combined effect when both the wanted signal and interference is undergoes fading. It is assumed that noise is negligible, we have $I_0/N_0 = 20$ dB. The average signal-to-interference ratio is $S_0/I_0 = 10$. We see that the larger of the two fading effects dominates the combined effect. The most dramatic effects are caused by the fading of the wanted signal.

Table 1. Required backoff values for mobility induced SINR variability.

S_0/S_{ave}	I_0/I_{ave}	Sig. Power	Intf. Power	Combined Effect
0	0	8.01	2.5	8.53
0	−10	8.01	6.76	11.30
−10	0	44.17	2.5	44.82
−10	−10	44.17	6.76	46.96

SINR variability caused by changes in precoders may be considered together with mobility-induced variability. The precoders used on interfering base stations may vary during the transmission. The effective interference is $I = \sum_{j=1}^J |\rho \mathbf{h}_{\tau,j} \mathbf{v}_{\tau,j} + \sqrt{1 - \rho^2} \tilde{\mathbf{h}}_j \mathbf{v}_{\tau,j}|$. For a given precoder $\mathbf{v}_{\tau,j}$, an individual interference can be modeled as a non-central chi-square distributed variable with PDF $f_I(i_j \mid \mathbf{v}_{\tau,j}) = \chi^2(i_j / \alpha_j; 2; \delta_j)$ where $\alpha_j = (1 - \rho^2) I_{ave,j}/2$, and the non-centrality is $\delta_j = \frac{2\lambda_j \rho^2}{(1-\rho^2)} \frac{|\mathbf{v}_j^H \mathbf{v}_{\tau,j}|^2}{I_{ave,j}}$. The unconditional PDF can be obtained by integrating over the distribution of the inner product $|\mathbf{v}_j^H \mathbf{v}_{\tau,j}|^2$. If we have $N_T = 2$ transmit antennas, this is a uniform distribution, and the integration can be performed in closed form, resulting in $f_I(i_j) = 1 - Q_1 \left(\sqrt{i_j}, \sqrt{\frac{2\lambda_j \rho^2}{(1 - \rho^s 2) I_{ave,j}}} \right)$. When there is one interferer, the outage probability for the joint effect of precoder, wanted signal, and interfering channel variability can thus be obtained in closed form as

$$P(\gamma_\tau \leq \gamma_t) = 1 - \int_0^\infty Q_1 \left(\sqrt{\delta_i}, \sqrt{\gamma_t(i + N_0)} \right) \left[1 - Q_1 \left(\sqrt{i}, \sqrt{\delta_j} \right) \right] di \tag{20}$$

where $\delta_i = \frac{\rho^2 |\mathbf{h}_0 \mathbf{v}|^2}{\alpha_i}$ and $\delta_j = \frac{\rho^2 \lambda_j}{\alpha_j}$ are the non-centrality parameters of the probability distributions of the power of the wanted signal and the interference with $\alpha = (1 - \rho^2) I_{ave}/2$. The required backoff value can be numerically evaluated. It is clear that for Rayleigh fading, the required backoff is dominated by the variability of the wanted signal power.

4. Conclusions

We investigated link adaptation for a mobile user, when the wanted signal and the interfering signals undergo fading, and when there may be changes in the transmissions of the interferers. Here, we consider MISO transmissions, and the variations in interfering transmission are related to the change of precoders in a cell. Mobility-induced signal and interference power changes and precoder changes cause SINR variation. Robust link adaptation is considered to meet a URC target of outage probability 10^{-5} with delay $\tau = 1$ ms. For this, we assume that at the time of SINR measurement, the instantaneous values of the wanted signal power, and the individual interferer powers are known, in addition to the average values, and the distribution of these quantities. A suitable backoff is then chosen based on the statistical characteristics of the realized SINR to avoid outage due to CQI misprediction.

Under Rayleigh fading assumption, we develop closed form expressions for the signal and interference power distributions, as well as the SINR distribution. Users experiencing a deep fade in either the interference or wanted signal power during the time of measurement require large backoffs to achieve ultra-reliable transmission with low outage. When the channel during the measurement is close to an average situation, small backoffs are required. This demonstrates that the accuracy of information of the current fading situations, as well as the fading statistics, are crucial for robust link adaptation. In comparison to the mobility-induced backoffs, backoffs related to variability of interference precoders are small, when the number of transmit antennas $N_T < 10$.

Acknowledgments: This research work has been partially supported by EIT ICT Labs under the EXAM and ACTIVE -projects.

Author Contributions: Udesh Oruthota, Furqan Ahmed, and Olav Tirkkonen conceived and planned the work; Udesh Oruthota played a leading role in the theoretical modeling; Udesh Oruthota, Furqan Ahmed, and Olav Tirkkonen wrote the paper.

Conflicts of Interest: The authors declare no conflict of interest.

Appendix A

The probability density function of $\sum_{i=1}^n \alpha_i (Z_i + \delta_i)^2$ where $Z_1, Z_2, ..., Z_n$ are mutually independent standard normal random variables, is given by [25]

$$f_n(\alpha, \delta, y) = \sum_{k=0}^{\infty} a_k \beta^{-1} \chi^2 \left(\frac{y}{\beta}; n + 2k; \Delta \right) \tag{21}$$

where $\chi^2(y/\beta; n + 2k; \Delta)$ is a non-central chi-square distribution with $n + 2k$ DoF and non-centrality parameter $\Delta = \sum_{i=1}^n \delta_i^2$. The parameter $\beta > 0$ have to be chosen appropriately to guarantee convergence. The coefficients a_k follow from a recursive formula [26];

$$a_0 = \prod_{j=1}^n (\beta/\alpha_i)^{\frac{1}{2}}$$

$$a_k = k^{-1} \sum_{r=0}^{k-1} b_{k-r} a_r, \ k \geq 1$$

with

$$b_1 = \frac{1}{2} \sum_{j=1}^n (1 - \delta_j)\theta_j$$

$$b_k = \frac{1}{2} \sum_{j=1}^n \theta_j^{k-1} \left(k\delta_j + (1 - k\delta_j)\theta_j \right) \ k \geq 2.$$

Here $\theta_j = 1 - \beta/\alpha_j$. If any of the $|\theta_j| > 1$, the ratios b_k/k grow without bound when $k \to \infty$. Accordingly, the ratio of the absolute values of two consecutive a_k is non-zero, and convergence in Equation (21) is either slow or absent. To guarantee convergence, one should select a suitable value for β to keep $-1 < \theta_j < 1$. A simple choice is to select β so that $\max_j |\theta_j|$ is minimized. By selecting $\beta = 2\alpha_{\min}\alpha_{\max}/(\alpha_{\min} + \alpha_{\max})$, the extrema of θ_j become $\theta_{\max} = (\alpha_{\max} - \alpha_{\min})/(\alpha_{\max} + \alpha_{\min})$ and $\theta_{\min} = -\theta_{\max}$ and all $|\theta_j| < 1$.

Appendix B

To obtain the outage probability for a combined effect of signal power and interference power variations, the integral $P_{out} = \int_0^\infty F_X(\gamma_t(y + N_0)) f_Y(y) dy$ needs to be evaluated. Here, $F_X(x)$ is the CDF of the desired signal power and $f_Y(y)$ denotes the PDF of interference power. The threshold SINR value is γ_t. Then, the integral would be

$$P_{out} = \int_0^\infty \left\{ 1 - Q_1 \left(\sqrt{\delta}, \sqrt{\frac{\gamma_t(y + N_0)}{\alpha}} \right) \right\} \sum_{n=0}^\infty a_n \beta^{-1} \chi^2 \left(\frac{y}{\beta}; 2(J + n), \Delta \right) dy.$$

Here, $\int_0^\infty \sum_{n=0}^\infty a_n \beta^{-1} \chi^2 \left(\frac{y}{\beta}; 2(J + n); \Delta \right) dy = 1$ as it represents the PDF of the total interference. Using the series representations of the Marcum-Q function (The series representation of Marcum-Q function is $Q_M(a, b) = e^{-\frac{a^2 + b^2}{2}} \sum_{k=1-M}^\infty \left(\frac{a}{b} \right)^k I_k(ab)$) and the modified Bessel function (The infinite series representation of a modified Bessel function is $I_k(x) = \sum_{m=0}^\infty \frac{1}{m! \Gamma(m+k+1)} \left(\frac{x}{2} \right)^{2m+k}$) the integral can be transformed to multiple sums,

$$P_{out} = 1 - \sum_{n=0}^\infty a_n \beta^{-1} \int_0^\infty Q_1 \left(\sqrt{\delta}, \sqrt{\frac{\gamma_t(y + N_0)}{\alpha}} \right) \chi^2 \left(\frac{x}{\beta}; 2(J + n), \Delta \right) dy$$

$$= 1 - \sum_{n=0}^\infty \frac{a_n \beta^{-1}}{2} \int_0^\infty e^{-\frac{\alpha\delta + \gamma_t(y + N_0)}{2\alpha}} \sum_{m=0}^\infty \left(\frac{\alpha\delta}{\gamma_t(y + N_0)} \right)^{\frac{m}{2}} I_m \left(\sqrt{\frac{\delta\gamma_t(y + N_0)}{\alpha}} \right)$$

$$\times e^{-\frac{y + \beta\Delta}{2\beta}} \left(\frac{y}{\beta\Delta} \right)^{\frac{J+n}{2} - \frac{1}{2}} I_{J+n-1} \left(\sqrt{\frac{\Delta y}{\beta}} \right) dy$$

$$= 1 - \sum_{n=0}^\infty \sum_{m=0}^\infty \sum_{p=0}^\infty \sum_{q=0}^\infty \frac{a_n}{2^{2(p+q)+m+J+n}} e^{-\left(\frac{\delta + \Delta}{2} + \frac{\gamma_t N_0}{2\alpha} \right)} \frac{\delta^{p+m} \gamma_t^p}{\alpha^p} \frac{\Delta^q}{\beta^{q+J+n}}$$

$$\frac{1}{p! q! (p + m)! (q + J + n - 1)!} \int_0^\infty e^{-\left(\frac{\gamma_t}{2\alpha} + \frac{1}{2\beta} \right) y} (y + N_0)^p y^{q+J+n-1}.$$

The infinite sum over m is straight forward, and the remaining integral can be expressed in terms of a confluent hypergeometric function $U(a, b, \bar{z})$ with $a = q + J + n$, $b = p + a + 1$ and $\bar{z} = \left(\frac{\gamma_t}{2\alpha} + \frac{1}{2\beta} \right) N_0$. Algebraic manipulations lead to

$$P_{out} = 1 - \frac{e^{-\left(\frac{\Delta}{2} + \frac{\gamma_t N_0}{2\alpha} \right)}}{2^{p+2q+m+J+n}} \sum_{n=0}^\infty \sum_{p=0}^\infty \sum_{q=0}^\infty \frac{a_n \Delta^q}{\alpha^p \beta^{q+J+n}} \frac{N_0^{p+q+J+n}}{(p!)^2 q!} \left(p! - p\Gamma \left(p, \frac{\delta}{2} \right) \right) U(a, b, \bar{z})$$

where $\Gamma(a, b)$ is the upper incomplete gamma function.

References

1. Osseiran, A.; Boccardi, F.; Braun, V.; Kusume, K.; Marsch, P.; Maternia, M.; Queseth, O.; Schellmann, M.; Schotten, H.; Taoka, H.; et al. Scenarios for 5G mobile and wireless communications: The vision of the METIS project. *IEEE Commun. Mag.* **2014**, *52*, 26–35.

2. Popovski, P. Ultra-reliable communication in 5G wireless systems. In Proceedings of the International Conference on Ubiquitous Connectivity for 5G, Levi, Finland, 26–28 November 2014; pp. 146–151.

3. Xu, D.; Li, Y.; Chiang, M.; Calderbank, A. Elastic Service Availability: Utility Framework and Optimal Provisioning. *IEEE J. Sel. Areas Commun.* **2008**, *26*, 55–65.

4. Lee, J.W.; Chiang, M.; Calderbank, A. Price-Based Distributed Algorithms for Rate-Reliability Tradeoff in Network Utility Maximization. *IEEE J. Sel. Areas Commun.* **2006**, *24*, 962–976.

5.   Ahmed, F.; Dowhuszko, A.A.; Tirkkonen, O.; Berry, R.   A distributed algorithm for network power minimization in multicarrier systems.   In Proceedings of the 2013 IEEE 24th International Symposium on Personal Indoor and Mobile Radio Communications (PIMRC), London, UK, 8–11 September 2013.

6.   Vicario, J.L.; Bel, A.; Salcedo, J.A.L.; Seco, G.   Opportunistic relay selection with outdated CSI: Outage probability and diversity analysis. *IEEE Trans. Wirel. Commun.* **2009**, *8*, 2872–2876.

7.   Torabi, M.; Haccoun, D. Capacity analysis of opportunistic relaying in cooperative systems with outdated channel information. *IEEE Commun. Lett.* **2010**, *14*, 1137–1139.

8.   Yu, C.; Tirkkonen, O. Rate adaptation of AMC/HARQ systems with CQI errors. In Proceedings of the 2010 IEEE 71st Vehicular Technology Conference (VTC 2010-Spring), Taipei, Taiwan, 16–19 May 2010; pp. 1–5.

9.   Ye, Z.; Krishnamurthy, S.; Tripathi, S.   A framework for reliable routing in mobile *ad hoc* networks.   In Proceedings of the IEEE Societies Twenty-Second Annual Joint Conference of the IEEE Computer and Communications (INFOCOM 2003), San Francisco, CA, USA, 30 March–3 April 2003; pp. 270–280.

10. Silva, I.; Guedes, L.A.; Portugal, P.; Vasques, F. Reliability and Availability Evaluation of Wireless Sensor Networks for Industrial Applications. *Sensors* **2012**, *12*, 806–838.

11. Schotten, H.; Sattiraju, R.; Gozalvez Serrano, D.; Ren, Z.; Fertl, P.   Availability indication as key enabler for ultra-reliable communication in 5G. In Proceedings of the 2014 European Conference on Networks and Communications (EuCNC), Bologna, Italy, 23–26 June 2014; pp. 1–5.

12. Love, R.; Ghosh, A.; Xiao, W.; Ratasuk, R.   Performance of 3GPP high speed downlink packet access (HSDPA).   In Proceedings of the 2004 IEEE 60th Vehicular Technology Conference (VTC2004-Fall), Los Angeles, CA, USA, 26–29 September 2004; pp. 3359–3363.

13. He, Z.; Zhao, F.   Performance of HARQ with AMC Schemes in LTE Downlink.   In Proceedings of the 2010 International Conference on Communications and Mobile Computing (CMC), Shenzhen, China, 12–14 April 2010; pp. 250–254.

14. Yu, C.; Tirkkonen, O. Rate adaptation design for adaptive modulation/coding systems with hybrid ARQ. In Proceedings of the International Conference on Wireless Communications and Mobile Computing: Connecting the World Wirelessly, IWCMC 2009, Leipzig, Germany, 21–24 June 2009; pp. 227–231.

15. Adhicandra, I.   Using AMC and HARQ to optimize system capacity and application delays in WiMAX networks. *J. Telecommun.* **2010**, *2*, 15–20.

16. Nakamura, M.; Awad, Y.; Vadgama, S. Adaptive control of link adaptation for high speed downlink packet access (HSDPA).   In Proceedings of the 5th International Symposium on Wireless Personal Multimedia Communications, Honolulu, HI, USA, 27–30 October 2002; pp. 382–386.

17. Oruthota, U.; Tirkkonen, O.   Link adaptation of precoded MIMO-OFDMA system with I/Q interference. *IEEE Trans. Commun.* **2015**, *63*, 780–790.

18. Jakes, W.C. *Microwave Mobile Communications*; Wiley: New York, NY, USA, 1974.

19. Rappaport, T.S.   Characterization of UHF multipath radio channels in factory buildings.   *IEEE Trans. Antennas Propegation* **1989**, *37*, 1058–1069.

20. Falahati, S.; Svensson, A.; Ekman, T.; Sternad, M.   Adaptive modulation systems for predicted wireless channels. *IEEE Trans. Commun.* **2004**, *52*, 307–316.

21. Ma, Y.; Jin, J.   Effect of channel estimation errors on M-QAM with MRC and EGC in Nakagami fading channels. *IEEE Trans. Veh. Technol.* **2007**, *56*, 1239–1250.

22. Shariatmadari, H.; Iraji, S.; Jantti, R. Analysis of transmission methods for ultra-reliable communications. In Proceedings of the 2015 IEEE 26th Annual International Symposium on Personal, Indoor, and Mobile Radio Communications (PIMRC), Hong Kong, China, 30 Augest–2 September 2015; pp. 2303–2308.

23. Durisi, G.; Koch, T.; Ostman, J.; Polyanskiy, Y.; Yang, W.   Short-packet communications over multiple-mntenna Rayleigh-fading channels. *IEEE Trans. Commun.* **2015**, *64*, 1–11.

24. Nuttall, A.H. Some integrals involving the Q_M function. *IEEE Trans. Inform. Theory* **1975**, *21*, 95–96.

25. Mathai, A.M.; Provost, S.B. *Quadratic Forms in Random Variables: Theory and Applications*; Marcel Dekker Inc.: New York, NY, USA, 1992.

26. Kotz, S.; Johnson, N.; Boyd, D. Series representations of distributions of quadratic forms in normal variables II. non-central case. *Ann. Math. Stat.* **1967**, *38*, 838–848.

27. Liua, H.; Tang, Y.; Zhang, H.H. A new chi-square approximation to the distribution of non-negative definite quadratic forms in non-central normal variables. *Comput. Stat. Data Anal.* **2008**, *53*, 853–856.

28. Pearson, E.S. Note on an approximation to the distribution of non-central χ^2. *Biometrika* **1959**, *46*, doi:10.2307/2333533.
29. Mukkavilli, K.K.; Abharwal, A.; Erkip, E.; Aazhang, B. On beamforming with finite rate feedback in multiple-antenna systems. *IEEE Trans. Inform. Theory* **2003**, *49*, 2562–2579.
30. Bradley, D.M.; Gupta, R.C. On the distribution of the sum of n non-identically distributed uniform random variables. *Ann. Inst. Stat. Math.* **2004**, *54*, 1–20.

4

Closed-Loop Feedback Computation Model of Dynamical Reputation Based on the Local Trust Evaluation in Business-to-Consumer E-Commerce

Bo Tian [1,*]**, Jingti Han** [1] **and Kecheng Liu** [2]

[1]   School of Information Management & Engineering, Shanghai University of Finance and Economics, Shanghai 200433, China; hanjt@mail.shufe.edu.cn
[2]   Informatics Research Center, University of Reading, Reading RG6 6UD, UK; k.liu@henley.ac.uk
*   Correspondence: youngtb@sina.com

Academic Editor: Willy Susilo

Abstract: Trust and reputation are important factors that influence the success of both traditional transactions in physical social networks and modern e-commerce in virtual Internet environments. It is difficult to define the concept of trust and quantify it because trust has both subjective and objective characteristics at the same time. A well-reported issue with reputation management system in business-to-consumer (BtoC) e-commerce is the "all good reputation" problem. In order to deal with the confusion, a new computational model of reputation is proposed in this paper. The ratings of each customer are set as basic trust score events. In addition, the time series of massive ratings are aggregated to formulate the sellers' local temporal trust scores by Beta distribution. A logical model of trust and reputation is established based on the analysis of the dynamical relationship between trust and reputation. As for single goods with repeat transactions, an iterative mathematical model of trust and reputation is established with a closed-loop feedback mechanism. Numerical experiments on repeated transactions recorded over a period of 24 months are performed. The experimental results show that the proposed method plays guiding roles for both theoretical research into trust and reputation and the practical design of reputation systems in BtoC e-commerce.

Keywords: reputation computation; local trust rating; beta distribution; closed-loop feedback

1. Introduction

Credit, payment, logistics, and authentication compose the supporting system of e-commerce. According to the 35th China Internet development statistics report of China Internet Network Information Center (CNNIC) on 3 February 2015, 54.5% of Internet users thought information on the Internet was trustworthy [1], which has greatly improved compared with five years ago. However, the degree of acceptance of the Internet in China is still relatively low. Mature Internet and mobile communication technologies laid a solid technical foundation for the development of e-commerce and mobile commerce. However, consumers are still reluctant to accept e-commerce in China. The low degree of trust in the information on the Internet is one of the main reasons. How to improve the level of trust consumers have in the new type of virtual trading mode is an urgent issue to be solved. Trust theory research and trust evaluation system design have become hotspots in the field of e-commerce. The main methods used to research trust in e-commerce at present are derived from the conclusions of interpersonal trust relations of social networks. Relationships of trustees and agents in the network environment are discussed, factors that affect the perceived trust are analyzed, and causal relationships between perceived trust and decision-making of network transactions are theoretically reasoned and empirically researched [2–4]. Different methods of qualitative analysis and computational models of trust are proposed gradually [4–7]. In the application of e-commerce, the degree of trust is obtained by the method of evaluation or rating; calculation methods are simple such as average or summary [6,8,9]. In recent years, the evaluation methods of trust based on the theories of mathematics have attracted attention [4,10–12].

The difficulty of computing trust and reputation is that a trust relationship has subjective and objective dual characteristics at same time. In human social networks, trust is prone to be subjective [13]. In machine networks such as the Internet, trust is regarded as a supplementary mechanism of reducing uncertainty [14]. The motivation driving trust research in business-to-consumer (BtoC) e-commerce lies in the fact that trust is an effective mechanism for lowering transaction complexity, because of the span of time and space and information asymmetry during the process of online transactions. The goal of trust research is to provide a theoretical basis and direction for practical e-commerce development. Unfortunately, recently proposed computation approaches of trust and reputation are mainly focused on peer-to-peer networks, *ad hoc* networks, sensor networks, semantic Web, autonomic computing, grid computing, and multi-agent systems in pervasive computing environments [10,15–17]. In addition, a trust mining method through feedback comments for e-commerce was proposed last year [9]. Our previous work on trust and reputation has mainly investigated the factors of trust in BtoC e-commerce [18], proposed a recommended trust evaluation method for BtoC e-commerce based on the fuzzy analytic hierarchy process [19], and established a reputation evaluation computation model based on the relationship of trust and reputation [20]. In this paper, a new dynamical computation model of reputation based on trust evaluation in BtoC e-commerce is further proposed. Components and multi-dimensional characteristics of trust in BtoC e-commerce are analyzed firstly. The ratings of each customer are set as basic trust scores with four dimensions, and periods of ratings constitute the probability distribution of trust. The time series of massive feedback ratings of customers are aggregated to formulate the local trust and dynamical reputation values. Based on the conceptions of local trust and overall reputation, an iterative computation model of reputation is proposed. In order to achieve this objective, a logical model of trust and reputation is established in which the time series of ratings are consulted. As for the situation of single goods with repeat transactions, an iterative mathematical model of trust and reputation is established. In the computation model, Bernoulli probability described by Beta distribution function is used to formulate the trust values of certain time intervals. Lastly, numerical experiments on repeated transactions records over a period of 24 months on Dangdang and Amazon are performed. Representative commodities such as books are used in both Dangdang and Amazon. More than 4000 ratings with four dimensions of each commodity over two years on each website are separated into 24 months as time series. Ratings for each month are used for independent probability distribution estimation, and trust and reputation are renewed iteratively. Experimental results illustrated the dynamical variation processes of reputation effectively. As a result, the proposed computation model can tell customers which agent they should choose in concrete situations. The proposed iterative computation model, with local trust and overall reputation, could play a guiding role for both the theoretical research into computation of trust and the practical design of reputation systems in BtoC e-commerce.

The remainder of this paper is organized as follows. Related works about trust and reputation are reviewed in Section 2. Meanings of trust and reputation for BtoC e-commerce are discussed in Section 3. Multi-dimensional characteristics and composition of trust in BtoC e-commerce are also analyzed. Additionally, relationship and motivation are introduced in this section. Then the logical and computational model of reputation is further proposed based on the concept of trust and the relationship between trust and reputation in BtoC e-commerce in Section 4. In addition, the time series of ratings are consulted to establish the iterative mathematical model of trust and reputation, and the Bernoulli distribution is discussed to estimate trust values in this section. Experimental results of reputation and trust computation for representative commodities in both Dangdang and Amazon are reported in Section 5. Data collection, rating aggregation, model organization, and numerical computation results are discussed in this section. Finally, conclusions are drawn in Section 6.

2. Related Works

Many surveys of different disciplines to classify and characterize computational trust and reputation models exist in the literature. Some of them are based on online trust-related systems [6,7]. Some of them are about trust and reputation in multi-agent systems [4]. Some reviews focus on concrete aspects or functionalities of trust or reputation management [3,14]. Others deal with more general network environments [10,11]. In the following, related works will be reviewed and discussed from four perspectives: trust-related research approaches in pervasive network environments, trust-related research approaches in e-commerce, trust-related computation methods in e-commerce, and the probability method in trust computation, the topic of which is from large domain to small field.

2.1. Trust-Related Research in Pervasive Networks

Trust relationships occur in many diverse contexts such as pervasive systems, social interactions, semantic networks, *ad hoc* networks, distributed systems, sensor networks, and so on. In pervasive computing environment, trust can be used as a natural way to achieve the goals that enhance security and reduce uncertainty. A wide variety of trust and reputation theories and models with different features have been developed in recent years. The work in [4] reviewed computational trust and reputation models for open multi-agent systems. Current research on trust management in distributed systems is surveyed, and some open research areas are explored in [21,22]. The work in [23] presented a model of reputation management in collaborative computing systems. The work in [24] presented a framework for building distributed, dependable reputation management systems, with counter measures against vulnerabilities. In [9], the authors defined a reputation evaluation method based on reputation value and reputation prediction variance value based on the aggregation of feedback. In [25], the authors introduced an adaptive and dynamic reputation-based trust model to evaluate trustworthiness, based on community feedback about participants' past behavior. The paper [26] proposed a computational model for trust establishment based on a reputation mechanism, which incorporates direct experiences and information disseminated from past experiences in pervasive systems. The paper [27] proposed an adaptive and attribute-based trust model for service-level agreement guarantees in cloud computing. A more general social trust computational approach is researched in [10]. The objective of these research methods is the computation of general trust and reputation in network environments, which can provide a reference for research into trust and reputation in e-commerce.

2.2. Trust Research Approaches in E-Commerce

The range of theoretical research in e-commerce includes related technologies, application modes, value chains, legal ethics, consumption decision behavior research, and so on [28]. The research into trust in e-commerce mainly uses consumer decision-making theory and analyzes the role of perceived trust in consumer decision-making, in which trust acts as a sort of soft safety mechanism in the transaction procession. Empirical analysis is the main research method. The theory of consumer decision-making includes attitude intention behavior theory, innovation diffusion theory, Task-Technology Fit (TTF) theory and the Technology Acceptance Model (TAM) model, *etc.* [28,29]. The main research methods are borrowed from psychology, social science, economics, and marketing science. Based on the concept of general trust, the particularity of electronic commerce is incorporated. Related aspects and factors of trust during the transaction processes are analyzed. Conceptual models related to the roles of risk and trust in the purchase decision are established, and different hypotheses are put forward and empirically researched [30–33]. Computation methods of trust in e-commerce usually employ artificial intelligence, graph theory, game theory, probability, and stochastic process theories, in which the trust relationships are described and the trust evaluations are measured and forecast [4,7,11]. According to the difference of mechanisms, trust can be divided into identity-based trust models, role-based trust models, trust-negotiation models, and reputation-based trust models [28].

According to the difference of mathematical tools used in the trust computation, the concrete methods can be based on deterministic mathematics theory, probability theories, and uncertainty theories [6,9,11]. The trust computation models mainly involve the expression of measurement of the concept of trust, a description of the relationship between reputation and trust, and a calculation of trust, which will be discussed thoroughly.

2.3. Trust-Related Computation Methods in E-Commerce

Computation methods of trust in e-commerce are analyzed as follows. Most practically applied methods of trust computation are based on simple operations such as average or sum [7,26]. This kind of method is widely used in the process of evaluation of e-commerce websites. The method refers to the trust evaluation among people in social networks, and the method is simple and easy to understand. At present, a weighted averaging method is used in Auction, Eigen, and Trust eBay. The main shortcomings of this method are that the evaluation is simple and cannot reflect the real trust values of the reviewers and the real trust status of the object to be evaluated.

Trust is a kind of psychological relationship; therefore, subjective logic can be used to describe it. Jøsang adopted the evidence space and the concept space to describe the trust relationships [34]. The author put forward that conjunction, consensus, and recommendation constitute the subjective logic operation associated with trust degree and integrated computation. Ternary group is used to express the degree of trust. However, the model cannot effectively eliminate the impact of malicious feedback evaluation. Evidence reasoning theory is used to compute reputation in [35].

Fuzzy reasoning is normally used to compute the uncertainty of research objects and has been used in trust computation in recent years. The paper [36] proposed a reputation-based trust system Regret. The paper [37] proposed a trust calculation framework that is based on fuzzy reasoning. The three stages of fuzzy reasoning are fuzzy processing, fuzzy reasoning, and defuzzification. The paper [38] proposed a P2P reputation system named Power Trust based on fuzzy logic reasoning. The authors illustrated that the number of user transactions follows a power-law distribution by analysis of a dataset of eBay, and, additionally, that only small parts of super nodes have a decisive role in the trust evaluation of a node. Zhou proposed a Gossip trust model for realizing trust computation by chat [39]. Wang proposed a fuzzy evaluation method of trust in the service environment [40]. The fuzzy inference methods solve the problem of imprecise input in the reasoning process, and simplify the reasoning process; however, prior knowledge is necessary to select the membership function.

Trust reflects the network relationships of human beings, so connective graph network methods can be used to describe trust. The paper [41] computed trust value through connectivity relationships of trust networks, in which the starting node sends a request to its neighboring nodes, and if the neighbors have no relevant information, the request gradually spreads to other neighbors. In the search path, trust evaluation provided by the node with low trust degree will be ignored, and all the trust values are averaged by the starting node finally. The model is based on t social networks between human beings. The paper [36] used the method of hierarchical structure of social networks to analyze different types of reputation in order to compute the trust value of the final node.

Different research methods have been proposed by others. Game theory is used in [42]. Cho [43] proposed a reputation computing system based on collaborative filtering. Gutowska [5] put forward a reputation simulation calculation model in BtoC e-commerce. Wang [44] proposed an evaluation method based on evidence probability. Liu [45] recently proposed a trust computing model based on a prototype. Furthermore, probability-related methods are an important kind of trust computation in e-commerce, which will be reviewed separately.

2.4. Probability Methods in Trust Computation

Trust is the expectation of behavior of the trustee in uncertain and incomplete environments [13]. Therefore, probability theory is adopted to evaluate trust and reputation. Despotovic proposed the method of maximum-likelihood estimation to calculate trust of nodes in P2P environment [46].

Beth [47] put forward a trust computing model based on experience and probability statistics. Experience is divided into two kinds: positive and negative, in the model. Trust is defined as the probability of a successful completion of the target entity. Based on Bayesian theory, posterior probability of the 0–1 events (satisfaction or dissatisfaction) is described by beta distribution function, which evaluates the trust scores [48,49], and trust is expressed by the expectation of the Beta probability density function. Jøsang [50] proposed the Dirichlet reputation system. A Bayesian network is used to model the trust under different conditions in [51]. By using Bayesian network, the requester can calculate the confidence probability of service providers according to the content he or she cares about. Each value of probability expresses the credibility of a node in the networks. Based on the concept of group, Bayesian model of trust and reputation was researched in [52]. We noticed that probability methods used in soft trust computation are employed mainly in general and broad network environments such as pervasive networks. In this paper, a trust-related computation method based on probability theory in BtoC e-commerce is proposed. Meanings, multi-dimensional characteristics, and composition of trust in BtoC e-commerce are analyzed. Based on the relationship of trust and reputation in BtoC e-commerce, iterative computation models of trust and reputation are established. Experimental results illustrated that the proposed model can effectively simulate the dynamical variation processes of reputation in BtoC e-commerce.

3. Relationship of Trust and Reputation

In order to establish a computational model of trust and reputation, the relative concepts, components, and hierarchical structure of trust are discussed. In addition, the logical relationship between trust and reputation in BtoC e-commerce is analyzed.

3.1. Meanings of Trust

The concept and meanings of trust have been defined by different disciplines. For instance, trust is considered as part of personal qualities, namely the beliefs, expectations, and feelings developed during individual psychological processes [7]. Trust is regarded as a form of organizational control used to reduce uncertainty as well as transaction cost in management [53]. Trust is essentially personal relationships, according to Mayer [54]. McKnight differentiates trust belief from trust intention [13]. It has been noted that trust in a person is a commitment to an action based on a belief that the future actions of that person will lead to good outcomes. Trust (or distrust) is the level of subjective probability with which an agent assesses that another agent will perform a particular action. Online trust refers to an individual's willingness to trust another individual (or entity) under the existence of uncertainties in e-commerce circumstances. BtoC e-commerce is the consumer purchase of products and services through online shopping or from firms on the Internet. So, trust in BtoC e-commerce is associated with the experience of consumers, asymmetry of information, interval of space and time of transaction, transaction risk, uncertainty, and so on. The concept of trust in BtoC e-commerce can be described as follows. Trust in BtoC e-commerce is the subjective psychological expectation of consumers that relies on the promise made by online firms, their websites, or a transaction environment under certain circumstances. The psychology of intuition and reliance are brought out from subjective beliefs, expectations, and feelings of consumers towards their trading counterparty, its website, and the virtual environment. The subjective psychological expectation of consumers can be described by probability formulation, which is determined by consumers, the trading counterparty, and the transaction environment. Its target is to reduce transaction risk and uncertainty because of information asymmetry, time-space interval, and trading vitality in BtoC e-commerce.

3.2. Components of Trust

The subjective probability of psychological expectation or trust in BtoC e-commerce is affected by consumers, goods, online companies, and their websites as well as the environment. Components of trust in BtoC e-commerce can be further established, as shown in Figure 1. Moreover, components relating to the trustor, trustee, and environment are shown in Table 1 in our previous work [18]. Three component factors of trust in BtoC e-commerce will be discussed separately.

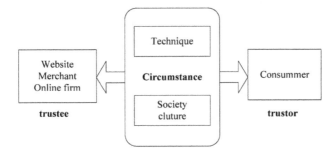

Figure 1. The components of trust system chart of business-to-consumer (BtoC) e-commerce.

Table 1. Components of the trust system of BtoC e-commerce.

Trustor	Consumer	Disposition to trust, purchase history ,attitude towards online shopping, attitude towards information technique, personal values, age, education and gender, subjective perceptive risk
Trustee	Online firm	Brand, reputation, offline presence, predictability, dependence, faith, cooperation, familiarity, benevolence, history of the firm
	Merchant	Quality, satisfaction, price, service, transference, familiarity
	Website	Likeability, convenience, usability, efficiency, reliability, portability, integrity, privacy, security, branding
Circumstance	Technique	Privacy, security, transparency, credibility of information, characteristics of computer technique, Internet technique, information technique, encryption, third-party certification
	Society	General attitude towards trust, Internet and e-commerce, policy, law, morality, culture

Components relating to the trustor include disposition to trust, purchase history, attitude towards online shopping, attitude towards information techniques, personal values, age, education, gender, subjective perceptive risk, and so on. Trustor-related factors can be further refined to include the following respects: (A1) experience of using the Internet, (A2) experience of trading online, (A3) attitude towards risk, which usually involves three types: risk preference, risk neutral, and risk aversion. People who belong to risk preference are more likely to accept online transactions. The final factor is (A4) trust propensity: the willingness to trust an individual, developed through long-term growth in society, which reveals the trend of consumers' trust towards general things, including their Internet trust trend.

Components relating to the trustee include the e-commerce website, the merchant and the online service provider that include the brand, offline presence, faith, cooperation, familiarity, benevolence, history of the firm, quality of merchant, price, and website quality aspects such as convenience, usability, efficiency, reliability, privacy, and security. Merchant-related factors are as follows: (B1) types of goods—generally speaking, search goods have a lower perceived risk than experience goods; (B2) brand of goods—a good brand can reduce consumers' perceived risks; (B3) price of goods—under the premise of the law of value, the lower the price, the more attractive it is to consumers. On the contrary, too high or too low a price deviates from the law of value and will lead to consumers' distrust. Finally, (B4) is instructions about goods—appropriate instructions will improve consumers' purchase intention, while vague or exaggerated descriptions will easily cause distrust in certain consumers. Website-related factors are as follows: (C1) website reputation and popularity; (C2) website security, which includes transaction security, privacy protection, and third-party certification; (C3) navigation system, namely the ease of use of the website; (C4) transaction implementation convenience; and (C5) website style, consisting of layout design, image and content design, namely the usefulness of the website. Online company-related factors are as follows: (D1) reputation and popularity; (D2) history and business scale; (D3) willingness to make customized products for consumers; and (D4) consumer familiarity with the company.

Components of the environment of trust include technique and social factors. Components relating to techniques are privacy, security, transparency, credibility of information, Internet-relative technique, information technique, encryption, and third-party certification, among others. Social components include policy, law, morality, and culture, among others. As the information transmission medium, security of data transmission and privacy of transaction are prerequisites of online transaction [6]. Social environment, information technology, relevant laws and regulations, as well as trust management are effective means of lowering BtoC E-commerce information asymmetry [53,55]. The following environment-related factors have an influence on consumers' perceived trust: (E1) social and cultural; (E2) legal; and (E3) commercial and operational. The following technology environment-related factors have an impact on consumers' perceived trust: (E4) network technology maturity; (E5) information access facility; (E6) network system stability; and (E7) website authority safety certification.

3.3. Hierarchical Structure of Online Trust

The trust relationships between interpersonal social networks are established mainly through three channels, namely (1) objective institutional trust; (2) direct trust; and (3) indirect trust [28]. In BtoC e-commerce, objective institutional trust includes customary and trading rules, e-commerce related laws, third-party authentication, access control and guarantees, and other trust forms. The situational norm and structure guarantee are two facets of objective trust. Situational norms refer to trust that is judged through common habits and rules embedded in the transaction process. The structure guarantee means that there are factors such as legal norms, guarantees, or regulations in the specific transaction environment that influence trust.

In BtoC e-commerce, subjective direct trust of a customer is relative to their individual personality, psychological characteristics, and life experience. It is found that this personal factor is the most important factor for online perceived trust [6]. The recommendation information includes the local individual recommendation and the reputation of the public as a whole. The individual recommendation is also looked upon as one component that directs trust because individual recommendation trust is determined by life experience. If a person's friends are prone to trust more in BtoC e-commerce, he or she will be more prone to shopping online. Reputation is the expectation of the behavior of the object through the global trust in the historical behavior of the object [3,6]. Therefore, in BtoC e-commerce, the reputation of the public is regarded as the trust resource of general indirect recommendation, which contains other factors except the consumer's direct perceived trust.

Thus, trust in BtoC e-commerce is composed of subjective perceived trust and objective institutional trust. Subjective perceived trust includes direct perception trust and general recommendation trust. Objective trust is the environmental basis of trust in BtoC e-commerce. Direct perception trust is the inclination of the customer to trust an object. When direct trust is not enough to make a judgment regarding the trust objects or to determine the online trust of a strange transaction, other sources of information such as reputation or recommendation by friends will be applied to strengthen the trust so as to finish the transaction. Based on the analysis of the components of trust, a hierarchical structure of online trust in BtoC e-commerce can be constructed, as shown as Table 2. The components that influence trust in BtoC e-commerce can be classified as direct trust, indirect trust, and environment trust, based on which an integrated evaluation model of trust and reputation is established.

Table 2. Hierarchical structure of online trust in BtoC e-commerce.

Total Trust	Objective Trust	Institutional Trust	Situation norm	C1-C6, D3, E6-E7
			Structure guarantee	A8, C7-C9, D5, E1-E4, E8
	Subjective Trust	Direct Trust	Direct perceived trust	A1-A8, B1-B4, C1-C9, D1-D5, E1-E8
			Individual recommendation	A1, A7
		Indirect Trust	reputation	A1, A3, A8, B2, C1, D1

3.4. Logical Relationship between Trust and Reputation

Reputation systems collect, process, and aggregate information about participants or services to help future users make optimal decisions. In service-oriented network environments, reputation systems should encourage trustworthy behavior and punish dishonest participation. In the following, a general trust computation model for BtoC e-commerce is formulated to represent the relationship between trust and reputation. Based on the logical relationship between trust and reputation, iterative dynamical trust and reputation computation models will be derived in the next section.

In the hierarchical structure of online trust in BtoC e-commerce shown in Table 2, objective trust is invariable or changes slowly over a period, which constitutes the background knowledge of perceived trust during the transaction process. Direct perceived trust and individual recommendation trust compose direct trust. Reputation is often regarded as recommendation trust in the literature. Reputation and direct trust compose subjective trust. Subjective trust and objective trust compose the total trust. On the other hand, the factors of trust previously described (A1–E7) are usually considered in some practical trust and reputation evaluation systems such as Dang and Amazon. Therefore, these factors are refined to a multi-dimensional trust computation model, which includes reputation. Trust depends on potentially quantified trustworthiness qualities and context of transaction. Trustworthiness, or degree of trust, is the objective probability that the trustee performs a particular action on which the interests of the trustor depend. Reputation is a social evaluation or public estimation of standing for merit, achievement, reliability, *etc.* Reputation is the opinion of a community toward a person or someone else. Reputation may be used as a basis for trust. However, they are different notions, as pointed out by Jøsang [6]. Trust is local, temporary, and subjective, while reputation is global, long-term, and relatively objective. Both trust and reputation provide soft security mechanisms for online transactions. The relationship between trust and reputation constitutes the basic structure for the model of reputation computation, which is described by Figure 2.

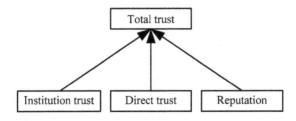

Figure 2. Schematic diagram of trust and reputation.

Based on the relationship between trust and reputation, a general mathematical description of the relationship of trust with reputation can be established as:

$$T = f(T_e, T_d, R) \tag{1}$$

where total trust T is the function of institutional trust T_e, direct perspective trust T_d, and reputation R. Linear function and product form are usually adopted to simulate the function relationship f of the total trust and its factor in the literature [17]. In our proposed method, the probability model is used. Because the objective institutional trust is slowly changing or invariable during a period, it is assumed to be constant and will not be considered when computing trust and reputation.

4. The Proposed Model

Based on the relationship of trust and reputation, a dynamical reputation and trust model will be proposed in this section. Firstly, the three variables denoted as total trust, direct trust, and reputation used in the proposed model are clarified, and the multi-dimensional trust concept of quantitative computation is derived. Then, the iterative mathematical relationship of trust and reputation is formulated. Finally, a probability computational model is established to compute reputation values.

4.1. Variables in the Model

Because the objective institutional trust T_e in Equation (1) is assumed to be constant, this factor will not be considered any more. The objective institutional trust is the total background trust factor from societies formulated over a long time, which has been mentioned in [13,28]. Thus, the total trust T is modeled on the function of direct perspective trust T_d and reputation R:

$$T = f(T_d, R). \tag{2}$$

In some practical reputation evaluation systems and research works, trust scores are used as basic elements in the computation of reputation [9,56–59]. However, direct trust and total trust are not distinguished. In the evaluation systems of Dangdang and Amazon, some examples of different aspects of evaluations are provided by customers, shown in Table 3, which correspond to the components of trust shown in Tables 1 and 2. Quality, price, logistics, and servers are the four different aspects of f trust in BtoC e-commerce transactions used in our proposed method.

Table 3. Examples of four aspects of evaluations provided by evaluation systems of Dangdang and Amazon.

Dimension	Dangdang	Amazon	Trust-Related Factors
Quality	Content is good	Quality is fine	B1–B2,B4,C1,D1–D3
Price	Price is reasonable	It is expensive, comparatively	B3
Logistics	Logistics are slow	Logistics are very fast	E2–E3,D1–D4
Servers	I connect to servers easily	Relative information is useful	A1–A4,B4,C1–C5,D1–D4,E4–E7

When we use the comments of customers to formulate trust and reputation, trust evaluation becomes a multi-dimensional concept. Furthermore, the evaluation-based trust is direct perceptive trust, which is expressed as the overall direct trust score T_d for the selling party of the transactions and the weighted aggregation of multi-dimensional trust scores for different aspects is shown as:

$$T_d = f(T_d^{(1)}, T_d^{(2)}, ..., T_d^{(k)}), \tag{3}$$

where $T_d^{(k)}$ represents the trust score for dimensions k ($k = 1, 2, ..., C$) such as quality, price, logistics, and convenience. Computation examples of multi-dimensional components of trust will be illustrated in Section 5.

From the relationship between reputation and trust discussed previously, reputation is the formation of long-term and global macro-concept. It is the result of the accumulation of trust. Therefore, reputation can be simplified as the representation of the average value of trust after a series of transactions for any given merchandise. If m transactions or transaction time units for the same merchandise occur, and the total trust of each transaction or transaction time unit is $T(i), i = 1, 2, ..., m$, then the reputation can be calculated as follows:

$$R = \frac{1}{m} \sum_{i=1}^{m} T(i). \tag{4}$$

The concrete form of the function relationship f of the total trust, direct perceptive trust, and reputation is a linear function in our proposed method, which is shown as:

$$T = \lambda * T_d + (1 - \lambda) * R, \tag{5}$$

where λ is the weighted factor that balances the roles of direct trust T_d and reputation R. If the values of total trust T, direct trust T_d, and reputation R are known, λ can be estimated by the regression method.

4.2. Iterative Model of Reputation and Trust

Reputation values are based on the average values of trust, which is usually calculated by the expectation function of probability variables [48]. Practical experience in BtoC e-commerce shows that a change in business reputation is caused by a change in trust of a large number of customers. Reputation influences consumers' perceived trust in return, and they both interact with each other. Therefore, by using closed-loop feedback control theory, the closed-loop evolution model of reputation and trust can be further illustrated as in Figure 3.

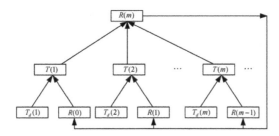

Figure 3. Iterative closed-loop computation model of reputation and trust.

In Figure 3, the values of reputation before the m-th transaction (or time interval) and after the m-th transaction (or time interval) are recorded as $R(m-1)$ and $R(m)$ respectively, the total trust of the m-th transaction (or time interval) is $T(m)$, and the direct trust of the m-th transaction (or time interval) is $T_d(m)$, $(m \in Z^+)$. As for repeated transactions of the same single commodity, the computational model can be established when considering the time series characteristics of the transactions. The reputation value of the last time is the basis of the next total trust calculation, and a renewal of trust will cause changes to the reputation. From Equation (4), the relationship of $R(m)$, $R(m-1)$ and the m-th total trust of $T(m)$ is shown as:

$$R(m) = \frac{m-1}{m}R(m-1) + \frac{1}{m}T(m), m \in Z^+. \tag{6}$$

From Figure 3 and Equation (5), the relationship of the m-th total trust of $T(m)$, $m \in Z^+$, direct trust T_d and the m-th reputation $R(m-1)$ is established as

$$T(m) = \lambda * T_d(m) + (1-\lambda) * R(m-1), m \in Z^+. \tag{7}$$

If the direct trust T_d of each transaction (or time interval) is known, and the parameters of Equations (6) and (7) are given, the iterative total trust and reputation values can be calculated. As discussed above, trust is the probability formulation for the counterpart of transactions. Therefore, the trust score on a dimension for a counterpart of a transaction is the probability that the consumer expects the seller to carry out transactions satisfactorily, which corresponds to the rating in practical evaluation systems. Following, the simple dimension direct trust component of T_d will be modeled by 0–1 distribution or Beta distribution, and the multi-dimensional direct trust component of T_d is computed by multi-dimensional probability distribution.

4.3. Computation of Direct Trust

A direct trust computation is performed when customers are attempting to interact with agents, making transactions, and giving their comments or star evaluations. In this situation, the direct trust computation is based on direct observation and derived from personal perception or the identity information embodied in online systems. Direct trust will be computed by using Beta distribution.

4.3.1. Characteristics of Beta Distribution

The Beta distribution is an important notion that describes the probability distribution of binary events in probability theory [48]. In Bayesian inference, Beta distribution can be used as a prior distribution by means of the probability density function, which in turn can be used for decision making. Bayesian inference is a statistical process through which the current state of the observed distribution is evaluated. Several researchers have exploited trust computation methods by using the Beta distribution and Bayesian frameworks [58]. Posterior probabilities of binary events can be represented as Beta distributions. The Beta-family of probability density functions is a continuous family of functions indexed by the two parameters α and β. The Beta probability distribution density function f can be expressed by using the gamma function as:

$$f(t; \alpha, \beta) = \frac{\Gamma(\alpha + \beta)}{\Gamma(\alpha)\Gamma(\beta)} t^{\alpha-1}(1 - t)^{\beta-1}, 0 \leqslant t \leqslant 1, \alpha > 0, \beta > 0 \tag{8}$$

where $\Gamma(\alpha) = (\alpha - 1)!$. In binomial distribution, it is desirable to compute the trust value of transactions. The notation T is used to represent the probability that a satisfactory evaluation will be provided by buyers. Considering repeated transactions for the same goods, the two parameters used in the beta distribution to represent the observations are α and β, respectively; n_s is the number of previous satisfactory evaluations; and n_u is the number of previous unsatisfactory evaluations. By setting $\alpha = n_s + 1$ and $\beta = n_u + 1$, the estimated value of T is obtained by computing the expectation value of the probability distribution function of the Beta distribution as:

$$T = E(f(t; \alpha, \beta)) = \frac{\alpha}{\alpha + \beta} = \frac{n_s + 1}{n_s + n_u + 2}. \tag{9}$$

In Equation (9), the values of n_s and n_u are obtained by counting the history of satisfactory and unsatisfactory evaluations. The local direct trust value is based on the expected value of the Beta distribution (see Equation (9)). For the same trust values, there may be several combinations of different values of n_s and n_u. In other words, if trust values are constant, large and small numbers of satisfactory evaluations and unsatisfactory evaluations may lead to the same level of trust. However, in practice, a greater number of evaluations would ensure more accurate trust computations. Therefore, a new characteristic parameter named confidence is used to distinguish between trust values that are estimated using different numbers of evaluations [17]. Level of confidence is denoted as $Conf$, and is defined via the variance of the Beta distribution as:

$$Conf(T) = 1 - Var(f(t; \alpha, \beta)) = 1 - \frac{\alpha\beta}{(\alpha + \beta)^2(\alpha + \beta + 1)} = 1 - \frac{(n_s + 1)(n_u + 1)}{(n_s + u + 2)^2(n_s + u + 3)} \tag{10}$$

where Var is the variation value of the probability distribution function. Considering the combination of values of n_s and n_u shown in Table 4, the result is equal trust and different levels of confidence. Figure 4 shows the same trust values with different variation values. It can be seen that the value of $Conf$ is higher when values of n_s and n_u increase. Therefore, the parameter $Conf$ is suitable to describe the level of confidence of trust.

Table 4. Same trust values with different samples of trust computation.

Total n	n_s	n_u	T	Var	$Conf$
6	2	4	0.375	0.0260	0.9740
14	5	9	0.375	0.0138	0.9862
22	8	14	0.375	0.0094	0.9906
30	11	19	0.375	0.0071	0.9929
38	14	24	0.375	0.0057	0.9943
46	17	29	0.375	0.0048	0.9952
54	20	34	0.375	0.0041	0.9959
62	23	39	0.375	0.0036	0.9964
70	26	44	0.375	0.0032	0.9968
78	29	49	0.375	0.0029	0.9971

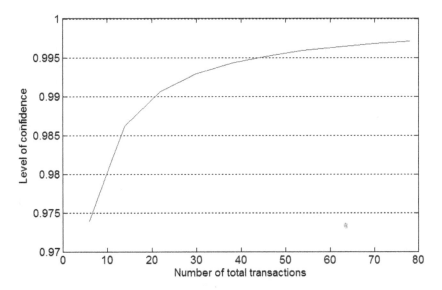

Figure 4. The relationship between level of confidence and transaction times.

4.3.2. Multi-Dimensional Beta Distribution

As for multi-dimensional trust scores with different respects $T_d^{(1)}, T_d^{(2)}, ..., T_d^{(k)}$, when each aspect is assumed to be independent from the others, the probability distribution density function f of $T_d^{(1)}, T_d^{(2)}, ..., T_d^{(k)}$, can be expressed as:

$$f(t_1, \alpha_1, \beta_1; t_2, \alpha_2, \beta_2, ..., t_C, \alpha_C, \beta_C) = \frac{\Gamma(\alpha_1 + \beta_1)}{\Gamma(\alpha_1)\Gamma(\beta_1)} t_1^{\alpha_1-1}(1-t_1)^{\beta_1-1} \frac{\Gamma(\alpha_2 + \beta_2)}{\Gamma(\alpha_2)\Gamma(\beta_2)} t_2^{\alpha_2-1}(1-t_2)^{\beta_2-1}$$

$$... \frac{\Gamma(\alpha_C + \beta_C)}{\Gamma(\alpha_C)\Gamma(\beta_C)} t_C^{\alpha_C-1}(1-t_C)^{\beta_C-1}, 0 \leqslant t_i \leqslant 1, \alpha_i > 0, \beta_i > 0, i = 1, 2, ..., C. \tag{11}$$

Therefore, the estimated value of T_d with multi-dimensional factors is obtained by computing the expectation of probability distribution function $f(t_1, \alpha_1, \beta_1; t_2, \alpha_2, \beta_2; ...; t_C, \alpha_C, \beta_C)$ as:

$$T_d = E(f(t; \alpha, \beta)) = \prod_{i=1}^{C} T_i = \prod_{i=1}^{C} \frac{n_{s_i} + 1}{n_{s_i} + n_{u_i} + 2}, \tag{12}$$

The level of confidence $Conf$ defined from the variance of the beta distribution is shown as:

$$Conf(T) = 1 - Var(f(t; \alpha, \beta)) = (\prod_{i=1}^{C} \frac{n_{s_i} + 1}{n_{s_i} + n_{u_i} + 2})^2 - \prod_{i=1}^{C} \frac{(n_{s_i} + 1)(n_{s_i} + 2)}{(n_{s_i} + n_{u_i} + 2)(n_{s_i} + n_{u_i} + 3)} + 1. \tag{13}$$

4.3.3. Dynamical Reputation Computation Processes

From Equations (4) and (11), it can be seen that the values will not change with an increase in the number of transactions if the reputation is stable. When the number of transactions increases, trust values only become more accurate. However, the reputation of trustees in the process of transactions changes gradually in practice. Especially in BtoC commerce, there are so many competitors. As a result, the number of transactions may change drastically. Therefore, in order to establish the dynamical reputation computation model, the transactions are regarded as a time series of events, and divided into equal time intervals. For example, there are $N_1, N_2, ..., N_m$ transactions in m equal time intervals. After each transaction, the customer provides a binomial distribution evaluation (good or bad). In the i-th time interval, there are $n_s(i)$ satisfactory evaluations and $n_u(i)$ unsatisfactory evaluations. The direct local $T_d(i)$ can be calculated with Equation (9). Given the value of parameter λ and initial value of

$R(0)$, the total trust value $T(i)$ can be computed, $i = 1, 2, ..., m, m \in Z^+$. The cumulative reputation can be computed using Equation (8).

As for multi-dimensional components of trust, similar computation steps will be completed. After each transaction, the customer provides a binomial distribution evaluation (good or bad) for each dimensional component of trust. In the i-th time interval, there are $n_{sj}(i)$ satisfactory evaluations and $n_{uj}(i)$ unsatisfactory evaluations for the j dimension, $j = 1, 2, ..., C$, where C is the number of dimensions. The direct local $T_d(i)$ can be calculated by Equation (11). Similarly, total trust values and cumulative reputation can be computed using Equations (8) and (9).

5. Experimental Results

In this section, numerical experiments are performed to illustrate the variation of total dynamic reputation with local computed trust. Firstly, data are collected on two online firms. Original two-year language evaluations of four aspects of trust in relation to online transactions are collected and these transaction evaluations are separated into 24 different time intervals. Then the value of direct trust is estimated by using the expected value of the probability distribution function of the Beta distribution, and the values and reputation are renewed by an iterative algorithm. The reputation of the same commodity from two online business firms is computed. From the computational results, it is noted that there are different characteristics of different firms.

5.1. Data Collection

In most BtoC transaction platforms, consumers can write reviews about a variety of topics from consumer durables to household electrical appliances. In China, Dangdang (http://www.dangdang.com/) and Amazon (http://www.amazon.cn/) are two famous BtoC firms especially with regard to the sale of books. Therefore, the proposed computational method of reputation was used to analyze the trust and reputation of these two firms. Piracy has become a serious problem in China in the 10 ten years, and online book sales have become an important channel for pirated books, which are inferior in quality to the genuine books. For this study, the same books with more than 4000 effective evaluations in the last three years were chosen. If readers want to know the details of the evaluation systems, please visit the website. The evaluations are divided into 24 monthly periods. In each month, positive and negative evaluations of quality, price, logistics, and servers are counted manually from the language evaluations of the different aspects of comments provided for customers in the evaluation systems of Dangdang and Amazon. In our experiment, evaluations of quality, price, logistics, and servers are assumed to be independent. Therefore, the multi-dimensional expected value of the probability distribution function of the Beta distribution can be used to compute the values of trust. Figure 5 shows the evaluation interference of Dangdang and Amazon. Table 5 shows the positive (marked "+") and negative (marked "−") evaluations of the four factors of trust of Dangdang and Amazon. The data are from June 2013 to May 2015. There are a total of 33,632 and 4057 effective evaluations of trust in the books on Dangdang and Amazon from June 2013 to May 2015.

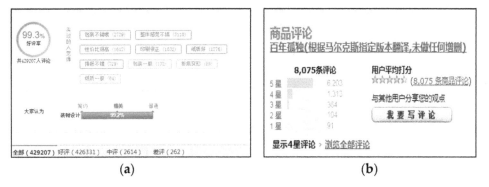

Figure 5. Evaluation interference of the same book on Dangdang and Amazon (Both in Chinese language). (**a**) Evaluation interference on Dangdang. (**b**) Evaluation interference on Amazon.

5.2. Computation Results

In order to compute the total local trust for a time interval by iterative formulation Equations (6) and (7), the initial value of reputation should be given in advance. In our method, the initial value of reputation $R(0)$ is set the same as $T_d(1)$, and the value of the parameter weighted factor λ is 0.6. By using the data shown in Table 5, direct trust for dimension k ($k = 1, 2, 3, 4$) named $T_d^{(k)}$ can be calculated using Equation (9), and total multi-dimensional direct trust T_d can be calculated using Equation (12). Computation results of one of four values of different dimensions of trusts (quality trust (Q-Tru), price trust (P-Tru), logistics trust (L-Tru), and servers trust (S-Tru)), different dimensions of reputation such as quality reputation (Q-Reput), price reputation (P-Reput), logistics reputation (L-Reput), and servers reputation (S-Reput), total trust (Total-Tru), and total reputation (Total-Reput) are shown in Table 6. In the last row of Table 6, there are values for the confidence of multi-dimensional direct trust computed using Equation (13). Figure 6 shows the dynamical variation of reputation, total multi-dimensional trust, and one of four different dimensions of trust (quality, price, logistics, and servers) for the book on Dangdang. Figure 7 shows the dynamical values of reputation, values of total multi-dimensional trust, and values of one of four dimensions of values of trust for the same book on Amazon. Finally, Figure 8 shows the variation of confidence of multi-dimensional direct trust of Dangdang and Amazon over 24 months from June 2013 to May 2015.

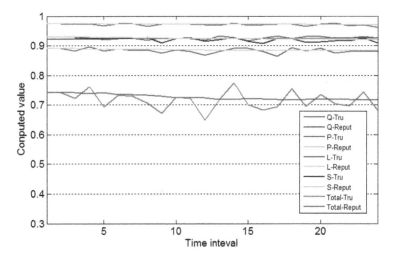

Figure 6. Dynamical reputation and trust for books on Dangdang over 24 months.

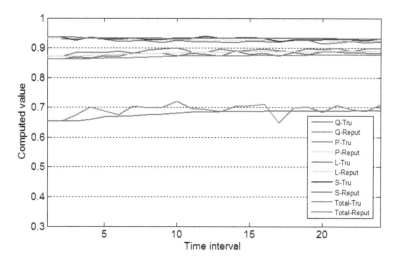

Figure 7. Dynamical reputation and trust for books on Amazon over 24 months.

Table 5. Number of evaluations of trust in books on Dangdang and Amazon during the 24 months.

Time Interval	Number of Evaluations of Dangdang								Number of Evaluations of Amazon							
	Quality		Price		Logistics		Servers		Quality		Price		Logistics		Servers	
	+	−	+	−	+	−	+	−	+	−	+	−	+	−	+	−
2013.06	223	18	324	08	285	34	327	24	24	3	26	3	26	1	28	1
2013.07	353	25	285	07	149	27	261	19	35	3	42	2	33	2	23	2
2013.08	395	17	427	09	392	35	298	31	22	2	29	1	47	2	44	2
2013.09	264	26	250	14	264	42	235	25	46	4	42	3	46	3	37	2
2013.10	354	29	418	11	317	39	173	16	35	3	43	2	37	4	41	3
2013.11	469	30	367	07	185	28	372	35	41	1	35	3	25	2	32	1
2013.12	358	41	294	18	378	52	264	19	64	4	52	2	53	5	37	3
2014.01	596	47	425	03	421	87	287	55	39	2	47	1	71	9	52	4
2014.02	397	32	358	10	258	34	232	21	22	2	39	0	45	3	32	1
2014.03	286	23	261	06	274	46	359	23	47	3	28	2	27	2	45	2
2014.04	243	28	174	05	152	39	285	41	35	3	31	3	34	3	37	0
2014.05	378	11	282	12	250	41	252	28	34	4	42	2	33	3	29	1
2014.06	412	25	467	02	376	32	274	15	53	2	37	3	38	4	48	2
2014.07	258	32	365	15	311	27	327	43	26	2	54	4	45	3	35	1
2014.08	395	28	391	12	285	43	163	30	41	3	40	2	31	2	42	2
2014.09	406	13	226	05	128	36	270	22	30	4	29	2	36	3	21	2
2014.10	378	29	362	08	380	29	361	27	51	3	30	3	57	2	36	3
2014.11	312	14	254	16	294	41	235	35	48	5	43	2	65	3	28	2
2014.12	659	31	258	05	459	40	196	28	39	2	58	4	46	6	31	2
2015.01	875	69	467	01	396	74	452	51	52	3	69	3	72	8	80	6
2015.02	457	32	357	19	238	37	239	27	21	1	32	3	47	3	34	2
2015.03	485	21	274	08	165	24	368	21	30	2	54	3	25	2	27	2
2015.04	266	19	187	14	271	36	227	35	27	2	41	2	42	3	43	2
2015.05	425	28	382	09	318	33	185	26	42	3	48	3	39	2	27	1

Table 6. Computational results of reputation and trust for books on Dangdang over 24 months.

Time Interval	Q-Tru.	Q-Reput.	P-Tru.	P-Reput.	L-Tru.	L-Reput.	S-Tru	S-Reput.	Total-Tru	Total-Reput	$Conf$
2013.06	0.9218	0.9218	0.9731	0.9731	0.8910	0.8910	0.9292	0.9292	0.7426	0.7426	0.99943
2013.07	0.9218	0.9218	0.9731	0.9731	0.8910	0.8910	0.9292	0.9292	0.7426	0.7426	0.99919
2013.08	0.9238	0.9218	0.9730	0.9731	0.8813	0.8910	0.9292	0.9292	0.7227	0.7426	0.99958
2013.09	0.9288	0.9225	0.9739	0.9730	0.8960	0.8877	0.9240	0.9292	0.7611	0.7376	0.99933
2013.10	0.9195	0.9240	0.9672	0.9732	0.8823	0.8898	0.9235	0.9279	0.6933	0.7423	0.99939
2013.11	0.9236	0.9231	0.9730	0.9720	0.8895	0.8883	0.9245	0.9270	0.7322	0.7341	0.99939
2013.12	0.9261	0.9232	0.9734	0.9722	0.8837	0.8885	0.9240	0.9266	0.7283	0.7339	0.99949
2014.01	0.9176	0.9236	0.9657	0.9724	0.8863	0.8878	0.9272	0.9262	0.7052	0.7332	0.99954
2014.02	0.9269	0.9229	0.9715	0.9715	0.8757	0.8876	0.9084	0.9263	0.6716	0.7301	0.99942
2014.03	0.9230	0.9233	0.9713	0.9715	0.8863	0.8863	0.9238	0.9244	0.7248	0.7242	0.99944
2014.04	0.9232	0.9233	0.9720	0.9715	0.8798	0.8863	0.9270	0.9243	0.7215	0.7243	0.99913
2014.05	0.9174	0.9233	0.9706	0.9715	0.8676	0.8857	0.9138	0.9245	0.6481	0.7240	0.99938
2014.06	0.9325	0.9228	0.9685	0.9715	0.8799	0.8842	0.9191	0.9236	0.7170	0.7182	0.99962
2014.07	0.9264	0.9235	0.9759	0.9712	0.8913	0.8839	0.9279	0.9233	0.7746	0.7181	0.99944
2014.08	0.9162	0.9237	0.9686	0.9716	0.8906	0.8844	0.9150	0.9236	0.6998	0.7219	0.99927
2014.09	0.9253	0.9232	0.9708	0.9714	0.8809	0.8848	0.9071	0.9231	0.6832	0.7205	0.99899
2014.10	0.9319	0.9234	0.9719	0.9713	0.8633	0.8846	0.9228	0.9221	0.6930	0.7183	0.99960
2014.11	0.9240	0.9239	0.9722	0.9714	0.8931	0.8833	0.9233	0.9221	0.7541	0.7169	0.99936
2014.12	0.9300	0.9239	0.9646	0.9714	0.8817	0.8839	0.9112	0.9222	0.6944	0.7188	0.99945
2015.01	0.9299	0.9242	0.9726	0.9711	0.8907	0.8837	0.9121	0.9216	0.7352	0.7176	0.99965
2015.02	0.9246	0.9245	0.9760	0.9711	0.8752	0.8841	0.9167	0.9211	0.7045	0.7185	0.99939
2015.03	0.9261	0.9245	0.9663	0.9714	0.8798	0.8837	0.9160	0.9209	0.6969	0.7178	0.99934
2015.04	0.9309	0.9246	0.9708	0.9711	0.8808	0.8835	0.9255	0.9207	0.7430	0.7169	0.99927
2015.05	0.9257	0.9248	0.9621	0.9711	0.8828	0.8834	0.9093	0.9209	0.6798	0.7180	0.99938

Table 7. Computational results of reputation and trust for books on Amazon over 24 months.

Time Interval	Q-Tru.	Q-Reput.	P-Tru.	P-Reput.	L-Tru.	L-Reput.	S-Tru	S-Reput.	Total-Tru	Total-Reput.	Conf
2013.06	0.8621	0.8621	0.8710	0.8710	0.9310	0.9310	0.9355	0.9355	0.6540	0.6540	0.99372
2013.07	0.8621	0.8621	0.8710	0.8710	0.9310	0.9310	0.9355	0.9355	0.6540	0.6540	0.99479
2013.08	0.8697	0.8621	0.8837	0.8710	0.9286	0.9310	0.9262	0.9355	0.6739	0.6540	0.99494
2013.09	0.8666	0.8646	0.8843	0.8752	0.9331	0.9302	0.9359	0.9324	0.7006	0.6589	0.99626
2013.10	0.8724	0.8651	0.8832	0.8775	0.9285	0.9309	0.9313	0.9333	0.6874	0.6673	0.99575
2013.11	0.8721	0.8666	0.8892	0.8786	0.9215	0.9304	0.9292	0.9329	0.6748	0.6706	0.99508
2013.12	0.8842	0.8675	0.8829	0.8804	0.9237	0.9290	0.9349	0.9323	0.7040	0.6712	0.99674
2014.01	0.8797	0.8699	0.8936	0.8807	0.9232	0.9282	0.9268	0.9326	0.6979	0.6753	0.99701
2014.02	0.8819	0.8711	0.8966	0.8824	0.9182	0.9276	0.9289	0.9319	0.7000	0.6778	0.99504
2014.03	0.8738	0.8723	0.9010	0.8839	0.9261	0.9265	0.9341	0.9316	0.7203	0.6800	0.99527
2014.04	0.8825	0.8724	0.8884	0.8856	0.9219	0.9265	0.9330	0.9318	0.6976	0.6837	0.99528
2014.05	0.8780	0.8734	0.8863	0.8859	0.9207	0.9261	0.9403	0.9319	0.6932	0.6849	0.99527
2014.06	0.8737	0.8737	0.8957	0.8859	0.9198	0.9256	0.9330	0.9326	0.6856	0.6855	0.99619
2014.07	0.8885	0.8737	0.8897	0.8867	0.9178	0.9252	0.9346	0.9326	0.7037	0.6855	0.99574
2014.08	0.8790	0.8748	0.8927	0.8869	0.9241	0.9246	0.9356	0.9328	0.7056	0.6867	0.99589
2014.09	0.8824	0.8751	0.8959	0.8873	0.9226	0.9246	0.9332	0.9330	0.7110	0.6879	0.99412
2014.10	0.8723	0.8755	0.8916	0.8878	0.9202	0.9245	0.9224	0.9330	0.6482	0.6893	0.99583
2014.11	0.8861	0.8753	0.8874	0.8880	0.9297	0.9242	0.9269	0.9324	0.6991	0.6870	0.99613
2014.12	0.8785	0.8759	0.8977	0.8885	0.9279	0.9245	0.9271	0.9321	0.7024	0.6876	0.99611
2015.01	0.8868	0.8761	0.8948	0.8888	0.9137	0.9247	0.9285	0.9318	0.6845	0.6884	0.99764
2015.02	0.8868	0.8766	0.9000	0.8894	0.9178	0.9242	0.9295	0.9316	0.7078	0.6882	0.99486
2015.03	0.8846	0.8771	0.8894	0.8894	0.9239	0.9239	0.9295	0.9315	0.6923	0.6891	0.99468
2015.04	0.8840	0.8774	0.8979	0.8894	0.9184	0.9239	0.9259	0.9314	0.6886	0.6892	0.99568
2015.05	0.8826	0.8777	0.8982	0.8897	0.9221	0.9236	0.9324	0.9312	0.7089	0.6892	0.99596

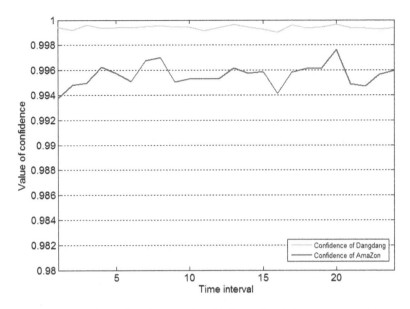

Figure 8. Variation values of confidence of multi-dimensional direct trust over 24 months.

5.3. Discussion

From Figures 6 and 7 the following conclusions can be drawn. In the case of Dangdang, single dimension values of reputation are, from high to low, price reputation (P-Repu), server reputation (S-Repu), quality reputation (Q-Repu), and logistics reputation (L-Repu). In the case of Amazon, single dimension values of reputation are, from high to low, server reputation (S-Repu), logistics reputation (L-Repu), price reputation (P-Repu), and quality reputation (Q-Repu). It can be noted that trust changed quickly because it was based directly on evaluations, whereas reputation changed slowly. Therefore, the model can correctly simulate local trust and global reputation. Comparing the total reputation shown in Figures 6 and 7 we can see that the reputation of Dangdang is higher than that of Amazon, and the former is decreasing slowly. The reputation of Amazon is lower than that of Dangdang and is increasing slowly. It can also be observed from Figure 8 that the values of confidence of total direct trust in Dangdang are higher than those of Amazon because there are more evaluations of Dangdang compared with Amazon.

6. Conclusions

A new closed-loop feedback computation model of dynamical reputation based on the trust evaluation in BtoC e-commerce has been proposed in this paper. Three concepts, namely direct trust, total trust, and reputation, are discussed initially. Based on the probability theory of evaluations of different dimensions of trust, a new dynamical computational model of trust and reputation is established. Multi-dimensional characteristics and the composition of trust in BtoC e-commerce are analyzed and the ratings of each customer are used as basic trust score events in the probability distribution. A logical model of trust and reputation is established based on the relationship between trust and reputation, and an iterative computation model of dynamical reputation is further proposed by using a closed-loop feedback mechanism. Furthermore, a time series of massive feedback ratings of customers are aggregated to formulate the sellers' local temporal trust scores using Beta distribution. Computational experiments on repeated transactions for the same commodity over a period of 24 months on Dangdang and Amazon are also performed. The results show that the proposed computational model can effectively simulate a variation in reputation. The proposed computational model for local trust and overall reputation can play a guiding role in both theoretical research into computational models of trust and reputation and the practical design of reputation systems in e-commerce. How to design a series of comparative experiments with a suitable method is not easy because of different mechanisms. Thus we did not design more comparative experiments. The information processing method derived in this paper is a trial. An advanced time-series signal processing method can also be used in the future. These directions are our next further research topics.

Acknowledgments: This research is supported by the National Natural Science Foundation of China (71302080), the Shanghai Natural Science Foundation (12ZR1409900), Ministry of Education Research of Social Sciences Youth Foundation projects (13YJC630149), and the Special Research Foundation for the Doctoral Program of Higher Education of China (20120078120001).

Author Contributions: All authors have made significant contributions to the paper. Bo Tian carried out a literature survey, proposed the trust and reputation computation system, and wrote the paper. Jingti Han and Kecheng Liu contributed to simulations and modification of the manuscript. All authors have read and approved the final manuscript.

Conflicts of Interest: The authors declare no conflict of interest.

References

1. China Internet Network Information Center. The Thirty-Fifth China Internet Network Development Status Report in February, 2015. Available online: https://www.cnnic.cn/hlwfzyj/hlwxzbg/hlwtjbg/201502/t20150203_51634.htm (accessed on 28 January 2016). (In Chinese).
2. Lin, W.-S.; Wang, C.-H. Antecedences to continued intentions of adopting e-learning system in blended learning instruction: A contingency framework based on models of information system success and task-technology fit. *Comput. Educ.* **2012**, *58*, 88–99. [CrossRef]
3. Wu, X.; Chen, Q.; Zhou, W.; Guo, J. A review of mobile commerce consumers' behavior research: Consumer acceptance, loyalty and continuance (2000–2009). *Int. J. Mob. Commun.* **2010**, *8*, 528–560. [CrossRef]
4. Pinyol, I.; Sabater-Mir, J. Computational trust and reputation models for open multi-agent systems: A review. *Artif. Intell. Rev.* **2013**, *40*, 1–25. [CrossRef]
5. Gutowska, A.; Sloane, A.; Buckley, K.A. On Desideratum for B2C E-Commerce Reputation Systems. *J. Comput. Sci. Technol.* **2009**, *24*, 820–832. [CrossRef]
6. Jøsang, A.; Ismail, R.; Boyd, C. A survey of trust and reputation systems for online service provision. *Decis. Support Syst.* **2007**, *43*, 618–644. [CrossRef]
7. Wang, Y.D.; Emurian, H.H. An overview of online trust: Concepts, elements, and implications. *Comput. Hum. Behav.* **2005**, *21*, 105–125. [CrossRef]
8. Qin, T.; Liu, X. DSRtrust: A dynamic trust model of distinguishing service and recommendation for internet-based virtual computing environment. *Int. J. Grid Distrib. Comput.* **2014**, *7*, 135–147. [CrossRef]
9. Zhang, X.; Cui, L.; Wang, Y. Commtrust: Computing multi-dimensional trust by mining e-commerce feedback comments. *IEEE Trans. Knowl. Data Eng.* **2014**, *26*, 1631–1643. [CrossRef]
10. Urbano, J.; Rocha, A.P.; Oliveira, E. An approach to computational social trust. *AI Commun.* **2014**, *27*, 113–131.
11. Sabater, J.; Sierra, C. Review on computational trust and reputation models. *Artif. Intell. Rev.* **2005**, *24*, 33–60. [CrossRef]
12. Kant, V.; Bharadwaj, K.K. Fuzzy computational models of trust and distrust for enhanced recommendations. *Int. J. Intell. Syst.* **2013**, *28*, 332–365. [CrossRef]
13. Marsh, S.P. Formalizing Trust as a Computational Concept. Ph.D. Thesis, University of Stirling, Stirling, UK, 1994.
14. Shankar, V.; Urban, G.L.; Sultan, F. Online trust: A stakeholder perspective, concepts, implications, and future directions. *J. Strateg. Inf. Syst.* **2002**, *11*, 325–344. [CrossRef]
15. Che, S.; Feng, R.; Liang, X.; Wang, X. A lightweight trust management based on Bayesian and entropy for wireless sensor networks. *Secur. Commun. Netw.* **2015**, *8*, 168–175. [CrossRef]
16. Shi, X.; Zhang, Y. Design and implementation of P2P trust model based on the classic Bayesian networks theory. *J. Theor. Appl. Inf. Technol.* **2012**, *45*, 129–135.
17. Denko, M.K.; Sun, T.; Woungang, I. Trust management in ubiquitous computing: A Bayesian approach. *Comput. Commun.* **2011**, *34*, 398–406. [CrossRef]

18. Zheng, Q.; Tian, B. A Trust Evaluation Model for B2C E-Commerce. In Proceedings of the 2007 IEEE International Conference on Service Operations and Logistics, and Informatics, Philadelphia, PA, USA, 27–29 August 2007.

19. Tian, B.; Yang, L. Dynamic Reputation Model in Service-Oriented Computing Environment. In Proceedings of the 2011 International Conference on Transportation, Mechanical, and Electrical Engineering (TMEE), Changchun, China, 16–18 December 2011.

20. Tian, B.; Wang, J.; Yang, L. Recommended trust evaluation in B2C E-commerce based on fuzzy analytic hierarchy process. *Int. J. Knowl. Syst. Sci.* **2012**, *3*. [CrossRef]

21. Ramchurn, S.D.; Huynh, D.; Jennings, N.R. Trust in multi-agent systems. *Knowl. Eng. Rev.* **2004**, *19*. [CrossRef]

22. Li, H.; Singhal, M. Trust management in distributed systems. *IEEE Comput.* **2007**, *40*, 45–53. [CrossRef]

23. Alvaro, E.A.; Benjamin, A.; Gheorghe, C.S. Reputation management in collaborative computing systems. *Secur. Commun. Netw.* **2010**, *3*, 546–564.

24. Srivatsa, M.; Liu, L. Securing decentralized reputation management using TrustGuard. *J. Parallel Distrib. Comput.* **2006**, *66*, 1217–1232. [CrossRef]

25. Xiong, L.; Liu, L. PeerTrust: Supporting reputation-based trust for peer-to-peer electronic communities. *IEEE Trans. Knowl. Data Eng.* **2004**, *16*, 843–857. [CrossRef]

26. Kraounakis, S.; Demetropoulos, I.N.; Michalas, A.; Obaidat, M.S.; Sarigiannidis, P.G.; Louta, M.D. A robust reputation-based computational model for trust establishment in pervasive systems. *IEEE Syst. J.* **2015**, *9*, 878–891. [CrossRef]

27. Li, X.; Du, J. Adaptive and attribute-based trust model for service level agreement guarantee in cloud computing. *IET Inf. Secur.* **2013**, *7*, 39–50. [CrossRef]

28. *Mobile Commerce and Wireless Computing Systems (Chin. Transl.)*; Chen, Z.B., Translator; Higher Education Press: Beijing, China, 2006.Elliott, G.; Phillips, N. Addison-Wesley: Boston, MA, USA, 2003.

29. Ponte, E.B.; Carvajal-Trujillo, E.; Escobar-Rodríguez, T. Influence of trust and perceived value on the intention to purchase travel online: Integrating the effects of assurance on trust antecedents. *Tour. Manag.* **2015**, *47*, 286–302. [CrossRef]

30. Hong, I.B. Understanding the consumer's online merchant selection process: The roles of product involvement, perceived risk, and trust expectation. *Int. J. Inf. Manag.* **2015**, *35*, 322–336. [CrossRef]

31. Moody, G.D.; Galletta, D.F.; Lowry, P.B. When trust and distrust collide online: The engenderment and role of consumer ambivalence in online consumer behavior. *Electron. Commer. Res. Appl.* **2014**, *13*, 266–282. [CrossRef]

32. Kim, K.; Hong, E.; Rho, S. The study of defined buying factors affecting trust building and service performance in financial management systems. *Math. Comput. Model.* **2013**, *58*, 38–48. [CrossRef]

33. Yen, D.C.; Wu, C.S.; Cheng, F.F.; Huang, Y.W. Determinants of users' intention to adopt wireless technology: An empirical study by integrating TTF with TAM. *Comput. Hum. Behav.* **2010**, *26*, 906–915. [CrossRef]

34. Jøsang, A. The Right Type of Trust for Distributed Systems. In Proceedings of the 1996 Workshop on New Security Paradigms (NSPW '96), Lake Arrowhead, CA, USA, 17–20 September 1996.

35. Yu, B.; Singh, M.P. An Evidential Model of Distributed Reputation Management. In Proceedings of the First International Joint Conference on Autonomous Agents and Multi-Agent Systems (AAMAS '02), Bologna, Italy, 15–19 July 2002.

36. Sabater, J.; Sierra, C. REGRET: A Reputation Model for Gregarious Societies. In Proceedings of the fifth International Conference on Autonomous Agents (AGENTS '01), Montreal, QC, Canada, 28 May–1 June 2001.

37. Schmidt, S.; Steele, R.; Dillon, T.S.; Chang, E. Fuzzy trust evaluation and credibility development in multi-agent systems. *Appl. Soft Comput.* **2007**, *7*, 492–505. [CrossRef]

38. Song, S.; Hwang, K.; Zhou, R.; Kwok, Y.K. Trusted P2P transactions with fuzzy reputation aggregation. *IEEE Internet Comput.* **2005**, *9*, 24–34. [CrossRef]

39. Zhou, R.; Hwang, K.; Cai, M. GossipTrust for fast reputation aggregation in Peer-to-Peer networks. *IEEE Trans. Knowl. Data Eng.* **2008**, *20*, 1282–1295. [CrossRef]

40. Wang, Y.; Lin, K.-J.; Wong, D.S.; Varadharajan, V. Trust management towards service-oriented applications. *Serv. Oriented Comput. Appl.* **2009**, *3*, 129–146. [CrossRef]

41. Golbeck, J.; Hendler, J. Accuracy of Metrics for Inferring Trust and Reputation in Semantic Web-Based Social Networks. In Proceedings of the 14th International Conference on Knowledge Engineering and Knowledge Management, Northamptonshire, UK, 5–8 October 2004.

42. Buragohain, C.; Agrawal, D.; Suri, S. A Game Theoretic Framework for Incentives in P2P Systems. In Proceedings of the Third International Conference on Peer-to-Peer Computing (P2P '03), Linköping, Sweden, 1–3 September 2003.

43. Cho, J.; Kwon, K.; Park, Y. Q-rater: A collaborative reputation system based on source credibility theory. *Expert Syst. Appl.* **2009**, *36*, 3751–3760. [CrossRef]

44. Wang, Y.; Hang, C.W.; Singh, M.P. A probabilistic approach for maintaining trust based on evidence. *J. Artif. Intell. Res.* **2011**, *40*, 221–267.

45. Liu, X.; Datta, A.; Rzadca, K. Trust beyond reputation: A computational trust model based on stereotypes. *Electron. Commer. Res. Appl.* **2013**, *12*, 24–39. [CrossRef]

46. Despotovic, Z.; Aberer, K. Maximum Likelihood Estimation of Peers' Performance in P2P Networks. Available online: http://www.eecs.harvard.edu/p2pecon/confman/papers/s2p3.pdf (accessed on 28 January 2016).

47. Beth, T.; Borcherding, M.; Klein, B. Valuation of trust in open networks. In Proceedings of the Third European Symposium on Research in Computer Security, Brighton, UK, 7–9 November 1994.

48. Ismail, R.; Jøsang, A. The Beta Reputation System. In Proceedings of the 15th Bled Electronic Commerce Conference, Bled, Slovenia, 17–19 June 2002.

49. Mui, L.; Mohtashemi, M.; Halberstadt, A. A Computational Model of Trust and Reputation. In Proceedings of the 35th Annual Hawaii International Conference on System Sciences, Big Island, HI, USA, 7–10 January 2002.

50. Jøsang, A.; Haller, J. Dirichlet Reputation Systems. In Proceedings of the Second International Conference on Availability, Reliability and Security (ARES '07), Vienna, Austria, 10–13 April 2007.

51. Wang, Y.; Vassileva, J. Bayesian Network-Based Trust Model. In Proceedings of the IEEE/WIC International Conference on Web Intelligence (WI 2003), Halifax, NS, Canada, 13–17 October 2003.

52. Teacy, W.L.; Luck, M.; Rogers, A.; Jennings, N.R. An efficient and versatile approach to trust and reputation using hierarchical Bayesian modeling. *Artif. Intell.* **2012**, *193*, 149–185. [CrossRef]

53. Kim, D.J.; Song, Y.I.; Braynov, S.B.; Rao, H.R. A multidimensional trust formation model in B-to-C e-commerce: A conceptual framework and content analyses of academia practitioner perspectives. *Decis. Support Syst.* **2005**, *40*, 143–165. [CrossRef]

54. Mayer, R.C.; Davis, J.H.; Schoorman, F.D. An integrative model of organizational trust. *Acad. Manag. Rev.* **1995**, *20*, 709–734.

55. Tian, B.; Zheng, Q. Recommended Trust Evaluation Model in Business-to-Consumer E-Commerce Based on DS Evidence Fusion Theory. *J. Manag. Sci.* **2008**, *21*, 98–104.

56. McKnight, D.H.; Choudhury, V.; Kacmar, C. Developing and validating trust measures for e-commerce: An integrative typology. *Inf. Syst. Res.* **2002**, *13*, 334–359. [CrossRef]

57. Tian, B.; Liu, K.C.; Chen, Y.Z. Dynamical Trust and Reputation Computation Model for B2C E-Commerce. *Future Internet* **2015**, *7*, 405–428. [CrossRef]

58. Thirunarayan, K.; Anantharam, P.; Henson, C.; Sheth, A. Comparative trust management with applications: Bayesian approaches emphasis. *Future Gener. Comput. Syst.* **2014**, *31*, 182–199. [CrossRef]

59. Kravari, K.; Bassiliades, N. HARM: A Hybrid Rule-Based Agent Reputation Model Based on Temporal Defensible Logic. In Proceedings of the 6th International Symposium on Rules: Research Based and Industry Focused, Montpellier, France, 27–29 August 2012.

5

Geospatially Constrained Workflow Modeling and Implementation

Feng Zhang and Yuetong Xu *

College of Geography and Environment, Shandong Normal University, Jinan, 250014, China; zfsrt@126.com
* Correspondence: yuetongxu@sina.com

Academic Editor: Willy Susilo

Abstract: With rapid development and application of mobile internet, geographic information in the field of business process is now more widely used. There are more and more researches in the field of the relationships between geographic information and workflow modeling. According to the workflow with geospatial constraints, this paper first discusses the geospatial constraints theory deeply, proposes a new concept of geospatial constraints unit, and then designs a geospatial constraint net model (GCNet). Secondly, this paper designs a new workflow model with geospatial constraints (GCWF-net) based on GCNet and workflow net (WF-net), and then analyzes some properties of the model. Finally, this paper discusses how to put GCWF-net into application practice from three aspects: extending PNML (Petri Net Markup Language) labels for GCWF-net, converting PNML to BPEL (Business Process Execution Language) and implementing BPEL.

Keywords: geospatial constraint; workflow; petri nets; WF-net; geospatial entity; PNML; BPEL

1. Introduction

A business process is "a procedure where documents, information or tasks are passed between participants according to defined sets of rules to achieve or contribute to an overall business goal" [1]. Workflow is "the computerized facilitation or automation of a business process, in whole or part" [1], and is an abstract, summary and description of business rule of the business process and the operation steps. Business professionals create business process models in order to get an understanding of who is involved and which resources are needed for the execution of a business process. Such business process models are required as a basis for knowledge transfer, quality purposes, regulations, communication between internal and external collaborative partners, or documentation in general [2]. At present, the technology of workflow modeling, analysis and simulation has been very mature and widely used in various sectors of society. With rapid development and application of mobile internet, geographic information in the field of business process is more widely used. There are some researchers beginning to study how to adapt to the demand of geographic information application in workflow modeling and the important role of geographic information in workflow automation and optimization. Traditional workflow uses mainly the geographic information as the static properties existing in workflow form or existing in the attribute information of the participating personnel, role, or organizations in a workflow, and its form is text, such as an address, a coordinate character string and so on.

Some researchers bring the geographic information into a workflow context, and mainly concentrate on the location-aware space. Chakraborty *et al.* [3] designed xBPEL language by extended BPEL. The xBPEL takes geographic location into consideration as an important context factor in the workflow operation mode, and based on this, a PerCallab system was designed. Wieland *et al.* [4] put forward the concept of context-aware workflow, and introduced what contextual factors should be considered in the workflow modeling and how to integrate them into the workflow implementation. They stressed the important role of location-aware, and the realization of the smart factory system

"NEXUS" location is one of the most important considerations. De Leoni *et al.* [5] designed a process-aware information systems framework based on YAWL (Yet Another Workflow Language). In this framework, the workflow tasks and resources are visualized on the map in order to assist the decision-making of the business process. Delker *et al.* [6] presented the concept of a location information constrained process, and extended UML (Unified Modeling Language) modeling with location information. Che *et al.* [7] used the language (GML) on the basis of Delker's conclusion to strengthen the role of location information. Zhang li *et al.* [8] designed location-aware workflow modeling and verification based on Petri Nets, and proposed six geographic relation primitives. Zhu Xinwei *et al.* clarified the concept of geospatial constraints, constructed the UML semantic framework of geospatial constraint [9], designed and verified the business process model with geospatial constraint based on Petri Nets [10]. For effective and efficient disaster emergency planning and management, Sackmann and Hofmann *et al.* [11,12] discussed the integration of place-related information in DRWfMS (Disaster Response workflow management systems), extended the knowledge base in BPM (Business Process Management) by formalizing "place" in process models and developed a framework for identifying and resolving place-related conflicts.

To sum up, the research on the relations of geospatial information and workflow modeling is increasing more and more. Researchers are extending the research focuses from geographic location to geographic information in the stage of workflow modeling, and have begun to research deeply the relations of workflow modeling and geospatial information in theory.

Based on the previous work, this paper discusses the relations between workflow modeling and geospatial information, proposes a novel modeling method based on Petri Nets. The contributions of this paper include the following: (1) Concepts: the level that the geospatial information impact on the business process is cleared, and the geospatial constraints subjects, objects, rules, states are discussed. The concept of geospatial constraints unit is put forward; (2) Models: the geospatial constraint net (GCNet) is designed based on geospatial constraint unit, and then workflow model with geospatial constraints (GCWF-net) is designed and analyzed according to GCNet and workflow net (WF-net); (3) Practices: this paper describes how to put GCWF-net into application practice from three aspects: extending PNML (Petri Net Markup Language) labels for GCWF-net, converting PNML to BPEL and the implement of BPEL.

The paper is organized as follows: Section 2 describes the concept of geospatial constraint unit (GCNet); Section 3 establishes and analyzes the workflow model with geospatial constraints (GCWF-net); Section 4 describes the implementation process of this model; and Section 5 provides conclusions and proposes future studies in this line of research.

2. Geospatially Constrained Net Model

2.1. Levels of Geospatial Information Impact on Workflow

In accordance with the participation degree, the levels of geospatial information impact on workflow can be described as the following:

(1)   First level—Geospatial information only describes the related information about workflow activities in text form, map visualization or other forms, and is always regarded as the attribute information of workflow activities, participant or organization, such as the location of activities implementation, the location of the person or organization.

(2)   Second level—Geospatial information influences the workflow activities in a decisive role, including the sites of participant or execution and the workflow trend. However, this geospatial information is previously defined in workflow design, and the workflow instances are implemented in accordance with the design.

(3)   Third level—Geospatial information influences the workflow activities in a decisive role too, but these influences is relative to geographic context of workflow activities. The geospatial

information asks workflow for positive responses, adjusting the workflow participants, execution locations or process trends in order to achieve the goals of workflow.

In the second and third levels above, workflow activities are constrained by geospatial information and must be in accordance with requirements of the geospatial information. Geospatial constraint is a statement that states the geospatial information of one or more activities in workflow scenarios or workflow instances [10]. To some extent, geospatial constraints that affect workflow activities are constraint mechanisms that constrain activities through the geospatial information related to these activities.

2.2. Subjects of Geospatial Constraints

Geospatial information is the performance and knowledge about the properties, characteristics and movement states of geographic entities. It describes the inherent quantities, qualities, distributions, relations and rules of spatial entities and environments, and it has positioning, quantitative, dynamic and multi-dimensional characteristics [14]. From an object oriented perspective, geographical spaces are composed of geographic entities. It is geographic entities or relationships that cause geospatial constraints on business process. Therefore, geographic entities can be regarded as the subjects of the geospatial constraints.

The geographic entity can be defined as a phenomenon that occupies a position in space that cannot be divided into similar phenomena in the real world, and can be expressed as simple abstract geometric objects, such as point entities, line entities, surface entities, body entities. Geographic entities in the real world do not exist in isolation. The distribution relationship of geographic entities in the geographic space is called a spatial relationship, including three basic types of spatial relationships: the topology, direction and measure relationships. The topological relationship describes the adjacent, correlative and containing relationships of entities. The direction relationship defines the position relationship between the entities. The measure relationship mainly refers to the distance relationship between entities.

Geographic entities have three characteristics: spatial characteristics, attribute characteristics and temporal characteristics. Spatial characteristics are used to describe the location and spatial relationships between things or phenomena, and they are also called the geometric or topological characteristics. Attribute characteristics are used to describe the attributes of things or phenomena. Temporal characteristics are used to describe things or phenomena changing with the time.

Definition 1. Geographic Entities Set E: E is a finite set of geographic entities related to workflow activities:

$$E = \{e_1, e_2, \cdots, e_{|E|}\}. \tag{1}$$

Every geographic entity is a five tuple:

$$e = (e_{ID}, e_{SC}, e_{PC}, e_{TC}, e_{metadata}). \tag{2}$$

e_{ID} is entity identification; e_{SC} is spatial characteristics set, including coordinates, geometric type, area, perimeter and topology relations, *etc.*; e_{PC} is an attribute characteristics set; e_{TC} is a temporal characteristics set; and $e_{metadata}$ is the meta data that describes the entity.

2.3. Geospatial Information Methods Set

Geospatial information constrains workflow activities through the results derived from geospatial information operations. The geospatial information operation is called spatial analysis. The use and analysis of spatial data is spatial analysis including all kinds of spatial operations, spatial reasoning and spatial data mining.

Definition 2. Geospatial Constraints Methods Set C: C is the methods set of geospatial constraints and should be a three tuple including inputs set, outputs set and methods set:

$$C = (E_I, E_O, F). \tag{3}$$

In the process of workflow modeling, the semantic description about the geospatial constraints methods set is needed. The following discusses the basic geospatial constraint methods.

The OGC (Open Geospatial Consortium) defines space component as four categories: point, line, surface and set. Geometry is the root of all space component, and Geometry operation interface covers most of the space component interface. According to the definitions of OGC and the actual business processes demands, this paper summed up the common measure relationships, direction relationships, topological relationships and basic spatial analysis methods in workflow modeling with geospatial constraints in Figure 1. In this figure, P and Q are two geographic entities.

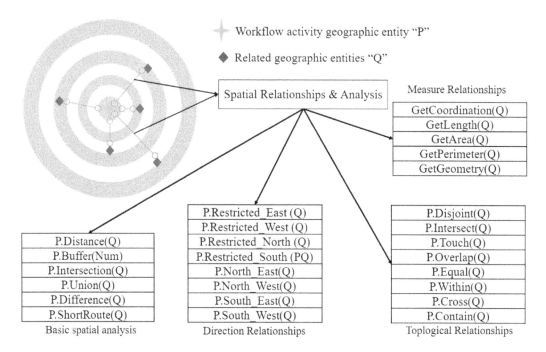

Figure 1. Semantic description of spatial relationships and basic analysis in workflow modeling.

2.4. Geospatial Constraints Rules

The geospatial constraints rules are the requirements of geospatial information to the workflow activities. These rules are complicated, but no matter what kind of requirements or constraints, they are related to three issues: (1) Who constrains others? (2) Who are constrained? (3) How to execute the constraints? Therefore, the rules of geospatial constraints on workflow activities should be made clear as follows: the subject of constraints, the object of constraints, and the constraint methods set. Thus, the geospatial constraints rule generally is a three tuple:

$$S_{rule} = (E, A, C). \tag{4}$$

E is geographic entities related to the geospatial constraints; A is the activities constrained in the workflow; C is the geographic information methods set in the geospatial constraints.

2.5. Geospatial Constraints States

Geospatial information constrains the workflow activities and affects the execution of the workflow. If the current workflow activity has been constrained by geospatial information, the activity is enabled, or else the current activity is not enabled. Therefore, the geospatial constraints have two states: the enabled or not enabled state. Then, monitoring the geospatial constraints states is required. A Boolean expression can monitor the states: $G(a) = true$ or $G(a) = false$. When $G(a) = true$, the current activity is enabled; otherwise, it is not enabled.

2.6. Geospatial Constraints Unit

In summary, the geospatial constraints unit is composed of the subjects, objects, rules, methods set, and states. These elements form the geospatial constraints unit to constrain workflow activities. Thus, the geospatial constraints unit should be a three tuple:

$$C_{unit} = (W_{wf}, S_{rule}, G). \tag{5}$$

W_{wf} is the related workflow; S_{rule} is the geospatial constraints rules including the subjects (geographic entity sets), objects (workflow activity) and geospatial information methods set; G is the geospatial constraint state monitor.

2.7. Geospatial Constraints Net Model

Petri Nets with a graphical formal semantics, a strict mathematical definition and precise syntax and semantics definition, relatively intuitive expression, have state-based process descriptions and rich model analysis methods, and can analyze workflow behaviors, states and performances. Yuan [15] defined C_net for implementing Petri Nets in programming. This paper uses some methods in C_net, and defines Geospatial Constraints Net(GCNet) based on Petri Nets and geospatial constraints unit.

Definition 3. Geospatial Constraints Net (GCNet): a six tuple GN= $(E, T; R, Wr, G, B)$ is a GCNet, if and only if:

(1) $E \cup T \neq \emptyset \wedge E \cap T = \emptyset$;
(2) $R \subseteq E \times T \wedge W_r \subseteq T \times E$;
(3) $dom(R) \cup cod(W_r) = E \wedge dom(R) \cup cod(W_r) = T$;
(4) $|T| = 1$;
(5) $\forall t \in T : G(t) \in \{true, false\}$.

E represents a geographic entities variables set, which is called E Place. If $|E| = 0$, then the transition is not constrained by geospatial information. R is reading relation, and W_r is writing relation. T is transition with geospatial constraints and is also the computing unit of geospatial constraints. T reads the geographic entities variables set E_R, calculates these variables and gets some results, and then writes the results to variable set E_{W_r}. $E_R \cup E_{W_r} = E$. The equation "$|T| = 1$" indicates that this is a geospatial constraints unit that only affects one workflow activity. According to geospatial constraints units previously defined, the geospatial constraints calculating unit is divided into two parts: one is the guard function G that is a Boolean expression monitoring the constraints state; another is the body function B corresponding to the constraint methods set.

Definition 4. If GN= $(E, T; R, Wr, G, B)$ is a GCNet, $\forall x \in E, \forall t \in T$, then

(1) $\bullet t, t\bullet, \bullet x, x\bullet$ have the same definitions with the pre-sets, post-set of directed nets.
(2) $r(t)$ is the reading set of t, and the set includes inputted geographic entities variables. $r(t) = \{x|(x,t) \in R\}.w(t)$ is the writing set of t, and the set includes the output variables. $w(t) = \{x|(x,t) \in W_r\}$. $r(t)$ and $w(t)$ must satisfy: $r(t) \subseteq E \wedge w(t) \subseteq E \wedge r(t) \cap w(t) = \emptyset \wedge r(t) \neq \emptyset \wedge w(t) \neq \emptyset$.

(3) tp(x) represents the geographic entities types of the variable x. When tp(x) is used as a set, it is in a range of x.

(4) Type=$\bigcup_{x \in E}$tp(x) is the type set of all geographic entity variables.

(5) M_E is called E_ marking of GCNet, if $\forall x \in E : M_E(x) \in$ tp (x).

(6) B is the body function of GCNet, if $B(t)$ is a geospatial constraints methods set expressed with semantics. B reads geographic entities variables from $r(t)$, writes the results into $w(t)$ after spatial operations with geospatial constraints methods set, and notices the results to G function finally.

(7) G is called a guard function of GCNet, if $G(t)$ is a Boolean expression, *i.e.*, whether the results from B satisfy the requirement of geospatial constraints.

In Figure 2, a geographic entity variable is represented with a double circle; the transition is divided into two parts: guard function and body function; reading relation and writing relation are represented by lines, with small circles at the endpoints,connecting the variables and transitions. If the small circle is at the transition side, it represents reading relation, otherwise writing relation.

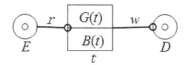

Figure 2. GCNet.

3. Geospatially Constrained Workflow Model

3.1. Definitions of Geospatially Constrained Workflow Model

In Petri Nets, "place" represents resources, and "transition" represents the qualitative or quantitative change of resources. For a transition, when the pre-sets can provide consumption resources and the post-sets can accommodate the produced resources, then the transition is enabled. Tokens are the resources flowing in the Petri Net. In van der Aalst's WF-net [17], transitions represent workflow activities, and places represents dependencies relationships between two activities. Token represents a case of business process. When the present activity is completed, according to the business rules, the next activity will be triggered by an artificial or by a workflow engine.

This section integrates the GCNet and WF-net to compose the geospatially constrained workflow model. In the model, if a transition is enabled, it must have two situations: one is the dependencies between activities, another is geospatial constraints.

Definition 5. Geospatially Constrained Workflow Model (GCWF-net): GCWF-net=$(P, E, T; F, R, W_r, M_T, G, B)$:

(1) P, T, F are the same definitions in WF-net, *i.e.*, WF-net=$(P, T; F)$.

(2) E, R, W_r, G and B are the same definitions in GCNet, and $W_r \cap R^{-1} = \varnothing$, or $W_r^{-1} \cap R = \varnothing$.

(3) M_T is called transition marking of GCWF-net and is a state of transition. $M_T = G(t) + B(t)$.

(4) M_P is the marking of P place in GCWF-net and is called P_ marking.

(5) M_E is the marking of E variable place of GCWF-net and is called E_ marking.

3.2. Transition Rules

Definition 6. Transition Rules: Let $M_T = (G + B)$ is transition marking of GCWF-net, $M = (M_P, M_E)$ is marking of GCWF-net, t is transition of GCWF-net:

(1) t is enabled by(M_T, M_E), *i.e.*, $(M_T, M_E)[t >$, if $G(t, M_E)$ is true, and the geographic entities in $G(t)$ are provided by M_E, and the geographic entities in $B(t, M_E)$ are provided by M_E too. The geospatial operation of methods in B can satisfy the geospatial constraints rules.

(2) t is enabled by M_P, i.e., $(M_T, M_P)[t >$, if t is enabled as the transition in WF-net.

(3) t is enabled by (M_T, M), i.e., $(M_T, M)[t >$, if t is enabled by (M_T, M_E) and is enabled by M_P, i.e., $(M_T, M)[t > \equiv (M_T, M_E)[t > \wedge (M_T, M_P)[t >$.

(4)   If $(M_T, M)[t >$, then t is enabled, (M'_T, M') is the successor of $(M_T, M)[t >$. $\forall t \in T, \forall x \in E$:

$$M'_P(p) = \begin{cases} M_P(p-1) & p \in {}^\bullet t - t^\bullet, \\ M_P(p+1) & p \in t^\bullet - {}^\bullet t, \\ M_P(p) & p \in {}^\bullet t \cup t^\bullet, \end{cases} \tag{6}$$

$$M'_E(x) = \begin{cases} B(x) & x \in w(t), \\ M_E(x) & p \in r(t). \end{cases} \tag{7}$$

B is the spatial operation methods set, $B(x)$ is the results set that is derived from the spatial operation, and should be written into x.

3.3. Workflow Routing Structures

It can be seen from the above definitions that WF-net is the base net of GCWF-net. For the token, GCWF-net and WF-net do not make any difference. The tokens all flow from i place to o place under the dependence relations of the front and rear activities. Based on WF-net, GCWF-net extends geospatial constraints, including variables, reading and writing relations, G, B, etc., and then geospatial constraints are able to play a better role. Moreover, as long as there is no reading and writing conflict on the same variable at the same time, the workflow routing structure of GCWF-net and WF-net are consistent.

A workflow process definition specifies how the cases are routed along the tasks that need to be executed [17]. In 1999, Workflow Management Coalition (WfMC) published the terminology and vocabulary (V3) that defines the four workflow routing. The following analyzes the basic workflow routing structures.

Sequential routing structure is used to execute activities in one thread and to deal with causal relationships between activities. Each transition in this routing has an obvious order. In conditional routing, routes of different instances in workflow execution may be different. The route of an instance depends on the workflow instance attribute, the behavior of the environment, the organization, or other relevant factors, such as geospatial constraints. However, for one instance, the related activities only have one order. For iterative routing, the workflow executes the same activity repeatedly. If the activity is constrained by geospatial information, then the related geographic entities variables would be written multiple times. Because we have specified the expression $r(t) \cap w(t) = \emptyset$ previously, the reading and writing conflict of geographic entities variables would not occur among activities.

Therefore, in these three GCWF-net routing structures, there would not be conflicts of reading and writing the same variable at the same time, and the GCWF-net and WF-net are consistent.

Parallel routing is used in situations where the order of execution is less strict. At the same time, there may be two or more activities being performed. Thus, there would be conflicts of reading and writing the same variables between activities. This conflicts are called E_conflicts. In addition, the conflict caused by insufficient tokens in the workflow place is called P_conflicts. The activities with neither P_conflict nor E_conflict can be concurrent.

If two transitions of GCWF-net have no reading and writing dependence, the formal expression is the following:

$$w(t_1) \cap (r(t_2) \cup w(t_2)) = \emptyset \wedge w(t_2) \cap (r(t_1) \cup w(t_1)) = \emptyset. \tag{8}$$

Both t_1 and t_2 would not write the variables in the pre-sets or post-sets of each other and would not write the same variable. If t_1 and t_2 are enabled at (M_T, M), but they have independent reading and writing, then t_1 and t_2 of GCWF-net have E_conflict at (M_T, M).

If Transition t_1 and t_2 are enabled at (M_T, M) and have neither P_conflict nor E_conflict, then t_1 and t_2 are concurrent at (M_T, M), i.e., $(M_T, M)[t_1, t_2 >$, The successors of the concurrent of t_1 and t_2 could be derived from themselves, respectively.

3.4. Validity of GCWF-Net

Compared to WF-net, GCWF-net extends geospatial constraints and affects the concurrent and enabled situation only. In other respects, GCWF-net and WF-net are consistent. The following defines the validity of GCWF-net.

Definition 7. Validity of GCWF-net: GCWF-net is validity, if and only if: for every reachable state M of i, there are trigger sequences from state M to state o:

$$\forall_M (i \xrightarrow{*} M) \Rightarrow M \xrightarrow{*} o. \tag{9}$$

State o is the only end state. When a workflow instance finishes, only the place o has one token, and the others are empty:

$$\forall_M (i \xrightarrow{*} M \wedge M \geq o) \Rightarrow M = o. \tag{10}$$

There is no dead transition in GCWF-net, i.e., every transition can be executed:

$$\forall_{t \in T} \exists_{M, M'} i \xrightarrow{*} M \xrightarrow{*} M'. \tag{11}$$

$\forall t \in T$, if t is geospatial constrained transition, then $M = (M_P, M_E), M' = (M'_P, M'_E)$, otherwise $M = M_P, M' = M'_P$.

4. Implement of GCWF-Net

This section gives an example for GCWF-net modeling first, and then discusses the other three processes. The Figure 3 describes the implement process of GCWF-net.

Figure 3. Implement process of GCWF-net.

4.1. GCWF-Net Modeling

Scenario Description: When a company's customer service center (CSC) receives a telephone for repair, if the repair request does not meet the acceptance conditions or could be settled on the phone, the process is over, else the CSC records the customer's address and other relevant information, and then hands this case over to the maintenance department; the maintenance department receives the task and assigns it to the nearest engineer to the customer; the engineer goes to inspect on-site, removes the damaged parts, and chooses the nearest maintenance station for repair; when the parts are repaired, the engineer installs the parts on-site, and then the maintenance department sends this case to another CSC; the CSC visits the customer by telephone; and the process is over.

In the repair process, the tasks with geospatial constraints are: the acceptance CSC could not be the return visit CSC; the on-site engineer assigned should be the nearest to the customer; parts repair should choose the nearest maintenance station. Figure 4 is the WF-net model of repair process. However, there are no descriptions about geospatial constraints in the model. Then, the important role of geographic information in the maintenance service process automation and optimization could not be seen.

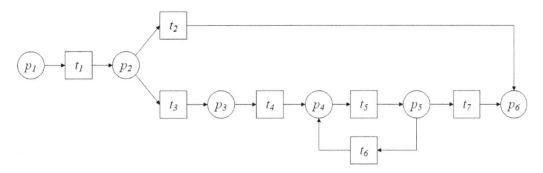

Figure 4. WF-net model of repair process. t_1: customer service center receives the telephone repair; t_2: the repair request does not meet the acceptance conditions or could be settled on the phone; t_3: repair engineer assignment; t_4: on-site inspection; t_5: on-site repair; t_6: back to maintenance station for repair; t_7: customer service center visit by telephone.

As is shown in Figure 5, GCWF-net model is designed to show the repair process with Geospatial Constraint Units, including E, G, B, R, W_r. Then, the model could show the descriptions of geospatial constraints and could be analyzed with analysis methods of Petri Nets or WF-net.

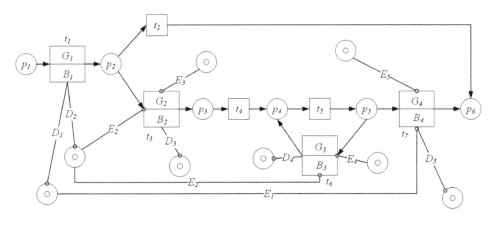

Reading Set:
E_1:CustomerServiceCenter
E_2:Customer
E_3:RepairMan
E_4:ServingStation
E_5:CustomerServiceCenter

Transition Calculation Unit:
G_1:D_1!=null&&D_2!=null
B_1:D_1=INPUT; D_2=INPUT
G_2:D_3!=null
B_2:D_3=E_2.ShortRoute((E_2.Buffer(10km)).Contain(E_3)?E_3:null)
G_3:D_4!=null
B_3:D_4=E_2.ShortRoute((E_2.Buffer(50km)).Contain(E_4)?E_4:null)
G_4:D_5!=null
B_4:D_5=!Random(E_5).Equals(E_1)

Writing Set:
D_1:CustomerServiceCenter
D_2:Customer
D_3:RepairMan
D_4:ServingStation
D_5:CustomerServiceCenter

Figure 5. GCWF-net model of repair process.

4.2. Representation of GCWF-Net in PNML

Due to the flexibility and the rapid development of Petri Nets, there has been a lot of versions, variants and characteristics [16]. These types and tools are different and incompatible to each other, so it is difficult to share and exchange the variant Petri Nets. In 2000, the International Conference on Theory and Application of Petri Nets began efforts on an exchange standardized format of Petri Nets, and PNML is one of the program [13]. PNML is an XML (Extensible Markup Language)-based Petri Nets file exchange format, and its main purpose is to solve the problem of non-uniform exchange format due to the different types of Petri Nets [17,18].

The PNML metamodel has no restrictions on the label, so PNML metamodel may represent any type of Petri Net. For a specific type of Petri Net, a legal label definitions model which is called Petri Net Type Definition (PNTD) is needed to extend the PNML metamodel. ISO/IEC15909-2 defines the type of Petri Nets for P/T Net, high-level Petri Nets and Symmetric nets, respectively [13].

Then, after the GCWF-net modeling, we should use PNML to describe this model.

4.3. Conversion from PNML to BPEL

The Web Service Business Process Execution Language (BPEL) has become the *de facto* standard for implementing business process. It is designed for web services orchestration and composition, but its XML expression is incomprehensible and difficult for the untrained user. The modeling advantage of Petri Nets is the strict mathematical definition, the graphical representation and rich analytical methods. Therefore, for business processes applications, we can use Petri Nets as a process design and analysis language, then BPEL as the process execution language.

For the conversion of WF-net to BPEL, van der Aalst *et al.* has proposed a conversion algorithm based on component [19,20]. Then, on this basis, GCWF-net adds geospatial constraints unit to WF-net. There are two aspects to pay attention to during the conversion process:

(1) Variables in GCWF-net correspond to the variables in BPEL; the names of variables in BPEL are automatically generated according to the conventional way of naming.
(2) G and B are the semantic expressions of guard function and operation methods set for geospatial constraint. The methods set corresponds to the geographic information services set, and spatial operation needs geographic information service combination.

According to the above aspects, we could develop a GCWF-net conversion tool.

4.4. Implementation of BPEL

Although the PNML of GCWF-net has converted to BPEL, only the main content of BPEL is converted successfully. BPEL should also include external services calls and some other content. All of these should to be improved, and then it needs to establish a demo system to verify the model. We use Oracle BPEL process manager (Oracle Corporation, Redwood Shores, CA, USA) as BPEL design and execution engine. According to the repair process, this paper established a web service providing system, mainly including the related web service and database table. In the process, the related web services are: repair reporting location web service; maintenance personnel dispatch web service; maintenance depot selection of web service; and the visit customer service center web service.

The web services and BPEL files could be configured in the Oracle BPEL process manager, and we can use maps as the main interface which can display geospatial information visually.

5. Conclusions

With the rapid development of mobile applications and spatial information technology, geographic information is more and more important to business processes. However, up to now, little research has been done about geospatial information impacts on workflow modeling. The existing research only focuses on geographic location and has not extended to the geospatial information. This paper discussed the geospatial constraints on workflow modeling, specified geospatial constraints content from several aspects—the levels, subjects, objects, methods, rules, states—put forward the concept of geospatial constraint unit, and established geospatial constraints net(GCNet) based on Petri Nets. Then, this paper combined the GCNet and workflow net, established geospatial constrained workflow model, and analyzed transition rules, and workflow routing. According to the standard of PNML, this paper used PNML to express GCWF-net and then converted the PNML to BPEL. Finally, the implementation process of the GCWF-net model was described.

With the limitation in space and time, there is more complex work to do, such as the following:

(1) Discussing specific geographic spatial constraint method models is required, so the next work is to carry out a detailed analysis for this content;
(2) Designing algorithms to analyze properties of GCWF-net will be necessary, such as validation, verification, performance, *etc.*
(3) Developing an application system using the GCWF-net.

Acknowledgments: This work was supported by the grants of the National Social Science Foundation Project of China (12BJY058), the Humanities and Social Sciences planning projects from the Education Ministry of China (12YJA790159), the Key Technology R&D Program of Shandong Province of China (2012GSF11718).

Author Contributions: Feng Zhang designed, performed the research and wrote the manuscript. Yuetong Xu reviewed the manuscript. Both authors have read and approved the final manuscript.

Conflicts of Interest: The authors declare no conflict of interest.

Abbreviations

The following abbreviations are used in this manuscript:

GCNet	Geospatial Constraints Net
GCWF-net	Geospatially Constrained Workflow Model
WF-net	Workflow net
PNML	Petri Net Markup Language
BPEL	Web Service Business Process Execution Language

References

1. Hollingsworth, D. Workflow Management Coalition the Workflow Reference Model. Available online: http://www.e-workflow.org/standards/ (accessed on 25 November 2015).
2. Born, M.; Kirchner, J.; Muller, J.P. Context-driven business process modeling. In Proceedings of the 1st International Workshop on Managing Data with Mobile Devices (MDMD 2009), Milan, Italy, 6–7 May 2009; pp. 6–10.
3. Chakraborty, D.; Lei, H. Pervasive enablement of business processes. *Perv. Mob.Comput.* **2004**, 87–97, doi:10.1109/PERCOM.2004.1276848.
4. Wieland, M.; Kopp, O.; Nicklas, D.; Leymann, F. Towards context-aware workflows. Available online: http://www-iaas.informatik.uni-stuttgart.de/RUS-data/INPROC-2007-18%20-%20Context4BPEL.pdf (accessed on 25 May 2016).
5. De Leoni, M.; Adams, M.; Van Der Aalst, W. M.; Ter Hofstede, A. H. Visual support for work assignment in process- aware information systems: Framework formalisation and implementation. *Decis. Support Syst.* **2012**, *54*, 345–361.
6. Decker, M. Modelling location-aware access control constraints for mobile workflows with uml activity diagrams. *Ubiquitous Comput. Syst.* **2009**, 263–268, doi:10.1109/ubicomm.2009.30.
7. Che, H.; Decker, M. Anomalies in business process models for mobile scenarios with location constraints. In Proceedings of the International Conference on Automation and Logistics, Hong Kong, China, 16–20 August 2010; pp. 306–313.
8. Zhang, L.; Zhao, J.; Jia, W.H.; Liu, Y.B. Location-aware workflow modeling and soundness verification method based on petri net. *Comput. Integr. Manuf. Syst.* **2012**, *18*, 1747–1756.
9. Zhu, G.; Zhu, X. A study on geospatial constrained process modeling using uml activity diagrams. *Asia Pac. Bus. Process Manag.* **2014**, *181*, 59–73.
10. Zhu, X.W.; Zhu, G.B. Business process modeling with geospatial constraints. *J. Softw.* **2015**, *26*, 584–599.
11. Sackmann, S.; Hofmann, M.; Betke, H. Towards a Model-Based Analysis of Place-Related Information in Disaster Response Workflows. In Proceedings of the 10th International Conference on Information Systems for Crisis Response and Management, Baden-Baden, Germany, 12–15 May 2013; pp. 78–83.
12. Hofmann, M.; Betke, H.; Sackmann, S. Automated analysis and adaptation of disaster response processes with place-related restrictions. In Proceedings of the 12th International Conference on Information Systems for Crisis Response and Management (ISCRAM 2015), Kristiansand, Norway, 24–27 May 2015.

13. Weber, M.; Kindler, E. The petri net markup language. In *Petri Net Technology for Communication-Based Systems*; Springer: Berlin/Heidelberg, Germany, 2003; pp. 124–144.

14. Wu, X.C. *Principles and Methods of Geographical Information System*, 2nd ed.; Publishing House of Electronics Industry: Beijing, China, 2011; pp. 3–4. (In Chinese)

15. Yuan, C.Y. *Application of Petri Nets*; Science Press: Beijing, China, 2013; pp. 119–139. (In Chinese)

16. Kindle, E. The Petri Net Markup Language and ISO/IEC 15909-2: Concepts, status, and future directions. *Tech. Rep.* **2006**, *9*, 35–55.

17. Van der Aalst, W.M. The application of petri nets to workflow management. *J. Circuits Syst. Comput.* **1998**, *8*, 21–66.

18. Billington, J.; Christensen,S.; Hee, K.V.; Kindler, E.; Kummer, O.; Petrucc, L.; Post, R.; Stehno, C.; Weber, M. The Petri Net markup language: Concepts, technology, and tools. *Appl. Theory Petri Nets* **2003**, *2679*, 483–505.

19. Van der Aalst, W.M.; Lassen, K.B. Translating Workflow Nets to BPEL. Available online: http://cms.ieis.tue.nl/beta/files/workingpapers/beta_wp145.pdf (accessed on 25 May 2016).

20. Lassen, K.B.; Van der Aalst, W.M. WorkflowNet2BPEL4WS: A tool for translating unstructured workflow processes to readable BPEL. *Move Mean. Intern. Syst.* **2006**, *4275*, 127–144.

A Specification-Based IDS for Detecting Attacks on RPL-Based Network Topology

Anhtuan Le [1], Jonathan Loo [2,*], Kok Keong Chai [1] and Mahdi Aiash [2]

[1]   School of Electroic Engineering and Computer Science, Queen Mary University of London, London E1 4NS, UK; a.le@qmul.ac.uk (A.L.); michael.chai@qmul.ac.uk (K.K.C.)

[2]   School of Science and Technology, Middlesex University, London NW4 4BT, UK; m.aiash@mdx.ac.uk

*   Correspondence: j.loo@mdx.ac.uk

Academic Editor: Willy Susilo

Abstract: Routing Protocol for Low power and Lossy network (RPL) topology attacks can downgrade the network performance significantly by disrupting the optimal protocol structure. To detect such threats, we propose a RPL-specification, obtained by a semi-auto profiling technique that constructs a high-level abstract of operations through network simulation traces, to use as reference for verifying the node behaviors. This specification, including all the legitimate protocol states and transitions with corresponding statistics, will be implemented as a set of rules in the intrusion detection agents, in the form of the cluster heads propagated to monitor the whole network. In order to save resources, we set the cluster members to report related information about itself and other neighbors to the cluster head instead of making the head overhearing all the communication. As a result, information about a cluster member will be reported by different neighbors, which allow the cluster head to do cross-check. We propose to record the sequence in RPL Information Object (DIO) and Information Solicitation (DIS) messages to eliminate the synchronized issue created by the delay in transmitting the report, in which the cluster head only does cross-check on information that come from sources with the same sequence. Simulation results show that the proposed Intrusion Detection System (IDS) has a high accuracy rate in detecting RPL topology attacks, while only creating insignificant overhead (about 6.3%) that enable its scalability in large-scale network.

Keywords: 6LoWPAN; RPL; internal threats; topology attacks; specification-based; IDS

1. Introduction

Routing Protocol for Low power and Lossy network (RPL) is a protocol developed specifically for the 6LoWPAN network, in order to bring the concept of Internet of Things (IoT) to the real life. RPL has many advantages such as the energy efficiency, optimal routing and minimal overhead, which makes it outperform other previous routing protocol [1]. As a result, the protocol is also proposed to apply in a lot of other situations such as Smart Grid and so on. For the overall operation of the protocol as well as the basic concepts of routing messages like DIO, DIS, and the trickle algorithm, readers can refer to [1–8] for more detail.

Internal threats on RPL-based network is a challenge due to the weak physical protections of the nodes, no centralized administration, low capability node that make strong cryptography not applicable, and lack of node co-operation. Internal threats can be categorized into two types: the performance attacks and the topology attacks [2]. The performance attacks focus on manipulating the network performance directly, for instance, making an adverse source dropping all the packets (black hole attack), dropping some of the packets (selective forwarding attack), or adding delay to the forwarding. On the other hand, topology attacks involve node operation to disrupt the optimal network topology, for example, creating loops, attracting traffic, or generating heavy overhead. Internal attackers often combine these two types of attacks to boost the effect of their attacks, for example, using topology attack to gain the traffic towards a malicious source and then manipulating those traffic through this source's performance.

The main focus of this paper is the topology attack. Several RPL topology attacks such as Sinkhole, Rank, Local Repair, Neighbor, and DIS attacks have been reported to have significant bad impact on network performance [3,5,8]. Cryptographic solutions cannot prevent the internal threats once the attackers tamper the nodes and obtain the secure keys [2]. Moreover, some security modes of RPL are considered impractical without the use of public key cryptography, which is believed to be too expensive in common [9]. Tsao *et al.* [9] also provided several countermeasures for a number of RPL attacks, however, such countermeasures mostly change the operations to overcome the attack impacts rather than specifying and eliminating the malicious sources, which can create long term issues for the network performance. Therefore, it is necessary to have an Intrusion Detection System (IDS) to monitor and detect the compromised nodes.

In RPL-based network, the two most applicable IDS approaches for detecting the internal threats are the anomaly-based and specification-based. Anomaly-based IDS identifies a node as intrusion when this node has too much deviation in behaviors compare to the normal baselines. The most important aspect for the accurateness of an anomaly-based IDS is to define the normal or legitimate behaviors and the threshold for the deviations, in which any node acts more than this threshold will be identified as the malicious. Anomaly-based IDS is used widely in securing routing protocols in wireless sensor and wireless ad hoc network from the internal threats. However, the work follows this approach in securing RPL is only in the initial step. Raza *et al.* [6] proposed SVELTE, the first anomaly-based IDS for securing the RPL protocol with two phases, including collecting and analyzing the IDS data. In the collecting phase, the Destination Oriented Directed Acyclic Graph (DODAG) root (also the monitoring node of all nodes in the network) will request its network members to send information about itself and its neighbors. The information that each member has to send includes the RPL Instance ID, the DODAG ID, the DODAG Version Number, all neighbors and their corresponding ranks, the parent ID, the node's rank and a timestamp. Once the information received, the monitoring node moves to the analyzing phase by using such data to form a network map, evaluate the rank consistency and check the legitimacy of the rank rules between any parent-child pair. This anomaly-based IDS also focuses on monitoring the deviation between normal and anomaly nodes behaviors. However, in case of topology attacks, malicious nodes perform similarly to normal nodes in terms of sending and receiving messages, hence, the difference in whether a node following the protocol rules cannot be effectively detected by the anomaly-based IDS.

On the other hand, the specification-based IDS detects the attackers if they do not follow a specified behavior reference of the routing protocol. This approach is effective in detecting the topology attacks because it can point out directly when the adverse nodes break the protocol rules. So far, specification-based detection has been applied to many similar situations, including securing different sensor and ad hoc network protocols [10,11]. In such environment, the routing protocols are usually profiled manually by experts through its theoretical specifications. There are also several RPL specification [4,7], but none of them satisfied the purpose of detecting the RPL topology attacks. In detail, in [4], we proposed only a prototype of RPL specification, which is lack of verification and implementation. On the other hand, the profile of RPL in [7] is only for the purpose of conformance testing, which mainly looks at verifying the implementation of the protocol from its documentation. Such profile is not effective when applying for the detection purpose because unlike the conformance tester, the IDS will not have the self-view of the node behaviors; its view is instead reflected from other IDS agent's report. The differences in the views bring issues like synchronization, data loss, data falsifying and so on, which make the profile not feasible to follow. Moreover, that RPL profile does not reflect any crucial behavior that the attackers may employ to attack the network performance, for example, a node needs to propagate consistent ranks with what are reflected from its neighbors, a node needs to follow the rank rule in any case, or a node needs to not generate redundant control messages.

Profiling technique also needs to be considered. Previous works mainly employed manually profiling techniques, which are based on the expert understanding of the protocol. This method is, however, lack of fast and accurate profile generations for a particular protocol, as well as difficult to verify. To overcome this problem, the authors in [12] propose a technique that based on Inductive Logic Programming (ILP) method to induce a hypothesis from individual observations and background knowledge. The authors collect examples of the protocol executions through extensive simulation traces and derive an abstract model of protocol behavior out of that. This solution has the advantage of fast profiling generation with the ability of validating the correctness of such specification.

This paper is the continuation of our on-going research on IDS for detecting the internal threats in IP-connected wireless sensor network [2–5], where we identified and evaluated prominent internal threats and proposed a general IDS framework to detect them. This work is the next concrete step to develop, implement, and verify a specification-based IDS to detect the topology attacks in RPL-based network. In detail, we first summarized the prominent topology attacks known to RPL from previous research [2,3,5,6,8]. We then profile the RPL operation based on a semi-auto specifying technique, which is inspired from [12] and involves the use of simulation trace files to generate an Extended Finite State Machines (EFSM—a Finite State Machine with statistic information about transitions and states) for RPL. Such profile will be transformed as a set of rules applied for checking monitoring data from the network nodes regarding relevant properties. We employ the cluster monitoring architecture, in which the network will be divided into multiple smaller clusters, the IDS agent will stay as the head in the center of each cluster to monitor the cluster members according to the set of rules implemented. This architecture can decrease the storage and computation work load for the IDS agents, while keeping a low rate of overhead. The simulation results show that our IDS can effectively detect most of the topology attacks with small amount of overhead.

The rest of this paper is organized as follows: Section 2 gives a short summary of prominent known RPL topology attacks. Section 3 describes two phases of building our specification-based IDS, including profiling the RPL protocol and implementing it into the network. Section 4 evaluates the proposed solution and Section 5 discusses further consideration of expanding the IDS to deal with more kind of internal threats. Finally, Section 6 concludes the paper.

2. Topology Attacks on RPL

Our works [2–5] have discussed some of the particular topology attacks on RPL including the Rank, the Local repair, the Neighbor, and the DIS attack. Attacks with the same nature in wireless sensor or ad hoc network can also apply for RPL, as discussed in [2,6]. We will summarize some of the prominent attacks from those that work as the targets for our IDS to detect as follow.

- **The Rank attack:** after the attack is triggered, the malicious node changes the way it processes the DIO messages from other neighbors so that it will get the node with the worst rank as the preferred parent. This kind of attack will create un-optimized route for all the packets that go through the malicious nodes, and it also creates more traffic to the victim.
- **The Sinkhole attack:** the malicious node will propagate its rank with a good value, normally the same rank of the sink. As a result, its neighbors will select it as their preferred parent and send traffic to that node. The Sinkhole attack is often combined with the Selective Forwarding attack (a performance attack which is out of scope of this paper) to drop all the traffic attracted.
- **The Local repair attack:** after the attack is triggered, the malicious node starts broadcasting local repair messages periodically, though there is no problem with the link quality around the node. Other node upon receiving the local repair messages will need to recalculate the route that is related to the malicious nodes. This kind of attack creates more control overhead messages, as well as some packet dropping because of temporarily unavailable route.

- **The Neighbor attack:** after the attack is triggered, the malicious node will replicate any DIO messages that it receives and broadcast them again. The victims who receive this type of messages may think that it has a new neighbor, which is not in range. Moreover, if the new neighbor advertises a good rank then the victims may request it as the preferred parent and change the route to the out range neighbors.
- **The DIS attack:** after the attack is triggered, the malicious nodes will send the DIS messages periodically to its neighbors. The DIS messages can be sent two ways, which will lead to a different response from the receivers. The first way is to broadcast DIS, the receivers upon receive will have to reset the DIO timer as they realize that there is something with the topology around. The second way is to unicast this DIS message to all nodes in the neighbor list, the receivers upon receive will unicast DIO message to the sender. Both of these ways add more control overhead on the network.

All of these presented attacks are practically shown to affect significantly RPL performance [2,3,5]. The attacks can be summarized in Table 1 below.

Table 1. Summary of potential internal threats towards RPL topology performance.

Type of Attacks	Attack Descriptions	Misuse Goal
Rank attack	An attacker does not send packets to preferred parent	Route disruption—redirect traffic
Sinkhole attack	The attacker propagates the sink's rank as its rank	Redirect traffic
Local repair	An attacker sends local repair periodically	Route disruption, resource consumption
Neighbor attack	An attacker forward the DIO messages to other neighbors without changing	False route, route disruption, resource consumption
DIS attack	The attackers send DIS messages with a fake IP address so let the other node have to generate the DIO messages so increase the overhead	Resource consumption

3. A specification-Based IDS for RPL to Detect the Topology Attacks

In this section, we introduce our specification-based IDS for RPL to detect the topology attacks as presented in the previous section. Our solution consists of two phases. In the first phase, we specify the RPL in the EFSM form using the ILP technique. In detail, we simulate the RPL network operation in the normal condition extensively to get the trace files. We then define all the states that relate to the network topology stability and analyze the transitions between those states based on similar algorithms presented in [12]. As discussed in Section 1, the approach of using the trace file to generate the operation rules has multiple advantages to compare with the manual approach of profiling a protocol from its documents. The generated module cannot only be improved by expert knowledge added from understanding the protocol, but also be used as a verification module for the detection. We also record the statistic of the states and their transitions as we know that the more transitions between the states, the more instable the network is. In the second phase, we translate the knowledge of the RPL profile of the detection algorithms that are implemented in the IDS agents. We discuss the process from IDS placement, how the monitoring data are collected, and how the IDS agents obtain the detections.

3.1. Profiling RPL

To profile the RPL protocol, we used the traces of legitimate protocol behaviors generated from the Contiki-Cooja simulation platform [13]. We only consider behaviors that related to the optimal and stable topology, in particular the route establishment and the route maintenance processes.

We develop two simple algorithms to extract the states, transitions, and their statistics as below. Algorithm 1 is to analyze the potential states, transitions and statistics in each node while Algorithm 2 is to merge all the different operations found in each node, which are generated from Algorithm 1, to form an abstract of RPL node operations.

Algorithm 1. Extracting states and transitions

Require: Trace file from simulation with marking relevant states
1: **for** $k = 1$ **to** n **do**
2:    **for** $i = 1$ **to** $N_k - 1$ **do**
3:        $PState = StateExtract(N_i)$ // Get previous state from N_i
4:        $CState = StateExtract(N_{i+1})$ // Get current state from N_{i+1}
5:        $CTran = NewTran(PState, CState)$ // Get current transition
6:        **if** $CTran \notin AllTrans[k]$ **do**
7:            $AllTrans[k] = Add(AllTrans[k], CTran)$ // Add transition to list
8:            $AllTransStatistic[k] = AddStatistic(AllTrans[k], CTran)$ // Add statistic
9:        **else**
10:            $AllTransStatistic[k] = AddStatistic(AllTrans[k], CTran)$ // Add statistic
11:       **end if**
12:   **end for**
13: **end for**

At the end of Algorithm 1, we generate a set of concrete states, transitions, and corresponding statistic data for each node. For example, we extract the relevant trace to node 3 and observe the following messages: [Node 3 broadcasts DIS—Node 3 receives DIO from node 5—Node 3 receives DIO from node 7—Node 3 receives DIO from node 9—Node 3 calculates the preferred parent and send a new DIO]. This trace then will be recorded as [Node 3 broadcast DIS—Node 3 receives DIOs (3 times)—Node 3 process received DIO—Node 3 send a new DIO]. Figure 1 illustrates an example of the results recorded from Algorithm 1 for node 3. As can be seen from the figure, the flow of the in and out control messages to node 3 is represented in CM [3] on the left, while the transition merge and relevant statistics are represented in AllTrans [3] on the right.

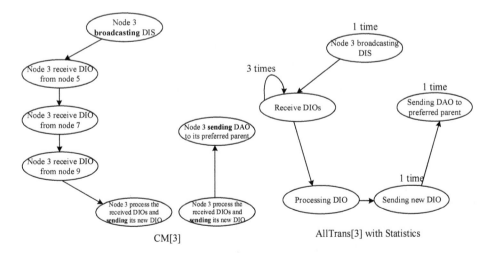

Figure 1. Example of the results of Algorithm 1.

The results of the Algorithm 1 are sets of states, transitions and corresponding statistic for each node. Algorithm 2 will merge those sets one by one to form an abstract of RPL operation. The results of the Algorithm 1 are sets of states, transitions and corresponding statistic for each node. Algorithm 2 will merge those sets one by one to form an abstract of RPL operation.

Algorithm 2. Form the specification-based IDS for RPL

Require: *AllTrans[k], AllTransStatistic[k], k = 1,..., n*
1: *FinalSpe = AllTrans[1]*
2: *FinalSpeStatistic = AllTransStatistic[1]*
3: **for** *k = 1* **to** *n* **do**
4:    *FinalSpe = Merge(FinalSpe, AllTrans[k])*
5:    *FinalSpeStatistic = Merge(FinalSpeStatistic, AllTransStatistic[k]*
6: **end for**

The Merge function first compares the states that two Transitions have. It only adds to the FinalSpe the states and transitions that it does not have yet. It also compares the statistic pattern and only record the pattern with significant different trend.

At the end of Algorithm 2, we obtain a Specification-based module as shown in Figure 2 below.

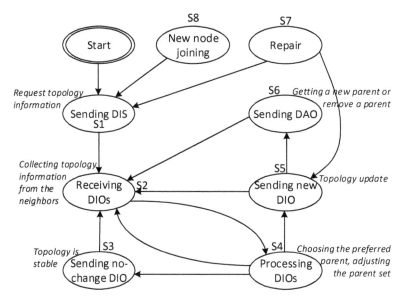

Figure 2. Specification-based IDS for RPL through trace file analysis.

The generated RPL specification module consists of 8 states: The *sending DIS, sending DIO, receiving DIO (DIOr), sending no-change DIO, processing DIOs, sending new (changed) DIO, Sending DAO, repair,* and *new node joining*. From the statistical data recorded, we obtain the following observations:

(i)   Nodes only move to the *Sending DIS* state when it first starts, joins, or involves in a link repair procedure. As a result, nodes only visit the *Sending DIS* state few times during the network performance.

(ii) Nodes in the center tend to have more transitions to nodes in the border. The reasons are that center nodes have more neighbors than border nodes, while their neighbors are also more likely to update the routing information than the border nodes' neighbors.

(iii) In the *processing DIOs* state, nodes have to strictly follow the rank rule.

(iv) After a long enough time of running, when the network topology becomes stable, the node will visit mostly the *Sending no-change DIO* state. However, such visit is not too often, because the DIO trickle time is always extended in a stable network.

(v)   The five states *sending DIS, sending new DIO, sending DAO, repair,* and *new node joining* indicate the instability of the network topology. When the node is in one of these states, the transitions are expected to happen more often, because the DIO trickle time is set to minimum.

In the next section, we will use the knowledge obtained from this section to design and implement a Specification-based IDS in the RPL network.

3.2. Design and Implementation of the Specification-Based IDS for RPL-Based Network

3.2.1. Placement of IDS Agents

IDS agents are placed into the network through the three common methods, the host-based, network-based or the hybrid. The host-based IDS implements the detection module in every node of the network. Each node will act as a monitoring node to monitor the operation of all of its neighbors. This method creates heavy overhead and requires a lot of memory and calculation resources from the node. On the other hand, the network-based IDS implement the detection module at the sink. The necessary information for detection decision will be asked, collected from all the nodes in the network to send to the sink. This method also creates extra communication overhead, and does not guarantee that the sink will have all the information it needs, for instance, in the case when partial of the network is compromised, information from such part will not be able for the sink anymore.

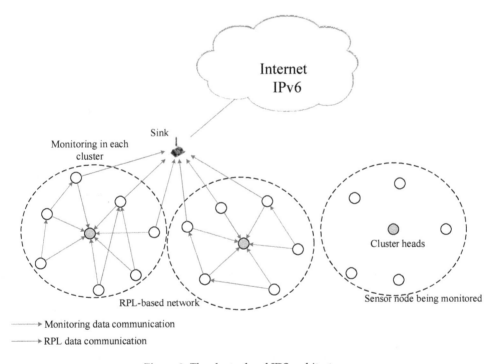

Figure 3. The cluster head IDS architecture.

The monitoring architecture employed in this paper is the hybrid or the clustering architecture, which we found to have multiple advantages to compare with the other approaches. An illustration for this architecture is given in Figure 3 below. In this approach, the network is divided into clusters, each has similar size in terms of the number of nodes. In each cluster, there will be one cluster head, which has direct communication to all the other nodes in this cluster. Each cluster head is placed in a way that it can cover the whole network, and allow every node in the network to find the cluster head to register for the monitoring purposes. The number of nodes in each cluster is depending on the network density in this area. More detail about the cluster-based IDS design and algorithms to select the cluster head positions can be found in [14]. In this design, we will place the IDS agent in each cluster head. In detail, they will record relevant information of its cluster members either through overhearing the communication or the members report themselves upon requested. Such recorded data will be checked by the built-in IDS algorithms also integrated in the cluster head to detect malicious behaviors. There is always a trade-off on choosing which algorithms to apply, for example, strong algorithms may detect the threats better, however, they will consume more resource and require more data storage, which shorten the lifetime of the cluster head. In this paper, the built-in IDS algorithms (the details are in Section 3.2.3) are obtained from the RPL profile in Section 3.1, which only require simple threshold-comparison on collected data, so they are light-weight and will not affect significantly the operation of the cluster heads. Moreover, as being assigned the data collection and decision making roles, cluster head can be usually provided more resource like battery power and memory to deal with such additional IDS work. This architecture can reduce the communication overhead significantly to compare with the host-based method, while providing more robust decision than the network-based method due to full and quick access to the detection information it needs.

3.2.2. IDS Data Collection

Similar to [6], we do not make the cluster head to change to promiscuous mode to eavesdrop all the radio communication around because it will drain its battery out quickly, while the obtained information in this case also has only limited use. Instead, we make the cluster head to request its members to report its topology information periodically. The period is set up depends on the particular scenario. Once the members receive such request, they need to send their neighbor lists with corresponding ranks, the preferred parent, and its own rank. Such information are already stored in the routing table of each node for the purpose of selecting its preferred parent, therefore, there will be no additional cost on storing and computation. By doing so, we save the resource for the cluster head while expanding the view to even nodes which are outside the cluster.

As nodes report information of its neighbors, a cross-check of the collected data is required. However, the cross-check process suffers from the synchronization issue when the IDS agent cannot check whether the data from the neighbor is collected later or sooner than data from the node itself. This issue was first pointed out by Matsunaga et al. [15], through the example illustrated in Figure 4 as follows. Let A is a normal node in the network and N is its neighbor. At time t_1 when A broadcasting its DIO, its rank is 3 and N record rank of A as 3 in its memory. At time t_2, A updates its rank to 4 but because it is not the time to send the new DIO yet, so A does not send any new DIO, and N still store the rank of A as 3. Soon after t_2, at t_3, the root requests nodes to send IDS information. In this case, node A will send its rank as 4 (its current rank) while node N informs the root that the actual rank of A is 3. The rank information of node A that it and node N reported is not the same because the recording time was not synchronized. This synchronization issue makes the root consider that the rank of A is not consistent, hence detect A as malicious node, which create a false detection.

Matsunaga et al. [15] proposes an improvement by letting the nodes send only the rank information in its latest broadcast DIO, rather than the latest rank it has. Moreover, they separate the rank inconsistent threshold when detecting the consistency, in which if there is time difference when receiving the report rank (information from the node itself) and the monitor rank (information from the node's neighbors), the threshold will be higher than it in the case there is no time difference. However, this solution still cannot overcome the synchronization issue in some of the cases. For instance, based on Figure 4, in Figure 5, we added node P as node A's parent and N is the neighbor of both A and P. At time t_1, P has rank 2, A has rank 3. In time t'_1, P update its rank to 3, hence it broadcasts this new information to the neighbors. At time t_2, node A receives this information and increase its new rank to 4 without updating its rank for the neighbor yet. At time t_3, the root request every node to send IDS information. According to Matsunaga, P will report its rank as 3 because it already sends the new DIO before the root request. On the other hand, node A will also report its rank as 3 because its next DIO is scheduled after the root asking for report. Both of these reports are considered consistent under the view of node N. Now, A and P has the same rank as 3, both are considered consistent, but according to the rank rule, P is the parent of A so it should have a lower rank than A. As a result, both A and P may be considered as malicious source.

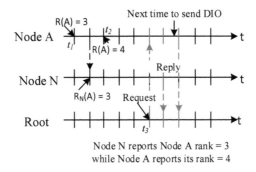

Node N reports Node A rank = 3
while Node A reports its rank = 4

Figure 4. Synchronization issue in Raza's solution.

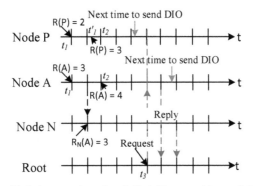

Node A reports its rank as 3, Node N reports A has rank 3
Node P reports its rank as 3, Node N reports P has rank 3
P is the parent of A and has the same rank with A
Both A, P may be detected as malicious

Figure 5. Synchronization issue in Matsunaga's solution.

In order to solve the synchronization issue as raised above, we propose to add the sequence number information in the DIO and DIS messages in order to make the cross-check more reliable. We will use the reserved bytes in the DIO and DIS message format (readers can refer to [1] for the format of DIO and DIS message) for this purpose, so the actual size of such messages will remain the same. The synchronization issue is solved because the sequence number indicates specifically which packets the information belongs to; hence the agent can cross-check only the sources that have the same sequence to eliminate any mistake caused from the unsynchronized communication.

Finally, the IDS agent will record the following information for each of its members:

- DIS sequence, number of DIS received
- DIO sequence, number of DIO received
- List of neighbors, each neighbor has
  - Node ID
  - Rank
  - The sequence of the DIO that provides this info
  - DIS sequence, number of DIS received
  - DAO sequence, number of DAO received, and a parent bit (if there is no DAO message sent, or if there is a DAO message require to remove the parent relationship, then the parent bit is 0, otherwise it will be set to 1)
- Preferred parent ID

Such information will be collected and sent periodically to the IDS agents. Upon receiving the IDS data, the IDS agents will apply relevant algorithms to detect any malicious behaviors of the cluster members.

3.2.3. Detection at the IDS Agent

Algorithm 3 shown a detection algorithm that we developed based on the RPL profile discussed in Section 3.1 and the collected data given in Section 3.2.2. The detection algorithm would be executed as an IDS agent at Cluster head. The algorithm consists of 5 modules:

- Module 1: Checking the DIS message, alarm if the received DIS is fake or sending too much.
- Module 2: Checking the sequence of DIO message, alarm if the received DIO is fake
- Module 3: Checking the rank consistency, alarm if the rank of the member is different to the rank reported by its neighbors or the cluster head, given the same DIO sequence. Penalize the neighbors if they do not have the latest DIO message. Alarm if there is any DIO message reported by the neighbors or cluster head that has newer DIO sequence than the member itself
- Module 4: Check the rank rule between every pair of parent and child
- Module 5: Check the instability of the network area around a member through the relevant states and observations in Section 3.1. Penalize if there is any instability.

The detail algorithm is as below.

Algorithm 3. Detecting topology attacks from cluster head view

---

Module 1: Check whether DIS message is illegitimate

1: **On receiving** DIS {
2:    **record** $SourceID, DIS\_seq\_new$;
3:    $DIS\_count[SourceID]$++;
4:    **if** $DIS\_seq\_new \leqslant DIS\_seq\_current$ **then**
5:       **alarm** *fake DIS*;
6:       **else** $DIS\_seq\_current = DIS\_seq\_new$
7:    **end if**
8:    **if** $DIS_count[SourceID] > $ threshold$_{DIS\_count}$ **then**
9:       **alarm** *DIS attack*;
10:   **end if** }

Module 2: Check whether there is any fake DIO

1: **On receiving** DIO {
2:    **record** $SourceID, DIO\_seq\_new, rank$;
3:    $DIO\_count[SourceID]$++;
4:    **if** $DIO\_seq\_new \leqslant DIO\_seq\_current$ **then**
5:       **alarm** *fake DIO*;
6:       **else** $DIO\_seq\_current = DIO\_seq\_new$
7:    **end if** }

Module 3: Check the rank inconsistency

1:    After receiving reports from all of the members {
2:       **for each** *Member* in *Cluster* **do** {
3:          **if** $Member.DIO\_seq < CH.Member.DIO\_seq$ **then**
4:             **alarm** *fake DIO*;
5:          **end if**

Algorithm 3. Detecting topology attacks from cluster head view

---

Module 3: Check the rank inconsistency

6:      **for each** *Neighbour* in *Member.Neighbour* **do**
7:        **if** Member.DIO_seq < Neighbour.Member.DIO_seq **then**
8:          **alarm** *fake DIO;*
9:        **else if** *Member.DIO_seq < Neighbour.Member.DIO_seq* **then**
10:            *Neighbour.fault = Neighbour.fault + 0.5 //penalised*
11:        **else if** *Member.DIO_seq = Neighbour.Member.DIO_seq* **then**
12:          **if** *Member.rank != Neighbour.Member.Rank* **then**
13:            **alarm** *fake DIO;*
14:          **end if**
15:        **end if**
16:      **end for**
17:    **end for** } }

Module 4: Check the rank rule

1:    **for each** *Member* in *Cluster* **do**
2:      **if** *Member.rank + MinHopRankIncrease < Member.parent.rank* **then**
3:        **alarm** *rank attack;*
4:      **end if**
5:      **for each** *Neighbour* in *Member.Neighbour* **do** {
6:        **if** *Member.DAO.parent == 1* **then**
7:          **if** *Member.rank − MinHopRankIncrease > Member.child.rank* **then**
8:            **alarm** *rank attack;*
9:          **end if**
10:        **end if**
11:      **end for**
12: **end for** }

Module 5: Check the stability of the network part which relate to a cluster member

---

//Setting the initial stability evaluation for each member in cluster
1: **for each** *Member* in *Cluster* **do**
2:      *Member.stability = threshold$_{stability}$*
3: **end for**
//Penalise if stability condition is observed to be not satisfied
4: **for each** *Member* in *Cluster* {
5:      **if** *IsRepairAfterPeriod* **then**
6:          *Member.stability -= 2 // penalised −2 on stability*
7:      **end if**
8:      **if** *IsChangeAfterPeriod(Member.DIO)* | | *IsChangeAfterPeriod(Member.DAO)* | |
          IsNewNodeJoiningAfterPeriod **then**
9:          *Member.stability -= 0.5 // penalised 0.5 on stability*
10:      **end if** }
//Checking every period of time
11: **if** *IsCheckingPeriod* **then**
12:      **for each** *Member* in *Cluster* **do**
13:          **if** *Member.stability < 0* **then**
14:              **alarm** *Member instability;*
15:          **end if**

Algorithm 3. Detecting topology attacks from cluster head view
Module 5: Check the stability of the network part which relate to a cluster member

16:	**if** $Member.fault > threshold_{fault}$ **then**
17:	**alarm** $Member\ fault$; // member fault is recorded in module 3
18:	**end if**
19:	**end for**
20: **end if**	

The thresholds used in the algorithm are summarized in Table 2 below.

Table 2. The thresholds used in the algorithm.

Threshold	Meaning
$threshold_{DIS\_count}$	Alarm if a node visit the DIS state more than $threshold_{DIS\_count}$ in the monitoring time.
$threshold_{fault}$	Alarm if a node not updating info from the neighbours
$threshold_{instability}$	Alarm if node visit the instability states $S1, S5, S6, S7, S8$ more than a $threshold_{instability}$ in the monitoring time

4. Evaluation Results and Discussion

To investigate further the effectiveness of the IDS, we implement the five types of attacks as discussed in Section 3 in Contiki-Cooja [13] and see how the IDS module can detect them. This session first presents the simulation setup, evaluation metrics, and then discuss about the results achieved.

4.1. Simulation Set up

Our simulation scenario consists of a total of 100 nodes placed randomly in a 600×600 m area, each node has a transmission range of 50 m. The topology setup is shown in Figure 6 below. There is one sink placed in the center (node ID: 1 with dot pattern in Figure 6) and 11 IDS cluster heads (the grey nodes) to cover the operation of the remaining 88 nodes in the network (the white nodes). Every node sends packet to the sink at the rate of 1 packet every 60 s. Data specified in Section 3.2.2 is collected and sent to the cluster heads every 2 min. We implement the specification-based module from Section 3 in the IDS cluster heads to analyze the collected trace data. The thresholds are set up based on analyzing the statistical data in the trace files with the following values: $threshold_{DIS\_count} = 3$, $threshold_{fault} = 2$, and $threshold_{instability} = 10$.

We implemented each of the five types of attacks as discussed in Section 2 in random positions of 88 normal senders. For each of the attack scenario, there will be one random node in the 88 normal nodes to be injected the relevant attack code. The attacks are initiated after 3 min when the topology establishment phase is done. The summary of the simulation parameters is shown in Table 3 below.

Table 3. The simulation parameters.

Parameters	Value
Simulation platform	Cooja Contiki 2.6
Number of nodes	99 senders, 1 sink
Number of cluster head	11
Number of attackers	1
Traffic model	Constant bit rate
Sending rate	1 packet every 60 s
IDS require info every	2 min
Simulation run time	30 min

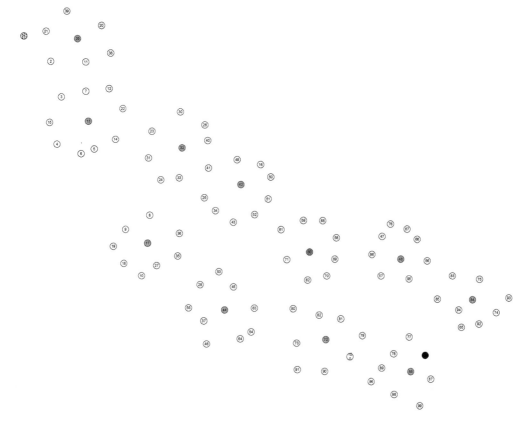

Figure 6. Topology set up.

4.2. Evaluation Metrics

Evaluation metrics include metric to evaluate the accuracy of the IDS and the level of overhead to compare with the network operating without IDS. Metrics to evaluate the accuracy of an IDS is mainly the True Positive Rate and the False Positive Rate. The True Positive rate can also be called the Detection Rate as it shows how good the IDS is at detecting the malicious behaviors. On the other hand, the False Positive rate represents the falsification of the IDS as it shows how bad the IDS can be at falsifying to detect a legitimate behaviors. The formula to calculate these two metrics are:

$$\textbf{True Positive Rate (TPR):} \ \text{TP}_{\text{rate}} = \frac{\text{TP}}{\text{TP} + \text{FN}}$$

$$\textbf{False Positive Rate (FPR):} \ \text{FN}_{\text{rate}} = \frac{\text{FP}}{\text{FP} + \text{TN}}$$

where

- True Positive (TP): is the total correctly detected malicious behaviours. This happens when the IDS correctly raise alert on a malicious event.
- False Positive (FP): happens when the IDS erroneously raises a false alarm over a legitimate behaviour in the network.
- True Negative (TN): happens when the IDS correctly judging a legitimate behaviour as normal.
- False Negative (FN): happens when the IDS erroneously judging a malicious event as normal.

The impacts to the resource consumption are evaluated utilizing the network energy usage and node power consumption as presented in [6]. The formula to calculate these metrics are as follow:

Energy usage (mJ)

$$= (19.5\text{mA} \times \text{transmit} + 21.8\text{mA} \times \text{listen} + 1.8\text{mA} \times \text{CPU} \tag{1}$$
$$+ 0.0545 \times \text{LPM}) \times 3 \text{ V}/4096 \times 8$$

$$\textbf{Power Consumption (mW)} = \frac{\text{Energyusage (mJ)}}{\text{Time (s)}} \tag{2}$$

The more energy and power the network uses, the shorter its lifetime is.

4.3. Simulation Results and Discussion

4.3.1. Detection Efficency

We divided the attacks into two groups which have similar results when detected by our IDS. The first group contains the Rank attack, Sinkhole attack, and Neighbor attack—the threats which are detected only by the specified states. The second group includes the local repair and the DIS attacks, which involved both the specification states and statistic collection to reveal.

Table 4 below shows the TPR and FPR of the Rank attack, Sinkhole attack and the Neighbor attack after 4 min, when the Rank attack already initiated (at the third minute) and the IDS has just collected the first two IDS data packets from its neighbor. As can be seen from the table, we obtained ideal IDS results, where the TPR is 100% and the FPR is 0%. These results can be explained as follows.

The DIO sequence checking in Modules 2 and 3 ensure that there is no inconsistency in DIO and Rank information between the IDS data reported by the neighbours. As a result, the cluster head will know most of the parent—child relationships and their accurate corresponding ranks.

Regarding the Rank attack, given its nature which is choosing the worst parent as the preferred parent and changing it frequently, the cluster head will detect the behaviour of breaking the rank rule and raise alarm about the child node for choosing inappropriate parent. Therefore, the Rank attack is detected quickly with high accuracy.

Regarding the Sinkhole attack, our implementation lets the attacker keeps informing that it has the rank of the Sink to attract its neighbours. As the attacker is not the actual Sink, before initiating the attacks, it would have a preferred parent. Moreover, this parent-child relationship would be recorded by one of the cluster heads. When the attacker manipulates its new rank to the Sink's rank, such relationship will become illegal, because the child now has a better rank than the parent. This illegal relation will be detected by Module 4 of our IDS.

Regarding the neighbor attack, the neighbor attack involves some DIO replications, which will be detected by Modules 2 and 3 through the DIO duplication of the sequence number received. This detection is straightforward, fast and accurate because it does not need to collect much IDS information to decide.

Table 4. TPR and FPR of Rank attack, sinkhole attack and Neighbor attack after 4 min.

	FP	TP	FN	TN	TPR (%)	FPR (%)
RA	0	88	0	7656	100	0
SA	0	88	0	7656	100	0
NA	0	88	0	7656	100	0

Our IDS shows high accuracy results not long after the attack initiating. However, when letting the IDS works for a long time, when the TPR is still ideal, the FPR increases significantly and makes the IDS become less accurate. For example, the TPR and FPR after 10 min detecting RA, SA and

NA scenarios are shown in Table 5 below. The figure shows that the FPR increase to about 2%–5%. The reason is that the initiated attacks in the tampered nodes have affected its neighbors around, make those nodes work the same way as the attackers, and therefore become difficult to separate.

Table 5. TPR and FPR of Rank attack, sinkhole attack and Neighbor attack after 10 min.

	FP	TP	FN	TN	TPR (%)	FPR (%)
RA	402	88	0	7254	100	5.25
SA	251	88	0	7405	100	3.28
NA	202	88	0	7454	100	2.64

In order to minimize the FPR, the nodes which are detected as the malicious source should be removed from the network, for example, by adding to a blacklist and asking all other relevant nodes to skip nodes in that list. After removing the nodes, the IDS will stop judging for a certain time to help to stabilize the network before restarting in a new detection cycle.

The second group of attacks includes the Local repair and the DIS attack. The difference to compare with the first group is that in this group, observing that a node visit a state is not enough to conclude this node to be malicious. This observation is only considered as part of the statistic evidences. Only when a node visits a state more than a threshold of times during a period, the IDS has the right to raise alarm about the threat.

The mechanisms to detect attacks in the second group are as follows. In local repair attack, after initiating the local repair mechanism, the node sends the poison messages to the neighborhood in which its rank is reset to be infinite and it needs to resend the DIS to obtain the routing information around. The local repair will be reported after several times initiated according to Module 1. On the other hand, the local repair also invokes the high instability value in Module 5, so it will also be reported by this module.

In the DIS attack, the attacker needs to send DIS messages to force the neighbor to change the DIO trickle time, or to send the unicast DIO back. In any case, it will increase the DIS statistic in Module 1 and will be reported by the DIS.

Tables 6 and 7 below present the TPR and FPR detection of this group after 8 and 12 min. As can be seen from the figures, after 8 min, the IDS may not collect enough information in any of the cases so it cannot detect the Local repair attack and DIS attack, which results in a high FN and low TPR. On the other hand, after 12 min, the IDS collect all the needed information, so the FN and TPR are ideal. However, the Local repair and DIS attack is given long time enough to manipulate the neighbors around the malicious node to create the instability in the topology. Such instability is presented through the high rate of FP and FPR which make the IDS become less accurate because of detecting normal nodes as attackers. Therefore, there is a tradeoff between the TPR and FPR in detecting threats in this group.

Table 6. TPR and FPR of Rank attack, sinkhole attack and Neighbor attack after 8 min.

	FP	TP	FN	TN	TPR (%)	FPR (%)
LA	51	76	12	7605	86.36	0.67
DIS	232	83	5	7424	94.32	3.03

Table 7. TPR and FPR of Rank attack, sinkhole attack and Neighbor attack after 12 min.

	FP	TP	FN	TN	TPR (%)	FPR (%)
LA	519	88	0	7137	100	6.78
DIS	453	88	0	7203	100	5.92

Unlike the first group of attacks, where the attackers are always detected first before any FP happens, in the second group, a benign node can be detected as malicious before the attackers are revealed. Therefore, using a blacklist or other mechanism to eliminate the detected nodes in this case may not be appropriate. An alternative solution is to adjust the frequency threshold to adapt to the frequency of the corresponding Local repair/DIS attack in specific scenario through learning from simulation. A good chosen threshold will optimize the detection rate and accurateness of the IDS.

It is worth to mention that in general, the specification-based IDS has the ability to detect the new attacks because it focuses on checking the legitimacy of the protocol operation rather than on any specific attack behaviors. Similarly, our proposed IDS aims at monitoring the optimal network topology and its stability as a whole, which is broader than just verifying illegitimate behaviors created by some specific internal attacks. Hence, it will also have the ability to detect other topology attacks which are not mentioned in this paper, if those attacks breaking the optimal topology or create network instability.

4.3.2. Energy Efficiency

We run the simulation in RPL-collect network (the sink collect environment data from every other nodes) with and without our IDS integration and obtain the energy and power consumption as calculated in Formulas (1) and (2) in Section 4.2. In normal RPL network, the energy is around 190J, while in the RPL with IDS integration, the average energy consumption is about 202J, which represents an increase of 6.3%. This is a lot more saving to compare with the IDS in [6], where the overhead is 30% for a setup of 64 nodes (the overhead would be larger if they setup for the same 100 nodes like our setup). The reason for this saving is that we only limit the IDS work locally, where monitoring nodes only need to deal with 8–12 nodes in average, instead of sending all the IDS data to one IDS center. In this paper, we implement between 8 and 12 nodes in each cluster for the experiment set-up. In other scenarios with denser network, the number of nodes in each cluster can be higher, which leads to slightly more energy consumption. Besides, the average power consumption in each node increases slightly 6.3% with 1.2 mW in IDS integration scenario to compare with 1.05 mW in normal scenario. This indicates that the network lifetime will not be affected much once implementing the IDS.

5. Further Considerations on Expanding the IDS Capability to Detect More Internal Threats

Topology attack is only one type of internal threats that can happen with the RPL-based network. The nature of the specification-based IDS makes it suitable to detect this type of attack because all the collected monitoring data and set of rules can be used straight forward for detect the illegitimate protocol behaviors with small amount of overhead and little requirement on storage and computing. As aforementioned, this work is only part of our on-going research on detecting the internal threats. In detail, besides topology attacks, there are still other internal threats that aim at performance directly, as discussed comprehensively in our previous work [2]. Apart from the protocol side, node behaviors also depend on other conditions such as applications, environments and so on. The set of protocol rules obtained from the specification-based IDS cannot reflect node behaviors regarding such aspects, therefore, it may not be effective in dealing with the performance-type internal threats. For example, internal adverse can follow the protocol operation yet still manipulating other performance behaviors such as sending, forwarding or controlling activities at the lower layer. To deal with this type of internal threats, a more proper anomaly-based IDS technique needs to be applied. As the accuracy of any anomaly-based IDS will correlate to the robustness of the detection algorithm and the amount of monitoring data that the system collected, the storage and computation capability need to be extended more. Note that the specification-based IDS in this paper collects only a small amount of monitoring data, while using simple comparing and checking algorithms, therefore, the cluster head can still adapt with the storage and computation workload. However, if we want to employ anomaly-based IDS with larger monitoring data and more robust detection algorithm such as Bayesian network or other data mining techniques, the cluster monitoring architecture will not be able to deliver.

To enable the use of a more robust anomaly-based IDS working on a larger amount of monitoring data, we envisage an architecture that can extend the computation and storage capability of the IDS massively, yet still keep the network overhead low and acceptable for operating. In detail, we extend the cluster monitoring architecture by first making benefit from the multiple-interface design that allows the sensor devices to communicate in different channels. One real life example is the Libelium Waspmote devices that allow many wireless communication standards such as Wifi, 3G, GSM, GPRS, LoRa, and so on apart from sensor data transmission [16]. We can use the multi-interface sensor devices as the cluster heads to communicate both in RPL-based network and another overlay network, which supports high speed, long distance, and low power consumption transmission. There are many options for such overlay network, for example, the IEEE 802.11, LTE, 3G, *etc.* By doing so, we aim at transferring the IDS monitoring data directly to an IDS server through the overlay network by the extra interface. To compare with the network-based architecture, sending IDS data to the server through the overlay channel will eliminate many communicational issues such as overhead, delay, packet loss, *etc.* Moreover, we propose to implement the Cloud Computing [17] application at the IDS server. The IDS work deal by the server only before now can be delegated to many other computers in the Cloud, which helps to enable the IDS computation and storage capability massively. The additional cost for implementing this architecture is only a little, given the reasonable price of multi-interface cluster heads, IDS data collection, and Cloud Computing service. The benefit of this architecture will be the allowance to use many robust IDS algorithms on large amounts of IDS data, so as to have higher accuracy in dealing with many other internal threats effectively, while can be scalable well in large-scale network. An illustration of this vision can be seen in Figure 7 below.

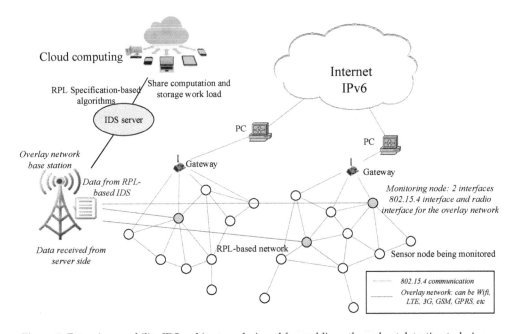

Figure 7. Extensive capability IDS architecture designed for enabling other robust detecting techniques.

6. Conclusions

This paper aimed at detecting the attacks on the RPL based network topology that jeopardizing the network operational optimality and stability. The considered attacks include the Rank, the Sinkhole, the Local Repair, the Neighbor, and DIS attack. These threats can affect different aspects of network performance, from directly such as increase the end to end delay or create more packet loss, to indirectly like exhausting the resources of the nodes by communicational and computational overhead. Our detection solution involves semi-auto building a specification-based IDS model for protecting RPL-based network topology. The main idea is to learn the states, transitions, and relevant statistic based on the analyzing the trace file. The generated model will be integrated in the IDS server, which connects to the network through many cluster interfaces. The simulation results show that our IDS is energy efficiency and applicable for the large-scale networks, while providing high detection rates and accurateness in revealing most of the topology attacks. In the future, with the envisaged IDS architecture in Section 5, we would like to develop a more robust anomaly-based IDS for detecting performance-attacks type of the internal threats, for example, the black hole, selective forwarding or wormhole attack. We believe the extension of IDS capability in storage and computation will allow detection of internal threats more accurately and efficiently.

Acknowledgments: We thank our colleagues from Middlesex University and Queen Mary University of London who provided insight and expertise that greatly assisted the research on its early design. We are also grateful to the two anonymous reviewers for their valuable suggestions.

Author Contributions: Jonathan Loo jointly conceived the study with Anhtuan Le designed the attack experiment, IDS architecture, profiling model, and prepared the manuscript; Anhtuan Le implemented the model and experiments, created the analytic model with contributions from Kok Keong Chai and Mahdi Aiash; Kok Keong Chai supervised the analysis on RPL profile and IDS detection, and edited the manuscript; Mahdi Aiash edited the manuscript. All authors have read and approved the final manuscript.

Conflicts of Interest: The authors declare no conflict of interest.

Abbreviations

The following abbreviations are used in this manuscript:

6LoWPAN	IPv6 over Low-power Wireless Personal Area Network
DAO	Destination Advertisement Object
DIO	Destination Oriented DAG Information Objective
DIS	DODAG Information Solicitation
FN	False Negative
FP	False Positive
FPR	False Positive Rate
LA	Local Repair Attack
LTE	Long-Term Evolution
NA	Neighbor Attack
IDS	Intrusion Detection System
IoT	Internet of Things
RA	Rank attack
RPL	Routing Protocol for Low Power and lossy network
SA	Sinkhole Attack
TN	True Negative
TP	True Positive
TPR	True Positive Rate

References

1. Winter, T.; Thubert, P.; Brandt, A.; Hui, J.; Kelsey, R.; Levis, P.; Pister, K.; Struik, R.; Vasseur, J.P.; Alexander, R. *RPL: IPv6 Routing Protocol for Low-Power and Lossy Network*; Internet Engineering Task Force (IETF): Fremont, CA, USA, 2012.
2. Le, A.; Loo, J.; Lasebae, A.; Aiash, M.; Luo, Y. 6LoWPAN: A study on QoS security threats and countermeasures using intrusion detection system approach. *Int. J. Commun. Syst.* **2012**, *25*, 1189–1212. [CrossRef]
3. Le, A.; Loo, J.; Lasebae, A.; Vinel, A.; Chen, Y.; Chai, M. The impact of rank attack on network topology of routing protocol for low-power and lossy networks. *IEEE Sens. J.* **2013**, *13*, 3685–3692. [CrossRef]
4. Le, A.; Loo, J.; Luo, Y.; Lasebae, A. Specification-based IDS for securing RPL from topology attacks. In Proceedings of the 2011 IFIP Wireless Days (WD), Niagara Falls, ON, Canada, 10–12 October 2011; pp. 1–3.
5. Le, A.; Loo, J.; Luo, Y.; Lasebae, A. The impacts of internal threats towards Routing Protocol for Low power and lossy network performance. In Proceedings of the 2013 IEEE Symposium on Computers and Communications (ISCC), Split, Croatia, 7–10 July 2013; pp. 789–794.

6.   Raza, S.; Wallgren, L.; Voigt, T. SVELTE: Real-time intrusion detection in the Internet of Things. *Ad Hoc Netw.* **2013**, *11*, 2661–2674. [CrossRef]
7.   Tang, J.; Huang, X.; Qian, J.; Viho, C. A FSM-based test sequence generation method for RPL conformance testing. In Proceedings of the Green Computing and Communications (GreenCom), 2013 IEEE and Internet of Things (iThings/CPSCom), IEEE International Conference on and IEEE Cyber, Physical and Social Computing, Beijing, China, 20–23 August 2013; pp. 591–597.
8.   Wallgren, L.; Raza, S.; Voigt, T. Routing attacks and countermeasures in the RPL-based Internet of Things. *Int. J. Distrib. Sens. Netw.* **2013**, *2013*, 794326. [CrossRef]
9.   Tsao, T.; Alexander, R.; Dohler, M.; Daza, V.; Lozano, A.; Richardson, M. A Security Threat Analysis for Routing Protocol for Low-Power and Lossy Networks (RPL). Available online: https://tools.ietf.org/html/draft-ietf-roll-security-threats-06 (accessed on 6 May 2016).
10. Panos, C.; Xenakis, C.; Stavrakakis, I. A novel intrusion detection system for MANETs. In Proceedings of the 2010 International Conference on Security and Cryptography (SECRYPT), Athens, Greece, 26–28 July 2010; pp. 1–10.
11. Tseng, C.-Y.; Balasubramanyam, P.; Ko, C.; Limprasittiporn, R.; Rowe, J.; Levitt, K. A specification-based intrusion detection system for AODV. In Proceedings of the 1st ACM Workshop on Security of Ad Hoc and Sensor Networks, Washington, DC, USA, 27–30 October 2003.
12. Stakhanova, N.; Basu, S.; Wensheng, Z.; Wang, X.; Wong, J.S. Specification synthesis for monitoring and analysis of MANET protocols. In Proceedings of the 21st International Conference on Advanced Information Networking and Applications Workshops, AINAW '07, Niagara Falls, ON, Canada, 21–23 May 2007; pp. 183–187.
13. Contiki. Available online: http://www.contiki-os.org/ (accessed on 6 May 2016).
14. Mitrokotsa, A.; Karygiannis, A. Intrusion detection techniques in sensor networks. In *Wireless Sensor Network Security*; Lopez, J., Zhou, J., Eds.; IOS press: Amsterdam, The Netherlands, 2008; pp. 251–272.
15. Matsunaga, T.; Toyoda, K.; Sasase, I. Low false alarm rate RPL network monitoring system by considering timing inconstancy between the rank measurements. In Proceedings of the 2014 11th International Symposium on Wireless Communications Systems (ISWCS), Barcelona, Spain, 26–29 August 2014; pp. 427–431.
16. Libelium. Wireless Interfaces Supported in Waspmote. Available online: http://www.libelium.com/products/waspmote/interfaces/ (accessed on 6 May 2016).
17. Armbrust, M.; Fox, A.; Griffith, R.; Joseph, A.D.; Katz, R.; Konwinski, A.; Lee, G.; Patterson, D.; Rabkin, A.; Stoica, I.; *et al.* A view of cloud computing. *Commun. ACM* **2010**, *53*, 50–58. [CrossRef]

7

On-Body Smartphone Localization with an Accelerometer

Kaori Fujinami

Department of Computer and Information Sciences, Tokyo University of Agriculture and Technology, 2-24-16 Naka-cho Koganei, Tokyo 184-8588, Japan; fujinami@cc.tuat.ac.jp

Academic Editors: James Park, Marek R. Ogiela and Yang Xiao

Abstract: A user of a smartphone may feel convenient, happy, safe, *etc.*, if his/her smartphone works smartly based on his/her context or the context of the device. In this article, we deal with the position of a smartphone on the body and carrying items like bags as the context of a device. The storing position of a smartphone impacts the performance of the notification to a user, as well as the measurement of embedded sensors, which plays an important role in a device's functionality control, accurate activity recognition and reliable environmental sensing. In this article, nine storing positions, including four types of bags, are subject to recognition using an accelerometer on a smartphone. In total, 63 features are selected as a set of features among 182 systematically-defined features, which can characterize and discriminate the motion of a smartphone terminal during walking. As a result of leave-one-subject-out cross-validation, an accuracy of 0.801 for the nine-class classification is shown, while an accuracy of 0.859 is obtained against five classes, which merges the subclasses of trouser pockets and bags. We also show the basic performance evaluation to select the proper window size and classifier. Furthermore, the analysis of the contributive features is presented.

Keywords: smartphone; on-body position; device localization; accelerometer; machine learning; feature selection; activity recognition; opportunistic sensing; intelligent systems; wearable computing

1. Introduction

Mobile phones are getting smarter due to the advancement of technologies, such as microelectromechanical systems (MEMS), high performance and low power computation, also called a *smartphone*. Various sensors are embedded in or attached to a device, and a wide variety of contextual information can be extracted, which is about the user, the device and/or the environment. These sensors are (or will) not only utilized for explicit usage of the terminal's functionalities, like user authentication [1], display orientation change and backlight intensity control [2], but also for activity recognition [3,4], indoor person localization [5,6], pedestrian identification [7], environmental monitoring [8,9], *etc*. A phone carrying survey revealed that 17% of people determine the position of storing a mobile phone based on contextual restrictions, e.g., no pocket in the T-shirt, too large a phone size for a pants pocket, comfort for an ongoing activity [10]. These factors are variable throughout the day, and thus, users change their positions in a day. This suggests that the context, *on-body device position*, has great potentials for improving the usability of a smartphone and the quality of sensor-dependent services, facilitating human-human communication, the reduction of unnecessary energy consumption, *etc*. In this article, we deal with nine popular storing positions for a smartphone, including four types of bag. We attempt to find a set of features that can characterize and discriminate the motion of a smartphone during walking, using an embedded accelerometer. The contributions of the paper are as follows:

- Recognition features are analyzed from a microscopic point of view, in which a systematic feature selection specified 63 classifier-independent features that are more predictive of classes and less correlated with each other. Especially, we found that: (1) features derived from the y-axis are the most contributive; (2) the correlation between the y-axis and the magnitude of three axes, *i.e.*, the force given to the device, might be useful to capture the characteristics of the propagated ground reaction force within nine storing positions; and (3) the selected features were also effective at classifying three additional classes, *i.e.*, wrist, upper arm and belt.
- A "compatibility" matrix is introduced and showed the possibilities of improving the accuracy by removing a "noisy" dataset of particular persons from a training dataset and training a classifier using a dataset with similar characteristics of the acceleration of a device during walking.
- The high precision against "neck" and "trouser pocket" under leave-one-subject-out cross validation (0.95) allows reliable placement-aware environmental risk alert.

The rest of the article is organized as follows: Section 2 presents the importance of on-body position recognition with examples in three categories, and a literature survey is shown in Section 3. Section 4 describes our approach, followed by the performance evaluation in Section 5. Discussions based on the evaluation are presented in Section 6. Finally, Section 7 concludes the article.

2. Importance of On-Body Position Recognition

In this section, the importance of taking into account the on-body position of a device as the context of a system is presented.

2.1. Device Functionality Control

In our preliminary study, an audio notification is perceived with significantly smaller sound volume when a smartphone is hanging from the neck, compared to the case of putting it into a trouser pocket and a jacket pocket. This may also be experienced by a number of people. The case with a chest pocket comes in the middle of "neck" and "trouser pockets". One static solution is to set an audio level sufficiently high, so that a user could perceive it at any storing position; however, it is annoying in the vicinity when the smartphone is hanging from the neck, because a user can notice it with an even lower audio level at the position. Therefore, the audio volume can be adjusted at a minimum level by the information of the storing position, so that only the user can receive the notification, as Diaconita et al. intended [11,12]. Other functionalities, such as a display component and a keypad, can be controlled to avoid power drain due to an invisible display, as well as accidental inputs when a smartphone is inside a bag or pocket [13].

2.2. Accurate Activity Recognition

A context-aware system does not work as designed when the context is not correctly recognized. In the work on activity recognition using body-mounted sensors, including smartphones, the sensing device is often assumed to be at the intended positions [3,4,14]. Pirttikangas et al. showed that an accelerometer hanging from the neck had contributed to discriminate certain kinds of movement of the upper body, such as brushing teeth and sitting while reading a newspaper [4]. Atallah et al. showed the variations in activity recognition performance by the position of body-worn sensor [15], in which sensors placed on the wrist and the chest had contributed to discriminate medium level activities, such as walking in a corridor and vacuuming. These findings imply that particular activities are not recognized accurately when the sensor is removed from the contributive position to another. In such a case, by utilizing the positional information, a system can ask a user to keep putting a smartphone into a chest pocket or turn the sensing component off to avoid noisy measurement based on application requirements.

2.3. Reliable Environmental Sensing

Smartphone-based environmental sensing is getting attention due to the popularity of smartphones and the existence of communication infrastructure [8,16], by which dense environmental information is easily collected without deploying a dedicated sensing system from scratch. The storing position of a smartphone is regarded as a key element of reliable measurement in such human-centric sensing, because the measurements are affected by storing positions [16–18]. Especially, "outside a container" is important in such a case of noise sensing [9] and humidity/temperature sensing [18]. In [18], a difference in the readings from a relative humidity sensor and a thermometer is observed due to the effect of body heat propagation. Furthermore, the positioning information on the Earth, e.g., latitude, longitude and the orientation, is usually captured by a GPS receiver, magnetometer and gyroscope along with the target sensor measurement. Vaitl *et al.* [19] and Blum *et al.* [20] report that even these sensors are affected by the storing position. In these cases, storing positional information can be utilized to build and select models to correct the measurement or notify a user of the state of storing into unintended positions, which is required to offer reliable sensing results.

3. Related Work

On-body position sensing is getting the attention of researchers in machine learning and ubiquitous computing communities [21–23], which starts from the work of Kunze *et al.* [24]. Table 1 summarizes the comparison of the major work on on-body device localization with our work regarding the target positions, sensor types, evaluation method, number of subjects and position recognition accuracy.

The research direction is on the type of device that is actually realized or intended to be utilized in the future as a wearable device [23–25] or a smartphone [11–13,17,22,26–29]. The type of device relates to the selection of target positions. In the wearable device approach, the target positions range from the head to the ankle, including fine-grained discrimination, such as upper arm *vs.* forearm and shin *vs.* thigh [23]. A device is usually attached firmly using a belt or a special mounting fixture. This indicates that the direction of the device might not change so irregularly within a specific activity in a frequent manner, given that small displacement might occur during activities [30]. By contrast, a smartphone terminal is usually stored into containers, such as the pockets of a jacket, chest and trouser pockets and a wide variety of bags, as well as in a user's hand, hanging from the neck and on a table, as surveyed in [10,27]. In this case, the degree of freedom of irregular movement in a large container, e.g., jacket pocket or handbag, would increase. In this article, we focus on the smartphone localization in nine storing positions on the body and carrying items, *i.e.*, bags. We equally collect data from four types of bags, which is a unique aspect of our work. In existing work, the type of bag is not clearly defined [27] or limited to a backpack [11] and messenger bag [29]. Therefore, the trained classifier has a bias on the collected types of bags.

Table 1. Related work on on-body localization of a device. The brackets in the accuracy column indicate the condition of the evaluation. LOSO, leave-one-subject-out.

	Target Position (Total Number)	Sensor	Evaluation	Subjects	Accuracy (%)
Kunze et al. [24]	Head, trousers, breast, wrist (4)	Accelerometer	10-fold	6	94.0 (walking)
Harrison & Hudson [13]	Backpack, jacket, jeans hip, desk, etc. (27)	Multispectral light (active sensing w/ Ir light)	10-fold	16	94.8 (N/A)
Miluzzo et al. [17]	In or out of a pocket (2)	Microphone	2-fold	1	80 (N/A)
Vähdatpour et al. [23]	Upper arm, forearm, waist shin, thigh, head (6)	Accelerometer	5-fold	25	89 (walking)
Shi et al. [22]	Trouser front/back, breast, hand (4)	Accelerometer, gyroscope	5-fold	4	91.69 (walking)
Fujinami et al. [26]	Chest, jacket, trouser front/back of neck, 4 types of bags (9)	Accelerometer	LOSO / 10-fold	20	74.6 (walking) / 99.4 (walking)
Wiese et al. [27]	Pocket, bag, out of body, hand (4)	Accelerometer, proximity, capacitive	LOSO	15	85 (mixed)
Diaconita et al. [11]	Pocket, backpack, desk, hand (4)	Microphone (active sensing w/ vibration)	10-fold	Not given	97 (stationary)
Diaconita et al. [12]	Pocket, hand, bag, desk (4)	Accelerometer (active sensing w/ vibration)	10-fold	Not given	99.2 (mixed)
Mannini et al. [25]	Ankle, thigh, hip, arm, waist (5)	Accelerometer	LOSO / 10-fold	33	91.2 (walking) / 96.4
Alanezi et al. [28]	Trouser front/back, jacket, hand holding, talking on phone, watching a video (6)	Accelerometer, Accelerometer, gyro	10-fold	10	88.5 (walking) / 89.3 (walking)
Incel [29]	Trousers, jacket, 2 types of bags, wrist, hand, arm, belt (8)	Accelerometer	LOSO	max/min/ave 35/10/15.6	85.4 (walking) / 76.4 (stationary) / 84.3 (mobile)
	Trouser left/right, upper arm, belt, wrist (5)	Accelerometer, gyro	LOSO	10	95.9 (mixed)
This work	Neck, chest, jacket, trouser front/back, 4 types of bags (9) / Merged: "trousers", "bags" (5)	Accelerometer	LOSO / 10-fold / LOSO	20	80.5 (walking) / 99.9 (walking) / 85.9 (walking)

Another aspect is the modality of sensing, in which an accelerometer is dominant due to its low power operation and the availability in most commercial smartphones and wearable devices. Shi *et al.* [22], Alanezi *et al.* [28] and Incel [29] utilized a gyroscope in combination with an accelerometer, in which the combined approach slightly improved the accuracy [28,29]; however, considering the power-hungry nature of a gyroscope [31], the improvement would not be the reason for utilizing a gyroscope. Harrison and Hudson [13] utilized a multispectral light sensor to discriminate the device position based on light components. Although the recognition system was tested with a wide variety of positions, *i.e.*, 27, from 16 people, the robustness on real-world usage seems to be still an issue. For example, a bag with cellular fabric might pass light inside, which may have similar light components even with active sensing. Active sensing methods were also utilized in [11,12] to regulate the environment that sensors capture. However, as pointed out by Jung and Choi [32], a vibration motor is a relatively high power component in a smartphone. Frequent activation, like a sliding-window approach, is not a practical solution; however, activation on receiving a phone call could work well as intended by Diaconita *et al.* [11,12]. An advantage of an active sensing approach seems that the classification performance might not be so influenced between individuals, rather by the materials around. We consider that this helps the data collection tasks that need great human, time and monetary resources, although data collection from many variations of material is still required.

In this article, we extend our previous work [26], while utilizing the same dataset, by: (1) introducing the magnitude of three axes of acceleration as an axis for feature calculation (Section 4.4) that is found to be effective; (2) providing an analysis of contributive features from a microscopic point of view (Section 5.3); and (3) discussing the possibility of classifier-tuning based on the analysis of the compatibility of the dataset among people (Section 5.5). Recent work by Incel [29] shows an extensive study on acceleration-based phone localization, which proposes recognition features that represent the movement, rotation and orientation of devices during diverse activities of a person, e.g., walking, sitting, biking. Furthermore, Wiese *et al.* [27] and Diaconita *et al.* [12] trained and tested with a dataset from various users' conditions in addition to walking. By contrast, as outlined in Section 4.3, we primarily recognize the device position when a person is walking based on the thought that walking is the most frequent and consistent activity throughout the day. We have a mechanism of identifying the period of walking using constancy detection, which is intended to be applied before classification. Leave-one-subject-out (LOSO) cross-validation was carried out against an integrated dataset from 35 persons in total in [29]; however, the number of persons varies between positions (35 persons for trouser pocket, 25 for backpack, 15 for hand and 10 for messenger bag, jacket, belt and wrist), and the average number is 15.6. On the other hand, we tested with LOSO-CV with 20 persons who equally provided data from all target positions. By comparing to our previous work [26], the accuracy with the new set of features is much better, by six points, while still lower than the work by Incel [29], although it is hard to compare directly because of the difference in the target position and evaluation method, as well as the number of subjects.

4. On-Body Smartphone Localization Method

In this section, the method of localizing a smartphone on the body is described.

4.1. Target Positions

Nine popular positions shown in Figure 1 are selected as the targets of recognition: (1) around the neck (hanging); (2) chest pocket; (3) jacket pocket (side); (4) front pocket of trousers; (5) back pocket of trousers; (6) backpack; (7) handbag; (8) messenger bag; and (9) shoulder bag. People often carry smartphones in their hands during texting, calling, *etc.* We consider that such states could be detected by the application logging information of the terminal more precisely. Therefore, we excluded them in this study.

Including a bag as a storing position is technically challenging due to its diverse shape and the carrying style; however, as the survey [10] shows, a bag is a major location for storing a smartphone, especially for women (about 60%), and about 50% of them do not notice incoming calls/messages in their bags, which motivated us to detect a situation of carrying a smartphone in a bag. The four types of bags were specified as popular ones based on our observations on streets in Tokyo. We determined to recognize these types separately, rather than handle them as one single type of "bag". This is because the movement patterns that we utilize in recognizing a storing position are very different from each other, as shown in Table 2. Therefore, we considered it difficult to find powerful features to describe a general "bag". Instead, the result of fine-grained recognition can later be merged into one class "bag".

Figure 1. Target storing positions.

Table 2. Characteristics of the four types of bags.

Type	Way of Slinging	Relationship with Body
Backpack	Over both shoulders	On the back (center of the body)
Handbag	Holding with hand	In the hand (side of the body)
Messenger bag	On the shoulder opposite the bag	Side or back of the body
Shoulder bag	On the same side of the shoulder as the bag	Side of the body

4.2. Sensor Modality

A three-axis accelerometer is utilized to obtain signals that characterize the movement patterns generated by dedicated storing positions while a person is walking. As surveyed in Section 3, accelerometer-based on-body device localization is popular. By contrast, although Shi *et al.* showed the effectiveness of a gyroscope in storing position recognition, a gyroscope is a more power hungry sensor than an accelerometer [31] and not popular for low-end terminals; other multi-sensor approaches, e.g., [27], may also encounter similar issues. A vibration motor-based active sensing-based approach, such as [11,12], is not suitable for continuous position sensing due to the power consumption of a vibration motor, although a microphone and an accelerometer are available in today's smartphones. Typical raw acceleration signals from the target positions are shown in Figure 2. Note that the x-, y- and z-axes of the accelerometer in the terminal (NexusOne) are set to the direction of *width*, *height* and *thickness* in portrait mode, respectively, as shown in Figure 3.

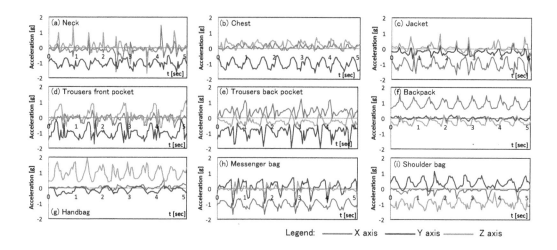

Figure 2. Raw acceleration signals from the nine target positions of a person during walking.

Figure 3. The definition of the axes of an accelerometer in an Android smartphone.

4.3. Flow of Localization

Figure 4 illustrates the data processing flow from sensor readings to an event of placement change. The localization is carried out window-by-window to recognize the class of a position from the nine candidate positions based on the similarity of the patterns of the acceleration signals. Our approach primarily recognizes the storing position of a device while a person is walking. This is in line with the principles of Vahdatpour *et al.* [23] and Mannini *et al.* [25], which are based on the thoughts that walking is the most frequent and consistent activity throughout the day. Nevertheless, non-periodic motions, such as jumping and sitting, can be included in the stream of the acceleration signal. Such states are eliminated based on the constancy of the acceleration signal, as proposed in [33]. The storing position of a previous recognition result is carried over against a window that is judged as "not walking".

Once a window contains a period of walking, a feature vector is obtained, in which features are calculated against linear acceleration signals. Linear acceleration is obtained by removing gravity components from the measured signals. Sophisticated linear acceleration signal estimation methods have been proposed by combining the gyroscope and magnetometer, e.g., [34]; however, we utilize only the accelerometer for the same reason as the choice of an accelerometer as a modality of storing position recognition. We adopted the method proposed by Cho *et al.* [35], in which the gravity components are approximately removed from the raw acceleration signals by subtracting the mean of accelerations in a window (Formula (1)), where $a_{linear,\{x|y|z\},i}$ and $a_{raw,\{x|y|z\},i}$ indicate the i-th component of a dedicated axis of the linear acceleration signal and the raw acceleration signal, respectively. Furthermore, $\overline{a_{raw,\{x|y|z\}}}$ denotes the mean raw acceleration signals of the x-, y- and z-axes in a window.

$$a_{linear,\{x|y|z\},i} = a_{raw,\{x|y|z\},i} - \overline{a_{raw,\{x|y|z\}}} \tag{1}$$

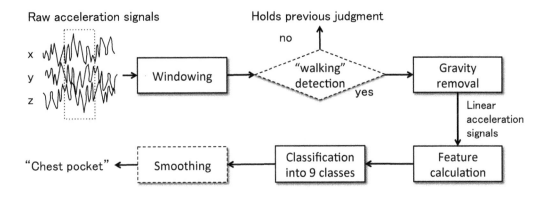

Figure 4. Localization process: the components with a dotted-line have been implemented, but are not the focus of this article.

A feature vector is then given to a nine-class classifier, which is modeled by a machine-learning technique in advance. *Temporal smoothing* is carried out to reject a different pulsed output, since an output of the classifier is window based. Here, majority voting is applied among successive outputs. In this way, one position recognition is performed. We have already implemented the entire process on an Android platform and confirmed that the walking detection works pretty well; however, in this article, we focus on recognition features from a microscopic point of view, and the classification against single windows is performed, in which a dataset obtained during walking is utilized in an offline manner.

4.4. Recognition Features

We take the approach of listing candidates of features from the literature and the observation of waveforms (Figure 2), as well as selecting relevant and non-redundant features based on a machine learning technique. In addition to the three axes, *i.e.*, x, y and z, utilized in our previous work [26], we introduce the magnitude of the acceleration signal (m) as the forth dimension (Formula (2)).

$$a_{linear,m,i} = \sqrt{a_{linear,x,i}^2 + a_{linear,y,i}^2 + a_{linear,z,i}^2} \tag{2}$$

We systematically calculate the candidates of features from a window of a four-dimensional vector of linear acceleration signals by the combination of feature types and the axes. In total, 182 features are obtained (38 types × 4 axes for individual axes and 5 types × 6 pairs for correlation-based features). The feature selection is described in Section 5.3.

Table 3. Classification features (x-, y- and z-axes and the magnitude (m) of the three axes).

Type	Description
$sdev_{time}$	Standard deviation of time series data
min_{time}	Minimum value of time series data
max_{time}	Maximum value of time series data
$3^{rd}Q_{time}$	3rd quartile of time series data
IQR_{time}	Inter-quartile range of time series data
RMS_{time}	Root mean square of time series data
$bin1_{time}$	1st bin of the binned distribution of time series data
$bin2_{time}$	2nd bin of the binned distribution of time series data
$bin3_{time}$	3rd bin of the binned distribution of time series data
$bin4_{time}$	4th bin of the binned distribution of time series data
$bin5_{time}$	5th bin of the binned distribution of time series data
$bin6_{time}$	6th bin of the binned distribution of time series data
$bin7_{time}$	7th bin of the binned distribution of time series data
$bin8_{time}$	8th bin of the binned distribution of time series data
$bin9_{time}$	9th bin of the binned distribution of time series data
$bin10_{time}$	10th bin of the binned distribution of time series data
$max_{freq,all}$	Maximum value in an entire frequency spectrum
$fMax_{freq,all}$	Frequency that gives $max_{freq,all}$
$3^{rd}Q_{freq,all}$	3rd quartile value in the frequency spectrum
$IQR_{freq,all}$	Inter-quartile range of the values in the frequency spectrum
$2^{nd}Max_{freq,all}$	2nd maximum value of the frequency spectrum
$f2^{nd}Max_{freq,all}$	Frequency that gives $2^{nd}Max_{freq,all}$
$max_{freq,low}$	Maximum value in the low-frequency range
$max_{freq,mid}$	Maximum value in the mid-frequency range
$max_{freq,high}$	Maximum value in the high-frequency range
$sdev_{freq,low}$	Standard deviation in the low-frequency range
$sdev_{freq,mid}$	Standard deviation in the mid-frequency range
$sdev_{freq,high}$	Standard deviation in the high-frequency range
$maxSdev_{freq,all}$	Maximum $sdev$ in subwindows in the frequency spectrum
$fMaxSdev_{freq,all}$	Central frequency of the subwindow that gives $maxSdev_{freq,all}$
$sumPower_{freq,all}$	Sum of the entire range power
$sumPower_{freq,low}$	Sum of the power in the low-frequency range
$sumPower_{freq,mid}$	Sum of the power in the mid-frequency range
$sumPower_{freq,high}$	Sum of the power in the high-frequency range
$entr_{freq,all}$	Frequency entropy in the entire range
$entr_{freq,low}$	Frequency entropy in the low-frequency range
$entr_{freq,mid}$	Frequency entropy in the mid-frequency range
$entr_{freq,high}$	Frequency entropy in the high-frequency range

Table 3 shows the features calculated from the four axes individually. The time domain features, except for the binned distribution, are basic and popular ones in acceleration-based activity recognition. The *binned distribution*, however, is defined as follows: (1) the range of values for each axis is determined by subtracting the minimum value from the maximum one; (2) the range is equally divided into 10 bins; and (3) the number of values that fell within each of the bins is counted [3].

Regarding the frequency domain features, max_{freq}, $fMax_{freq}$, $3^{rd}Q_{freq}$, IQR_{freq}, $2^{nd}Max_{freq}$ and $f2^{nd}Max_{freq}$ are specified to represent the shape of the frequency spectrum, as shown in Figure 5a. The feature $maxSdev_{freq}$ is obtained in a way similar to "sliding window average"; a subwindow with a 2.9 Hz range is created in an entire frequency spectrum to calculate the standard deviation ($sdev$); the subwindow is slid by 0.1 Hz throughout the frequency spectrum; and the maximum $sdev$ is found. $fMaxSdev_{freq}$ is the central frequency of a particular subwindow that gives $maxSdev_{freq}$. An example is shown in Figure 5b, where the third subwindow (sw_3) gives the largest standard deviation in N-frequency subwindows as $maxSdev_{freq}$, and the central frequency for subwindow sw_3 corresponds to fMaxSdev$_{freq}$. The size and sliding width (0.1 Hz) of the subwindow were heuristically determined. A feature calculated as the sum of squared values of frequency components (Formula (3)) is sumPower$_{freq}$ (also know as "Fast Fourier Transform (FFT) energy" in [26]) [14]. The FFT entropy (entr$_{freq}$) is then calculated as the normalized information entropy of FFT component values of acceleration signals (Formula (4)), which represents the distribution of frequency components in the frequency domain [14]. Note that the frequency spectrum is equally divided into three "frequency ranges" and assigned subscripts *low*, *mid* and *high*, which correspond to 0.0–4.2 Hz, 4.2–8.4 Hz and 8.4–12.5 Hz, respectively. In addition, the subscript *all* indicates the entire frequency range of 0.0–12.5 Hz.

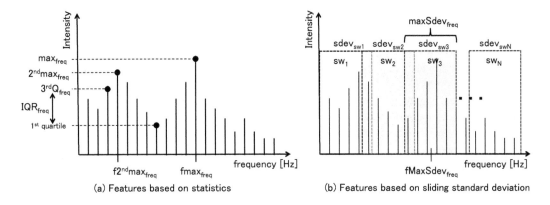

(a) Features based on statistics   (b) Features based on sliding standard deviation

Figure 5. Features obtained in the frequency domain.

$$sumPower_{freq} = \sum_{i=1}^{N/2} f_i^2 \tag{3}$$

$$entr_{freq} = -\sum_{i=1}^{N/2} p_i \times log_2\, p_i \quad where \;\; p_i = \frac{f_i^2}{sumPower_{freq}} \tag{4}$$

Table 4 shows the features regarding the correlation of two axes, *i.e.*, the *correlation coefficient*. The correlation coefficient is represented by Formula (5), where s and t represent two axes of time series data in the time domain or those of frequency spectra in the frequency domain, and M indicates the number of samples. We expected that (positively or negatively) high correlation indicates the characteristics of rotation in a particular storing position.

$$corr = \frac{\sum_{i=1}^{M}(s_i - \bar{s})(t_i - \bar{t})}{\sqrt{\sum_{i=1}^{M}(s_i - \bar{s})^2}\sqrt{\sum_{i=1}^{M}(t_i - \bar{t})^2}} \tag{5}$$

Table 4. Classification features based on correlation coefficients between two axes.

Type	Description
corr$_{time}$	Correlation coefficient in time series data
corr$_{freq,all}$	Correlation coefficient in an entire frequency spectrum
corr$_{freq,low}$	Correlation coefficient in the low-frequency range
corr$_{freq,mid}$	Correlation coefficient in the mid-frequency range
corr$_{freq,high}$	Correlation coefficient in the high-frequency range

5. Experiment

5.1. Dataset

Unlike in well-established areas, such as machine vision [36] and speech recognition [37], reference dataset, *i.e.*, the corpus, has not yet been recognized in on-body device localization. Combining datasets from different device localization projects is an option to cover a wide variety of storing positions and the diversity of people; however, this approach makes it difficult to separate the dataset for each person and, thus, to carry out LOSO-CV. Furthermore, we could find a very limited number and types of datasets publicly available for device localization [38]. Therefore, we utilized the dataset collected in our previous study [26], which was performed as summarized in Table 5. Twenty graduate/undergraduate students (2 females and 18 males) participated to the experiment, in which they were asked to walk about 5 min (30 s/trial × 10 trials) for each storing position. We asked the participants to walk as usual, so that the data could be collected from a naturalistic condition, and no special instruction about the orientation of the device was given. They wore their own clothes; we only lent them clothes in the case that they did not have clothes with pockets. Regarding bags, we utilized one typical bag for each type of category of bag, and we asked the participants to carry bags as designed; that is, for example, carrying the handbag with one hand, not slinging it over the shoulder like a "shoulder bag". In total, we obtained about 150,000 samples per position. The applicability to other dataset in terms of different activities and other positions will be examined in Sections 5.6 and 5.7 using a dataset [38].

Table 5. Condition of data collection.

Condition	Value
Way of walking and orientation of a terminal	Unconstrained
Number of subjects	20 (2 females and 18 males)
Trials per position	10
Duration of walking per trial	30 s
Terminal	NexusOne (HTC)
Sampling rate	25 Hz

5.2. Basic Performance Evaluation

We compared the combinations of the window size and the classifier (classification algorithm), which are important tuning parameters in the recognition task.

5.2.1. Method

Three classes of window size were tested, *i.e.*, 128, 256 and 512, which correspond to 5.12, 10.24 and 20.48 s, respectively. A window is generated by sliding 25 samples (1.00 s) in the data sequences. Regarding the classifier, we utilized five types of classifiers: (1) J48 tree as a decision-tree method; (2) naive Bayes as a Bayesian method; (3) a support vector machine (SVM) classifier; (4) multi-layer perceptron (MLP) as an artificial neural network-based method; and (5) RandomForest as an ensemble learning method. Here, the number of trees in RandomForest was set to 50. Ten-fold cross-validation (10-fold CV) was utilized to understand the basic classification performance, which is often utilized except for the active sensing approach (see Table 1) [13,17,22–24,28]. The Weka machine learning toolkit (version 3.6.9, University of Waikato, Hamilton, New Zealand) [39] was utilized, and the specific parameters for classifiers in Weka are summarized in Table 6.

Note that, prior to the evaluation, feature selection was performed to reduce the number of features for high generalization (avoiding overfitting to the training data) and lightweight computation. The number of selected features is 62, 63 and 61 among 182 features for window sizes of 128, 256 and 512, respectively. This means that the feature dimension was reduced to 1/3 of the original feature set. The details of the feature selection are described in Section 5.3.

Table 6. Classifier parameters in Weka.

Classifier	Parameter
J48	-C 0.25 -M 2
Naive Bayes	N/A
Support Vector Machine (SVM)	-S 0 -K 2 -D 3 -G 2.0 -R 0.0 -N 0.5 -M 40.0 -C 1.0 -E 0.0010 -P 0.1 -Z
Multi-Layer Perceptron (MLP)	-L 0.3 -M 0.2 -N 50 -V 0 -S 0 -E 20 -H a
RandomForest	-I 50 -K 0 -S 1

5.2.2. Results and Analysis

Table 7 summarizes the classification accuracy for each window size and classifier. Here, the classification accuracy is defined by Formula (6). From the table, we can understand that the accuracy basically gets higher as the window size grows and that the SVM and RandomForest classifiers performed the best at high accuracy, *i.e.*, 0.999. By taking into account the ease of parameter tuning and the processing speed, we determine to utilize RandomForest in later experiments. Regarding the window size, it seems that the accuracy of the RandomForest classifier was saturated up to 256. The window size has an impact not only on the computational cost of features, but also on the reactivity to signal changes. That is, the classifier may fail to decide the correct class on a window if a position change is detected in a window; the duration of incorrect classification depends on the size of the window, *i.e.*, the smaller window makes a duration in which the mixed patterns appear shorter. Therefore, we take 256 as the window size for the later experiment, which is 10.24 s.

$$accuracy = \frac{The\ number\ of\ correct\ classifications}{The\ number\ of\ total\ classifications} \tag{6}$$

Table 7. Basic performance in the relationship between classification accuracy *vs.* window size and the classifier (10-fold CV).

Window Size	J48	Naive Bayes	SVM	MLP	RandomForest
128	0.964	0.798	0.997	0.984	0.994
256	0.979	0.810	0.999	0.994	0.999
512	0.989	0.813	0.999	0.994	0.999

5.3. Feature Selection

In this section, we describe the method of feature selection, in which the result is focused on the window size of 256.

5.3.1. Method

We utilized a correlation-based feature selection (CFS) [40]. CFS has a heuristic evaluation function *merit*, which can specify the subset of features that are highly correlated with classes, *i.e.*, more predictive of classes, but uncorrelated with each other, *i.e.*, more concise. As described in Section 4.4, a large number of features were listed up, which may contain redundant features. Therefore, we considered that the capability of CFS was suitable for this problem. The forward selection algorithm was utilized to generate a ranking on feature subsets, which begins with no features and greedily adds features one by one. Note that CFS is a classifier-independent method of feature selection.

In the feature selection process, the window sliding width was set to 64 samples, while the other evaluations (Sections 5.2 and 5.4) were carried out with the sliding width of 25. This indicates that the evaluations were fairer than an experiment that utilizes the same sliding width as the one at feature selection. This is because the values of calculated features were almost different from each other.

5.3.2. Results and Analysis

Figure 6 shows the relationship between the size of the feature subset and the merit score of the feature subset. From the figure, three phases in the relationship are found: (1) the quick increase with up to 10 features; (2) the slight increase up to 63 features; and (3) gradual degradation to the end. Therefore, we specified a feature subset with 63 features that provides the highest merit score. Table 8 summarizes the list of selected features, in which rank-N indicates the order of participation in the selected feature subset. Furthermore, to summarize the contribution of categories, such as axis and domain from Table 8, the medians of the rank are shown in Table 9.

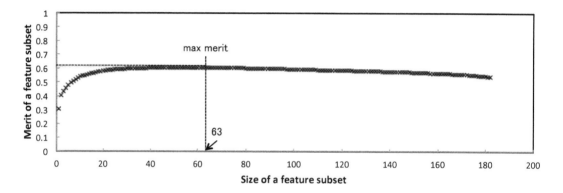

Figure 6. The relationship between the size of the feature subset and the merit score (window size: 256).

Table 8. Selected features with ranks.

Rank	Name	Rank	Name	Rank	Name
1	$\mathrm{sumPower}_{freq,mid,y}$	22	$\mathrm{f2^{nd}Max}_{freq,all,y}$	43	$\mathrm{sdev}_{freq,low,z}$
2	$\mathrm{corr}_{time,my}$	23	$\mathrm{max}_{time,z}$	44	$\mathrm{corr}_{freq,all,yz}$
3	$\mathrm{sumPower}_{freq,high,y}$	24	$\mathrm{corr}_{freq,high,mz}$	45	$\mathrm{min}_{time,y}$
4	$\mathrm{entr}_{freq,low,z}$	25	$\mathrm{corr}_{freq,low,yz}$	46	$\mathrm{bin9}_{time,x}$
5	$\mathrm{corr}_{time,mz}$	26	$\mathrm{IQR}_{freq,all,y}$	47	$\mathrm{sumPower}_{freq,high,m}$
6	$\mathrm{entr}_{freq,low,x}$	27	$\mathrm{3^{rd}Q}_{freq,all,z}$	48	$\mathrm{bin4}_{time,y}$
7	$\mathrm{3^{rd}Q}_{freq,all,y}$	28	$\mathrm{corr}_{freq,low,zx}$	49	$\mathrm{corr}_{freq,low,xy}$
8	$\mathrm{sumPower}_{freq,high,x}$	29	$\mathrm{max}_{freq,all,x}$	50	$\mathrm{bin5}_{time,z}$
9	$\mathrm{corr}_{freq,high,my}$	30	$\mathrm{sumPower}_{freq,mid,x}$	51	$\mathrm{sumPower}_{freq,low,y}$
10	$\mathrm{corr}_{freq,all,zx}$	31	$\mathrm{entr}_{freq,low,y}$	52	$\mathrm{corr}_{time,yz}$
11	$\mathrm{RMS}_{time,m}$	32	$\mathrm{corr}_{freq,mid,mz}$	53	$\mathrm{bin3}_{time,m}$
12	$\mathrm{corr}_{freq,all,xy}$	33	$\mathrm{fMax}_{freq,all,x}$	54	$\mathrm{entr}_{freq,mid,z}$
13	$\mathrm{maxSdev}_{freq,all,y}$	34	$\mathrm{sumPower}_{freq,mid,m}$	55	$\mathrm{sumPower}_{freq,mid,z}$
14	$\mathrm{corr}_{freq,mid,my}$	35	$\mathrm{bin6}_{time,x}$	56	$\mathrm{bin2}_{time,x}$
15	$\mathrm{entr}_{freq,all,z}$	36	$\mathrm{corr}_{freq,all,my}$	57	$\mathrm{max}_{time,y}$
16	$\mathrm{entr}_{freq,all,x}$	37	$\mathrm{max}_{freq,mid,y}$	58	$\mathrm{max}_{freq,high,x}$
17	$\mathrm{sdev}_{freq,mid,y}$	38	$\mathrm{min}_{time,x}$	59	$\mathrm{IQR}_{time,z}$
18	$\mathrm{entr}_{freq,all,y}$	39	$\mathrm{corr}_{freq,mid,mx}$	60	$\mathrm{f2^{nd}Max}_{freq,all,x}$
19	$\mathrm{3^{rd}Q}_{freq,all,x}$	40	$\mathrm{corr}_{time,xy}$	61	$\mathrm{corr}_{freq,mid,xy}$
20	$\mathrm{corr}_{time,mx}$	41	$\mathrm{sdev}_{freq,high,y}$	62	$\mathrm{bin1}_{time,z}$
21	$\mathrm{max}_{freq,high,y}$	42	$\mathrm{bin6}_{time,z}$	63	$\mathrm{IQR}_{freq,all,m}$

Table 9. Median of the rank and the ratio of selected features for each category.

	Calculation Target		Domain	
	Single Axis	Multi Axes (Correlation)	Time	Frequency
Median of rank	34	26.5	45	27.5
Proportion of selection	45/63	18/63	19/63	44/63

	Individual Axis (Axes) Series									
	x	y	z	m	xy	zx	yz	mx	my	mz
Median of rank	34	24	43	40.5	44.5	44	19	29.5	11.5	24
Proportion of definition	12/38	16/38	11/38	6/38	4/5	3/5	2/5	2/5	4/5	3/5

Note: in the case of an even number of features, the average of two central successive values was utilized.

With respect an individual axis, the y-axis is most contributive to classification. We consider that this is because a ground reaction force mainly influences the vertical direction, which is the y-axis in the usual cases of neck, chest pocket and trouser pockets. The propagated ground reaction force may have different acceleration patterns in such storing positions.

The correlation-based features ($corr_{time|freq}$) generally performed well, as shown in Table 9, *i.e.*, the rows of the "median of rank" in the upper part (26.5) and the "proportion of definition" in the lower part (more than 0.4). The effectiveness of the correlation between the magnitude of linear acceleration m and the other axes, e.g., $corr_{time,my}$, indicates that the force is dominantly given to the axis. A scatter plot in Figure 7a shows the distribution of the value of $corr_{time,my}$, in which (1) "neck" and (2) "chest pocket" have a clear negative and/or positive correlation between the y- and m-axes. We consider that this is because a smartphone stored in these positions basically faces toward the front in the portrait orientation and moves up-and-down due to the strong influence of the ground reaction force. By contrast, the high correlation between the x-, y- and z-axes represents rotational motions. For example, the high correlation between the x- and y-axes indicates a motion around the yaw angle when a smartphone is placed in portrait orientation. We consider that such a yaw angle motion might be well observed when a terminal is put in the trouser pocket, because a terminal in portrait orientation swings with the motion of the legs. We also consider that this is a reason why a weak correlation is observed in positions, except for "neck" and "chest pocket", in Figure 7a. Similarly, there might be a particular linear and rotational motion patterns in each storing position. The effectiveness of rotational elements is consistent with the findings in [29], in which rotational information, *i.e.*, pitch and roll, was calculated per sample, and some features, such as "mean" and "root mean square", were calculated in a window of such rotational information. In this case, the degree of rotational change is utilized to characterize the storing positions. We consider that our correlation-based features represent the level of dominance of the rotational axis in a window for specific storing positions, which is regarded as another aspect of the classification feature.

Regarding the comparison with the domains, 44 out of 63 features were originated from the frequency domain, which indicates that the features obtained from the frequency domain are contributive. Especially, eight out of the top 10 features are frequency domain-originated ones, as shown in Table 8, in which three "sum of power ($sumPower_{freq}$)" and two "frequency entropy ($entr_{freq}$)" were ranked within the top 10. As described in Section 4.4, $sumPower_{freq}$ represents the intensity of movement in a certain time window, while $entr_{freq}$ is a measure of the frequency distribution of the frequency components. The difference of the ground reaction force propagated through the body and the container of a smartphone might have different intensities. Figure 7b shows the distribution of the value of $sumPower_{freq,mid,y}$, where large values can be found in (4) the trouser front pocket and (5) the trouser back pocket. We consider that this is because the ground reaction force is directly transmitted to the trouser pockets. Regarding entropy, Figure 7c is an example ($entr_{freq,low,z}$), where the frequency entropy of "neck" is relatively high. This might indicate that the signal obtained from the z-axis at the "neck" contains diverse frequency components with relatively uniform power. As inferred above, the y-axis is the dominant axis at the "neck", and conversely, the z-axis is subject to disordered force.

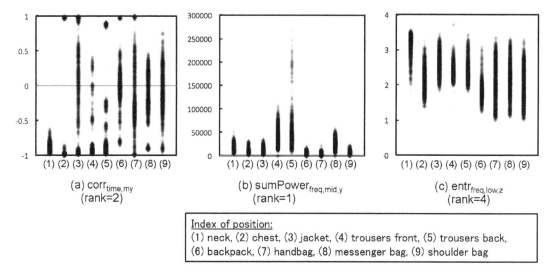

(a) corr$_{time,my}$
(rank=2)

(b) sumPower$_{freq,mid,y}$
(rank=1)

(c) entr$_{freq,low,z}$
(rank=4)

Index of position:
(1) neck, (2) chest, (3) jacket, (4) trousers front, (5) trousers back,
(6) backpack, (7) handbag, (8) messenger bag, (9) shoulder bag

Figure 7. Scatter plot of the distribution of features by target positions. The thick and dark portion indicates dense plots.

5.4. Evaluation with Unknown Subjects

5.4.1. Method

The performance evaluation based on n-fold CV shows an optimistic result because $(n-1)/n$ of data from each person are included in the training dataset in theory, and hence, the classifier mostly "knows" about the subjects in advance. To see the capability of the robustness of the recognition system between individuals, we carried out LOSO cross-validation with the same dataset as 10-fold CV. LOSO-CV is carried out by testing a dataset from a particular person with a classifier that is trained without a dataset from the person. The result of the LOSO test can represent the performance in a realistic situation, such that a person purchases an on-body placement-aware functionality from a manufacturer or a third-party, because the data from a particular person are not utilized to train the classifier. Therefore, LOSO-CV is regarded as a fairer and practical test method, which has recently been getting attention [26–29].

5.4.2. Results and Analysis

Table 10 summarizes the confusion matrix of the average number of classified results per person. Here, *recall* and *precision* are defined by Formula (7) and Formula (8), respectively. The average accuracy per person is 0.805 with a maximum of 0.977, a minimum of 0.610 and a median of 0.828. By comparing to the work [26], which does not contain the m-axis and utilized a different classifier, *i.e.*, SVM, the average accuracy was improved by 0.059 (5.9 points in percentage). "Neck" was classified very accurately, while "jacket" was the most difficult case. The shape and the size of jacket pockets are relatively diverse and large. Furthermore, the bottom of a jacket sometimes flaps as a person walks, which makes the movement of a smartphone diverse. We consider that this is a reason why the recall of "jacket" is low, *i.e.*, 0.633. Additionally, the positions on the body are similar to each other in the case of "jacket" and "shoulder bag", as shown in Figure 1. Such similarity of position might cause the wrong determination of the movement of a smartphone.

$$recall_i = \frac{The\ number\ of\ cases\ correctly\ classified\ into\ class_i}{Total\ number\ of\ test\ cases\ in\ class_i} \tag{7}$$

$$precision_i = \frac{The\ number\ of\ cases\ correctly\ classified\ into\ class_i}{Total\ number\ of\ cases\ classified\ into\ class_i} \tag{8}$$

Table 10. Confusion matrix of LOSO-CV for the 9-class classification (averaged per person).

Answer\decision	a	b	c	d	e	f	g	h	i	Recall
a. neck	187	3	3	0	0	0	0	0	0	0.970
b. chest	0	168	17	0	0	0	1	0	3	0.889
c. jacket	8	14	119	5	3	12	2	7	19	0.633
d. trouser front	1	0	6	146	20	0	1	16	0	0.768
e. trouser back	1	3	7	29	145	0	0	9	1	0.744
f. backpack	0	10	1	0	0	156	14	1	15	0.794
g. handbag	0	11	4	0	0	12	162	0	9	0.818
h. messenger bag	0	11	12	0	0	1	1	171	3	0.853
i. shoulder bag	0	0	17	0	0	1	19	5	155	0.785
Precision	0.945	0.767	0.639	0.810	0.856	0.862	0.813	0.823	0.751	0.805

Moreover, the table shows two groups of frequent misclassification, *i.e.*, (1) trouser front and back pockets and (2) backpack, handbag, messenger bag and shoulder bag. By taking into the semantic similarity between "trouser front pocket" and "trouser back pocket", these two classes are merged into a higher level of positional context "trousers (pockets)". Similarly, the four types of bag are integrated into "bags". Table 11 shows the confusion matrix by the merge operation, in which the merged rows and columns were averaged. As a result, the accuracy was improved to be 0.859.

Let us analyze the variation of classification performance in individuals. Figure 8 shows the sorted individual accuracy. Based on the fact that the median accuracy of the 9-class classification is larger than the averaged accuracy, we consider that there are some persons whose accuracies are very low. The figure implies that the classification for 6 persons, *i.e.*, Persons J, M, D, T, G and B, degraded the overall accuracy. The common characteristics of these 6 persons are basically consistent with what was described above, *i.e.*, large confusion within "bags" and "trousers", as well as confusion between "jacket" and "bags".

Table 11. Confusion matrix of LOSO-CV for the merged 5-class classification (averaged per person).

Answer\decision	a	b	c	x	y	Recall
a. neck	187	3	3	0	0	0.970
b. chest	0	168	17	0	4	0.889
c. jacket	8	14	119	8	40	0.633
x. trousers	1	2	7	170	13	0.883
y. bag	0	8	9	0	181	0.914
Precision	0.953	0.867	0.776	0.949	0.761	0.859

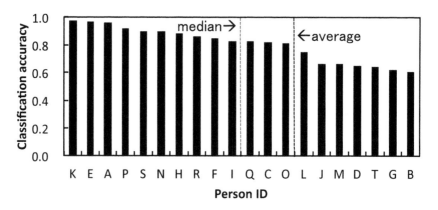

Figure 8. Classification accuracy per person sorted by the value.

5.5. Compatibility Analysis

The compatibility of the classifier among subjects was analyzed.

5.5.1. Method

Classifiers are trained per individuals, and a particular classifier was tested with the datasets from the remaining persons, which was repeated with all persons.

5.5.2. Results and Analysis

Table 12 shows the "compatibility matrix". The number placed in a cell with row i and column j is the averaged accuracy against the dataset from person j that is tested with a classifier trained with the dataset from person i. For example, the value 0.69 at (A, E) means that the dataset from Person E was classified with an accuracy of 0.69 by a classifier trained by Person A. An exception is the values on the diagonal line, in which training and testing were carried out against the dataset from the same person by 10-fold CV. Therefore, the case is considered to be an ideal case, in which a classifier is personalized for the person. In the table, the values 0.0 and 1.0 are white and black, and the other values ranges are grayscale colors.

The rightmost column is the average of the values on each row, which indicates how well a classifier trained by the dataset from a particular person fits to other persons. Therefore, the value can be referred to as "average fitness". Here, a classifier by Person A's dataset is the best fit one, *i.e.*, 0.58 on average, while the average fitness of Person G is the least suitable one (0.35). In training a classifier, reducing the weight on the dataset from persons whose average fitness is low, e.g., Persons C, D and G, would improve LOSO-CV accuracy by a single classifier.

By contrast, the analysis of the averages per column suggests the possibility of selective classifier tuning. The undermost row is the average on each column, which represents the generality of the dataset from a person. The best-classified dataset on average is the one from Person E (0.57), and Person J's dataset failed to be classified well on average with classifiers by the dataset from others (0.37). The classifiers trained by the datasets from Persons B, I and L did not perform well against the dataset from Person J with an accuracy of 0.18, 0.21 and 0.22, respectively. By contrast, classifiers trained by the datasets from Persons A, N and S classified Person J's dataset relatively well (0.54, 0.62 and 0.51, respectively). This suggests that the LOSO-CV accuracy might be improved if a classifier can be tuned for a person using datasets from others who have similar characteristics.

Table 12. Compatibility matrix of the accuracy obtained by training and testing with person-by-person.

Person ID whose dataset was used for testing.

Person ID whose dataset was used for training.	A	B	C	D	E	F	G	H	I	J	K	L	M	N	O	P	Q	R	S	T	ave.
A	1.00	0.41	0.34	0.43	0.69	0.61	0.31	0.66	0.57	0.54	0.60	0.76	0.62	0.67	0.67	0.66	0.67	0.69	0.74	0.43	0.58
B	0.37	1.00	0.43	0.66	0.38	0.51	0.43	0.49	0.39	0.18	0.39	0.37	0.47	0.38	0.49	0.34	0.58	0.33	0.45	0.39	0.42
C	0.41	0.32	1.00	0.52	0.62	0.35	0.39	0.28	0.32	0.41	0.36	0.28	0.29	0.47	0.51	0.19	0.42	0.15	0.34	0.30	0.37
D	0.38	0.50	0.37	1.00	0.55	0.37	0.34	0.32	0.43	0.28	0.50	0.44	0.25	0.35	0.37	0.45	0.27	0.57	0.41	0.45	0.40
E	0.67	0.43	0.54	0.58	1.00	0.55	0.47	0.52	0.57	0.47	0.75	0.49	0.33	0.80	0.55	0.67	0.46	0.45	0.62	0.47	0.55
F	0.53	0.40	0.48	0.49	0.57	1.00	0.32	0.65	0.30	0.40	0.41	0.60	0.32	0.51	0.41	0.35	0.63	0.56	0.36	0.25	0.45
G	0.28	0.28	0.37	0.49	0.47	0.26	1.00	0.26	0.39	0.32	0.45	0.26	0.38	0.27	0.44	0.43	0.29	0.23	0.43	0.30	0.35
H	0.65	0.49	0.27	0.41	0.48	0.66	0.30	1.00	0.45	0.30	0.53	0.23	0.54	0.53	0.65	0.50	0.64	0.58	0.36	0.30	0.47
I	0.68	0.44	0.45	0.53	0.74	0.50	0.71	0.59	1.00	0.21	0.53	0.42	0.44	0.53	0.64	0.59	0.61	0.60	0.44	0.32	0.52
J	0.44	0.25	0.48	0.22	0.54	0.51	0.43	0.44	0.35	1.00	0.49	0.37	0.34	0.57	0.49	0.61	0.34	0.38	0.67	0.43	0.44
K	0.50	0.55	0.53	0.52	0.71	0.43	0.41	0.65	0.55	0.36	1.00	0.54	0.68	0.58	0.67	0.68	0.47	0.56	0.74	0.54	0.56
L	0.53	0.50	0.19	0.53	0.50	0.62	0.32	0.36	0.36	0.22	0.56	1.00	0.39	0.33	0.45	0.43	0.64	0.75	0.39	0.33	0.44
M	0.51	0.50	0.20	0.27	0.28	0.37	0.48	0.65	0.45	0.27	0.79	0.22	1.00	0.32	0.54	0.58	0.40	0.42	0.54	0.54	0.44
N	0.52	0.46	0.59	0.44	0.76	0.52	0.41	0.61	0.47	0.62	0.56	0.54	0.25	1.00	0.54	0.64	0.65	0.55	0.53	0.41	0.53
O	0.62	0.46	0.50	0.44	0.71	0.52	0.63	0.62	0.67	0.42	0.60	0.37	0.71	0.68	1.00	0.43	0.46	0.43	0.43	0.32	0.53
P	0.74	0.53	0.49	0.39	0.49	0.51	0.45	0.61	0.55	0.35	0.68	0.50	0.62	0.54	0.57	1.00	0.51	0.69	0.68	0.40	0.54
Q	0.67	0.49	0.45	0.38	0.52	0.62	0.37	0.57	0.48	0.37	0.45	0.60	0.41	0.47	0.50	0.54	1.00	0.42	0.53	0.46	0.49
R	0.57	0.44	0.32	0.50	0.68	0.65	0.27	0.61	0.44	0.45	0.62	0.59	0.38	0.53	0.54	0.60	0.53	1.00	0.44	0.37	0.50
S	0.75	0.50	0.42	0.49	0.55	0.47	0.41	0.50	0.50	0.51	0.67	0.57	0.45	0.58	0.47	0.57	0.53	0.56	1.00	0.65	0.53
T	0.39	0.26	0.50	0.45	0.52	0.43	0.31	0.41	0.32	0.38	0.57	0.38	0.49	0.47	0.42	0.35	0.52	0.34	0.57	1.00	0.43
ave.	0.54	0.43	0.42	0.46	0.57	0.50	0.41	0.52	0.45	0.37	0.55	0.45	0.44	0.50	0.52	0.51	0.51	0.49	0.51	0.40	

5.6. Robustness of Selected Features against New Positions

In Section 5.3, 63 features were selected for what are less redundant and more predictive of 9 classes defined in Section 4.1. In this section, the applicability of the feature set to other storing positions is examined.

5.6.1. Method

A dataset collected in [38] was utilized. The dataset was collected from four positions of 10 people, *i.e.*, "trouser front pocket", "wrist", "upper arm and belt", using a Samsung Galaxy SII smartphone during seven activities of "walking", "jogging", "biking", "upstairs", "downstairs", "standing" and "sitting", among which, we picked the data from "wrist", "upper arm" and "belt" during walking. Therefore, the classification targets increased to 12 positions. The data were down-sampled by 1/2, so that the sampling rate could be consistent with ours, *i.e.*, 25 Hz, since the data were sampled at 50 Hz. The data were then merged into our original dataset, and a 10-fold CV using a RandomForest classifier was carried out.

5.6.2. Results and Analysis

The F-measure of the 10-fold CV of 12-class classification was proven to be at the same level of that of the 9-class classification, *i.e.*, 0.999 (see Table 7 for the 9-class classification). Notably, the F-measures for the added classes were 1.00. We consider that "wrist" and "upper arm" had quite different movements from other positions, as pointed out by Incel [29]. Regarding the position of "belt", we consider that a device on a belt should have a certain degree of uniqueness, because it is fixed, *i.e.*, not stored in a free-moving position, such as a jacket pocket and a backpack, and placed between the lower and upper body.

5.7. Storing Position Recognition during Periodic Motions other Than Walking

In this article, we focused on the recognition of the storing position of a device during walking based on the thought that walking is the most frequent and consistent activity throughout a day. As described in Section 4.3, a preprocessing was employed to pass through a segment of periodic motion that we regard as a walking period. However, due to the characteristics of the algorithm, other periodic motions, such as "jogging" and "biking", could still be passed through. To understand the robustness of the recognition against such accidental cases, a small-scale experiment was carried out.

5.7.1. Method

A classifier was trained by our original dataset (see Section 5.1) with the selected 63 features, which was obtained from 20 people during walking. As a dataset for testing during other activities, the dataset collected in [38] was again utilized. We removed "standing" and "sitting" because these two non-periodic activities can be easily filtered out at the preprocessing based on constancy detection. In addition, although the dataset were collected from four positions, *i.e.*, "trouser front pocket", "upper arm", "wrist" and "belt", we only utilized "trouser front pocket", because it was included in the original dataset. Classification was carried out per person, and the *recalls* (Formula (7)) were averaged.

5.7.2. Results and Analysis

Table 13 summarizes the recalls for "trouser front pocket" and the names of the most confused classes with their recalls.

A window obtained from "trouser front pocket" during biking was misrecognized as "jacket" with a recall of 0.321. We consider that this is because the jacket hem in which the device is stored touches the thigh during biking and that this made the movement of the device in the trouser front pocket similar to that of the jacket. Regarding stepping up and down activities, "downstairs" was pretty low with a recall of 0.150, while that of "upstairs" was relatively high with a recall of 0.815. We consider that the difference comes from the impact with the ground. The motion of stepping down looks relatively different from walking compared to stepping up due to the strong downward force, which might have made the recognition difficult.

Table 13. Averaged recalls per person against the dataset obtained during various activities.

	Biking	Jogging	Upstairs	Downstairs
Recall of trousers front pocket	0.009	0.673	0.815	0.150
Most confused class and	Jacket	Trousers back	Neck	Neck
the false recognition for the class	0.321	0.240	0.118	0.806

6. Discussions

6.1. Improving the Recognition Performance against an Unknown Person

The compatibility matrix presented in Section 5.5 suggests that the LOSO-CV accuracy might be improved if a classifier can be tuned for a person using datasets from others who have similar characteristics. The selection needs not to be person based. Instead, tuning a classifier based on the selection of an appropriate subset from all data might work better. In either case, the dataset for tuning a classifier needs to be identified when a person starts utilizing the system for the first time, which is a challenging issue, because no label to a class, *i.e.*, storing position, is given for the first time usage. We will examine the possibility of identifying an appropriate dataset based on the position-independent variables, such as walking frequency.

6.2. Storing Position Recognition during Various Activities

As described in Section 4.3, when non-periodic motions, such as "standing" and "sitting", are detected, a previous decision during a periodic motion is carried over. Therefore, an issue to be considered is the occurrence of periodic motions other than the original "walking", although we take a stance that walking is the most frequent and consistent activity throughout the day. In Section 5.7, the data labeled as "trouser front pocket" were utilized to evaluate if they are correctly recognized during various periodic motions. The result showed that "biking" and "stepping down stairs" were difficult to handle when a device is put into the trouser front pocket.

The functionality of filtering out the period of biking activity needs to be investigated by paying attention to the key difference between a biking activity and the other "walking"-related activities. We consider that the key difference is the existence of the influence of the ground reaction force. Once the period of biking activity is identified, it can be handled in the same way as other non-periodic motions, *i.e.*, carrying over the previous decision. Note that, we can ignore the case with upper body positions, because a device stored in a chest pocket, for example, moves less periodically than in a trouser pocket, which is easily filtered out by the current preprocessing.

Regarding stepping up and down activities, especially in the case of "downstairs", the difference in acceleration from "walking" might not be so large as in "biking". Therefore, it might be difficult to filter out; however, a workaround is to apply temporal smoothing from the long-term point of view, because the stepping up and down activities keep up for a couple of minutes at most.

6.3. Valid Applications with the Current Recognition Performance

The importance of on-body position recognition is described in Section 2. As shown in Table 11, "neck" and "trouser pockets" were classified very well, which is suitable for a class of applications that monitor environmental conditions, such as temperature and humidity. The measurement from the neck often differs from the trouser pockets due to the effect of body heat and sweat [18]. An application can take an appropriate action, e.g., correction to the value assumed to be measured outside and alerting a user, when a monitoring device (smartphone) is inside a trouser pocket. Furthermore, a placement-aware audio volume adaptation would work well.

Moreover, the high *precision* for "neck" allows a sensor placement-aware activity recognition to recognize activities related to the upper part of the body, e.g., brushing teeth [4]. A position-specific activity recognizer might be chosen in the case that the position recognition result is reliable, *i.e.*, a position with high precision, such as the "neck"; by contrast, a common recognizer can be utilized against positions with low precision, such as "jacket" and "bag", in order to avoid significant degradation of the recognition due to the wrong choice of a recognizer.

7. Conclusions

In this article, we proposed a method of localizing a smartphone on the body. An accelerometer is utilized to recognize the storing position from nine candidate positions based on the similarity of acceleration patterns during walking. We systematically defined 182 features calculated from the axes of an accelerometer, including the magnitude of the x-, y- and z-axes. As a result of correlation-based feature selection, 63 contributive features were selected that are more predictive and less redundant features than the remaining 119 features. Through the analysis of the contribution of each feature, we found that: (1) the features originated from y-axis are the most contributive; (2) the features calculated based on the correlation between two axes generally performed well compared to single-axis-originated ones, and the correlation between the magnitude axis and one of the other three axes is especially powerful; and (3) the features in the frequency domain are more powerful than the ones in the time domain; especially the sum of the power and frequency entropy are powerful. These findings would contribute to defining other features to accomplish the position recognition performance.

Furthermore, the selected features were proven to be effective against new activities, *i.e.*, "wrist", "upper arm" and "belt", which were not considered during the selection process.

The LOSO-CV evaluation with 20 subjects showed that the accuracy of nine-class classification was 0.801. Meanwhile, the accuracy against merged-class classification was 0.859, in which trouser front and back pockets were integrated into one category of "trouser pocket", and four types of bags were merged into "bag". Although a fair comparison among existing work is not practical due to the diversity of the system and environmental parameters, we consider that the accuracy falls into the category of being good. The "compatibility matrix" showed the possibilities of improving LOSO-CV accuracy by selecting an appropriate dataset prior to training a single classifier or customizing a classifier for each unknown user on the fly. In addition, we need to make the system robust against various activities that appear in daily life to improve the accuracy of recognition.

Acknowledgments: This work was supported by Ministry of Education, Culture, Sports, Science and Technology (MEXT) Grants-in-Aid for Scientific Research (A) No. 23240014.

Conflicts of Interest: The author declares no conflict of interest.

References

1. Okumura, F.; Kubota, A.; Hatori, Y.; Matsumoto, K.; Hashimoto, M.; Koike, A. A Study on Biometric Authentication based on Arm Sweep Action with Acceleration Sensor. In Proceedings of the International Symposium on Intelligent Signal Processing and Communications (ISPACS '06), Yonago, Japan, 12–15 December 2006; pp. 219–222.

2. Gellersen, H.; Schmidt, A.; Beigl, M. Multi-Sensor Context-Awareness in Mobile Devices and Smart Artifacts. *J. Mob. Netw. Appl.* **2002**, *7*, 341–351.

3. Kwapisz, J.R.; Weiss, G.M.; Moore, S.A. Activity recognition using cell phone accelerometers. *SIGKDD Explor. Newsl.* **2011**, *12*, 74–82.

4. Pirttikangas, S.; Fujinami, K.; Nakajima, T. Feature Selection and Activity Recognition from Wearable Sensors. In Proceedings of the International Symposium on Ubiquitous Computing Systems (UCS 2006), Seoul, Korea, 11–13 October 2006; pp. 516–527.

5. Blanke, U.; Schiele, B. Sensing Location in the Pocket. In Proceedings of the 10th International Conference on Ubiquitous Computing (Ubicomp 2008), Seoul, Korea, 21–24 September 2008.

6. Rai, A.; Chintalapudi, K.K.; Padmanabhan, V.N.; Sen, R. Zee: Zero-effort Crowdsourcing for Indoor Localization. In Proceedings of the 18th Annual International Conference on Mobile Computing and Networking (MobiCom 2012), Istanbul, Turkey, 22–26 August 2012.

7. Sugimori, D.; Iwamoto, T.; Matsumoto, M. A Study about Identification of Pedestrian by Using 3-Axis Accelerometer. In Proceedings of the IEEE 17th International Conference on Embedded and Real-Time Computing Systems and Applications (RTCSA), Toyama, Japan, 28–31 August 2011; pp. 134–137.

8. Goldman, J.; Shilton, K.; Burke, J.; Estrin, D.; Hansen, M.; Ramanathan, N.; Reddy, S.; Samanta, V.; Srivastava, M.; West, R. Participatory Sensing: A Citizen-Powered Approach to Illuminating the Patterns that Shape Our World. Available onlie: https://www.wilsoncenter.org/sites/default/files/participatory _sensing.pdf (accessed on 23 March 2016).

9. Stevens, M.; D'Hondt, E. Crowdsourcing of Pollution Data using Smartphones. In Proceedings of the 1st Ubiquitous Crowdsourcing Workshop, Copenhagen, Denmark, 26–29 September 2010.

10. Cui, Y.; Chipchase, J.; Ichikawa, F. A Cross Culture Study on Phone Carrying and Physical Personalization. In Proceedings of the 12th International Conference on Human-Computer Interaction, Beijing, China, 22–27 July 2007; pp. 483–492.

11. Diaconita, I.; Reinhardt, A.; Englert, F.; Christin, D.; Steinmetz, R. Do you hear what I hear? Using acoustic probing to detect smartphone locations. In Proceedings of the IEEE International Conference on Pervasive Computing and Communication Workshops (PerCom Workshops), Budapest, Hungary, 24–28 March 2014; pp. 1–9.

12. Diaconita, I.; Reinhardt, A.; Christin, D.; Rensing, C. Inferring Smartphone Positions Based on Collecting the Environment's Response to Vibration Motor Actuation. In Proceedings of the 11th ACM Symposium on QoS and Security for Wireless and Mobile Networks (Q2SWinet 2015), Cancun, Mexico, 2–6 November 2015.

13. Harrison, C.; Hudson, S.E. Lightweight material detection for placement-aware mobile computing. In Proceedings of the 21st annual ACM symposium on User interface software and technology (UIST 2008), Monterey, CA, USA, 19–22 October 2008.

14. Bao, L.; Intille, S.S. Activity recognition from user-annotated acceleration data. In Proceedings of the 2nd International Conference on Pervasive Computing (Pervasive 2004), Linz/Vienna, Austria, 18–23 April 2004.

15. Atallah, L.; Lo, B.; King, R.; Yang, G.Z. Sensor Placement for Activity Detection Using Wearable Accelerometers. In Proceedings of the 2010 International Conference on Body Sensor Networks (BSN), Singapore, 7–9 June 2010; pp. 24–29.

16. Lane, N.D.; Miluzzo, E.; Lu, H.; Peebles, D.; Choudhury, T.; Campbell, A.T. A survey of mobile phone sensing. *IEEE Commun. Mag.* **2010**, *48*, 140–150.

17. Miluzzo, E.; Papandrea, M.; Lane, N.; Lu, H.; Campbell, A. Pocket, Bag, Hand, *etc.*-Automatically Detecting Phone Context through Discovery. In Proceedings of First International Workshop on Sensing for App Phones (PhoneSense 2010), Zurich, Switzerland, 2 November 2010.

18. Fujinami, K.; Xue, Y.; Murata, S.; Hosokawa, S. A Human-Probe System That Considers On-body Position of a Mobile Phone with Sensors. In *Distributed, Ambient, and Pervasive Interactions*; Streitz, N., Stephanidis, C., Eds.; Springer: Berlin/Heidelberg, Germany, 2013; Volume 8028, pp. 99–108.

19. Vaitl, C.; Kunze, K.; Lukowicz, P. Does On-body Location of a GPS Receiver Matter? In *International Workshop on Wearable and Implantable Body Sensor Networks (BSN'10)*; IEEE Computer Society: Los Alamitos, CA, USA, 2010; pp. 219–221.

20. Blum, J.; Greencorn, D.; Cooperstock, J. Smartphone Sensor Reliability for Augmented Reality Applications. In *Mobile and Ubiquitous Systems: Computing, Networking, and Services*; Zheng, K., Li, M., Jiang, H., Eds.; Springer: Berlin/Heidelberg, Germany, 2013; Volume 120, pp. 127–138.

21. Fujinami, K.; Jin, C.; Kouchi, S. Tracking On-body Location of a Mobile Phone. In Proceedings of the 14th Annual IEEE International Symposium on Wearable Computers (ISWC 2010), Orlando, FL, USA, 9–14 July 2010; pp. 190–197.

22. Shi, Y.; Shi, Y.; Liu, J. A rotation based method for detecting on-body positions of mobile devices. In Proceedings of the 13th International Conference on Ubiquitous Computing, ACM (UbiComp '11), Beijing, China, 17–21 September 2011; pp. 559–560.

23. Vahdatpour, A.; Amini, N.; Sarrafzadeh, M. On-body device localization for health and medical monitoring applications. In Proceedings of the 2011 IEEE International Conference on Pervasive Computing and Communications, Seattle, WA, USA, 21–25 March 2011; pp. 37–44.

24. Kunze, K.; Lukowicz, P.; Junker, H.; Tröster, G. Where am I: Recognizing On-body Positions of Wearable Sensors. In Proceedings of International Workshop on Location- and Context-Awareness (LoCA 2005), Oberpfaffenhofen, Germany, 12–13 May 2005; pp. 264–275.

25. Mannini, A.; Sabatini, A.M.; Intille, S.S. Accelerometry-based recognition of the placement sites of a wearable sensor. *Perv. Mob. Comput.* **2015**, *21*, 62–74.

26. Fujinami, K.; Kouchi, S. Recognizing a Mobile Phone's Storing Position as a Context of a Device and a User. In *Mobile and Ubiquitous Systems: Computing, Networking, and Services*; Zheng, K., Li, M., Jiang, H., Eds.; Springer: Berlin/Heidelberg, Germany, 2013; Volume 120, pp. 76–88.

27. Wiese, J.; Saponas, T.S.; Brush, A.B. Phoneprioception: Enabling Mobile Phones to Infer Where They Are Kept. In Proceedings of the SIGCHI Conference on Human Factors in Computing Systems (CHI '13), Paris, France, 27 April–2 May 2013.

28. Alanezi, K.; Mishra, S. Design, implementation and evaluation of a smartphone position discovery service for accurate context sensing. *Comput. Electr. Eng.* **2015**, *44*, 307–323.

29. Incel, O.D. Analysis of Movement, Orientation and Rotation-Based Sensing for Phone Placement Recognition. *Sensors* **2015**, *15*, 25474–25506.

30. Kunze, K.; Lukowicz, P. Dealing with Sensor Displacement in Motion-based Onbody Activity Recognition Systems. In Proceedings of the 10th International Conference on Ubiquitous Computing (UbiComp '08), Seoul, Korea, 21–24 September 2008.

31. Zhang, L.; Pathak, P.H.; Wu, M.; Zhao, Y.; Mohapatra, P. AccelWord: Energy Efficient Hotword Detection Through Accelerometer. In Proceedings of the 13th Annual International Conference on Mobile Systems, Applications, and Services (MobiSys'15), Florence, Italy, 19–22 May 2015.

32. Jung, J.; Choi, S. Perceived Magnitude and Power Consumption of Vibration Feedback in Mobile Devices. In *Human-Computer Interaction. Interaction Platforms and Techniques*; Jacko, J., Ed.; Springer: Berlin/Heidelberg, Germany, 2007; Volume 4551, pp. 354–363.

33. Murao, K.; Terada, T. A motion recognition method by constancy-decision. In Proceedings of the 14th International Symposium on Wearable Computers (ISWC 2010), Seoul, Korea, 10–13 October 2010; pp. 69–72.

34. Hemminki, S.; Nurmi, P.; Tarkoma, S. Gravity and Linear Acceleration Estimation on Mobile Devices. In Proceedings of the 11th International Conference on Mobile and Ubiquitous Systems: Computing, Networking and Services (MobiQuitous 2014), London, UK, 2–5 December 2014; pp. 50–59.

35. Cho, S.J.; Choi, E.; Bang, W.C.; Yang, J.; Sohn, J.; Kim, D.Y.; Lee, Y.B.; Kim, S. Two-stage Recognition of Raw Acceleration Signals for 3-D Gesture-Understanding Cell Phones. In Proceedings of the Tenth International Workshop on Frontiers in Handwriting Recognition, La Baule, France, 23–26 October 2006.

36. Li, F.-F.; Fergus, R.; Perona, P. One-shot learning of object categories. *IEEE Trans. Pattern Anal. Mach. Intell.* **2006**, *28*, 594–611.

37. Paul, D.B.; Baker, J.M. The Design for the Wall Street Journal-based CSR Corpus. In Proceedings of the Workshop on Speech and Natural Language, Pacific Grove, CA, USA, 19–22 February 1991; pp. 357–362.

38. Shoaib, M.; Bosch, S.; Incel, O.D.; Scholten, H.; Havinga, P.J.M. Fusion of Smartphone Motion Sensors for Physical Activity Recognition. *Sensors* **2014**, *14*, 10146–10176.

39. *Weka 3—Data Mining with Open Source Machine Learning Software in Java.* Machine Learning Group at University of Waikato, Hamilton, New Zealand. Available online: http://www.cs.waikato.ac.nz/ml/weka/ (accessed on 15 March 2016).

40. Hall, M.A. Correlation-Based Feature Selection for Machine Learning. Ph.D. Thesis, The University of Waikato, Hamilton, New Zealand, 1999.

8

Nearest Neighbor Search in the Metric Space of a Complex Network for Community Detection

Suman Saha * and Satya P. Ghrera

Department of Computer Science and Engineering, Jaypee University of Information Technology, Waknaghat, Solan 173215, India; sp.ghrera@juit.ac.in
* Correspondence: suman.saha@juit.ac.in

Academic Editors: Ana Paula Couto da Silva and Pedro O. S. Vaz de Melo

Abstract: The objective of this article is to bridge the gap between two important research directions: (1) nearest neighbor search, which is a fundamental computational tool for large data analysis; and (2) complex network analysis, which deals with large real graphs but is generally studied via graph theoretic analysis or spectral analysis. In this article, we have studied the nearest neighbor search problem in a complex network by the development of a suitable notion of nearness. The computation of efficient nearest neighbor search among the nodes of a complex network using the metric tree and locality sensitive hashing (LSH) are also studied and experimented. For evaluation of the proposed nearest neighbor search in a complex network, we applied it to a network community detection problem. Experiments are performed to verify the usefulness of nearness measures for the complex networks, the role of metric tree and LSH to compute fast and approximate node nearness and the the efficiency of community detection using nearest neighbor search. We observed that nearest neighbor between network nodes is a very efficient tool to explore better the community structure of the real networks. Several efficient approximation schemes are very useful for large networks, which hardly made any degradation of results, whereas they save lot of computational times, and nearest neighbor based community detection approach is very competitive in terms of efficiency and time.

Keywords: complex network; nearest neighbor; metric tree; locality sensitive hashing; community detection

1. Introduction

The nearest neighbor (NN) search is an important computational primitive for structural analysis of data and other query retrieval purposes. NN search is very useful for dealing with massive data sets, but it suffers from the curse of dimension [1,2]. Though nearest neighbor search is a extensively studied research problem for low dimensional data, a recent surge of results shows that it is the most useful tool for analyzing very large quantities of data, provided a suitable space partitioning the data structure is used, like, kd-tree, quad-tree, R-tree, metric-tree and locality sensitive hashing [3–6]. One more advantage of using nearest neighbor search for large data analysis is the availability of efficient approximation scheme, which provides almost same results in very less time [7,8].

Though nearest neighbor search is very successful and extensively used across the research domains of computer science, it is not studied rigorously in complex network analysis. Complex networks are generally studied with a graph theoretic framework or spectral analysis framework. One basic reason for this limitation may be the nodes of the complex networks do not naturally lie on a metric space, thus restricting the use of nearest neighbor analysis which is done using metric or nearness measures.

Other than graphs, the complex networks are characterized by small "average path length" and a high "clustering coefficient". A network community (also known as a module or cluster) is typically a group of nodes with more interconnections among its members than the remaining part of the network [9–11]. To extract such group of nodes from a network one generally selects an objective function that captures the possible communities as a set of nodes with better internal connectivity than external [12,13]. However, very little research has been done for network community detection, which tries to develop nearness between the nodes of a complex network and use the nearest neighbor search for partitioning the network [14–20]. The way metric is defined among the nodes should be able to capture the crucial properties of complex networks. Therefore, we need to create the metric very carefully so that it can explore the underlying community structure of the real life networks [21].

Extracting network communities in large real graphs such as social networks, web, collaboration networks and bio-networks is an important research direction of recent interest [11,22–25]. In this work, we have developed the notion of nearness among the nodes of the network using some new matrices derived from the modified adjacency matrix of the graph which is flexible over the networks and can be tuned to enhance the structural properties of the network required for community detection.

The main contributions of this work are, (1) development of the concept of nearness between the nodes of a complex network; (2) comparing the proposed nearness with other notions of similarities; (3) study and experiment on approximate nearest neighbor search for complex network using M-tree and LSH; (4) design of efficient community detection algorithm using nearest neighbor search. We observed that nearest neighbor between network nodes is a very efficient tool to explore better community structure of the real networks. Further several efficient approximation scheme are very useful for large networks, which hardly made any degradation of results, whereas saves lot of computational times.

The rest of this paper is organized as follows. Section 2 describes the notion of nearness in complex network and proposed method to compute distance between the nodes of a complex network. Sections 3 and 4 describe the algorithm of the nearest neighbor search over complex network using of metric tree and locality sensitive hashing methods respectively. In Section 5, the proposed algorithm for network community detection using nearest neighbor search is discussed. The results of the comparison between community detection algorithms are illustrated in Section 6.

2. Proposed Notion of Nearness in Complex Network

The notion of nearness between the nodes of a graph is used in several purposes in the history of literature of graph theory. Most of the time the shortest path and edge connectivity are popular choices to describe nearness of nodes. However, the edge count does not give the true measure of network connectivity. A true measure of nearness in a complex network should able to determine how much one node can affect the other node to provide a better measure of connectivity between nodes of a real life complex network. Research in this direction need special attention in the domain of complex network analysis, one such is proposed in this article and described in the following subsections.

2.1. Definitions

Definition 1 (Metric space of network). *Given, a graph $G = (V, E)$ the metric is defined over the vertex set V and d, a function to compute the distance between two vertices of V. Pair (V, d) distinguished metric space if d satisfies reflexivity, non-negativity, symmetry and triangle inequality.*

Definition 2 (Nearest neighbor search on network). *The nearest-neighbor searching problem in complex network is to find the nearest node in a graph $G = (V, E)$ between a query vertex v_q and any other vertex of the graph $V \{v_q\}$, with respect to a metric space $M(V, d)$ associated with the graph $G = (V, E)$.*

Definition 3 (Approximate nearest neighbor search on network). *For any $v_q \in V$, An ϵ approximate NN of $v_q \in V$ is to find a point $v_p \in V\{v_q\}$ s.t. $d(v_p, v_q) \leq (1+\epsilon)d(v, v_q) \forall v \in V\{v_q\}$.*

2.2. Nearness in Complex Network

Methods based on node neighborhoods. For a node x, let $N(x)$ denote the set of neighbors of x in a graph $G(V, E)$. A number of approaches are based on the idea that two nodes x and y are more likely to be affected by one another if their sets of neighbors $N(x)$ and $N(y)$ have large overlap.

Common neighbors: The most direct implementation of this idea for nearness computation is to define $d(x, y) := |N(x) \cap N(y)|$, the number of neighbors that x and y have in common.

Jaccard coefficient: The Jaccard coefficient, a commonly used similarity metric, measures the probability that both x and y have a feature f, for a randomly selected feature f that either x or y has. If we take features here to be neighbors in $G(V, E)$, this leads to the measure $d(x, y) := |N(x) \cap N(y)| / |N(x) \cup N(y)|$.

Preferential attachment: The probability that a new edge involves node x is proportional to $|N(x)|$, the current number of neighbors of x. The probability of co-authorship of x and y is correlated with the product of the number of collaborators of x and y. This corresponds to the measure $d(x, y) := |N(x)| \times |N(y)|$.

Katz measure: This measure directly sums over the collection of paths, exponentially damped by length to count short paths more heavily. This leads to the measure $d(x, y) := \beta \times |paths(x, y)|$ where, $paths(x, y)$ is the set of all length paths from x to y. (β determines the path size, since paths of length three or more contribute very little to the summation.)

Commute time: A random walk on G starts at a node x, and iteratively moves to a neighbor of x chosen uniformly at random. The hitting time $H(x, y)$ from x to y is the expected number of steps required for a random walk starting at x to reach y. Since the hitting time is not in general symmetric, it is also natural to consider a commute time $C(x, y) := H(x, y) + H(y, x)$.

PageRank: Random resets form the basis of the PageRank measure for Web pages, and we can adapt it for link prediction as follows: Define $d(x, y)$ to be the stationary probability of y in a random walk that returns to x with probability α each step, moving to a random neighbor with probability $1 - \alpha$.

Most of the methods are developed for different types of problems like information retrieval, ranking, prediction e.t.c. and developed for general graphs. In the article [21], the authors studied a measure specially designed for complex network.

2.3. Proposed Nearness in Complex Network

In this subsection, we developed the notion of nearness among the nodes of the network using some linear combination of adjacency matrix A and identity matrix of same dimension for the network $G = (V, E)$. The similarities between the nodes are defined on matrix $L = \lambda I + A$ as spherical similarity among the rows and determine by applying a concave function ϕ over the standard notions of similarities like, Pearson coefficient(σ_{PC}), Spacerman coefficient(σ_{SC}) or Cosine similarity(σ_{CS}). $\phi(\sigma)()$ must be chosen using the chord condition, *i.e.*, metric-preserving ($\phi(d(x_i, x_j)) = d_\phi(x_i, x_j)$), concave and monotonically-increasing, to obtain a metric. It works by picking a pair of rows from L and computing the distance defined in the $\phi(\sigma)()$. The function ϕ converts a similarity function (Pearson coefficient (σ_{PC}), Spacerman coefficient (σ_{SC}) or cosine similarity (σ_{CS})) into a distance matrix. In general, the similarity function satisfies the positivity and similarity condition of the metric, but not the triangle inequality. ϕ is a metric-preserving ($\phi(d(x_i, x_j)) = d_\phi(x_i, x_j)$), concave and monotonically-increasing function. The three conditions above are referred to as the chord condition. The ϕ function is chosen to have minimum internal area with the chord.

The choice of λ and $\phi(\sigma)()$ in the above sub-modules play a crucial role in the graph to metric transformation algorithm to be used for community detection. The complex network is characterized by a small average diameter and a high clustering coefficient. Several studies on network structure analysis reveal that there are hub nodes and local nodes characterizing the interesting structure of the complex network. Suppose we have taken $\phi = arccos$, σ_{CS} and constant $\lambda \geq 0$. $\lambda = 0$ penalizes the effect of the direct edge in the metric and is suitable to extract communities from a highly dense graph. $\lambda = 1$ places a similar weight of the direct edge, and the common neighbor reduces the effect of the direct edge in the metric and is suitable to extract communities from a moderately dense graph. $\lambda = 2$ sets more importance for the direct edge than the common neighbor (this is the common case of available real networks). $\lambda \geq 2$ penalizes the effect of the common neighbor in the metric and is suitable for extracting communities from a very sparse graph.

3. Nearest Neighbor Search on Complex Network Using Metric Tree

There are numerous methods developed to compute the nearest neighbor search for points of a metric space. However, finding the nearest neighbor search on some data where dimension is high suffer from curse of dimension. Some recent research in this direction revealed that dimension constrained can be tackled by using efficient data structures like metric tree and locality sensitive hashing. In this section we have explored metric tree to perform the nearest neighbor search on complex network with the help of metric mapping of complex network described in the previous section.

3.1. Metric-Tree

A metric tree is a data structure specially designed to perform the nearest neighbor query for the points residing on a metric space and perform well on high dimension particularly when some approximation is permitted. A metric tree organizes a set of points in a spatial hierarchical manner. It is a binary tree whose nodes represent a set of points. The root node represents all points, and the points represented by an internal node v is partitioned into two subsets, represented by its two children. Formally, if we use $N(v)$ to denote the set of points represented by node v, and use $v.lc$ and $v.rc$ to denote the left child and the right child of node v, then we have $N(v) = N(v.lc) \cup N(v.rc)$ $\phi = N(v.lc) \cap N(v.rc)$ for all the non-leaf nodes. At the lowest level, each leaf node contains very few points.

An M-Tree [26] consists of leaf node, internal node and routing object. Leaf nodes are set of objects N_v with pointer to parent object v_p. Internal nodes are set of routing objects N_{RO} with pointer to its parent object v_p. Routing object v_r store covering radius $r(v_r)$ and pointer to covering tree $T(v_r)$, Distance of v_r from its parent object $d(v_r, P(v_r))$. Feature values stored in the object v_j are object identifier oid (v_j) and distance of v_j from its parent object $d(v_j, P(v_j))$

The key to building a metric-tree is how to partition a node v. A typical way is as follows: We first choose two pivot points from $N(v)$, denoted as $v.lpv$ and $v.rpv$. Ideally, $v.lpv$ and $v.rpv$ are chosen so that the distance between them is the largest of all distances within $N(v)$. More specifically, $||v.lpv - v.rpv|| = max_{p_1,p_2 \in N(v)}||p_1 - p_2||$. A search on a metric-tree is performed using a stack. The current radius r is used to decide which child node to search first. If the query q is on the left of current point, then $v.lc$ is searched first, otherwise, $v.rc$ is searched first. At all times, the algorithm maintains a candidate NN and there distance determines the current radius, which is the nearest neighbor it finds so far while traversing the tree. The algorithm for nearest neighbor search using metric tree is (Algorithm 1) given below.

3.2. Nearest Neighbor Search Algorithm Using M-Tree

The theoretical advantage of using metric tree as a data structure for nearest neighbor search is: Let $M = (V, d)$, be a bounded metric space. Then for any fixed data $V \in R^n$ of size n, and for constant $c \geq 1$, $\exists \epsilon$ such that we may compute $d(q, V)|_{\epsilon}$ with at most $c \cdot \lceil \log(n) + 1 \rceil$ expected metric evaluations [27].

Algorithm 1 NN search in M-Tree

Require: $M = (V, d) \, \& \, q$
Ensure: $d(q, v_q)$
  1: Insert root object v_r in stack
  2: Set current radius as $d(v_r, q)$
  3: Successively traverse the tree in search of q
  4: PUSH all the objects of traversal path into stack
  5: Update the current radius
  6: If leaf object reached
  7: POP objects from stack
  8: For all points lying inside the ball of current radius centering q, verify for possible nearest neighbor and update the current radius.
  9: **return** $d(q, v_q)$

---

4. Nearest Neighbor Search on Complex Network Using Locality Sensitive Hashing

Metric trees, so far represent the practical state of the art for achieving efficiency in the largest dimension possible. However, many real-world problems consist of very large dimension and beyond the capability of such search structures to achieve sub-linear efficiency. Thus, the high-dimensional case is the long-standing frontier of the nearest-neighbor problem. The approximate nearest neighbor can be computed very efficiently using Locality sensitive hashing.

4.1. Approximate Nearest Neighbor

Given a metric space (S, d) and some finite subset S_D of data points $S_D \subset S$ on which the nearest neighbor queries are to be made, our aim to organize S_D s.t. NN queries can be answered more efficiently. For any $q \in S$, NN problem consists of finding single minimal located point $p \in S_D$ s.t. $d(p, q)$ is minimum over all $p \in S_D$. We denote this by $p = NN(q, S_D)$.

An ϵ approximate NN of $q \in S$ is to find a point $p \in S_D$ s.t. $d(p, q) \leq (1 + \epsilon) d(x, d) \, \forall \, x \in S_D$.

4.2. Locality Sensitive Hashing (LSH)

Several methods to compute first nearest neighbor query exists in the literature and locality-sensitive hashing (LSH) is most popular because of its dimension independent run time [28,29]. In a locality sensitive hashing, the hash function has the property that close points are hash into same bucket with high probability and distance points are hash into same bucket with low probability. Mathematically, a family $H = \{h : S \rightarrow U\}$ is called (r_1, r_2, p_1, p_2)-sensitive if for any $p, q \in S$

- if $p \in B(q, r_1)$ then $Pr_H[h(q) = h(p)] \geq p_1$
- if $p \notin B(q, r_2)$ then $Pr_H[h(q) = h(p)] \leq p_2$

where $B(q, r)$ denotes a hyper sphere of radius r centered at q. In order for a locality-sensitive family to be useful, it has to satisfy inequalities $p_1 > p_2$ and $r_1 < r_2$ when D is a distance, or $p_1 > p_2$ and $r_1 > r_2$ when D is a similarity measure [4,5]. The value of $\delta = log(1/P_1)/log(1/P_2)$ determines search performance of LSH. Defining a LSH as $a(r, r(1 + \epsilon), p1, p2)$, the $(1 + \epsilon)$ NN problem can be solved via series of hashing and searching within the buckets [5,30,31].

4.3. Locality Sensitive Hash Function for Complex Network

In this sub-section, we discuss the existence of locality sensitive hash function families for the proposed metric for complex network. The LSH data structure stores all nodes in hash tables and searches for nearest neighbor via retrieval. The hash table is contain many buckets and identified by bucket id. Unlike conventional hashing, the LSH approach tries to maximize the probability of collision of near items and put them into same bucket. For any given the query q the bucket $h(q)$

considered to search the nearest node. In general k hash functions are chosen independently and uniformly at random from hash family H. The output of the nearest neighbor query is provided from the union ok k buckets. The consensus of k functions reduces the error of approximation. For metric defined in the previous Section 2 we considered k random points from the metric space. Each random point r_i define a hash function $h_i(x) = sign(d(x, r_i))$, where d is the metric and $i \in [1, k]$. These randomized hash functions are locality sensitive [32,33].

Algorithm 2 NN search in LSH

Require: $M = (V, d)$ & q
Ensure: $d(q, V)$
  1: Identify buckets of query point q corresponding to different hash functions.
  2: Compute nearest neighbor of q only for the points inside the selected buckets.
  3: **return** $d(q, V)$

The theoretical advantage of using locality sensitive hashing as a data structure for nearest neighbor search is: Let $M = (V, d)$, be a bounded metric space. Then for any fixed data $V \in R^n$ of size n, and for constant $c \geq 1$, $\exists \epsilon$ such that we may compute $d(q, V)|_\epsilon$ with at most $mn^{O(1/\epsilon)}$ expected metric evaluations, where m is the number of dimension of the metric space. In case of complex network $m = n$ so expected time is $n^{O(2/\epsilon)}$ [27,34].

5. Proposed Community Detection Based on Nearest Neighbor

In this section we have described the algorithm proposed for network community detection using nearest neighbor search. Our approach differs from the existing methods of community detection. The broad categorization of the available algorithms is generally based on graph traversal, semidefinite programming and spectral analysis. The basic approach and the complexity of very popular algorithms are listed in the Table 1. There are more algorithms developed to solve network community detection problem a complete list can be obtained in several survey articles [11,35,36]. Theoretical limitations and evaluation strategies of community detection algorithms are provided in the articles [37–41]. Content based node similarity (discussed in [42,43]) methods uses additional information of the network node and not available in general complex networks. A partial list of algorithms developed for network community detection purpose is tabulated in Table 1. The algorithms are categorized into three main group as spectral (SP), graph traversal based (GT) and semi-definite programming based (SDP). The categories and complexities are also given in Table 1.

Table 1. Algorithms for network community detection and their complexities.

Author	Reference	Category	Order
Van Dongen	(Graph clustering, 2000 [44])	GT	$O(nk^2), k < n$ parameter
Eckmann & Moses	(Curvature, 2002 [45])	GT	$O(mk^2)$
Girvan & Newman	(Modularity, 2002 [46])	SDP	$O(n^2m)$
Zhou & Lipowsky	(Vertex Proximity, 2004 [47])	GT	$O(n^3)$
Reichardt & Bornholdt	(spinglass, 2004 [48])	SDP	parameter dependent
Clauset et al.	(fast greedy, 2004 [49])	SDP	$O(n log_2 n)$
Newman & Girvan	(eigenvector, 2004 [12])	SP	$O(nm^2)$
Wu & Huberman	(linear time, 2004 [50])	GT	$O(n + m)$
Fortunato et al.	(infocentrality, 2004 [51])	SDP	$O(m^3n)$
Radicchi et al.	(Radicchi et al. 2004 [25])	SP	$O(m^4/n^2)$

Table 1. *Cont.*

Author	Reference	Category	Order
Donetti & Munoz	(Donetti and Munoz, 2004 [52])	SDP	$O(n^3)$
Guimera *et al.*	(Simulated Annealing, 2004 [53])	SDP	parameter dependent
Capocci *et al.*	(Capocci *et al.* 2004 [54])	SP	$O(n^2)$
Latapy & Pons	(walktrap, 2004 [14])	SP	$O(n^3)$
Duch & Arenas	(Extremal Optimization, 2005 [15])	GT	$O(n^2 log n)$
Bagrow & Bollt	(Local method, 2005 [55])	SDP	$O(n^3)$
Palla *et al.*	(overlapping community, 2005 [56])	GT	$O(exp(n))$
Raghavan *et al.*	(label propagation, 2007 [57])	GT	$O(n+m)$
Rosvall & Bergstrom	(Infomap, 2008 [58])	SP	$O(m)$
Ronhovde & Nussinov	(Multiresolution community, 2009 [59])	GT	$O(m\beta log n), \beta \approx 1.3$
De Meo *et al.*	(Mixing information, 2014 [41])	SDP	$O(n^3)$
Jin *et al.*	(Geometric Brownian motion, 2014 [60])	SDP	$O(n^3)$

5.1. Distance Based Community Detection

There exist no algorithms in the literature of network community detection which compute direct nearest neighbor between nodes to the best of our knowledge; however, concepts of nearness used in some of the algorithms and they are described below.

Walktrap Algorithm (WT): This algorithm by Pons and Latapy [14] uses a hierarchical agglomerative method. Here, the distance between two nodes is defined in terms of random walk process. The basic idea is that if two nodes are in the same community, the probability to get to a third node located in the same community through a random walk should not be very different. The distance is constructed by summing these differences over all nodes, with a correction for degree. The complexity of the algorithm is $O(n^3)$ as reported in Latapy & Pons (walktrap, 2004 [14]).

Label Propagation Algorithm (LP): This algorithm by Raghavan *et al.* [57] uses the concept of node neighborhood and the diffusion of information in the network to identify communities. Initially, each node is labeled with a unique value. Then an iterative process takes place, where each node takes the label which is the most spread in its neighborhood. This process goes on until the conditions, no label change, is met. The resulting communities are defined by the last label values with the complexity $O(n+m)$ for each iteration as reported in Raghavan *et al.* (label propagation, 2007 [57]).

Geometric Brownian motion (GBM): This concept was borrowed from statistical physics by Zhou *et al.* [47] and extended by Jin *et al.* [60] with the inclusion of the concept of bispace. This method develops the notion of Brownian motion on networks to compute the influences between the nodes, which used to discover communities of social networks. The complexity of the algorithm is $O(n^3)$ as reported in Jin *et al.* (GBM, 2014 [60]).

5.2. Proposed Algorithm for Network Community Detection Using Nearest Neighbor Search

In this subsection we have described k-central algorithm for the purpose of network community detection by using the nearest neighbor search in a complex network. The community detection methods based on partitioning of graph is possible using nearest neighbor search, because the nodes of the graph are converted into the points of a metric space. This algorithm for network community detection converges automatically and does not compute the value of objective function in iterations therefore reduce the computation compared to standard methods. The k-central algorithm for community detection is (Algorithm 3) given below.

Algorithm 3 k-central algorithm

Require: $M = (V, d)$
Ensure: $T = \{C_1, C_2, \ldots, C_k\}$ with minimum $cost(T)$
 1: Initialize centers $z_1, \ldots, z_k \in R^n$ and clusters $T = \{C_1, C_2, \ldots, C_k\}$
 2: **repeat**
 3:    **for** $i = 1$ to k **do**
 4:      **for** $j = 1$ to k **do**
 5:        $C_i \leftarrow \{x \in V \; s.t. \; |z_i - x| \leq |z_j - x|\}$
 6:      **end for**
 7:    **end for**
 8:    **for** $j = 1$ to k **do**
 9:      $z_i \leftarrow Central(C_i)$; where $Central(C_i) \in C_i$
10:    **end for**
11: **until** $|cost(T_t) - cost(T_{t+1})| = 0$
12: **return** $T = \{C_1, C_2, \ldots, C_k\}$

5.3. Complexity And Convergence

Complexity of the network community detection algorithms are the least studied research topic in network science. However, the rate of convergence is one of the important issues of algorithmic complexity and low rate of convergence is the major pitfall of the most of the existing algorithms. Due to the transformation into the metric space, our algorithm is equipped with the quick convergence facility of the k-partitioning on metric space by providing a good set of initial points. Another crucial pitfall suffer by majority of the existing algorithms is the validation of the objective function in each iteration during convergence. Our algorithm converges automatically to the optimal partition thus reduces the cost of validation during convergence.

Theorem 4. *During the course of the k center partitioning algorithm, the cost (community-wise total distance from the corresponding centers) monotonically decreases.*

Proof. Let $Z^t = \{z_1^t, \ldots, z_k^t\}$, $T^t = \{C_1^t, \ldots, C_k^t\}$ denote the centers and clusters at the start of the tth iteration of k partitioning algorithm. The first step of the iteration assigns each data point to its closest center; therefore $cost(T^{t+1}, Z^t) \leq cost(T^t, Z^t)$

On the second step, each cluster is re-centered at its mean; therefore $cost(T^{t+1}, Z^{t+1}) \leq cost(T^{t+1}, Z^t)$. $\square$

The main achievement of our algorithm is to use the rich literature of clustering using nearest neighbor. Clustering is easy NP-Hard in metric space, whereas graph partitioning is NP-Hard. Our algorithm converges automatically to optimal clustering. It does not require verifying the value of objective function guide next iteration, like popular approaches, thus saving the time of computation.

6. Experiments and Results

In this section we described in details several experiments to asses the, proposed nearness measure for the nodes of the network, efficiency of several approximation scheme to compute node nearness and performance of proposed algorithm for community detection. Several experiments conducted in this regard are detailed below along with their parameter settings, results and conclusions.

6.1. Experimental Designs

We performed three different experiments to asses the performance of the proposed network nearest neighbor search for community detection. The first experiment is designed to evaluate the nearness measure, the second experiment is designed to explore the effectiveness of approximate nearest neighbor search for network community detection and the third experiment is designed to verify behavior of the algorithm and the time required to compute the algorithm. One of the major goals of the last experiment is to verify the behavior of the algorithm with respect to the performance of other popular methods exists in the literature in terms of standard modularity measures. Experiments are conducted over several real networks Table 2 to compare the results (Tables 5 and 6) of our algorithm with the state-of-the-art algorithms (Table 1) available in the literature in terms of modularity most preferred by the researchers of the domain of network community detection. The details of the several experiments and the analysis of the results are given in the following subsections.

6.2. Performance Indicator

Modularity: The notion of modularity is the most popular for the network community detection purpose. The modularity index assigns high scores to communities whose internal edges are more than that expected in a random-network model which preserves the degree distribution of the given network.

6.3. Datasets

A list of real networks taken from several real life interactions are considered for our experiments and they are shown in Table 2 below. We have also listed the number of nodes, number of edges, average diameter, and the k value used in Subsection 5.2. The values of the last column can be used to assess the quality of detected communities.

Table 2. Complex network datasets and values of their parameters.

Name	Type	# Nodes	# Edges	Diameter	k
DBLP	U	317,080	1,049,866	8	268
Arxiv-AstroPh	U	18,772	396,160	5	23
web-Stanford	D	281,903	2,312,497	9.7	69
Facebook	U	4039	88,234	4.7	164
Gplus	D	107,614	13,673,453	3	457
Twitter	D	81,306	1,768,149	4.5	213
Epinions1	D	75,879	508,837	5	128
LiveJournal1	D	4,847,571	68,993,773	6.5	117
Orkut	U	3,072,441	117,185,083	4.8	756
Youtube	U	1,134,890	2,987,624	6.5	811
Pokec	D	1,632,803	30,622,564	5.2	246
Slashdot0811	D	77,360	905,468	4.7	81
Slashdot0922	D	82,168	948,464	4.7	87
Friendster	U	65,608,366	1,806,067,135	5.8	833
Amazon0601	D	403,394	3,387,388	7.6	92
P2P-Gnutella31	D	62,586	147,892	6.5	35
RoadNet-CA	U	1,965,206	5,533,214	500	322
Wiki-Vote	D	7115	103,689	3.8	21

6.4. Experiment 1: Experiment with Nearness Measure

In this experiment we tried to asses the usefulness of proposed nearness measure between the nodes of complex network. For this purpose we have equiped our algorithm with different measures of nearness along with our measure. Experimental steps are as follows:

Nearness measures: Six different measures are taken for construction the distance based community detection. They are jaccard coefficient (JA), preferential attachment (PA), Katz measure (KM), commute time (CT), page rank (PR) and proposed metric (PM). details of the measures are already discussed in Subsection 2.2 and proposed metric is detailed in Subsection 2.3.

Algorithm: The community detection algorithm proposed in Section 5 is used and exact nearest neighbor between nodes are considered and computed communities besed on those different nearness measures.

Network data: Different types of real network data is taken, small, large, very sparse and relatively dense and they are discussed in Table 2.

Results: Compared the community structure obtained by algorithms, equipped with different measures of node nearness, in terms of modularity and shown in Table 3.

Observation: It can be observed from Table 3 that algorithm based on proposed metric (shown in column PA) provides better modularity than other for community detection.

Table 3. Experiment 1: Experiment with nearness measure.

Name	JC	PA	KM	CT	PR	PM
Facebook	0.4806	0.4937	0.5037	0.4973	0.5206	0.5434
Gplus	0.3061	0.3253	0.3411	0.3309	0.3671	0.3998
Twitter	0.3404	0.3465	0.3508	0.3481	0.3582	0.3691
Epinions1	0.0667	0.0816	0.0943	0.0861	0.1150	0.1401
LiveJournal1	0.1010	0.1097	0.1167	0.1122	0.1284	0.1432
Pokec	0.0183	0.0205	0.0222	0.0211	0.0251	0.0288
Slashdot0811	0.0066	0.0080	0.0087	0.0082	0.0101	0.0127
Slashdot0922	0.0086	0.0105	0.0116	0.0109	0.0137	0.0171
Friendster	0.0360	0.0395	0.0422	0.0405	0.0467	0.0526
Orkut	0.0424	0.0476	0.0518	0.0491	0.0587	0.0675
Youtube	0.0375	0.0483	0.0574	0.0515	0.0724	0.0903
DBLP	0.4072	0.4103	0.4118	0.4110	0.4148	0.4207
Arxiv-AstroPh	0.4469	0.4590	0.4682	0.4624	0.4837	0.5045
web-Stanford	0.3693	0.3738	0.3765	0.3749	0.3815	0.3896
Amazon0601	0.2057	0.2174	0.2266	0.2207	0.2419	0.2615
P2P-Gnutella31	0.0180	0.0246	0.0302	0.0266	0.0394	0.0503
RoadNet-CA	0.0701	0.0893	0.1051	0.0949	0.1312	0.1633
Wiki-Vote	0.0874	0.1109	0.1308	0.1179	0.1633	0.2023

6.5. Experiment 2: Experiment on Approximation

In this experiment we explore the effectiveness of several approximation techniques of nearest neighbor search on complex network designed via metric tree and locality sensitive hashing. For this purpose we have equiped our algorithm with different data structures (metric tree and LSH) with varying approximation ratio. Experimental steps are as follows:

Metric and algorithm: The algorithms considered in this experiment used proposed measures of node nearness detailed in Subsection 2.3. The community detection algorithm proposed in Section 5 is used in this experiment.

Approximation: Computed communities using approximate nearest neighbor via metric tree and locality sensitive hashing. Different precision of approximation is considered ranges from 0–0.5 and computed five times each over both the scheme of approximation.

Network data: Different types of real network data is taken to verify the acceptablity of degradation over the networks and is shown in Table 4.

Results: Compared the community structure obtained by algorithms, equipped with approximate nearest neighbor instead of exact measures of node nearness, in terms of modularity and shown in Table 4.

Observations: Observed that both the approximation schemes are very good for community detection and slightly degrade the results under ranges of Approximations Table 4.

Table 4. Experiment 2: Experiment on approximation.

Name	Exact	0.1 Mtree	0.1 Lsh	0.2 Mtree	0.2 Lsh	0.3 Mtree	0.3 Lsh	0.4 Mtree	0.4 Lsh	0.5 Mtree	0.5 Lsh
Facebook	0.5472	0.5468	0.5462	0.5463	0.5452	0.5459	0.5441	0.5454	0.5431	0.5450	0.5421
Gplus	0.4056	0.4053	0.4049	0.4050	0.4042	0.4047	0.4035	0.4044	0.4028	0.4041	0.4021
Twitter	0.3709	0.3706	0.3701	0.3702	0.3693	0.3699	0.3685	0.3695	0.3677	0.3692	0.3669
Epinions1	0.1447	0.1446	0.1445	0.1445	0.1443	0.1445	0.1441	0.1444	0.1439	0.1443	0.1437
LiveJournal1	0.1458	0.1456	0.1454	0.1455	0.1450	0.1453	0.1447	0.1452	0.1443	0.1450	0.1439
Pokec	0.0295	0.0294	0.0293	0.0294	0.0292	0.0293	0.0290	0.0293	0.0289	0.0292	0.0287
Slashdot0811	0.0125	0.0124	0.0123	0.0123	0.0122	0.0121	0.0120	0.0120	0.0119	0.0119	0.0117
Slashdot0922	0.0168	0.0167	0.0167	0.0167	0.0166	0.0166	0.0164	0.0166	0.0163	0.0165	0.0162
Friendster	0.0536	0.0535	0.0534	0.0534	0.0532	0.0533	0.0529	0.0532	0.0527	0.0531	0.0525
Orkut	0.0690	0.0689	0.0688	0.0688	0.0685	0.0687	0.0683	0.0686	0.0680	0.0685	0.0678
Youtube	0.0936	0.0936	0.0935	0.0935	0.0934	0.0935	0.0932	0.0934	0.0931	0.0934	0.0930
DBLP	0.4215	0.4211	0.4206	0.4207	0.4197	0.4204	0.4189	0.4200	0.4180	0.4196	0.4171
Arxiv-AstroPh	0.5081	0.5077	0.5072	0.5073	0.5063	0.5069	0.5053	0.5065	0.5044	0.5061	0.5035
web-Stanford	0.3908	0.3904	0.3900	0.3901	0.3891	0.3897	0.3883	0.3894	0.3874	0.3890	0.3866
Amazon0601	0.2650	0.2647	0.2644	0.2645	0.2638	0.2642	0.2633	0.2640	0.2627	0.2637	0.2621
P2P-Gnutella31	0.0523	0.0523	0.0523	0.0523	0.0523	0.0523	0.0523	0.0523	0.0523	0.0523	0.0523
RoadNet-CA	0.1692	0.1690	0.1686	0.1687	0.1681	0.1685	0.1675	0.1682	0.1670	0.1680	0.1664
Wiki-Vote	0.2095	0.2094	0.2093	0.2093	0.2090	0.2092	0.2088	0.2091	0.2085	0.2090	0.2083

6.6. Experiment 3: Experiment to Evaluate Proposed Algorithm

In this experiment we have compared several algorithms for network community detection with our proposed algorithm developed using the nearest neighbor search in complex network, which is discussed in Section 5. The experiment is performed on a large list of network data sets Table 2. Two versions of the experiment are developed for comparison purposea based on modularity and time taken. The results are shown in the Tables 5 and 6 respectively.

Table 5. Comparison of our approaches with other best methods in terms of modularity.

Name	Spectral	SDP	GT	WT	LP	GBM	NN-Search	M-Tree	LSH
Facebook	0.4487	0.5464	0.5434	0.5117	0.5042	0.4742	0.5472	0.5450	0.5421
Gplus	0.2573	0.4047	0.3998	0.3528	0.3412	0.2963	0.4056	0.4041	0.4021
Twitter	0.3261	0.3706	0.3691	0.3545	0.3513	0.3375	0.3709	0.3692	0.3669
e Epinions1	0.0280	0.1440	0.1401	0.1034	0.0940	0.0589	0.1447	0.1443	0.1437
LiveJournal1	0.0791	0.1455	0.1432	0.1220	0.1169	0.0966	0.1458	0.1450	0.1439
Pokec	0.0129	0.0294	0.0288	0.0235	0.0223	0.0172	0.0295	0.0292	0.0287
Slashdot0811	0.0038	0.0130	0.0127	0.0095	0.0090	0.0060	0.0125	0.0119	0.0117
Slashdot0922	0.0045	0.0176	0.0171	0.0127	0.0119	0.0078	0.0168	0.0165	0.0162
Friendster	0.0275	0.0536	0.0526	0.0443	0.0423	0.0343	0.0536	0.0531	0.0525
Orkut	0.0294	0.0689	0.0675	0.0549	0.0519	0.0398	0.0690	0.0685	0.0678
Youtube	0.0096	0.0934	0.0903	0.0640	0.0573	0.0319	0.0936	0.0934	0.0930
DBLP	0.4011	0.4214	0.4207	0.4136	0.4125	0.4060	0.4215	0.4196	0.4171
Arxiv-AstroPh	0.4174	0.5079	0.5045	0.4755	0.4688	0.4410	0.5081	0.5061	0.5035
web-Stanford	0.3595	0.3908	0.3896	0.3791	0.3772	0.3673	0.3908	0.3890	0.3866
Amazon0601	0.1768	0.2649	0.2615	0.2336	0.2269	0.1999	0.2650	0.2637	0.2621
P2P-Gnutella31	0.0009	0.0522	0.0503	0.0343	0.0301	0.0146	0.0523	0.0523	0.0523
RoadNet-CA	0.0212	0.1690	0.1633	0.1168	0.1053	0.0603	0.1692	0.1680	0.1664
Wiki-Vote	0.0266	0.2093	0.2023	0.1451	0.1306	0.0752	0.2095	0.2090	0.208

Table 6. Comparison of our approaches with other best methods in terms of time.

Name	Spectral	SDP	GT	WT	LP	GBM	NN-Search	M-Tree	LSH
Facebook	6	7	11	13	7	8	6	4	1
Gplus	797	832	1342	1512	877	948	661	390	115
Twitter	462	485	786	886	509	554	398	235	68
Epinions1	411	419	667	749	452	475	292	174	56
LiveJournal1	1297	1332	2129	2394	1427	1514	969	576	179
Pokec	1281	1305	2075	2330	1410	1480	901	538	173
Slashdot0811	552	561	891	1000	608	636	382	228	74
Slashdot0922	561	570	906	1017	618	647	389	232	75
Friendster	2061	2105	3352	3766	2269	2390	1477	880	280
Orkut	1497	1529	2435	2736	1647	1735	1074	640	203
Youtube	829	844	1340	1505	913	957	578	345	111
DBLP	381	403	655	739	420	461	341	201	57
Arxiv-AstroPh	217	230	375	423	239	263	197	116	33
web-Stanford	498	525	852	960	549	600	437	258	74
Amazon0601	653	678	1089	1225	719	771	520	308	93
P2P-Gnutella31	182	184	293	328	200	209	124	74	24
RoadNet-CA	758	785	1261	1419	834	894	599	355	107
Wiki-Vote	54	55	88	99	59	63	39	23	7

Experimental steps are as follows:

Design of experiment: In this experiment we have compared three groups of algorithms for network community detection with one based on nearest neighbor search, described above. Two versions of the experiment are developed for comparison purposes based on modularity and time taken in seconds.

Best of literature: Regarding the three groups of algorithms; the first group contain algorithms based on semi-definite programming and the second group contain algorithms based on graph traversal approaches. For each group, we have taken the best value of modularity in Table 5 among all the algorithms in the groups. All the algorithms considered in this experiment are detailed in Section 5.

Other distance based methods: Three different methods of network community detection are also considered for our comparison which indirectly use the influence between the nodes in their algorithms. These methods are walktrap (WT), label propagation (LP) and geometric brownian motion (GBM) and already discussed in Section 5 along with their references and complexities.

Proposed methods: Three versions of proposed algorithm are compared with other algorithms, the proposed algorithm based on exact nearest neighbor, approximated nearest neighbor computed using metric tree and approximate nearest neighbor computed using locality sensitive hashing.

Network data: A long list of real network data is taken for evaluation of modularity and timedescribed in Table 4.

Efficiency and time: Compared the community structure obtained in terms of modularity and time (seconds) taken by the algorithms, shown in the Tables 5 and 6, respectively.

The results obtained with our approach are very competitive with most of the well known algorithms in the literature and this is justified over the large collection of datasets. On the other hand, it can be observed that time (second) taken (Table 6) by our algorithm is quite less compared to other methods and justify the theoretical findings.

6.7. Results Analysis and Achievements

In this subsection, we have described the analysis of the results obtained in our experiments shown. The results obtained in the first experiment justify that the proposed distance is more useful for complex network to extract the community structure compared to other measures of similarity. The results obtained in the second experiment verify that the approximate distance is also useful for network community detection especially for large data where time is a major concern. The results obtained in the third experiment justify that the proposed algorithm for community detection is very efficient compared to other existing methods in terms of modularity and time.

7. Conclusions

In this paper, we studied the interesting problem of the nearest neighbor within the nodes of a complex networks and applied this for community detection. We have used a geometric framework for network community detection instead of the traditional graph theoretic approach or spectral methods. Processing the nearest neighbor search in complex networks cannot be achieved straightforwardly; we presented the transformation of the graph to metric space and efficient computation of the nearest neighbor therein using metric tree and locality sensitive hashing. To validate the performance of proposed nearest neighbor search designed for complex networks, we applied our approaches on a community detection problem. Through several experiments conducted in this regard and we found community detection using nearest neighbor search is very efficient and time saving for large networks due to good approximations. The results obtained on several network data sets prove the usefulness of the proposed method and provide motivation for further application of other structural analysis of complex network using the nearest neighbor search.

Acknowledgments: This work is supported by the Jaypee University of Information Technology.

Author Contributions: Suman Saha proposed the algorithm and prepared the manuscript. Satya P. Ghrera was in charge of the overall research and critical revision of the paper. Both authors have read and approved the final manuscript.

Conflicts of Interest: The authors declare no conflict of interest.

References

1. Uhlmann, J.K. Satisfying general proximity/similarity queries with metric trees. *Inf. Proc. Lett.* **1991**, *40*, 175–179.
2. Ruiz, E.V. An algorithm for finding nearest neighbours in (approximately) constant average time. *Pattern Recognit. Lett.* **1986**, *4*, 145–157.
3. Panigrahy, R. Entropy based nearest neighbor search in high dimensions. In Proceedings of the Seventeenth Annual ACM-SIAM Symposium on Discrete Algorithm (SODA '06), Miami, FL, USA, 22–24 January 2006.
4. Indyk, P.; Motwani, R. Approximate nearest neighbors: Towards removing the curse of dimensionality. In Proceedings of the Thirtieth Annual ACM Symposium on Theory of Computing (STOC '98), Dallas, TX, USA, 23–26 May 1998.
5. Gionis, A.; Indyk, P.; Motwani, R. Similarity search in high dimensions via hashing. In Proceedings of the 25th International Conference on Very Large Data Bases (VLDB '99), Edinburgh, UK, 7–10 September 1999.
6. Dasgupta, S.; Freund, Y. Random projection trees and low dimensional manifolds. In Proceedings of the Fortieth Annual ACM Symposium on Theory of Computing (STOC '08), Victoria, BC, Canada, 17–20 May 2008.
7. Akoglu, L.; Khandekar, R.; Kumar, V.; Parthasarathy, S.; Rajan, D.; Wu, K.L. Fast nearest neighbor search on large time-evolving graphs. In Proceedings of the European Conference on Machine Learning and Knowledge Discovery in Databases, Nancy, France, 15–19 September 2014.
8. Liu, T.; Moore, A.W.; Gray, E.; Yang, K. *An Investigation of Practical Approximate Nearest Neighbor Algorithms*; MIT Press: Cambridge, MA, USA, 2004; pp. 825–832.
9. Weiss, R.; Jacobson, E. A method for the analysis of complex organisations. *Am. Sociol. Rev.* **1955**, *20*, 661–668.
10. Schaeffer, S.E. Graph clustering. *Comput. Sci. Rev.* **2007**, *1*, 27–64.
11. Fortunato, S. Community detection in graphs. *Phys. Rep.* **2010**, *486*, 75–174.
12. Newman, M.E.J.; Girvan, M. Finding and evaluating community structure in networks. *Phys. Rev. E* **2004**, *69*, 026113.
13. Luxburg, U. A tutorial on spectral clustering. *Stat. Comput.* **2007**, *17*, 395–416.
14. Pons, P.; Latapy, M. Computing communities in large networks using random walks. *J. Graph Algorithms Appl.* **2004**, *10*, 284–293.
15. Duch, J.; Arenas, A. Community detection in complex networks using Extremal Optimization. *Phys. Rev. E* **2005**, *72*, 027104.
16. Chakrabarti, D. AutoPart: Parameter-Free Graph Partitioning and Outlier Detection. *Knowledge Discovery in Databases: PKDD 2004*; Boulicaut, J.F., Esposito, F., Giannotti, F., Pedreschi, D., Eds.; Springer: Berlin/Heidelberg, Germany, 2004; Volume 3202, pp. 112–124.
17. Macropol, K.; Singh, A.K. Scalable discovery of best clusters on large graphs. *Proc. VLDB Endow.* **2010**, *3*, 693–702.
18. Levorato, V.; Petermann, C. Detection of communities in directed networks based on strongly p-connected components. In Proceedings of the 2011 International Conference on Computational Aspects of Social Networks (CASoN), Salamanca, Spain, 19–21 October 2011; pp. 211–216.
19. Brandes, U.; Gaertler, M.; Wagner, D. Experiments on Graph Clustering Algorithms. *Algorithms - ESA 2003*; Battista, G.D., Zwick, U., Eds.; Springer: Berlin/Heidelberg, Germany, 2003; Volume 2832, pp. 568–579.
20. Bullmore, E.; Sporns, O. Complex brain networks: Graph theoretical analysis of structural and functional systems. *Nat. Rev. Neurosci.* **2009**, *10*, 186–198.
21. Saha, S.; Ghrera, S.P. Network community detection on metric space. *Algorithms* **2015**, *8*, 680–696.
22. Freeman, L.C. Centrality in social networks conceptual clarification. *Soc. Netw.* **1978**, *1*, 215–239.
23. Carrington, P.J.; Scott, J.; Wasserman, S. (Eds.) *Models and Methods in Social Network Analysis*; Cambridge University Press: Cambridge, UK, 2005.

24. Newman, M. The structure and function of complex networks. *SIAM Rev.* **2003**, *45*, 167–256.

25. Radicchi, F.; Castellano, C.; Cecconi, F.; Loreto, V.; Parisi, D. Defining and identifying communities in networks. *Proc. Natl. Acad. Sci. USA* **2004**, *101*, 2658–2663.

26. Ciaccia, P.; Patella, M.; Zezula, P. M-tree: An efficient access method for similarity search in metric spaces. In Proceedings of the 23rd International Conference on Very Large Data Bases (VLDB'97), Athens, Greece, 25–29 August 1997.

27. Ciaccia, P.; Patella, M.; Zezula, P. A cost model for similarity queries in metric spaces. In Proceedings of the 16th ACM SIGACT-SIGMOD-SIGART Symposium on Principles of Database Systems (PODS '97), Seattle, WA, USA, 1–4 June 1998.

28. Motwani, R.; Naor, A.; Panigrahy, R. Lower Bounds on Locality Sensitive Hashing. *SIAM J. Discret. Math.* **2007**, *21*, 930–935.

29. Paulevé, L.; Jégou, H.; Amsaleg, L. Locality sensitive hashing: A comparison of hash function types and querying mechanisms. *Pattern Recognit. Lett.* **2010**, *31*, 1348–1358.

30. Joly, A.; Buisson, O. A posteriori multi-probe locality sensitive hashing. In Proceedings of the 16th ACM International Conference on Multimedia, Vancouver, BC, Canada, 27–31 October 2008; pp. 209–218.

31. Datar, M.; Immorlica, N.; Indyk, P.; Mirrokni, V.S. Locality-sensitive hashing scheme based on p-stable distributions. In Proceedings of the Twentieth Annual Symposium on Computational Geometry (SCG '04), Brooklyn, NY, USA, 9–11 June 2004.

32. Andoni, A.; Indyk, P. Near-optimal Hashing Algorithms for Approximate Nearest Neighbor in High Dimensions. *Commun. ACM* **2008**, *51*, 117–122.

33. Charikar, M.S. Similarity Estimation Techniques from Rounding Algorithms. In Proceedings of the Thiry-fourth Annual ACM Symposium on Theory of Computing (STOC '02), Montreal, QC, Canada, 19–21 May 2002.

34. Indyk, P. A Sublinear Time Approximation Scheme for Clustering in Metric Spaces. In Proceedings of the 40th Annual Symposium on Foundations of Computer Science, New York, NY, USA, 17–19 October 1999; pp. 154–159.

35. Leskovec, J.; Lang, K.J.; Mahoney, M.W. Empirical comparison of algorithms for network community detection. In Proceedings of the 19th International Conference on World Wide Web, Raleigh, NC, USA, 26–30 April 2010.

36. Yang, J.; Leskovec, J. Defining and Evaluating Network Communities Based on Ground-Truth. In Proceedings of the ACM SIGKDD Workshop on Mining Data Semantics, Beijing, China, 12–16 August 2012.

37. Zarei, M.; Samani, K.A.; Omidi, G.R. Complex eigenvectors of network matrices give better insight into the community structure. *J. Stat. Mech. Theory Exp.* **2009**, *2009*, P10018.

38. Pan, G.; Zhang, W.; Wu, Z.; Li, S. Online community detection for large complex networks. *PLoS ONE* **2014**, *9*, e102799.

39. Lee, C.; Cunningham, P. Community detection: Effective evaluation on large social networks. *J. Complex Netw.* **2014**, *2*, 19–37.

40. Aldecoa, R.; Marin, I. Exploring the limits of community detection strategies in complex networks. *Sci. Rep.* **2013**, *3*, doi:10.1038/srep02216.

41. De Meo, P.; Ferrara, E.; Fiumara, G.; Provetti, A. Mixing local and global information for community detection in large networks. *J. Comput. Syst. Sci.* **2014**, *80*, 72–87.

42. De Meo, P.; Nocera, A.; Terracina, G.; Ursino, D. Recommendation of similar users, resources and social networks in a social internetworking scenario. *Inf. Sci.* **2011**, *181*, 1285–1305.

43. Becker, H.; Naaman, M.; Gravano, L. Learning similarity metrics for event identification in social media. In Proceedings of the Third ACM International Conference on Web Search and Data Mining (WSDM '10), New York, NY, USA, 3–6 February 2010.

44. Van Dongen, S. *A Cluster Algorithm For Graphs*; Technical Report INS-R 0010; CWI: Amsterdam, The Netherlands, 2000.

45. Eckmann, J.P.; Moses, E. Curvature of co-links uncovers hidden thematic layers in the World Wide Web. *Proc. Natl. Acad. Sci. USA* **2002**, *99*, 5825–5829.

46. Girvan, M.; Newman, M.E.J. Community structure in social and biological networks. *Proc. Natl. Acad. Sci. USA* **2002**, *99*, 7821–7826.

47. Zhou, H.; Lipowsky, R. Network brownian motion: A new method to measure vertex-vertex proximity and to identify communities and subcommunities. *Computational Science - ICCS 2004*; Springer: Berlin/Heidelberg, Germany, 2004; Volume 3038, pp. 1062–1069.

48. Reichardt, J.; Bornholdt, S. Detecting fuzzy community structures in complex networks with a Potts model. *Phys. Rev. Lett.* **2004**, *93*, 218701.

49. Clauset, A.; Newman, M.E.J.; Moore, C. Finding community structure in very large networks. *Phys. Rev. E* **2004**, doi:10.1103/PhysRevE.70.066111.

50. Wu, F.; Huberman, B. Finding communities in linear time: A physics approach. *Eur. Phys. J. B* **2004**, *38*, 331–338.

51. Fortunato, S.; Latora, V.; Marchiori, M. Method to find community structures based on information centrality. *Phys. Rev. E* **2004**, *70*, 056104.

52. Donetti, L.; Muñoz, M.A. Detecting network communities: A new systematic and efficient algorithm. *J. Stat. Mech. Theory Exp.* **2004**, *2004*, P10012.

53. Guimera, R.; Amaral, L.A.N. Functional cartography of complex metabolic networks. *Nature* **2005**, *433*, 895–900.

54. Capocci, A.; Servedio, V.D.P.; Caldarelli, G.; Colaiori, F. Detecting communities in large networks. *Physica A* **2004**, *352*, 669–676.

55. Bagrow, J.P.; Bollt, E.M. Local method for detecting communities. *Phys. Rev. E* **2005**, *72*, 046108.

56. Palla, G.; Derenyi, I.; Farkas, I.; Vicsek, T. Uncovering the overlapping community structure of complex networks in nature and society. *Nature* **2005**, *435*, 814–818.

57. Raghavan, U.N.; Albert, R.; Kumara, S. Near linear time algorithm to detect community structures in large-scale networks. *Phys. Rev. E* **2007**, *76*, 036106.

58. Rosvall, M.; Bergstrom, C.T. Maps of random walks on complex networks reveal community structure. *Proc. Natl. Acad. Sci.* **2008**, *105*, 1118–1123.

59. Ronhovde, P.; Nussinov, Z. Multiresolution community detection for megascale networks by information-based replica correlations. *Phys. Rev. E* **2009**, *80*, 016109.

60. Jin, F.; Khandpur, R.P.; Self, N.; Dougherty, E.; Guo, S.; Chen, F.; Prakash, B.A.; Ramakrishnan, N. Modeling mass protest adoption in social network communities using geometric brownian motion. In Proceedings of the 20th ACM SIGKDD International Conference on Knowledge Discovery and Data Mining (KDD '14), New York, NY, USA, 24–27 August 2014.

9

Efficient Dynamic Integrity Verification for Big Data Supporting Users Revocability

Xinpeng Zhang [1,2,*], Chunxiang Xu [1], Xiaojun Zhang [1], Taizong Gu [2], Zhi Geng [2] and Guoping Liu [2]

[1]   School of Computer Science and Engineering, University of Electronic Science and Technology of China, Chengdu 611731, China; chxxu@uestc.edu.cn (C.X.); xiaojunzhang_019@126.com (X.Z.)

[2]   Logistic Information Center, Joint Logistics Department, Chengdu Military Region, Chengdu 610015, China; gutaizhong2015@tom.com (T.G.); gengzhi2016@21cn.com (Z.G.);18981990008@189.cn (G.L.)

*   Correspondence: carriage1029@163.com

Academic Editor: Gordana Dodig-Crnkovic

Abstract: With the advent of the big data era, cloud data storage and retrieval have become popular for efficient data management in large companies and organizations, thus they can enjoy the on-demand high-quality cloud storage service. Meanwhile, for security reasons, those companies and organizations would like to verify the integrity of their data once storing it in the cloud. To address this issue, they need a proper cloud storage auditing scheme which matches their actual demands. Current research often focuses on the situation where the data manager owns the data; however, the data belongs to the company, rather than the data managers in the real situation which has been overlooked. For example, the current data manager is no longer suitable to manage the data stored in the cloud after a period and will be replaced by another one. The successor needs to verify the integrity of the former managed data; this problem is obviously inevitable in reality. In this paper, we fill this gap by giving a practical efficient revocable privacy-preserving public auditing scheme for cloud storage meeting the auditing requirement of large companies and organization's data transfer. The scheme is conceptually simple and is proven to be secure even when the cloud service provider conspires with revoked users.

Keywords: cloud storage; privacy-preserving; integrity verification; user revocation

---

1. Introduction

Nowadays, a large amount of data has been gathered and produced by individuals, companies and organizations. Moore's law is broken by the rapid growth of the data scale. The growth of the data scale is far more than the growth of the processing and storage capacity of computer. For companies and organizations, the volumes of those data are often so tremendous that they cannot process and manage it effectively by themselves. In fact, some of them even don't have sufficient disk space to store their data because it's an enormous burden to purchase such a large number of disks. Facing this reality, companies and organizations have to turn to cloud service provider (CSP) for help, e.g., Dropbox, Google Drive and skyDrive.

As one of the dominate services in cloud computing, cloud storage allows users to store data on clouds instead of their local computing systems. By data outsourcing, this kind of new storage service has many advantages such as relieving users' burden in terms of data management and maintenance, universal data access with independent geographical locations and avoiding capital cost on hardware and software. However, at the meantime, cloud storage also brings a number of challenging security problems [1–3] despite its appealing features. Security concerns still deter potential consumers from using the service. One of the major security concerns [1] on the cloud storage service is whether the cloud could ensure the integrity of the stored data. Integrity challenges of data corruption are inevitable [4–6], but cloud service providers may not be fully trusted from the view of the interests. Cloud Security Alliance (CSA) conducted a systematic investigation into reported vulnerabilities in cloud computing such as outages, downtimes, and data loss. CSA also released a white paper [7] in 2013 which revealed that the top three threats were "Insecure Interfaces & APIs", "Data Loss & Leakage" and "Hardware Failure". These three threats accounted for 64% of all cloud outage incidents while "Data Loss & Leakage" accounted for 25%. Consequently, guaranteeing the integrity of the data, or data auditing, in cloud is a highly desirable security demand for secure cloud storage. Many researches have been done on checking the integrity for outsourcing data in the cloud. Despite a number of cloud data auditing schemes [8–15] have been proposed with different requirements so far, they are all designed for traditional cloud storage environment without considering the applications for user revocable.

We notice that almost all of the previous public auditing systems are fixed by the user who computes the block tags. In other words, those auditing schemes require that the user of the cloud storage service is always the same one during the entire data period. However, it is impractical. On one hand, the verification information of an auditing system such as the user's public key may expire after a period of time. On the other hand, the user may be a data manager of a company for a time and may leave for some reasons. For example, the data manager may go to work in another company for a higher salary. Therefore, for practical considerations, an auditing scheme should support efficient user revocation.

Recently, a few public auditing schemes for cloud storage systems with user revocation have been presented, e.g., [16–18]. However those schemes are designed for auditing shared cloud data rather than for revoking inappropriate users when auditing owned cloud data. Moreover, we note that the existing users revocable public cloud storage auditing schemes are either involved or less secure. Specifically, the revocable public cloud storage auditing schemes in [17] and [18] employ the unwieldy dynamic broadcast encryption [19] and group signature [20] techniques respectively. Although the scheme in [16] is more efficient, it can't resist collusion attacks between the cloud and a revoked user. That is, the collusion of the cloud and a revoked user could always deceive an incumbent user into belief that the data in the cloud remains intact even if it's actually not. Thus collusion attack resistance is indispensable in a revocable public cloud storage auditing schemes. As a result, it's crucial to design efficient and collusion-resistant user revocable public auditing schemes.

1.1. Related Work

Juels *et al.* proposed an auditing scheme called Proofs Of Retrievability (POR) while the auditing scheme proposed by Ateniese *et al.* is called Provable Data Possession (PDP). Shacham-Waters used BLS signature constructed an efficient public verifiable POR scheme [13]. Based on their research, many cloud storage auditing schemes have been proposed to verify the data integrity without needing to retrieve entire data [8–13]. However, the privacy protection of user's data has not yet been considered in most of these schemes [11,13]. This shortcoming can greatly affect the safety of these schemes. Therefore, the auditing process should not leak the knowledge of the challenged files to the third-party auditor. In 2013, Wang *et al.* [9] presented a privacy-preserving public auditing scheme for cloud storage; it resorts to the homomorphic authenticator technique and random masking technique to realize privacy-preserving public auditing and take advantage of the technique of bilinear aggregate signature to realize batch auditing.

All the auditing schemes mentioned above do not consider the user revocation problem, thus those schemes can only be applied to static users. However, user revocation is an obviously inevitable problem. Recently, a few auditing schemes supporting user revocation are published for realizing multi-user shared cloud storage audit. In 2012 Wang *et al.* [21] first introduced the shared cloud storage auditing issue and proposed a private auditing scheme with user revocation based on group signature [20]. In 2013, Wang *et al.* [17] presented a public auditing scheme with user revocation for shared cloud storage, based on the dynamic broadcast encryption scheme of [19] and the bidirectional proxy re-signature scheme of [21]. Later, using a group signature like technique, Yuan and Yu proposed a public version of the scheme in [18]. As group signature and dynamic broadcast encryption techniques are both involved, the above revocable auditing schemes are all less efficient in practice. To address this problem, in 2015 Wang *et al.* presented an efficient revocable public auditing scheme in [16] by just using the bidirectional proxy re-signature scheme of [22]. However, we note that the bidirectional proxy re-signature scheme cannot resist the collusion attack of the cloud and a revoked user since an incumbent user's secret key can be recovered from the cloud's update key and a revoked user's secret key.

We also notice that all the previous papers focus on the data integrity and security are under the shared cloud storage model [23,24]. Although these schemes involve user revocation problem, the main research is still cloud data sharing, where security problems cannot be ignored. Therefore, we analyze the revocation need of companies and organizations cloud storage data users, propose the model of user revocable auditing schemes and design an efficient dynamic integrity verification scheme for big data supporting user revocability. This is the major work we are doing in this paper.

1.2. Our Contributions

Motivated by above, in this paper, an efficient dynamic integrity verification for big data supporting users revocability and third-party privacy-preserving auditing scheme be proposed. To achieve this, we make the following contributions: we analyze the revocation need of companies and organizations cloud storage data users. Based on technique of bilinear aggregate signature, a specific revocable public cloud storage third-party auditing scheme be presented. It can help the current user audit the data which was sent to the cloud by all the previous users, and can satisfy the user transfer demand of large companies and organizations. Meanwhile cloud users can delegate a third party (TPA) to perform security auditing tasks as it is not economically feasible for them to handle it by themselves. By given a precise definition of security that collusion resistance is mandatory. At last by analyzing the performance of scheme and the results, we demonstrate that our scheme is efficient.

1.3. Paper Organization

The remainder of this paper is organized as follows. Preliminaries is described in Section 2. Section 3 formalizes the concept of revocable third-party privacy-preserving auditing scheme for cloud storage and also presents our design goals. The revocable third-party privacy-preserving auditing scheme for cloud storage is given in Section 4. Section 5 analyzes the scheme security. Section 6 analyzes the performance of it. Finally, Section 7 concludes this paper.

2. Preliminaries

2.1. The User Data Stored in the Cloud

As illustrated in Figure 1, a basic cloud storage auditing system involves two main entities: a user and the CSP. The user would be a company or an organization (more precisely, it is usually a data manager of them who uses the cloud storage service to store its superabundant data. The CSP is cloud service provider who has ample storage space, and could offer economical and professional storage services to users. Specifically, a cloud storage auditing scheme works as follows. A user first splits the data M into n blocks such that each block is m_i in Z_p, i.e., $M = (m_1, \ldots, m_n) \in (Z_p)^n$, $M \in \{0,1\}^*$, $i \in \{1, \cdots, n\}$, and computes the signatures of all blocks using its secret key like $\sigma = (\sigma_1, \ldots, \sigma_n)$. Here the signatures are known as block tags. Then the user sends the data and all tags to the cloud, and deletes them locally. When their outsourced data needs to be checked, the user picks a random set of data blocks and sends a corresponding $Q = \{(i, v_i)\}$ to the cloud, where i and v_i

indicate the identity and random coefficient of a selected data block respectively. After receiving Q, the cloud calculates and returns a proof by using those data blocks as well as the corresponding tags. Finally, the user verifies the validity of the proof. If the proof is invalid then the user can confirm that its data has been damaged. Otherwise, it may be intact; the user could repeat the challenge verification procedure until getting a confirmation. It obviously shows that the cloud only stored the user data block and the corresponding blocks tags.

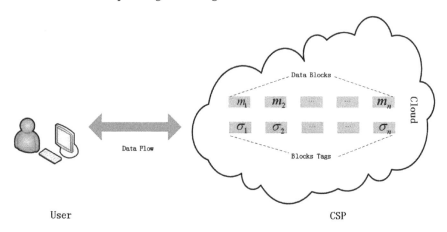

Figure 1. The user data stored in the cloud.

2.2. Multi-User Data Stored in the Cloud with the Revocable System

As shown in Figure 2, cloud storage system supporting revocable user is quite different from the basic cloud storage auditing system, as there are many users who are able to manage the same piece of data. In reality, the data stored in the cloud belongs to the company, not to the data manager. In a specific period, there is usually one data manger that is responsible for managing the data, but in a longer time period, there might be many users who are able to managing the data. That is, after some time, a data manager who is responsible for managing the data is no longer suitable to manage the data, e.g., the data manager leaves the company and work for another company, thus, a successor of the data manager is needed.

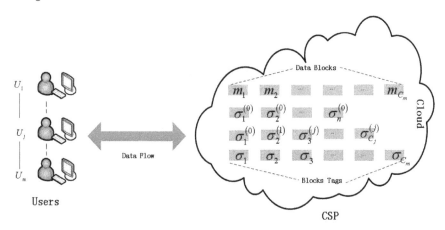

Figure 2. Multi-user data stored in the cloud.

We assume that there is an initial user who uploads the company's data to the cloud on behalf of the company, we regard this initial user as U_0, then the company recruit a data manger to manage those data stored on the cloud. Clearly the data manager is not tenure. Before leaving, a data manger needs to transfer all data he managed to his successor. The successor also needs to verify these data to make sure all the data stored on the cloud is intact. Assume that a company or organization only needs one data manager to manage the data in a specific period. Then we have $U_1, U_2, \cdots, U_m$ users in the company or organization where m is a positive integer. So the data management period is divided into $T_1, T_2, \cdots, T_m$ accordingly. And the user has to transfer the data to the successor at the end of the period. (Note: In the paper the initial user U_0 can't do anything except uploads the data to the cloud. Only $U_1, U_2, \cdots, U_m$ can management the data.)

The initial user U_0 first divides all the files into n blocks, and calculates its corresponding tag σ using his secret key, then uploads the data and tag to the cloud. U_1 manages the data during the period of T_1, then U_1 will be replaced by its successor U_2 at the end of T_1, U_2 will also be replaced by U_3 some time later, and so on till the U_j replaces U_{j-1}, where $j \in \{0, \cdots, m\}$ and U_j is the current user.

As the tag is signed by the user, if a user has been revoked, the tags computed by the user should be modified. An obvious approach to update those tags is re-computing the tags of data blocks using the current user's secret key. However, this is not a cloud storage auditing scheme supporting user revocation, as this method introduces large communication and computation overhead. All the data manager can add, modify and delete the data which is stored on the cloud. For the current user U_j all these operations can only happen during the T_j period. For the add operation, U_j divides the data into blocks, computes the tags of each block and sends all the blocks and tags to the cloud. For the modify operation, U_j first retrieves the data which needs to be modified and its corresponding tags. U_j verifies the correctness of the data, and discards the tags. If the data is intact, then U_j modifies the data and computes the tags for the data using his secret key and uploads the data and tags to the cloud. For simplicity, we assume that the cloud server can handle the delete operation effectively. (e.g., if some deleted data are selected by a challenge, all the data are set to 0, this will not affect the alter verification process of the data. In fact, those deleted data will no longer take any space on the cloud server.) Thus for serial number of blocks, its value will never decrease.

The value of the $i - th$ of blocks C is related to the period T and the operation P. Assume that $C_1, \cdots, C_m$ are the $i - th$ of blocks at the end of period $T_1, T_2, \cdots, T_m$, and $c_1, \cdots, c_m$ are the increment of the data block at the end of period $T_1, T_2, \cdots, T_m$, and $p_{j,1}, p_{j,2}, \cdots, p_{j,\theta}$ are the increment of the data block by the operation $P_{j,1}, P_{j,2}, \cdots, P_{j,\theta}$ during the period T_j. Then we get $C_j = n + \sum_{\ell \in [1,j]} c_\ell = C_{j-1} + c_j$, where $\ell \in \{1, \cdots j\}$, and $\sum_{k \in [1,\theta]} p_{j,k} = c_j$, where $p_{j,k}$ is a positive integer and $k \in \{1, \cdots \theta\}$. So at the auditing time the value of the $i - th$ of blocks is $C_{j,k} = C_{j-1} + p$, where $p = p_{j,1} + p_{j,2} + \cdots + p_{j,k}$.

For a more realistic cloud storage system supporting user revocation, all the data stored on the cloud included the data $m_1, \ldots, m_{C_m}$ and its corresponding tags $\sigma_1, \ldots, \sigma_{C_m}$, and its corresponding period $T_1, T_2, \cdots, T_m$. They are uploaded by the initial users U_0 and all the other data managers $U_1, U_2, \cdots, U_m$. So as shown in Figure 3, the integrity verification of m_i will be verified by σ_i, C, T.

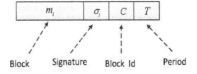

Figure 3. Each block is attached with a signature, a block id and a current period.

As mentioned above, U_j can only add and modify data at the time period of T_j, and compete the tags of data blocks using his own secret key. In order to distinguish those tags, we use $\sigma_i^{(j)}$ to represent the tags computed by the user U_j for data block m_i. For the current user, he has to not only manage the data blocks $m_{C_{(j-1)+1}}, \ldots, m_{C_{j,k}}$ and their corresponding tags, but also manage all the data blocks and tags which were uploaded to the cloud by all of his predecessors. Some of the tags might be signed by different users. For example, in time period T_1, user U_1 did modify operation which gets data block m_2 and tag $\sigma_2^{(1)}$; at the current period, user U_j modifies data block m_i and computes its tag $\sigma_i^{(j)}$.

2.3. The Revocable Scheme Supported Third-Party Privacy-Preserving Auditing

Due to reason of the online burden which potentially brought by the periodic storage correctness verification, cloud users tend to delegate a third-party auditor (TPA) to execute security auditing tasks. Through the TPA automatic execution periodic auditing tasks can save communication resources effectively. Therefore, the third-party auditing schemes are more desirable in the real world. As illustrated in Figure 4, a revocable cloud storage third-party auditing scheme works as follows. When the user wants to check its outsourced data, it sends a verify request to the TPA. When the TPA receives the request, it picks a random set of data blocks and sends a corresponding $Q = \{(i, v_i)\}$ to the cloud, where i and v_i indicate the identity and random coefficient of a selected data block respectively. After receiving Q, the cloud calculates and returns a proof using those data blocks as well as the corresponding tags. Then, the user verifies the validity of the proof. If the proof is invalid then the TPA can confirm that its data has been damaged. Otherwise, it may be intact; the TPA could repeat the challenge verification procedure until getting a confirmation. Finally, the TPA sends the result to the user. It is obvious that the cloud only stored the user's data block and the corresponding blocks tags.

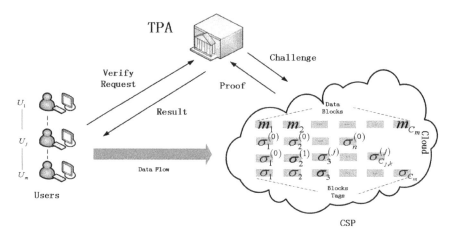

Figure 4. An efficient and security revocable third-party privacy-preserving auditing scheme for cloud storage.

3. Formalization and Definitions

Without loss of generality , a revocable third-party privacy-preserving auditing scheme for cloud is assumed as shown in Figure 4, which involves in $m + 1$ authorized users for some $m \in Z > 0$ and their sequence is $U_0, U_1, U_2, \cdots, U_m$, corresponding the manager period $T_1, T_2, \cdots, T_m$. (Notice that unauthorized users can be easily recognized and additionally they cannot impair the integrity of the outsourced data. Thus it can be assumed that there is no unapproved user in our auditing schemes.) Then such an auditing scheme can be defined as below.

3.1. Definition 1: Revocable Third-Party Privacy-Preserving Auditing Scheme for Cloud Storage

A revocable third-party privacy-preserving auditing scheme for cloud storage consists of six probabilistic polynomial time (PPT) algorithms (*Setup, SigGen, Update, Challeng, ProofGen, ProofVerify*), where:

Setup: This algorithm is to generate each user's public/secret keys and run by each user U_j, where $j \in \{0, \cdots, m\}$. For the $j-th$ user U_j, the algorithm takes as input a security parameter λ and outputs $U_j's$ public-secret key pair (pk_j, sk_j).

SigGen: This algorithm is to generate the tags of the stored data. It consists of three child probabilistic polynomial time algorithms($SigGen\,(U_0)$, $SigGen\,(U_j)$, $SigGen\,(U_\ell \rightarrow U_j)$).

SigGen (U_0): This algorithm is to generate the initial block tags of the stored data in the initial time and thus will be run by the initial user U_0 The algorithm takes as input $U_0's$ secret key sk_0 and block data $(m_1, \ldots, m_n)$, $m_i \in \{0,1\}^*$, $i \in \{1, \cdots, n\}$, and outputs the verification metadata V of $(m_1, \ldots, m_n)$ associated with the user U_0. After that, U_0 sends V and $(m_1, \ldots, m_n)$ to the cloud and deletes them locally.

SigGen (U_j): This algorithm is to generate the block tags of the stored data in the period T_j on the operation $p_{j,k'}$, $k \in \{1, \cdots, \theta\}$, $k' \in \{1, \ldots, k\}$ and thus will be run by the current user U_j. The algorithm takes as input $U_j's$ secret key sk_j and block data $\left(m_{C_{j,(k'-1)}+1}, \ldots, m_{C_{j,k'}}\right)$, $m_i \in \{0,1\}^*$, where $C_{j,k'}$ is a positive integer. And the output of verification metadata V of $\left(m_{C_{j,(k'-1)}+1}, \ldots, m_{C_{j,k'}}\right)$ is associated with the user U_j. After that, U_j sends V and $\left(m_{C_{j,(k'-1)}+1}, \ldots, m_{C_{j,k'}}\right)$ to the cloud and then deletes them locally.

SigGen $(U_\ell \rightarrow U_j)$: This algorithm is to generate the block tags of the stored data in the period T_j when U_j wants to update the data which the previous user U_ℓ uploaded to the cloud. So it will be run by the current user U_j. The algorithm first retrieving the data block $m_i$and it corresponding tags, then verified it if invalid turn out, if valid U_j replaced the m_i by m_i^* (For simple reason we also record it as m_i too). Later the algorithm takes $U_j's$ secret key sk_j and block data m_i as input and the outputs of verification metadata V of m_i associated with the user U_j. After that, U_j sends V and m_i to the cloud and then deletes them locally.

Update: This is an interactive algorithm for updating users. Suppose the user U_j needs to be replaced by the user U_{j+1}, then U_{j+1} will initiate the algorithm. After the algorithm ends, U_{j+1} would obtain an update $uk_{j\rightarrow j+1}$ for the cloud, and finally sends it to the cloud.

Challeng: This is an interactive algorithm for users send checking order. Assume U_j is the current user and wants to check its outsourced data, it sends a verify request to the TPA. When TPA received the request, it picks a random set of data blocks and sends a corresponding $Q = \{(i, v_i)\}$ to the cloud, where i and v_i indicate the identity and random coefficient of a selected data block respectively.

ProofGen: After receiving *Challeng*, the cloud would run the algorithm to return a response. To do this, the algorithm takes as input the *Challeng*, the block data m_i, $i \in Q$ and the verification metadata V of $\{m_i\}_{i\in Q}$, and outputs a verification *proof*.

ProofVerify: This algorithm is run by the TPA to verify the correctness of the *proof*. The algorithm takes as input $U_j's$ public key pk_j, the *Challeng* and the corresponding *proof*, and outputs VALID if *proof* is valid; INVALID otherwise. Finally, the TPA sends the result to the U_j.

For easier understanding, the revocable third-party privacy-preserving auditing scheme for cloud storage intuition behind the definition is given here. The basic idea of our security definition is: if the data in the cloud is indeed damaged but the cloud cannot admit, even by colluding with the revoked users, fool the current user into believing that the data remains intact. Let the cloud be an adversary A. To model the collusion between the cloud and revoked users, we permit to query a Corrupt oracle which takes a revoked user's identity as input and outputs the user's secret key. However, according to the aforementioned reasons we prohibit A from querying the Corrupt oracle on the user's identity. Additionally, like other security models, our security model also allows A to query *SigGen* oracle, *Update* oracle as well as the *ProofGen* oracle for obtaining the initial block tags, all update keys and valid proofs of any challenges.

3.2. Definition 2: Security Model

Now we describe the security definition of revocable third-party privacy-preserving auditing scheme for cloud storage. A revocable third-party privacy-preserving auditing scheme for cloud storage is secure if for any polynomial time adversary A the probability wins the following game played between a challenger C and the adversary A is negligible.

Setup: The challenger C first runs the algorithm $\text{KeyGen}(\lambda)$ to generate $U_j's$ public-secret key pair (pk_j, sk_j) for all $j \in \{0, \cdots, m\}$, and then sends all public $\{pk_j\}_0^m$ to the adversary A.

Query: The adversary A could query the following oracles adaptively.

SigGen-Oracle: For any data block $m \in \{0,1\}^*$, if A wants to get the initial block tags of m, it will query the oracle on m. After receiving the query, the challenger C first runs the algorithm $SigGen(sk_0, m)$ to produce a result V_0 and then returns V_0 as response.

Update-Oracle: When A believes some user is not suitable for auditing, A will query the oracle on the user's identity to replace the user with its successor. Assume the user to be replaced is U_{j+1} for $j \in \{1, \cdots, m-1\}$. The challenger C first runs the algorithm $Update\ (U_{j+1})$ to produce a update key $uk_{j \to j+1}$ and then sends it to A. After receiving $uk_{j \to j+1}$, A could generate the verification metadata V_{j+1} of a data block m associated with the user U_{j+1} using the update key $uk_{j \to j+1}$, the data block m and the verification metadata V_j of m associated with U_j.

Corrupt-Oracle: Suppose all revoked users at present are $U_0, U_1, \cdots, U_d$ for some $d \in \{0, \ldots, m-1\}$, then the adversary A could query the oracle on any of them, with the exception of only U_0. When receiving such a query on the user U_ℓ for $\ell \in \{1, \ldots, d\}$, the challenger C returns $U_\ell's$ secret key sk_ℓ as response.

Proof. In order to verify whether the data block m stored in the cloud is the same as before, the challenger C generates a random challenge $Chal$ and requests the adversary A to return a proof of m associated with user U_j where $j \in \{0, \ldots, m\}$. On input the challenge $Chal$, the data block m and the verification metadata U_j of M associated with U_j, the adversary A outputs a proof as response. $\square$

Forgery. When the above process ends, the adversary A finally outputs a proof of some challenge $Chal$ on file M with respect to user U_j, where $j \in \{0, \ldots, m\}$. We say A wins the game if the following conditions hold:

1.   *Verification* $(pk_\ell,\ chal,\ proof) \to Valid$;
2.   The data block m is not the original one.

3.3. Design Goals

To support secure and efficient user revocable and data privacy preserving in a public cloud data auditing scheme, we have the following design goals:

(i)   TPA is allowed to verify the correctness of the cloud data. It executes data auditing without retrieving entire data and introduces none additional online burden to the user.
(ii)   Storage correctness: If the cloud indeed stores entire data, then it would always output valid proofs.
(iii) Privacy-preserving: TPA learns no information of the stored data from information collected during the auditing process.
(iv)   Revocability: If a user is revoked, then its successor could establish a new auditing procedure efficiently.
(v)   Collusion resistance: If the data stored in the cloud is changed, then the auditing scheme should be able to detect it with high probability even though the cloud colludes with revoked users.
(vi)   Efficiency: the computation, communication and storage overhead should be as small as possible.

4. The Revocable Third-Party Privacy-Preserving Auditing Scheme for Cloud Storage

This section gives some preliminaries to be used in this work, including bilinear map and hardness assumptions.

4.1. Bilinear Map

Let G_1, G_2 and G_T be cyclic groups with the same prime order p. A map e: $G_1 \times G_2 \to G_T$ is called a bilinear map if it satisfies the following three properties.

1. Bilinearity: For all $a, b \in Z_p$, and $u \in G_1, v \in G_2$, we have $e(u^a, v^b) = e(u, v)^{ab}$.
2. Non-degeneracy: $e(g_1, g_2) \neq 1$.
3. Computability: There exists an efficient algorithm to compute the map e.
4. Exchangeability: $e(u_1 \cdot u_2, v) = e(u_1, v) \cdot e(u_2, v)$

4.2. Hardness Assumptions

The security of our constructions will rest on the Computational Diffie-Hellman (CDH) assumption and the Discrete Logarithm (DL) assumption.

Definition 3 (CDH Assumption). *The CDH assumption is given a group of prime order p, a generator g, and two random element $g^a, g^b \in G$ it's hard to output g^{ab}.*

Definition 4 (DL Assumption). *The DL assumption is given a group G of prime order p, a generator g, and a random element $g^c \in G$ it's hard to output c.*

4.3. Specification

In this section, the revocable third-party privacy-preserving auditing scheme for cloud storage is proposed. The auditing scheme is illustrated in Figure 4. Here, a semi-trusted TPA is needed to define, which is only responsible for auditing the integrity of data blocks honestly. However, it is curious and may try to reveal the user' primitive data blocks based on verification information. In this paper, the scheme includes of the following six algorithms: *Setup, SigGen, Update, Challeng, ProofGen, ProofVerify.*

Let G and G_T be two cyclic groups with the same prime order p, and g be a generator of G.t.

Let $e : G \times G \to G_T$ be a bilinear map and $H : \{0,1\}^* \to G, h : \{0,1\}^* \to G, f_{k_3} : \{0,1\}^* \to Z_p$ be a hash function. The auditing scheme is specified as follows.

Setup. On input a security parameter λ, each user U_j where $j \in \{0, \cdots, m\}$ does the following steps:

1. Select a random $x_j \in Z_p$.
2. Compute its public key g^{x_j}.
3. Output $pk_j = g^{x_j}$ and $sk_j = x_j$.

SigGen. This algorithm is to generate the tags of the stored data. It consists of three child algorithms ($SigGen\,(U_0), SigGen\,(U_j), SigGen\,(U_\ell \to U_j)$).

SigGen (U_0). When the companies and organizations delegate a trust user U_0 upload the initial data at the initial time period.

1. The initial user U_0 encodes all the files and then splits them into n block such that each block is in Z_p, i.e., $(m_1, \ldots, m_n) \in (Z_p)^n$.
2. For all $\{m_i\}$, $i \in \{1, \cdots, n\}$ compute the tag of $i - th$ data block m_i as $\sigma_i = (H(W_i) u^{m_i})^{x_0}$, $t_i = W_i || Sig_{ssk}(W_i)$, where u is a public parameter chosen randomly from G, $W_i = i || T_j$ and $j \in \{1, \cdots, m\}$.
3. Send the initial verification metadata $V = \{\sigma_i, t_i\}_{1 \leq i \leq n}$ and the data blocks $\{m_i\}_{1 \leq i \leq n}$ to the cloud and then deletes them locally.

SigGen (U_j). This algorithm is to generate the block tags of the stored data in the period T_j on the operation $p_{j,k'}, k \in \{1, \cdots, \theta\}, k' \in \{1, \ldots, k\}$.

1. The data blocks is processed as $\{m_i\}_{C_{j,(k'-1)} \leq i \leq C_{j,k'}}$ by current user U_j, where $C_{j,k'}$ is a positive integer. The increment of the data block by the operations denoted by $p_{j,k'}$, which user U_j will add these data to the cloud in the period T_j.

2. For all $\{m_i\}_{C_{j,(k'-1)}+1 \leq i \leq C_{j,k'}}$, U_j compute the tag of $i - th$ data block m_i as $\sigma_i = (H(W_i) u^{m_i})^{x_j}$, $t_i = W_i || Sig_{ssk}(W_i)$, where u is a public parameter chosen randomly from G, $W_i = i || T_j$ and $j \in \{1, \cdots, m\}$. Send the verification metadata $V = \{\sigma_i, t_i\}_{C_{j,(k'-1)}+1 \leq i \leq C_{j,k'}}$ and data blocks $\{m_i\}_{C_{j,(k'-1)}+1 \leq i \leq C_{j,k'}}$ to the cloud and then deletes them locally.

SigGen $(U_\ell \rightarrow U_j)$. This algorithm is to generate the block tags of the stored data in the period T_j. If the current user U_j wants to update the data of previous user U_ℓ do.

1. When the current user U_j wants to update the data m_i in the previous T_ℓ period for some reason, the m_i and $V = \{\sigma_i, t_i, C_\ell\}$ should be retrieved firstly.

2. Then the user U_j verified the $t_i = W_i || Sig_{ssk}(W_i)$ with the previous user public key. If wrong the auditing scheme ends, if right the user U_j deals with the data block as m_i and replaced the tag $\sigma_i^{(\ell)} = (H(W_i) u^{m_i})^{x_\ell}$ by $\sigma_i^{(j)} = (H(W_i) u^{m_i})^{x_j}$ At the same time the user U_j replaced $t_i = (i || T_\ell) || Sig_{ssk(U_\ell)}(i || T_\ell)$ by $t_i = (i || T_j) || Sig_{ssk(U_j)}(i || T_j)$.

3. At last the user U_j sends verification metadata $V = \{\sigma_i, t_i\}$ and the block m_i to the cloud and then deletes them locally.

Update. If the user U_{j+1} would take the place of the user U_j, then U_{j+1} computes the update key $uk_{j \rightarrow j+1}$ as $uk_{j \rightarrow j+1} = (g^{x_j})^{\frac{1}{x_{j+1}}} = g^{\frac{x_j}{x_{j+1}}}$, and sends it to the cloud.

The cloud does the following steps:

1. Set $\alpha_j = pk_j, \beta_{j+1} = uk_{j \rightarrow j+1}$.

2. For any $j \in \{0, \cdots, m-1\}$, let the verification metadata of block data m_i associated with user U_j be $V_i = (\sigma_i, t_i, \alpha_1, \ldots, \alpha_j, \beta_1, \ldots, \beta_j)$.

For the sake of clarity, we list some used signals in Table 1. The protocol is illustrated in Figure 5.

Table 1. Signal and its explanation.

Sig.	Repression
n	the number of the initial data block;
$T_1, T_2, \cdots, T_m$	the period of data manager's management;
T_j	the current period is correspondence the current user U_j;
C	the number of the total data blocks at the auditing time: $C_{j,k} = C_{j-1} + p$ where $p = p_{j,1} + p_{j,2} + \cdots + p_{j,k}$;
$C_1, \cdots, C_m$	the $i - th$ of blocks at the end of period $T_1, T_2, \cdots, T_m$;
$c_1, \cdots, c_m$	the increment of the data block at the end of period $T_1, T_2, \cdots, T_m$;
$p_{j,1}, p_{j,2}, \cdots, p_{j,\theta}$	the increment of the data block by the operation $P_{j,1}, P_{j,2}, \cdots, P_{j,\theta}$ during the period T_j ;
$\sigma_i^{(j)}$	the tag is generated by the U_j and data block m_i ;
Q	the set of index-coefficient pairs, i.e., $Q = \{(i, v_i)\}$;
t	it used to verify if the block i-th match the data block;
V	the response for the challenge Q;

TPA	The cloud server
(1) Retrieve file tag, verify its signature, and quit if fail; (2) Generate a challenge message challenge: $Q = \{(i,v_i)\}, i \in \{1, \ldots, C_{j,k}\};$ $\overrightarrow{Q = \{(i,v_i)\}}$	(3) Spilt this Q to $\{Q_{T_0}, \ldots, Q_{T_\ell}, \ldots, Q_{T_j}\};$ (4) Compute $\mu' = \sum_{i \in Q} v_i m_i,\ \sigma = \prod_{i \in Q} \sigma_i^{v_i} \in G_1;$ (5) compute $r = f_{k_3}(challenge) \in Z_p,$ $R = u^r \in G_1,\ \mu = \mu' + rh(R) \in Z_p,$ and $t = \{t_i\}_{i \in Q};$
$\overleftarrow{(\mu, \sigma, t, \alpha, \beta)}$	
(6) Compute: $r = f_{k_3}(challenge) \in Z_p;$ verify $PK_{(U_\ell)}\left(Sig_{ssk(U_\ell)}(W_i)\right) = (i\|T_\ell)$, then verify $(\mu, \sigma, t, \alpha, \beta)$ via the verification equation.	

Figure 5. Revocable third-party privacy-preserving auditing protocol.

Challeng. When the U_j wants to verify the integrity of the data block stored in the cloud in the period of T_j (U_j's period), it would send a verity request to the TPA.

ProofGen. When the TPA receives the request of user, it would issue a random set $Q = \{(i, v_i)\}$ and a communication key k_3 to the cloud as a *Challeng*, where $i \in \{1, \cdots, C_{j,k}\}$ and $v_i \in Z_p$. After receiving *Challeng*, the cloud can spilt this Q to $\{Q_{T_0}, \ldots, Q_{T_\ell}, \ldots, Q_{T_j}\}$ then computes and returns $(\mu, \sigma, t, \alpha, \beta)$ as a *proof*, where $r = f_{k_3}(challenge) \in Z_p$, $R = u^r \in G_1$, $\mu' = \sum_{i \in Q} v_i m_i$, $\mu = \mu' + rh(R) \in Z_p$, $\sigma = \prod_{i \in Q} \sigma_i^{v_i} \in G_1$, and $t = \{t_i\}_{i \in Q}$.

ProofVerify. When the TPA receives the *proof*, input the public key pk_ℓ of user U_ℓ, the *Challeng*, $Q = \{(i, v_i)\}$, k_3 and the *proof*, $(\mu, \sigma, t, \alpha, \beta)$, the algorithm outputs VALID to the U_j as the Result if the following equalities simultaneously hold.

First for each t_i verifies $PK_{(U_\ell)}\left(Sig_{ssk(U_\ell)}(W_i)\right) = (i\|T_\ell)$.

Second verifies the data block and tags $e(\sigma, g) = \prod_{\ell \in [0,j]} e\left(\alpha_\ell, u^\mu \cdot R^{-h(R)} \cdot \prod_{i \in Q_{T_\ell}} H(W_i)^{v_i}\right)$.

Third verifies the user $e(\alpha_{j-1}, g) = e(pk_j, \beta_j) e(\alpha_\ell, g) = e(\alpha_{\ell+1}, \beta_\ell)$ for $\ell \in \{0, \ldots, j-2\}$.

Remark 1. *The update process of the revocable third-party privacy-preserving auditing scheme is simple and is also efficient in terms of both computation and communication costs because it only needs to compute and send one update key $uk_{l \to l+1}$.*

Remark 2. *There is only one public key, i.e., the current user's public key, in the revocable third-party privacy-preserving auditing scheme for any period of time. All public keys of revoked users are not certified any more, and thus a malicious cloud could modify them discretionarily.*

5. Analysis of the Proposed Auditing Scheme

5.1. Correctness

Now we prove the correctness and security of our revocable third-party privacy-preserving auditing scheme.

Theorem 1. *The auditing scheme satisfies correctness.*

Proof. According to the above construction, that for any challenge $Q = \{(i, u_i)\}$, this challenge can be spilt to $Q = \left\{Q_{T_0}, \ \cdots, \ Q_{T_\ell}, \ \cdots, Q_{T_j}\right\}, \ell \in \{0, \ \cdots, \ j\}$, have

$$
\begin{aligned}
e(\sigma, g) &= e\left(\Pi_{i \in Q} \sigma_i^{v_i}, g\right) \\
&= \Pi_{\ell \in [0,j]} e\left(\Pi_{i \in Q_{T_\ell}} \sigma_i^{v_i}, g\right) \\
&= \Pi_{\ell \in [0,j]} e\left(\Pi_{i \in Q_{T_\ell}} (H(W_i) u^{m_i})^{v_i}, g^{x_\ell}\right) \\
&= \Pi_{\ell \in [0,j]} e\left(\alpha_\ell, u^{\mu - rh(R)} \cdot \Pi_{i \in Q_{T_\ell}} H(W_i)^{v_i}\right) \\
&= \Pi_{\ell \in [0,j]} e\left(\alpha_\ell, u^\mu \cdot R^{-h(R)} \cdot \Pi_{i \in Q_{T_\ell}} H(W_i)^{v_i}\right)
\end{aligned}
$$

Also, for any user U_j where $j \in \{1, \cdots, m\}$, we know that

$$
e(\alpha_{j-1}, g) = e(g^{x_{j-1}}, g) = e\left(g^{x_j}, g^{\frac{x_{j-1}}{x_j}}\right) = e(pk_j, \beta_j)
$$

and for all $\ell \in \{0, \cdots, j-2\}$ have

$$
e(\alpha_\ell, g) = e(g^{x_\ell}, g) = e\left(g^{x_{\ell+1}}, g^{\frac{x_\ell}{x_{\ell+1}}}\right) = e(\alpha_{\ell+1}, \beta_\ell)
$$

Therefore, the auditing scheme is correct. □

5.2. Security Analysis

Theorem 2. *The auditing scheme is secure in the random oracle model under the CDH assumption.*

Proof. According to Definition 2, if there exists a polynomial time adversary A who breaks the scheme with non-negligible probability ϵ, we construct an algorithm B that uses the adversary A as a subroutine to solve a hard CDH problem with probability ϵ too. Algorithm B does so by interacting with A as follows.

Setup. Given a security parameter λ, the algorithm B first randomly picks a generator g of G, $g^\alpha \in G$ and a hash function $H : \{0,1\}^* \to G$ that will be modeled as a random oracle in the proof. B also chooses random g^{x_0} from G for an unknown x_0 as U_0's public key and computes U_j's public key g^{x_j} for all $j \in \{0, \cdots, m\}$, where x_j is picked from Z_q. Then B sets $u = g^\alpha$ and sends the system parameters g, u and all users' public keys $\{g^{x_j}\}_0^m$ to the adversary A.

Query. The adversary A can query the following types of oracles adaptively. It is assumed that for any data block m_i, A will first make a H-Oracle query on the block before others.

H-Oracle. When A queries the oracle on a data block m_i, B looks up m_i in H-list, an initial empty list with the tuples $(m_i, s_i, H(W_i))$. If B finds a matched tuple, it outputs $H(W_i)$ as response. Otherwise B first picks a random value $s_i \in Z_p$ and then computes $H(W_i) = g^{s_i}/u^{m_i}$, stores $(m_i, s_i, H(W_i))$ in H-list and finally outputs $H(W_i)$ as response.

SignGen-Oracle. To get the tags of data blocks $\{m_i\}_{i \in [1, C_{j,k}]}$, A queries the oracle on the file. Upon receiving the query, for all $i \in \left\{1, \cdots, C_{j,k}\right\}, j \in \{1, \cdots, m\}, \ell \in \{0, \cdots, j\}$, B looks up

m_i in H-list, finds a matched tuple $(m_i, s_i, H(W_i))$, computes $\sigma_i = (g^{x_\ell})^{s_i}$ and finally outputs the set $V = \left(\sigma_1, \ldots, \sigma_{C_{j,k}} \right)$ as response. Since $\sigma_i = (H(W_i)u^{m_i})^{x_l}$, plugging $H(W_i) = g^{s_i}/u^{m_i}$ into the equality, we can see that $\sigma_i = (g^{x_\ell})^{s_i}$ for all $i \in \left\{ 1, \cdots, C_{j,k} \right\}$.

Update-Oracle. If A wants to replace the user U_j with its successor U_{j+1} for some $j \in \{1, \cdots, m-1\}$, A will query the oracle on U_j. Upon receiving the query, B first computes the update key $uk_{j \to j+1} = g^{x_j/x_{j+1}}$ using U_{j+1}'s secret key x_{j+1} and sends the result to A. Then A sets $\alpha_j = g^{x_j}$ and $\beta_{j+1} = uk_{j \to j+1}$, and adds them into U_j's verification metadata. Let $V_j = (\mu, \sigma, t, \alpha_1, \ldots, \alpha_{j-1}, \beta_1, \ldots, \beta_j)$ be U_j's verification metadata, then we know that U_{j+1}'s verification metadata is $V_{j+1} = (\mu, \sigma, t, \alpha_1, \ldots, \alpha_j, \beta_1, \ldots, \beta_{j+1})$.

Corrupt-Oracle. Let all revoked users at present be $U_1, \ldots, U_d$ for some $d \in \{1, \cdots, m-1\}$. If the adversary A queries the oracle on the user U_j where $j \in \{1, \cdots, d\}$, then B returns U_j's secret key x_j as response. $\square$

Proof. If B wants to verify whether the data block m stored in the cloud remains intact or not, it will issue a random challenge $Challeng(Q, k_3)$, $Q = \{(i, v_i)\}$ to A, where $i \in \left\{ 1, \cdots, C_{j,k} \right\}$ and $v_i \in Z_p$. Let $\left(m_1, \ldots, m_{C_{j,k}} \right) \in (Z_p)^n$ and the current user be U_j. Upon receiving $Challeng(Q, k_3)$, A computes $r = f_{k_3}(challenge) \in Z_p$, $R = u^r \in G_1$, $\mu' = \sum_{i \in Q} v_i m_i$, $\mu = \mu' + rh(R) \in Z_p$, $\sigma = \prod_{i \in Q} \sigma_i^{v_i}$, $t = \{t_i\}_{i \in Q}$, and returns a valid proof $V_j = (\mu, \sigma, t, \alpha_1, \ldots, \alpha_{j-1}, \beta_1, \ldots, \beta_j)$ to B.

Forgery. A with non-negligible probability ϵ outputs a valid proof $(\mu^*, \sigma^*, t, \alpha_1, \ldots, \alpha_{j-1}, \beta_1, \ldots, \beta_j)$ of a $Challeng(Q, k_3)$ on a damaged file $\{m_i\}_{i \in [1, C_{j,k}]}$ with respect to user U_j, where $j \in \{1, \cdots, m\}$.

Let the proof of the $Challeng(Q, k_3)$ on the unbroken data blocks $\{m_i\}_{i \in [1, C_{j,k}]}$ with respect to user U_j be (μ, σ), then we know $\mu \neq \mu^*$. Let $\Delta\mu = \mu^* - \mu$ Since $e(\sigma, g) = \prod_{\ell \in [0,j]} e\left(\alpha_\ell, u^\mu \cdot R^{-h(R)} \cdot \prod_{i \in Q_{T_\ell}} H(W_i)^{v_i} \right)$ and $e(\sigma^*, g) = \prod_{\ell \in [0,j]} e\left(\alpha_0, u^\mu \cdot R^{-h(R)} \cdot \prod_{i \in Q_{T_\ell}} H(W_i)^{v_i} \right)$, (by Definition 2), we have $e(\sigma^* \cdot \sigma^{-1}, g) = e(g^{x_0}, u^{\Delta\mu})$. As a result, we know $u^{x_0} = g^{ax_0} = (\sigma^* \cdot \sigma^{-1})^{\frac{1}{\Delta\mu}}$. That is, B with probability ϵ solves a CDH problem: given $g, g^a, g^{x_\ell} \in G$, output g^{ax_0}. $\square$

6. Performance Analysis

In this section, we analyze the communication and computation complexities of revocable third-party privacy-preserving auditing scheme for cloud storage. Particularly, we are only interested in the communication and computation costs of its frequent activities, and ignore the costs of the initial system setup that is the same as other conventional public auditing schemes.

NOTATION. Let $Pair$ denote one pairing operation, Exp denote one exponentiation operation in G, and MZ and MG respectively denote one multiplication operation in Z_p and G. We denote the bit size of the element in $\left\{ 1, \cdots, C_{j,k} \right\}$, $\{1, \cdots, n\}$, Z_p and G by $|C|$, $|n|$, $|p|$ and $|G|$ respectively. The number of the data blocks selected by a challenge user is assumed to be a constant c.

6.1. Communication Cost

We can see that the communication overhead of our scheme depends on the communication complexity of algorithm Proof. According to the Proof algorithm, the user U_j in one auditing process would first send a challenge $Q = \{(i, v_i)\}$ with size $c(|C| + |p|)$ to the cloud and then the cloud would send a proof $(\mu, \sigma, t, \alpha_1, \ldots, \alpha_{j-1}, \beta_1, \ldots, \beta_j)$ with size $|p| + 2j|G| + c|C| + |G|$ to the user U_j if it's the user U_j's first auditing query; otherwise the cloud would just send (μ, σ, t) with size $|p| + |G| + c|C|$ to the user U_j. Therefore, the total communication cost of one audit process in our scheme is $|p| + |G| + c(2|C| + |p|)$ bits.

6.2. Computation Cost

The computation cost includes update time and audit time. To update a user U_j, the Update algorithm only needs to compute g^{x_{j-1}/x_j}. Hence the update time of our scheme is Exp. To complete one audit, the cloud should output a proof and the auditing user should verify its correctness. We know that the audit time of our scheme for user U_j depends on the generation and verification costs of (μ, σ, t). Therefore, the audit time for user U_j is $(c+2j)\,MZ + jMG + (2c+j)\,Exp + (j+1)\,Pair$ (here we ignore the simple addition and hash operations).

Additional Comparison. We also give a comparison between our scheme and the revised scheme of [16] for auditing owned cloud storage. Table 2 shows the details of the comparison. We know that the auditing scheme in [16] is insecure under collusion attacks but it's the most efficient revocable public cloud storage auditing scheme in the literature. When a user U_j executes the Proof algorithm of [16], it would send a challenge $Q = \{(i, v_i)\}$ with size $c\,(|n|+|q|)$ to the cloud and the cloud would send a proof $\{\alpha, \beta, \{id_l, s_l\}_{l \in L}\}$ with size $j \cdot (|p|+|G|) + c \cdot |id|$ to the user U_j. Therefore, the total communication cost of one audit process in that scheme is $j \cdot (|p|+|G|) + c \cdot (|id|+|n|+|p|)$ bits. As the Update algorithm of [16] needs to recalculate all the tags of n data blocks, we know the update time of [16] is $nExp$. To complete one audit, the scheme in [16] first requests the cloud to output a proof $nExp$ and then instructs the auditing user to verify its correctness. Therefore, we know that the audit time of [16] for any user is $(c+2j)\,MZ + jMG + (c+j)\,Exp + (j+1)\,Pair$ (here the simple addition and hash operations are also ignored). From Table 2, we can see that the communication cost of our scheme will has superior efficiency than the [16] in some cases. And audit time of our scheme is (almost) the same as those of [16], while the update time of [16] is larger than that of our scheme. Therefore we know our scheme is more computationally efficient than the scheme in [16].

Table 2. The comparison of two revocable public cloud storage auditing schemes.

Scheme	Communication Cost	Computation Cost		Collusion Resistance
		Update Time	Audit Time	
[16]	$j \cdot (|p|+|G|) + c \cdot (|id|+|n|+|p|)$	$nExp$	$(c+2j)\,MZ + jMG + (c+j)\,Exp + (j+1)\,Pair$	NO
Our scheme	$|p|+|G|+c\,(2|C|+|p|)$	Exp	$(c+2j)\,MZ + jMG + (2c+j)\,Exp + (j+1)\,Pair$	YES

6.3. Experimental Results

As we know, the comparison of computation cost is obvious. Our Update time is Exp , it is much lower than the update time of [16]: $nExp$. Our auditing time is approximately equal the scheme in [16], it is only a difference of $cExp$. So we only need compare the communication cost of our auditing scheme with the work of [16] in experiments. Our experiments are implemented on a windows 7 system with an Intel Core 2 i5 CPU running at 2.53 GHz, 2 GB DDR 3 of RAM (1.74 GB available). All algorithms are implemented by C language, and our code uses the MIRACL library version 5.6.1. The elliptic curve we use is an MNT curve, the base field size is 159 bits and the embedding degree is 6. The security level is chosen to be 80 bit, and $|p| = |q| = 160$. For simplicity, we also set $k = 20$, $c = 300$. All the results of experiments are represented as the average of 30 trials. As described in Figure 6, the experimental results show that, compared with the auditing scheme in [16], the communication cost of our auditing scheme are much light-weight than the scheme in [16].

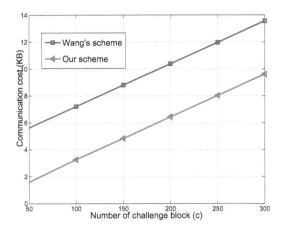

Figure 6. Comparison on the communication cost between our scheme and the scheme in [16].

7. Conclusions

In this paper, we have investigated the efficient user revocation problem in public cloud storage auditing systems and have proposed a dynamic revocable third-party privacy-preserving auditing scheme for cloud storage. We have proved that our scheme is secure against collusion attacks and have also demonstrated its effectiveness. In the light of the simplicity and extensibility of revocable third-party privacy-preserving auditing scheme for cloud storage, we believe the scheme would be much applicable in real-world cloud storage auditing systems.

Acknowledgments: This work is supported by the National Natural Science Foundation of China (No. 61370203) and the Science and Technology on Communication Security Laboratory Foundation(Grant No. 9140C110301110C1103).

Author Contributions: Theory: Xinpeng Zhang and Chunxiang Xu; Math analysis: Xinpeng Zhang and Xiaojun Zhang; Simulations: Xinpeng Zhang; Interpretation: Xinpeng Zhang and Xiaojun Zhang; Writing: Xinpeng Zhang, Taizong Gu, Zhi Geng and Guoping Liu. All authors have read and approved the final manuscript.

Conflicts of Interest: The authors declare no conflict of interest.

References

1. 9 worst cloud security threats. Available online: http://www.informationweek.com/byte/cloud/infras tructure-as-a-service/9-worst-cloud-security-threats/d/d-id/1114085 (accessed on 25 May 2016).
2. Cloud Security Alliance. Top Hreats to Cloud Computing. Available online: http://www.cloudsecurity alliance.org (accessed on 25 May 2016).
3. Kincaid, J. Mediamax/Helinkup Close Its Doors. Available online: http://techcrunch.com/2008/07/10/ mediamaxthelinkup-closes-its-doors/ (accessed on 25 May 2016).
4. Cloud Computing Users Are Losing Data, Symantec Finds. Available online: http://news.investors.com/ technology/011613-640851-cloud-computing-data-loss-high-in-symantec-study.htm (accessed on 25 May 2016).
5. Kher, V.; Kim, Y. Securing distributed storage: Challenges, techniques, and systems. In Proceedings of the 2005 ACM Workshop on Storage Security and Survivability, Fairfax, VA, USA, 11 November 2005; pp. 9–25.
6. Schroeder, B.; Gibson, G.A. Disk failures in the real world: What does an mttf of 1, 000, 000 hours mean to you? In Proceedings of the FAST '07: 5th USENIX Conference on File and Storage Technologies, San Jose, CA, USA, 14–16 Februery 2007; Volume 7, pp. 1–16.
7. Cloud Security Alliance. Cloud computing vulnerability incidents: a statistical overview. Available online: http://www.cert.uy/wps/wcm/connect/975494804fdf89eaabbdab1805790cc9/CloudComputing-Vulnerab ility-Incidents. pdf/?MOD=AJPERES (accessed on 25 May 2016).

8. Yu, S.; Wang, C.; Ren, K.; Lou, W.   Achieving secure, scalable, and fine-grained data access control in cloud computing.   In Proceedings of the 2010 Proceedings IEEE INFOCOM, San Diego, CA, USA, 14–19 March 2010; pp. 1–9.

9. Wang, C.; Chow, S.S.M.; Wang, Q.; Ren, K.; Lou, W. Privacy-preserving public auditing for secure cloud storage. *IEEE Trans. Comput.* **2013**, *62*, 362–375.

10. Wang, Q.; Wang, C.; Li, J.; Ren, K.; Lou, W. Enabling public verifiability and data dynamics for storage security in cloud computing. In *Computer Security—ESORICS 2009*; Springer: Medford, MA, USA, 2009; pp. 355–370.

11. Ateniese, G.; Burns, R.; Curtmola, R.; Herring, J.; Kissner, L.; Peterson, Z.; Song, D. Provable data possession at untrusted stores.   In Proceedings of the 14th ACM Conference on Computer and Communications Security, Alexandria, VA, USA, 29 October–2 November 2007; pp. 598–609.

12. Juels, A.; Kaliski, B.S., Jr.   Pors: Proofs of retrievability for large files. In Proceedings of the 14th ACM Conference on Computer and Communications Security, Alexandria, VA, USA, 29 October–2 November 2007; pp. 584–597.

13. Shacham, H.; Waters, B.   Compact proofs of retrievability.   In *Advances in Cryptology-ASIACRYPT 2008*; Springer: Medford, MA, USA, 2008; pp. 90–107.

14. Li, M.; Yu, S.; Ren, K.; Lou, W. Securing personal health records in cloud computing: Patient-centric and fine-grained data access control in multi-owner settings. In *Security and Privacy in Communication Networks*; Springer: Medford, MA, USA, 2010; pp. 89–106.

15. Zhang, X.; Xu, C.; Zhang, X. Efficient pairing-free privacy-preserving auditing scheme for cloud storage in distributed sensor networks. *Int. J. Distrib. Sens. Netw.* **2015**, *501*, 593759,

16. Wang, B.; Li, B.; Li, H. Panda: Public auditing for shared data with efficient user revocation in the cloud. *IEEE Trans. Serv. Comput.* **2015**, *8*, 92–106.

17. Wang, B.; Li, H.; Li, M.   Privacy-preserving public auditing for shared cloud data supporting group dynamics. In Proceedings of the 2013 IEEE International Conference on Communications (ICC), Budapest, Hungary, 9–13 June 2013; pp. 1946–1950.

18. Yuan, J.; Yu, S. Efficient public integrity checking for cloud data sharing with multi-user modification. In Proceedings of the IEEE Conference on Computer Communications (INFOCOM), Toronto, ON, Canada, 27 April–2 May 2014; pp. 2121–2129.

19. Delerablée, C.; Paillier, P.; Pointcheval, D.   Fully collusion secure dynamic broadcast encryption with constant-size ciphertexts or decryption keys.   In *Pairing-Based Cryptography—Pairing 2007*; Springer: Medford, MA, USA, 2007; pp. 39–59.

20. Chaum, D.; Van Heyst, E. Group signatures. In *Advances in Cryptology EUROCRYPT 91*; Springer: Medford, MA, USA, 1991; pp. 257–265.

21. Wang, B.; Li, B.; Li, H. Knox: Privacy-preserving auditing for shared data with large groups in the cloud. In *Applied Cryptography and Network Security*; Springer: Medford, MA, USA, 2012; pp. 507–525.

22. Ateniese, G.; Hohenberger, S.   Proxy re-signatures: New definitions, algorithms, and applications. In Proceedings of the 12th ACM conference on Computer and Communications Security, Alexandria, VA, USA, 7–10 November 2005; pp. 310–319.

23. Liu, Q.; Wang, G.; Wu, J. Efficient sharing of secure cloud storage services.   In Proceedings of the 2010 IEEE 10th International Conference on Computer and Information Technology (CIT), Bradford, UK, 29 June–1 July 2010; pp. 922–929.

24. Liu, Q.; Wang, G.; Wu, J. Time-based proxy re-encryption scheme for secure data sharing in a cloud environment. *Inf. Sci.* **2014**, *258*, 355–370.

Feature Engineering for Recognizing Adverse Drug Reactions from Twitter Posts

Hong-Jie Dai [1,2,*], **Musa Touray** [3], **Jitendra Jonnagaddala** [4,5,*] and **Shabbir Syed-Abdul** [3,6,*]

[1] Department of Computer Science & Information Engineering, National Taitung University, Taitung 95092, Taiwan

[2] Interdisciplinary Program of Green and Information Technology, National Taitung University, Taitung 95092, Taiwan

[3] Graduate Institute of Biomedical Informatics, Taipei Medical University, Taipei 11031, Taiwan; musatouray185@hotmail.com

[4] School of Public Health and Community Medicine, UNSW Australia, Sydney, NSW 2052, Australia

[5] Prince of Wales Clinical School, UNSW Australia, Sydney, NSW 2052, Australia

[6] International Center for Health Information Technology, Taipei Medical University, Taipei 11031, Taiwan

[*] Correspondence: hjdai@nttu.edu.tw (H.-J.D.); z3339253@unsw.edu.au (J.J.); drshabbir@tmu.edu.tw (S.S.-A.)

Academic Editors: Yong Yu and Yu Wang

Abstract: Social media platforms are emerging digital communication channels that provide an easy way for common people to share their health and medication experiences online. With more people discussing their health information online publicly, social media platforms present a rich source of information for exploring adverse drug reactions (ADRs). ADRs are major public health problems that result in deaths and hospitalizations of millions of people. Unfortunately, not all ADRs are identified before a drug is made available in the market. In this study, an ADR event monitoring system is developed which can recognize ADR mentions from a tweet and classify its assertion. We explored several entity recognition features, feature conjunctions, and feature selection and analyzed their characteristics and impacts on the recognition of ADRs, which have never been studied previously. The results demonstrate that the entity recognition performance for ADR can achieve an F-score of 0.562 on the PSB Social Media Mining shared task dataset, which outperforms the partial-matching-based method by 0.122. After feature selection, the F-score can be further improved by 0.026. This novel technique of text mining utilizing shared online social media data will open an array of opportunities for researchers to explore various health related issues.

Keywords: adverse drug reactions; named entity recognition; word embedding; social media; natural language processing

---

1. Introduction

An adverse drug reaction (ADR) is an unexpected occurrence of a harmful response as a result of consumption or administration of a pharmaceutical drug at a known normal prophylactic, diagnostic, or therapeutic dose. Even though drugs are monitored in clinical trials for safety prior to approval and marketing, not all ADRs are reported due to the short duration and number of patients registered in clinical trials. Therefore, post marketing surveillance of ADRs is of utmost importance [1,2]. Reporting of ADRs is commonly done by medical practitioners. However, the relevance of reports given by individual drug users or patients has also been emerging [3]. For example, MedWatch (http://www.fda.gov/Safety/MedWatch/) allows both patients and drug providers to submit ADRs manually. Although there are diverse surveillance programs developed to mine ADRs, only a very small fraction of ADRs was reported. Immediate observation of adverse events help not only the drug regulators, but also the manufacturers for pharmacovigilance. Therefore, currently existing methods rely on patients' spontaneous self-reports that attest problems. On the other hand, with more and more people using social media to discuss health information, there are millions of messages on Twitter that discuss drugs and their side-effects. These messages contain data on drug usage in much larger test sets than any clinical trial will ever have [4]. Although leading drug administrative agencies do not make use of online social media user reviews because of the highly time consuming and expensive process for manual ADR identification from unstructured and noisy data, the social media platforms presents a new information source for searching potential adverse events [5]. Researchers have begun diving into this resource to monitor or detect health conditions on a population level.

Text mining can be employed to automatically classify texts or posts that are assertive of ADRs. However, mining information from social media is not straightforward and often complex. Social media data in general is short and noisy. It is common to notice misspellings, abbreviations, symbols, and acronyms in Twitter posts. Tweets usually contain a special character. For example, in the tweet "Shouldn't have taken 80 mg of vyvanse today ... #cantsleep", the word "cantsleep" is preceded with the "#" symbol. The sign is called a hashtag, which is used to mark keywords or topics in a tweet. The symbol was used by twitter users to categorize messages. In this example, the hash-tagged word (can't sleep) is an ADR. In addition, the terms used for describing ADR events in social medial are usually informal and do not match clinical terms found in medical lexicons. Moreover, beneficial effects or other general mention types are usually ambiguous with ADR mentions.

In this study, an ADR event monitoring system that can classify Twitter posts regarding ADRs from Twitter is developed. The system includes an ADR mention recognizer that can recognize ADR mentions from a given Twitter post. In addition, because tweets mentioning ADRs may not always be ADR assertive posts, an ADR post classifier that can classify the given post for indication of ADR events is included in the system. The two systems were developed by using supervised learning approaches based on conditional random fields (CRFs) [6] and support vector machines (SVMs) [7], respectively. A variety of features have been proposed for supervised named entity recognition (NER) systems [8–10] in the newswire and biomedical domains. Supervised learning is extremely sensitive to the selection of an appropriate feature set. However, only limited studies focus on the impact of these features and their combinations on the effectiveness of mining ADRs from Twitter. In light of this, our study emphasizes the feature engineering for mining ADR events by analyzing the impact of various features taken from previous supervised NER systems. This study selected features widely used in various NER tasks to individually investigate their effectiveness for ADR mining, and conducted a feature selection algorithm to remove improper feature combinations to identify the optimal feature sets. Some previous works [11,12] demonstrated that the results of NER can be exploited to improve the performance of the classification task. Therefore, the output of the NER system is integrated with the features extracted for the ADR post classifier. The performance of both systems is finally reported on the manually annotated dataset released by the Pacific Symposium on Biocomputing (PSB) Social Media Mining (SMM) shared task [13].

2. Related Work

Identifying ADRs is an important task for drug manufacturers, government agencies, and public health. Although there are diverse surveillance programs developed to mine ADRs, only a very small fraction of ADRs was submitted. On the other hand, there are millions of messages on Twitter that discuss drugs and their side-effects. These messages contain data on drug usage in much larger test sets than any clinical trial will ever have [4]. Unfortunately, mining information related to ADRs from big social media reveals a great challenge. A series of papers has demonstrated how state-of-the-art natural language processing (NLP) systems perform significantly worse on social media text [14]. For example, Ritter *et al.* [15] presented that the Stanford NER system achieved an F-score of only 0.42 on the Twitter data, which is significantly lower than 0.86 on the CoNLL test set [16]. The challenges of mining information from Twitter can be summarized as follows [13,15,17,18]. (1) Length limits: Twitter's

140 character limit leads to insufficient contextual information for text analysis without the aid of background knowledge. The limit may somewhat lead to the use of shortened forms that leads to the second challenge; (2) The non-standard use of language, which includes shortened forms such as "ur" which can represent both "your" and "you're", misspellings and abbreviations like lol (laugh out loud) and ikr (i know, right?), expressive lengthening (e.g., sleeeeep), and phrase construction irregularities; (3) The final challenge is the lack of the ability to computationally distinguish true personal experiences of ADRs from hearsay or media-stimulated reports [19].

NER is one of the most essential tasks in mining information from unstructured data. Supervised NER that uses CRFs has been demonstrated to be especially effective in a variety of domains [20–22]. Several types of features have been established and widely used in various applications. Some features capture only one linguistic characteristic of a token. For example, the context information surrounding a word and its morphologic or part-of-speech (PoS) information. Zhang and Johnson [23] indicated that these basic features alone can achieve competitive levels of accuracy in the general domain. Conjunction features, on the other hand, consist of multiple linguistic properties, such as the combination of words within a context window. They are usually more sophisticated linguistic features and can also be helpful after feature selection [24]. Syntactic information, such as the shallow parsing (chunk), is usually considered a very useful feature in recognizing named entities since in most cases either the left or right boundary of an entity is aligned with either edge of a noun phrase. NER is also a knowledge-extensive task. Therefore, domain-specific features such as the lexicon (or gazetteers) feature [25] turned out to be a critical resource to improve recognition performance. For instance, Kazama and Torisawa [22] used the IOB tags to represent their lexicon features and showed an improvement of F-score by 0.03 in the task of recognizing four common entity categories. In addition, semi-supervised approaches based on unlabeled data have attracted lots of attentions recently, especially after the great success of employing word representation features in NLP tasks [26]. The idea of the feature could contribute to the pioneering n-gram model proposed by Brown *et al.* [27], which provides an abstraction of words that could address the data sparsity problem in NLP tasks [28]. Turian *et al.* [26] showed that the use of unsupervised word representations as extra word features could improve the quality of NER and chunking. The results of NER can also be exploited to improve the performance of the article classification task [11,12].

Based on the aforementioned works, several studies had adapted NLP techniques for utilizing social media data to detect ADRs. Pioneering studies [18,29] and systems developed in the recent PSB SMM workshop [13] implemented some of the conventional features described in their ADR mining systems. Nikfarjam *et al.* [18] introduced ADRMine, a CRF-based NER system that can recognize ADR-related concepts mentioned in data from DailyStrength and Twitter. In addition to the surrounding word, PoS, and lexicon features, they implemented a negation feature which indicates whether or not the current word is negated. Furthermore, they utilized word2vec [30] to generate 150-dimensional word vectors from data about drugs. Afterwards, the K-means clustering algorithm was performed to group the vectors into 150 clusters. The generated clusters were then used in the implementation of their word representation features. Lin *et al.* [29] studied the effect of different context representation methods, including normalization and word vector representations based on word2vec and global vector [31]. They observed that using either of them could reduce feature spaces and improve the recall and overall F-measure. Yates *et al.* [32] employed CRF model with two tag sets to recognize ADRs. They implemented surrounding word, PoS, lexicon, and syntactic features. The Stanford parser was employed to provide the syntactic dependency information. The orthographic features commonly used in biomedical NER were ignored because they believe that ADR expressions do not frequently follow any orthographic patterns.

Automatic classification of ADR containing user posts is a crucial task, since most posts on social media are not associated with ADRs [2]. Sarker and Gonzalez [33] considered the task as a binary classification problem and implemented a variety of features, including the n-gram features in which n was set from one to three, lexicon features, polarity features, sentimental score features, and topic modeling features. The system was then trained by using a data combining three different corpora. They observed that based on their features the SVM algorithm had the best performance. However, when multi-corpus training was applied, the performance cannot be further improved if dissimilar datasets are combined. Sarker *et al.* [34] manually annotated Twitter data and performed analyses to determine whether posts on Twitter contain signals of prescription medication abuse. By using the annotated corpus, they implemented the same *n*-gram features, lexicon features, and word representation features. The results once again demonstrated that the SVM algorithm achieved the highest F-score for the binary classification task of medication abuse. Paul and Dredze [35] improved their ailment topic aspect model by incorporating prior knowledge about diseases, and found that the new model outperformed the previous one without prior knowledge in the applications of syndromic surveillance.

3. Materials and Methods

Figure 1 shows the final flowchart of the developed systems for the task of ADR post classification (ADR-C) and the task of recognizing ADR mention (ADR-R) in the form of a pipeline. Because tweets in general are noisy, a few preprocessing steps were developed to address this issue. After preprocessing, we extracted various features to train the machine learning models for the ADR mention recognizer and the ADR post classifier. With the generated models, the same preprocessing steps and machine learning algorithms were used to classify the given Twitter post and recognize described ADR mentions.

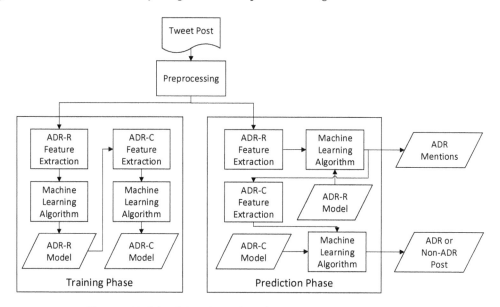

Figure 1. High level flowchart of the developed ADR mining system.

3.1. Preprocessing

Twokenizer [36] is used to tokenize the Twitter post into tokens and generate the PoS information for each of them. Each token is then processed by Hunspell (version 1.2.5554.16953, CRAWler-Lib, Neu-Ulm, Germany, http://hunspell.github.io/) to correct spelling errors. The spell checker is configured to use the English dictionaries for Apache OpenOffice and two other dictionaries. One dictionary contains ADR terms released by Nikfarjam *et al.* [18], and the other contains drug terms collected from the training set.

For ADR-R, the numerical normalization approach is employed to modify the numeral parts in each token to one representative numeral. The advantages of numerical normalization, including the reduction of the number of features, as well as the possibility of transforming unseen features to seen features, have been portrayed in several NER tasks [24,29] and could further improve the accuracy of feature weight estimation. In addition, the hashtag symbol "#" is deleted from its attached keywords or topics. The token prefixed with the "@" symbol is replaced with @REF. As a result, after the normalization preprocess, the example tweet "Shouldn't have taken 80 mg of vyvanse today ... #cantsleep" is convert into the following tokens "Shouldn't have taken 1mg of vyvanse today ... cantsleep".

For ADR-C, all tokens are lowercased and characters including web links, usernames, punctuations, and Twitter specific characters are deleted by using regular expressions. The Snowball stemmer (version C, open source tool, http://snowball.tartarus.org/) is then used to perform stemming. Finally, a custom stop word list created based on the training set is used to remove noisy tokens in tweets. The list mainly comprised of social media slang terms such as "retweet", "tweeter" and "tweetation", and words related to emails, inbox, and messages. For example, the tweet "©C4Dispatches Eeeeek! Just chucked my Victoza in the bin. I will take my chances with the diabetes #diabetes" is transformed to "eek chuck victoza i chanc diabet diabet" after the preprocessing step.

3.2. Development of the ADR Mention Recognizer

3.2.1. Machine Learning Algorithm and Formulation

The CRFs model has been successfully applied in many different NER tasks and showed a great performance. This study formulates the ADR-R task as a sequential labeling task by using the IOBES scheme with the CRF++ toolkit (version 0.58, open source tool, https://taku910.github.io/crfpp/) to develop the ADR mention recognizer. Figure 2 shows two example tweets after formulating ADR-R as the labelling task.

Shouldn't	have	taken	80 mg	of	vyvanse	today	...	#cantsleep	
O	O	O	O	O	O	O	O	S-ADR	
I	took	trazodone	last	night	and	it	really	helped-	but
O	O	O	O	O	O	O	O	O	O
it	was	difficult	to	wake	up	:/			
O	O	B-ADR	I-ADR	I-ADR	E-ADR	O			

Figure 2. The sequential labeling formulation with the IOBES scheme for the ADR-R task.

The IOBES scheme suggests the CRFs model to learn and recognize the Beginning, the Inside, the End, and the Outside of a particular category of ADR entities. The S tag is used to specifically represent a single-token entity. There are three ADR entity categories, resulting in a total of 13 tags ({ADR, Indication, Drug} × {B, I, E, S} + {O} = 13 tags.) for the ADR-R task.

3.2.2. Feature Extraction

The features extracted for ADR-R are elaborated as follows.

- Contextual features: For every token, its surrounding token is referred to as its context. For a target token, its context is described as the token itself (denoted as w_0) with its preceding tokens (denoted as $w_{-n}, w_{-n+1}, \ldots, w_{-1}$) and its following tokens (denoted as $w_1, w_2, \ldots, w_n$). In our implementation, the contextual features were extracted for the original tokens and the spelling checked tokens. All of the tokens were transformed into more compact representation with the process of normalization and stemming. As described later in the Results section, after the feature selection procedure, the context window was set to three, including $w_{-1}, w_0,$ and w_1.
- Morphology features: The feature set represents more information extracted from the current token. In our implementation, the prefixes and the suffixes of both the normalized and the spelling checked normalized tokens were extracted as features. The lengths of the prefix/suffix features were set to 3 to 4 within one-length context window.

- PoS features: The PoS information generated by Twokenizer for every token was encoded as features.

- Lexicon features: Three lexicon features were implemented to indicate a matching between the spelling corrected tokens with the entry in a lexicon. The first lexicon feature was implemented as a binary feature to indicate whether or not the current token partially matches with an entry in a given lexicon; the second feature further combines the matched token with the first feature to create a conjunction feature. Note that the conjunct spelling checked token may not be the same as the original token used for matching. The spelling checker may generate several suggestions for a misspelled token. In our implementation, the spelling checked contextual feature always uses the first suggestion generated by the checker, which may not match with the ADR lexicon. However, in the implementation of the lexicon feature, the matching procedure will match all suggestions against the ADR lexicon until a match is found, which may result in unmatched cases. The last lexicon feature encoded a match by using the IOB scheme that represents the matched position of the current token in the employed ADR lexicon. In some circumstances, especially when the post contains unique symbols such as hashtagged terms and nonstandard compound words, the spelling checker used in this study could decompose the tokens from the compound words. For example, "cant sleep" will be decomposed from the compound word "cantsleep". Each of the token will be matched with all of the entries in a lexicon. The ADR lexicon created by Leaman *et al.* [37] was employed as the lexicon for matching ADR terms. The sources of the lexicon include the UMLS Metathesaurus [38], the SIDER side effect resource [39], and other databases. The tokens annotated with the "Drug" tag were collected to form the lexicon for drugs. Take the Twitter post "Seroquel left me with sleep paralysis" as an example. The compound noun "sleep paralysis" matched with the ADR lexicon and their corresponding feature values are listed as follows.

  ○ Binary: 1, 1.
  ○ Conjunction: sleep/1, paralysis/1.
  ○ IOB: B-ADR, I-ADR.

- Word representation feature: The large unlabeled data from the Twitter website was utilized to generate word clusters for all of the unique tokens with the vector representation method [30]. The feature value for a token is then assigned based on its associated cluster number. If the current token does not have a corresponding cluster, its normalized and stemmed result will be used. The feature adds a high level abstraction by assigning the same cluster number to similar tokens. In order to create the unlabeled data, we searched the Twitter website for a predefined query to collect 7 days of tweets including 97,249 posts. The query was compiled by collecting each of the entries listed in the lexicon used for generating the lexicon feature, the described ADRs, their related drugs collected from the training set of the SMM shared task, as well as the hashtags annotated as ADRs in the training set. The final query contains 14,608 unique query terms. After the query was defined, the Twitter REST API was used to search for Twitter posts related to the collected ADR-drug pairs and hashtagged terms. Afterwards, Twokenizer was used on the collected dataset to generate tokens. The word2vec toolkit (open source tool, https://code.google.com/archive/p/word2vec/) was then used to learn a vector representation for all tokens based on their contexts in different tweets. The neural network behind the toolkit was set to use the continuous bag of words scheme, which can predict the word given its context. In our implementation, the size of context window was set to 5 with 200 dimension, and a total of 200 clusters were generated.

3.3. Development of the ADR Post Classifier

3.3.1. Machine Learning Algorithm

SVM with the linear kernel is used to develop the ADR post classifier. Due to the large class imbalance in the training set, instead of assigning class weight of 1 for both classes, we adjusted class weights inversely based on the class distribution. The cost parameter of the model is set to 0.5, which was optimized on the training set for better performance during the development.

3.3.2. Feature Extraction

Various feature sets are extracted, which include the linguistic, polarity, lexicon, and topic modelling based features.

- Linguistic features: We extracted common linguistic information like bag of words, bigrams, trigrams, PoS tags, token-PoS pairs, and noun phrases as features.
- Polarity features: The polarity cues developed by Niu *et al.* [40] were implemented to extract four binary features that can be categorized as "more-good", "less-good", "more-bad", and "less-bad". The categories are inferred based on the presence of polarity keywords in a tweet, which were then encoded as binary features for a tweet. For example, considering the tweet *"could you please address evidence abuutcymbalta being less effective than TCAs"*, the value of the feature "less good" would be 1 and the rest would take the value 0 because the token "less" and "effective" matched with the "less-good" polarity cue.
- Lexicon based features: The features were generated by using the recognition results of a string matching algorithm combined with the developed ADR mention recognizer. Tweets were processed to find exact matches of lexical entries from the existing ADR and drug name lexicons [18]. The presence of lexical entries were engineered as two binary features with the value of either 0 or 1. For example, in the Twitter post *"Antipsychotic drugs such as Zyprexa, Risperdal & Seroquel place the elderly at increased risk of strokes & death"*, both the ADR and the drug name lexical features take the value of 1.
- Topic modeling features: In our system, the topic distribution weights per tweet were extracted as features. The Stanford Topic Modelling Toolbox (version 0.4, The Stanford NLP Group, Stanford, CA, USA, http://nlp.stanford.edu/software/tmt/tmt-0.4/) was used to extract these features. The number of features depends on the number of topics to be obtained from the dataset. For example, if the topic model is configured to extract five topics, then the weights corresponding to the five topics are represented as the topic modeling features.

3.4. Dataset

The training set and development set released by the PSB SMM shared task [13] were used to assess the performance of the developed system. For the ADR-C task, a total of 7574 annotated tweets were made available, which contains binary annotations, ADR and non-ADR, to indicate the relevance of ADR assertive user posts. For the task of ADR-R, 1784 Twitter posts were fully annotated for the following three types of ADR mentions.

- Drug: A medicine or other substance which has a physical effect when ingested or otherwise introduced into the body. For example, "citalopram", "lexapro", and "nasal spray".
- Indication: A specific circumstance that indicates the advisability of a special medical treatment or method to describe the reason to use the drug. For example, "anti-depressant", "arthritis", and "autoimmune disease".
- ADR: A harmful or unpleasant reaction to the use of a drug. For instance, Warfarin (Coumadin, Jantoven) is used to prevent blood clots and is usually well tolerated, but a serious internal hemorrhage may occur. Therefore, the occurrence of serious internal bleeding is an ADR for Warfarin.

Nevertheless, during the preparation of this manuscript, some Twitter users removed their posts or even deactivated their accounts. As a result, some of the tweets from the original corpus are inaccessible. Only 1245 and 5283 tweets can be downloaded from the Twitter website for ADR-R and ADR-C, respectively. Therefore, the experiment results presented in the following section were based on a subset of the original dataset.

3.5. Evaluation Scheme

We devised an ADR mention recognizer which recognizes the text span of reported ADRs from a given Twitter post, and an ADR post classifier which categorizes the given posts as an indication of ADRs or not. Both systems were evaluated by using the following two paired criteria, precision (P) and recall (R), and the combined criterion, F-measure (F).

$$P = \frac{TP}{TP + FP} \tag{1}$$

$$R = \frac{TP}{TP + FN} \tag{2}$$

$$F = \frac{(2 \times P \times R)}{P + R} \tag{3}$$

In the equations, the notations of TP, FP and FN stand for true positives, false positives and false negatives, respectively. In the evaluation of the ADR-R task, the approximate-match criterion [41] is used to determine the TP/FP/FN cases. Therefore, a TP is counted if the recognized text span is a substring of the manually annotated span or vice versa, and its associated entity type is matched with the one given by domain experts. The modified version of the official evaluation tool evalIOB2.pl of the BioNLP/NLPBA 2004 Bio-Entity Recognition Task [42] was used to calculate the PRF scores. ADR-C can be considered as a binary classification task. Hence, an instance is considered as a TP when the predicted class is matched with the class manually determined by domain experts.

4. Results

4.1. Feature Engineering for the ADR Mention Recognizer

Here we report the performance of the developed ADR mention recognizer by different feature combinations. We started by handling the local contextual features, then studied the evaluation of external knowledge features. Tenfold cross validation (CV) was performed on the ADR-R training set to assess the performance during the development phase. Finally, all of the studied features were processed by a feature selection algorithm to sieve the most appropriate feature subsets. The performance of the model based on the selected features was evaluated on the training set and the development set of the SMM shared task.

4.1.1. Local Contextual Features

Table 1 reports the ADR-R performance when only the local information about a current token is used. As shown in configurations 1–7, it is not surprising that the ADR-R performance is poor with only contextual features. The best F-score obtained is the fourth configuration which only considers the normalized and stemmed tokens within three context-window size. Configurations 5 to 7 demonstrate that with larger context, the P of ADR-R can be improved but at the cost of decline in the R.

Table 1. Local contextual feature comparison on the training set. The best PRF-scores for each configuration set are highlighted in bold.

Configuration	Precision	Recall	F-Measure
(1) w_0	0.219	0.423	0.289
(2) w_0 (Normalized)	0.261	0.418	0.321
(3) w_0 (Normalized + Stemmed)	**0.353**	**0.429**	**0.387**
(4) (3) + w_{-1}, w_1 (Normalized + Stemmed)	0.743	**0.377**	**0.500**
(5) (4) + w_{-2}, w_2 (Normalized + Stemmed)	0.791	0.353	0.489
(6) (5) + w_{-3}, w_3 (Normalized + Stemmed)	0.790	0.322	0.457
(7) (4) + $w_{-1}/w_0, w_0/w_1$ (Normalized + Stemmed) [1]	**0.810**	0.358	0.496
(8) (3) + $\text{Prefix}_0, \text{Suffix}_0$ [2]	0.629	0.441	0.518
(9) (4) + $\text{Prefix}_0, \text{Suffix}_0$ [2]	0.735	**0.451**	**0.559**
(10) (4) + Shape_0	**0.793**	0.356	0.491

[1] The conjunction feature. [2] The length of three to four prefixes and suffixes were considered.

Configurations 8, 9, and 10 ignored surrounding context information but took the prefixes, suffixes, and shape features of the current token into consideration. The prefix and suffix features provided the recognizer good evidence of a particular token being a part of an ADR mention. However, the shape features did not increase the F-score of ADR-R.

4.1.2. External Knowledge Features

The external knowledge features studied include the spelling checking and PoS information for a token, the chunking information generated by a shallow parser, the lexicon information for ADR mentions, and the word representation information.

Table 2 compares the performance of the spelling checked contextual features with that of the unchecked contextual features. The results obtained in the configurations with spelling checked features such as 2, 4, 8, and 12 demonstrate the need for spelling check on Twitter posts. Precision improved when we replaced the original token with the spelling checked token, and recall can be further improved if the token is stemmed. Similar to the finding of Table 1, the performance drops with larger context, and the best size for the context window observed is three (configuration 8). Finally, by employing spelling check with normalized and stemmed prefixes and suffixes, the best F-score of 0.586 (configuration 12) was achieved.

Table 2. Impact of the spelling checking for the local contextual feature. The best PRF-scores for each configuration set are highlighted in bold.

Configuration	P	R	F
(1) w_0 (Normalized)	0.261	0.418	0.321
(2) w_0 (Normalized + Spelling Checked)	0.277	0.418	0.333
(3) w_0 (Normalized + Stemmed)	0.353	0.429	0.387
(4) w_0 (Normalized + SpellingChecked + Stemmed)	**0.377**	**0.439**	**0.406**
(5) (3) + w_{-1}, w_1 (Normalized + Stemmed)	0.743	0.377	0.500
(6) (4) + w_{-1}, w_1 (Normalized + SpellingChecked + Stemmed)	0.718	0.368	0.487
(7) (5) + (4)	0.729	0.426	0.538
(8) (6) + (3)	0.734	**0.436**	**0.547**
(9) (8) + w_{-2}, w_2 (Normalized + SpellingChecked + Stemmed)	0.728	0.420	0.532
(10) (8) + $w_{-1}/w_0, w_0/w_1$ (Normalized + Stemmed)	**0.792**	0.391	0.524
(11) (7) + $\text{Prefix}_0, \text{Suffix}_0$ (Normalized+Stemmed)	0.720	0.448	0.552
(12) (8) + $\text{Prefix}_0, \text{Suffix}_0$ (Normalized + SpellingChecked + Stemmed)	**0.752**	**0.480**	**0.586**
(13) (7) + Shape_0	0.802	0.402	0.535

Table 3 compares the ADR-R performance when we combined the local contextual features with the PoS information generated by two different PoS taggers—Twokenizer [36] and GENIA tagger [43].

The results shows that with the PoS information the precision of ADR-R can be boosted from 0.377 to 0.781 and 0.784, but the impact of these features on the F-score depends on the underlying PoS tagger.

Table 3. Comparison of the ADR-R performance based on different PoS information. The best PRF-scores for each configuration set are highlighted in bold.

Configuration	P	R	F
(1) w_0 (Normalized + SpellingChecked + Stemmed)	0.377	**0.439**	0.406
(2) (1) + PoS$_{GENIATagger0}$	**0.784**	0.295	0.428
(3) (1) + PoS$_{Twokenizer0}$	0.781 *	0.326	**0.460**
(4) (1) + w_{-1}, w_1 (Normalized + SpellingChecked + Stemmed)	0.718	**0.368**	0.487
(5) (4) + PoS$_{GENIATagger0}$	0.794	0.331	0.467
(6) (4) + PoS$_{Twokenizer0}$	0.809	0.364	**0.502**
(7) (6) + w_{-2}, w_2 (Normalized + SpellingChecked + Stemmed)	**0.833**	0.346	0.489

Table 4 displays the effect after including the parsing results created by the GENIA tagger in which a tweet was divided into a series of chunks that include nouns, verbs, and prepositional phrases. As shown in Table 4, although the P is improved after including the chunk information, the overall F-score was not improved with a larger context window.

Table 4. Effect of the chunk information on ADR-R. The best PRF-scores for each configuration set are highlighted in bold.

Configuration	P	R	F
(1) w_0 (Normalized + SpellingChecked + Stemmed)	0.377	**0.439**	0.406
(2) (1) + Chunking$_0$	**0.784**	0.301	**0.435**
(3) (1) + w_{-1}, w_1 (Normalized + SpellingChecked + Stemmed)	0.718	0.368	0.487
(4) (3) + Chunking$_0$	**0.798**	0.332	0.469
(5) (3) + w_0 (Normalized + Stemmed)	0.734	**0.436**	0.547
(6) (5) + Chunking$_0$	**0.815**	0.377	0.516

The impacts of the three implemented lexicon features were studied and illustrated in Table 5. In configuration 2, the IOB tag set was used. Configuration 3 represented the matching as a binary feature for the current token. The binary feature was further in conjunction with the matched spelling checked tokens in configuration 4. As indicated in Table 5, adding the three lexicon features improved the overall F-scores when a limited context window was employed. With the conjunct lexicon feature, the model performed better than that with just the binary feature. Considering the larger context window, the lexicon feature implemented by using the BIO tag set is the best choice.

Table 5. Comparison of the different representations for the lexicon features in the ADR-R task. The best PRF-scores for each configuration set are highlighted in bold.

Configuration	P	R	F
(1) w_0 (Normalized + SpellingChecked + Stemmed)	0.377	**0.439**	0.406
(2) (1) + ADR Lexicon-BIO$_0$	0.764	0.370	0.498
(3) (1) + ADR Lexicon-Binary$_0$	**0.773**	0.323	0.456
(4) (1) + ADR Lexicon-Binary$_0$/Matched Token	0.684	0.403	**0.507**
(5) (1) + w_{-1}, w_1 (Normalized + SpellingChecked + Stemmed)	0.718	0.368	0.487
(6) (5) + ADR Lexicon-BIO$_0$	0.747	**0.409**	**0.529**
(7) (5) + ADR Lexicon-Binary$_0$	**0.771**	0.349	0.480
(8) (5) + ADR Lexicon-Binary$_0$/Matched Spelling Checked Token	0.715	0.392	0.507

4.1.3. Word Representation Features

Table 6 exhibits the effect of the word representation features for ADR-R. From the results we can see that with the larger context window, inclusion of the word features can improve the recall and results in the increase of F-score.

Table 6. Comparison of the different word representation features in the ADR-R task. The best PRF-scores for each configuration set are highlighted in bold.

Configuration	P	R	F
(1) w_0 (Normalized + SpellingChecked + Stemmed)	0.377	**0.439**	0.406
(2) (1) + Word Representation$_0$	**0.463**	0.380	**0.418**
(3) (1) + w_{-1}, w_1 (Normalized + SpellingChecked + Stemmed)	0.718	0.368	0.487
(4) (3) + Word Representation$_0$	**0.748**	**0.397**	**0.519**
(5) (3) + w_{-2}, w_2 (Normalized + SpellingChecked + Stemmed)	**0.785**	0.352	0.486
(6) (5) + Word Representation$_0$	0.782	0.377	0.509

4.1.4. Backward/Forward Sequential Feature Selection Results

We integrated the features of all of the best configurations shown in the previous tables, and conducted a backward/forward sequential feature selection (BSFS/FSFS) algorithm [44] using tenfold CV of the training set to select the most effective feature sets. The procedure began with a feature space of 3,716,741 features, in which features were iteratively removed to examine whether the average F-score has improved. The algorithm then selected the subset of features that yields the best performance. The BSFS procedure terminated when no improvement of F-score can be obtained from the current subsets or there are no features available in the feature pool. The FSFS procedure then proceeds by adding the second-tier feature sets that could also improve the F-score but were not involved in the BSFS process. In each iteration, the FSFS procedure adds a feature set and selects the one with the best F-score for inclusion in the feature subset. The cycle repeats until no improvement is obtained from extending the current subset. Figure 3 displays the number of selected features and their corresponding F-scores.

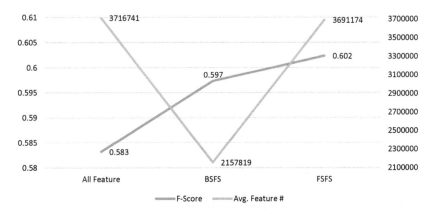

Figure 3. Comparison of the change in the number of features (the right y-axis) and F-scores (the left y-axis) after applying the feature selection procedure.

After the feature selection process, the F-score improved by 3.26%. The final PRF-scores of the developed ADR mention recognizer on the training set are 0.752, 0.502, and 0.602, respectively. Throughout this study, the organizers of the PSB SMM shared task have not released the gold annotations for their test set. Thus, the development set was used to compare the developed recognizer with a baseline system. The baseline system utilized a partial matching method based on the same lexicon used for extracting lexicon features, and all lexicon entries in the system were normalized for matching with the normalized Twitter posts.

As shown in Table 7, the recognizer with selected features can achieve an F-score of 0.588, which outperforms the same CRF-based recognizer with all features and the baseline system by 0.026 and 0.122, respectively.

Table 7. Performance comparison on the development set of the PSB SMM shared task.

Entity Type	Our Recognizer (All Features)			Our Recognizer (After Feature Selection)			Baseline System		
	P	R	F	P	R	F	P	R	F
Indication	0.600	0.120	0.200	0.667	0.160	0.258	0.000	0.008	0.000
Drug	0.000	0.000	0.000	0.000	0.000	0.000	0.000	0.000	0.000
ADR	0.797	0.490	0.606	0.800	0.521	0.631	0.670	0.394	0.496
Overall	0.789	0.437	0.562	0.788	0.469	0.588	0.392	0.579	0.466

4.2. Performance of the ADR Post Classifier

Table 8 reports the performance of the developed ADR post classifier on the development set. The first configuration uses a set of baseline features including the polarity, ADR-R, and linguistic features. The second configuration further includes the topic modeling feature that was set to extract three topics per tweet. The results suggest that the performance of the developed ADR post classifier can be improved with the topic modeling features.

Table 8. Performance of the developed ADR post classifier on the development set.

Configuration	P	R	F
(1) Baseline Feature Set	0.37	0.31	0.34
(2) 1 + Topic Modeling Features	0.43	0.38	0.40

4.3. Availability

All of the employed tools, datasets, and the compiled resources used in this study, including the stop word list and the word clusters generated from 7-days tweets, are available at https://sites.google.com/site/hjdairesearch/Projects/adverse-drug-reaction-mining.

5. Discussion

5.1. ADR Mention Recognition

We have demonstrated the results and performances of the feature selection based on the BSFS/FSFS algorithm. This approach is usually referred to as the wrapper method because the learning algorithm is wrapped into the selection process [45]. Wrappers are often criticized due to the requirement of intensive computation. On the other hand, the filter method is another feature selection method that makes an independent assessment based only on the characteristics of the data without considering the underlying learning algorithm. Here we implemented a filter-based feature selection algorithm, the simple information gain (IG) algorithm proposed by Klinger and Friedrich [46], to compare its results with that of the BSFS/FSFS algorithm. Figure 4 shows the F-score curves of the developed model on the development set when using different percentages of all features.

It can be observed that when 30% of the features were used, the model achieved the best F-scores of 0.579, which improved the original model with all features by 0.017. When only 10% or 20% of the features were used, the F-scores dropped by 0.06 and 0.03, respectively. The F-scores also decreased when we increased the percentage of the employed features from 30% to 50%, but the scores were still better than that of the model with all features. The F-score curve lifted again after including around 60% to 80% of the features. This phenomena is similar to the results shown in Figure 3, in which including the additional feature sets selected by FSFS can improve the performance of the feature subset selected by BSFS. The results demonstrate that both the FSFS/BSFS algorithm and the IG selection algorithm could be employed for the task of ADR-R feature selection and in general they have compatible performance.

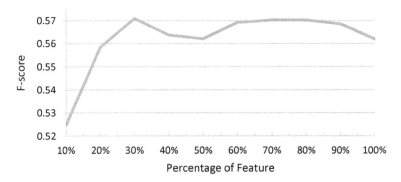

Figure 4. F-score curves of the filter-based feature selection with different percentages of all features.

Table 9 lists the features used for ADR-R after applying the BSFS/FSFS feature selection. The developed ADR mention recognizer with the selected features achieved an F-score of 0.631 for ADR mentions, which is significantly lower than the performance of the Stanford NER system in general domain. The Stanford NER system can achieve an F-score of 0.86 on the CoNLL test set [16]. As demonstrated by Ritter *et al.* [15], in which they reported the same system only achieved an F-score of 0.42 on the Twitter data, the results reveal the great challenge in mining information from big social media.

Table 9. Features selected for ADR-R.

Feature
w_{-1}, w_0, w_1 (Normalized + Stemmed)
w_0 (Normalized + Spelling Checked + Stemmed)
$Prefix_0, Suffix_0$ (Normalized + Stemmed)
$Prefix_0, Suffix_0$ (Normalized + Spelling Checked + Stemmed)
$PoS_{Twokenizer0}$
ADR Lexicon-BIO_0
Word Representation$_0$

One of the main reasons leading to the decrease of performance is that social media language is not descriptively accurate [17], which usually contains several non-standard spellings like "fx" for "affect", and word lengthening such as "killlerrr" for representing their subjectivity or sentiment [47]. We observed that certain ADR mentions are usually lengthening. For example, insomnia (UMLS CUI: C0917801) could be described in a tweet as "can't sleeeep" or "want to sleeeeep". The prefix and suffix features can capture the phenomenon and its implications. However, as shown in Table 2, the orthographic feature is less reliable for ADR-R. This is due to wide variety of letter case styles in Twitter posts. In the training set of ADR-R, 5.8% of tweets contain all lower case words, while 0.8% of the posts are all capitalized. Thus, the shape feature is not informative. Finally, the spelling variation leads to out-of-vocabulary (OOV) words, which requires the inclusion of the spell check token feature in the supervised machine learning model. Nonetheless, the suggestions generated by a spelling checker may not be perfect, so the original word is still an important feature for ADR-R. This is also supported by the distribution of the feature sets selected by the IG algorithm shown in Figure 5. We can observe that the top three important feature sets are the original word features, the spelling checked word features and the prefix/suffix features. The shape features only occupy 1% of the features.

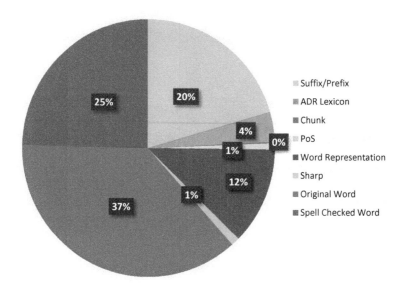

Figure 5. Feature distribution among the top 30% of features selected by the IG algorithm. Note that some feature sets were merged to simply the pie chart. For instance, the PoS information generated by either Twokenizer or GENIATagger were merged into the PoS feature set, and the original word feature set include the non-normalized, normallized, and stemmed word features.

Generally speaking, named entities such as person names or organization names are usually located in noun phrases. In most cases, named entities rarely exceed phrase boundaries, in which either the left or right boundary of an entity is aligned with either edge of a noun phrase [24]. However, the nomenclature for the entities in the ADR-R task are different from entities in general domains. Some ADR mentions are descriptive, like the ADR mention "feel like I cant even stand". Furthermore, off the shelf shallow parsers, such as the GENIATagger used in this study, have been observed to perform noticeably worse on tweets. Hence, addition of the chunk feature cannot improve the performance of ADR-R, which can also be interpreted from Figure 5, in which the chunk features occupy less than 1% of the features. Moreover, our results showed that larger context did not benefit the ADR-R either. In fact, during the BSFS procedure, features with larger contextual window except the chunk feature were the first few features to be removed from the feature space. Such behavior indicates that in the ADR-R task, the statistics of the dependency between the local context and the label of the token did not provide sufficient information to infer the current token's label, which is possibly due to the 140 character limit of Twitter post.

Previous work has shown that unlabeled text can be used to induce unsupervised word clusters which can improve the performance of many supervised NLP tasks [18,26,31]. Our results imply the similar conclusion. We observed that when the word representation feature is added, the recall of both the training and development sets improved, leading to an increase of F-score by 0.01. After manual analysis, the improvement can be attributed to the fact that the word representation feature enables the supervised learning algorithm to utilize the similarity between known ADR-related words and unknown words determined from the unlabeled data. An example of this is found in the 19th created word cluster, in which 49% of the tagged tokens are ADR-related. Another example can be observed in the development set. The token "eye" occurs only once in the training set. Both "eye" and the token "worse", which can compose the ADR mention "eyes worse", are not annotated as ADR-related terms in the training set. Fortunately, they are clustered into two clusters which contain ADR-related tokens in our word clusters. The token "eye" is within the cluster containing "dry" and "nose", while "worse" is in the cluster that consists of tokens like "teeth" and "reactions", which are known to be ADR-related terms in the training set. Therefore, the supervised learning algorithm is able to recognize the unseen mention as an ADR with this information.

The word clusters created by this study was based on a relatively small corpus compared with some publicly available word representation models trained on Twitter data. For example, the clusters generated by Nikfarjam et al. [18] were learned from one million tweets. Pennington et al. [31] released a pre-training model learned from two billion tweets by the global vector algorithm. It raises an interesting question about how well the performance of the developed model will be if the cluster information used by our word representation feature is replaced with the information from the two larger pre-trained clusters and vectors. We conducted an additional experiment to study the effect of this replacement, and the results are displayed in Table 10. In the configuration 2, the 150 clusters generated by Nikfarjam et al. was directly used. For the vectors created by Pennington et al., we applied the K-mean algorithm to create 150, 200, and 400 clusters and listed the results for each cluster in configuration 3, 4, and 5, respectively.

Table 10. ADR-R performance on the test set with different word clusters. The best PRF-scores are highlighted in bold.

Configuration	Precision	Recall	F-Measure
(1) With the Original 200 Clusters	**0.788**	0.469	0.5876
(2) With Nikfarjam et al.'s 150 Clusters	0.776	0.469	0.5843
(3) With Pennington et al.'s Vectors (150 Clusters)	0.771	0.455	0.5722
(4) With Pennington et al.'s Vectors (200 Clusters)	0.767	0.460	0.5746
(5) With Pennington et al.'s Vectors (400 Clusters)	0.779	**0.478**	**0.5922**

Similar to the observation in our previous work [48], it might be surprising to see that the replacement of larger clusters did not significantly improve the F-scores as shown in Table 10. The model with our clusters can achieve compatible performance in comparison to configuration 2. After examining the generated clusters and the manually annotated ADRs in the test set, we believe that it is owing to that the domain of our clusters is more relevant to ADR events because it was compiled using ADR-related keywords. The relevance of the corpus to the domain is more important than the size of the corpus [49]. It is noteworthy that clusters created by Nikfarjam et al. occasionally overlooked common ADR-related words such as "slept" and "forgetting". On the other hand, after checking Pennington et al.'s clusters used in configuration 3 and 4, we found that most of the ADR-related words such as "depression" are falling into the cluster consisting of words like "the", "for", and "do", implying that the number of pre-determined clusters may be insufficient to separate them from stop words. Therefore, we increased the number of clusters to 400 in configuration 5, and the results indicate an improvement in both R and F-scores. Several other studies have attempted to determine the optimal numbers of clusters or word embedding algorithms for implementing the word representation features, and it is beyond the scope of this study. Instead, we state that the number of clusters generated from vectors based on huge dataset is important, and we would like to further investigate this in our future work.

5.2. ADR Post Classification

As demonstrated in Table 6, although we included the output of ADR-R as a feature, which has shown to be an advantage over using the lexicon matching-based feature in a preliminary experiment, the performance of ADR-C is not satisfactory. We observed that the large number of error cases in the training and development set are due to the large class imbalance. SVM based classifier tends to be biased towards the majority class in an imbalanced dataset. Although the concern of class imbalance was addressed by assigning weights to the class based on the class distribution to a certain extent, applying more sophisticated class imbalance techniques, such as ensemble based classifiers, would further improve the ADR-C performance [50]. In addition, several issues remained despite various approaches during the preprocessing step have been exploited to reduce the noise in the data. For instance, several ill-formed special characters still remained after applying spelling check, which resulted in sparse feature space. Another major issue we noticed is the disambiguation of abbreviations. Many of the tweets included abbreviations or acronyms for ADRs and drug names that are ambiguous with general terms. Considering that there is an entirely different vocabulary of abbreviations and slang words adopted by Twitter users, we believe that a custom-built lexicon of abbreviations and acronyms for ADRs and drug names should mitigate the effect of these terms.

The performance of our ADR post classifier has increased with the addition of topic modeling based features. The improvement due to the addition of topic distribution weights per instance is consistent with the findings from previous studies in automatic text classification [51,52]. However, as shown in Figure 6, the performance varies, depending on the different number of extracted topics in the topic modeling features. The results indicate that when the topics are increased to five from three, the classification performance decreased in both the tenfold CV of the training set and the development set. This may be due to the fact that tweets are short, and extracting large number of topic related information creates sparse and noisy data. Moreover, the topic modeling features used only included per-tweet topic distribution weights. Topic modeling generates large amounts of useful information on a given dataset such as the number of terms in each topic and the weight of each term in a topic. Incorporating information of such might improve the effectiveness of the classifier.

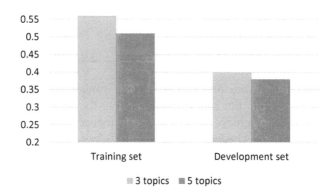

Figure 6. Comparison of F-scores with different number of topics.

6. Conclusions

In conclusion, this study presented methods to mine ADRs from Twitter posts using an integrated text mining system that utilizes supervised machine learning algorithms to recognize ADR mentions and to classify whether a tweet reports an event of an ADR. We implemented several features proposed for NER including local contextual features, external knowledge features, and the word representation features, and discussed their impact on ADR-R. After applying a feature selection algorithm, the best features included the current token, its surrounding tokens within the three context window, the prefix and suffix, the PoS of the current token, the lexicon feature, and the word representation features. In ADR-C, we proposed a method to automatically classify ADRs using SVM with the topic modeling, polarity, ADR-R, and linguistic features. The results demonstrated that the performance of the classifier could be improved by adding the topic modeling features, but would decline when the number of topics are increased. In the future, we aim to continually improve the performance of our methods by exploiting new features and ensemble based classifiers. In addition, the proposed methods for identifying ADRs will be evaluated in other social media platforms, as well as electronic health records.

Acknowledgments: This work was supported by the Ministry of Science and Technology of Taiwan (MOST-104-2221-E-143-005).

Author Contributions: Hong-Jie Dai conceived and designed the experiments; Musa Touray and Hong-Jie Dai performed the experiments; Jitendra Jonnagaddala and Hong-Jie Dai analyzed the data; Jitendra Jonnagaddala and Hong-Jie Dai developed the systems; Hong-Jie Dai, Jitendra Jonnagaddala, Musa Touray and Shabbir Syed-Abdul wrote the paper.

Conflicts of Interest: The authors declare no conflict of interest.

Abbreviations

The following abbreviations are used in this manuscript:

ADR	Adverse Drug Reaction
BSFS	Backward Sequential Feature Selection
CRF	Conditional Random Field
F	F-measure
FN	False Negative
FP	False Positive
FSFS	Forward Sequential Feature Selection
NER	Name Entity Recognition
NLP	Natural Language Processing
OOV	Out-Of-Vocabulary
P	Precision
PSB	Pacific Symposium on Biocomputing
PoS	Part of Speech
R	Recall
SMM	Social Media Mining
SVM	Support Vector Machine
TP	True Positive
UMLS	Unified Medical Language System

References

1. Lardon, J.; Abdellaoui, R.; Bellet, F.; Asfari, H.; Souvignet, J.; Texier, N.; Jaulent, M.C.; Beyens, M.N.; Burgun, A.; Bousquet, C. Adverse Drug Reaction Identification and Extraction in Social Media: A Scoping Review. *J. Med. Internet Res.* **2015**, *17*, e171. [CrossRef] [PubMed]

2. Sarker, A.; Ginn, R.; Nikfarjam, A.; O'Connor, K.; Smith, K.; Jayaraman, S.; Upadhaya, T.; Gonzalez, G. Utilizing social media data for pharmacovigilance: A review. *J. Biomed. Inform.* **2015**, *54*, 202–212. [CrossRef] [PubMed]

3. Blenkinsopp, A.; Wilkie, P.; Wang, M.; Routledge, P.A. Patient reporting of suspected adverse drug reactions: a review of published literature and international experience. *Br. J. Clin. Pharmacol.* **2007**, *63*, 148–156. [CrossRef] [PubMed]

4. Cieliebak, M.; Egger, D.; Uzdilli, F. Twitter can Help to Find Adverse Drug Reactions. Available online: http://ercim-news.ercim.eu/en104/special/twitter-can-help-to-find-adverse-drug-reactions (accessed on 20 May 2016).

5. Benton, A.; Ungar, L.; Hill, S.; Hennessy, S.; Mao, J.; Chung, A.; Leonard, C.E.; Holmes, J.H. Identifying potential adverse effects using the web: A new approach to medical hypothesis generation. *J. Biomed. Inform.* **2011**, *44*, 989–996. [CrossRef] [PubMed]

6. Lafferty, J.; McCallum, A.; Pereira, F. Conditional random fields: Probabilistic models for segmenting and labeling sequence data. In Proceedings of the 18th International Conference on Machine Learning (ICML), Williamstown, MA, USA, 28 June 2001.

7. Cortes, C.; Vapnik, V. Support-vector networks. *Mach. Learn.* **1995**, *20*, 273–297. [CrossRef]

8. Liu, S.; Tang, B.; Chen, Q.; Wang, X.; Fan, X. Feature engineering for drug name recognition in biomedical texts: Feature conjunction and feature selection. *Comput. Math. Methods Med.* **2015**, *2015*, 913489. [CrossRef] [PubMed]

9.   Dai, H.J.; Lai, P.T.; Chang, Y.C.; Tsai, R.T. Enhancing of chemical compound and drug name recognition using representative tag scheme and fine-grained tokenization. *J. Cheminform.* **2015**, *7*, S14. [CrossRef] [PubMed]

10. Tkachenko, M.; Simanovsky, A. Named entity recognition: Exploring features. In Proceedings of The 11th Conference on Natural Language Processing (KONVENS 2012), Vienna, Austria, 19–21 September 2012; pp. 118–127.

11. Gui, Y.; Gao, Z.; Li, R.; Yang, X. Hierarchical Text Classification for News Articles Based-on Named Entities. In *Advanced Data Mining and Applications*, Proceedings of the 8th International Conference, ADMA 2012, Nanjing, China, 15–18 December 2012; Zhou, S., Zhang, S., Karypis, G., Eds.; Springer: Berlin/Heidelberg, Germany, 2012; pp. 318–329.

12. Tsai, R.T.-H.; Hung, H.-C.; Dai, H.-J.; Lin, Y.-W. Protein-protein interaction abstract identification with contextual bag of words. In Proceedings of the 2nd International Symposium on Languages in Biology and Medicine (LBM 2007), Singapore, 6–7 December 2007.

13. Sarker, A.; Nikfarjam, A.; Gonzalez, G. Social media mining shared task workshop. In Proceedings of the Pacific Symposium on Biocomputing 2016, Big Island, HI, USA, 4–8 January 2016.

14. Gimpel, K.; Schneider, N.; O'Connor, B.; Das, D.; Mills, D.; Eisenstein, J.; Heilman, M.; Yogatama, D.; Flanigan, J.; Smith, N.A. Part-of-speech tagging for Twitter: Annotation, features, and experiments. In Proceedings of the 49th Annual Meeting of the Association for Computational Linguistics: Human Language Technologies, Portland, OR, USA, 19–24 June 2011.

15. Ritter, A.; Clark, S.; Etzioni, O. Named entity recognition in tweets: an experimental study. In Proceedings of the Conference on Empirical Methods in Natural Language Processing, Edinburgh, UK, 27–31 July 2011.

16. Finkel, J.R.; Grenager, T.; Manning, C. Incorporating non-local information into information extraction systems by Gibbs sampling. In Proceedings of the 43rd Annual Meeting on Association for Computational Linguistics, Ann Arbor, MI, USA, 25–30 June 2005.

17. Eisenstein, J. What to do about bad language on the internet. In Proceedings of the North American Chapter of the Association for Computational Linguistics (NAACL), Atlanta, GA, USA, 9–15 June 2013.

18. Nikfarjam, A.; Sarker, A.; O'Connor, K.; Ginn, R.; Gonzalez, G. Pharmacovigilance from social media: Mining adverse drug reaction mentions using sequence labeling with word embedding cluster features. *J. Am. Med. Inform. Assoc.* **2015**, *22*, 671–681. [CrossRef] [PubMed]

19. Harpaz, R.; DuMochel, W.; Shah, N.H. Big Data and Adverse Drug Reaction Detection. *Clin. Pharmacol. Ther.* **2016**, *99*, 268–270. [CrossRef] [PubMed]

20. Dai, H.-J.; Syed-Abdul, S.; Chen, C.-W.; Wu, C.-C. Recognition and Evaluation of Clinical Section Headings in Clinical Documents Using Token-Based Formulation with Conditional Random Fields. *BioMed Res. Int.* **2015**. [CrossRef] [PubMed]

21. He, L.; Yang, Z.; Lin, H.; Li, Y. Drug name recognition in biomedical texts: A machine-learning-based method. *Drug Discov. Today* **2014**, *19*, 610–617. [CrossRef] [PubMed]

22. Kazama, J.I.; Torisawa, K. Exploiting Wikipedia as external knowledge for named entity recognition. In Proceedings of the 2007 Joint Conference on Empirical Methods in Natural Language Processing and Computational Natural Language Learning, Prague, Czech Republic, 28–30 June 2007; pp. 698–707.

23. Zhang, T.; Johnson, D. A robust risk minimization based named entity recognition system. In Proceedings of the Seventh Conference on Natural language Learning at HLT-NAACL 2003, Edmonton, AB, Canada, 31 May–1 June 2003.

24. Tsai, R.T.-H.; Sung, C.-L.; Dai, H.-J.; Hung, H.-C.; Sung, T.-Y.; Hsu, W.-L. NERBio: Using selected word conjunctions, term normalization, and global patterns to improve biomedical named entity recognition. *BMC Bioinform.* **2006**, *7*, S11. [CrossRef] [PubMed]

25. Cohen, W.W.; Sarawagi, S. Exploiting dictionaries in named entity extraction: combining semi-Markov extraction processes and data integration methods. In Proceedings of the 10th ACM SIGKDD International Conference on Knowledge Discovery and Data Mining, Seattle, WA, USA, 22–25 August 2004.

26. Turian, J.; Ratinov, L.; Bengio, Y. Word representations: A simple and general method for semi-supervised learning. In Proceedings of the 48th Annual Meeting of the Association for Computational Linguistics, Uppsala, Sweden, 11–16 July 2010; pp. 384–394.

27. Brown, P.F.; de Souza, P.V.; Mercer, R.L.; Pietra, V.J.D.; Lai, J.C. Class-based *n*-gram models of natural language. *Comput. Linguist.* **1992**, *18*, 467–479.

28. Ratinov, L.; Roth, D. Design challenges and misconceptions in named entity recognition. In Proceedings of the 19th Conference on Computational Natural Language Learning, Boulder, CO, USA, 4–5 June 2009.

29. Lin, W.-S.; Dai, H.-J.; Jonnagaddala, J.; Chang, N.-W.; Jue, T.R.; Iqbal, U.; Shao, J.Y.-H.; Chiang, I.J.; Li, Y.-C. Utilizing Different Word Representation Methods for Twitter Data in Adverse Drug Reactions Extraction. In Proceedings of the 2015 Conference on Technologies and Applications of Artificial Intelligence (TAAI), Tainan, Taiwan, 20–22 November 2015.

30. Mikolov, T.; Sutskever, I.; Chen, K.; Corrado, G.S.; Dean, J. Distributed representations of words and phrases and their compositionality. In Proceedings of Advances in Neural Information Processing Systems (NIPS 2013), Lake Taheo, NV, USA, 5–10 December 2013; pp. 3111–3119.

31. Pennington, J.; Socher, R.; Manning, C.D. Glove: Global vectors for word representation. In Proceedings of the Empirical Methods in Natural Language Processing (EMNLP 2014), Doha, Qatar, 25–29 October 2014; Volume 12, pp. 1532–1543.

32. Yates, A.; Goharian, N.; Frieder, O. Extracting Adverse Drug Reactions from Social Media. In Proceedings of the Twenty-Ninth AAAI Conference on Artificial Intelligence (AAAI-15), Austin, TX, USA, 25–30 Jaunary 2015; pp. 2460–2467.

33. Sarker, A.; Gonzalez, G. Portable automatic text classification for adverse drug reaction detection via multi-corpus training. *J. Biomed. Inform.* **2015**, *53*, 196–207. [CrossRef] [PubMed]

34. Sarker, A.; O'Connor, K.; Ginn, R.; Scotch, M.; Smith, K.; Malone, D.; Gonzalez, D. Social Media Mining for Toxicovigilance: Automatic Monitoring of Prescription Medication Abuse from Twitter. *Drug Saf.* **2016**, *39*, 231–240. [CrossRef] [PubMed]

35. Paul, M.J.; Dredze, M. You Are What You Tweet: Analyzing Twitter for Public Health. In Proceedings of the Fifth International AAAI Conference on Weblogs and Social Media (ICWSM-11), Barcelona, Spain, 17–21 July 2011.

36. Owoputi, O.; O'Connor, B.; Dyer, C.; Gimpel, K.; Schneider, N.; Smith, N.A. Improved part-of-speech tagging for online conversational text with word clusters. In Proceedings of the Conference of the North American Chapter of the Association for Computational Linguistics, Atlanta, GA, USA, 9–14 June 2013.

37. Leaman, R.; Wojtulewicz, L.; Sullivan, R.; Skariah, A.; Yang, J.; Gonzalez, G. Towards internet-age pharmacovigilance: extracting adverse drug reactions from user posts to health-related social networks. In Proceedings of the 2010 Workshop on Biomedical Natural Language Processing, Uppsala, Sweden, 15 July 2010; pp. 117–125.

38. Bodenreider, O. The unified medical language system (UMLS): Integrating biomedical terminology. *Nucleic Acids Res.* **2004**, *32*, D267–D270. [CrossRef] [PubMed]

39. Kuhn, M.; Campillos, M.; Letunic, I.; Jensen, L.J.; Bork, P. A side effect resource to capture phenotypic effects of drugs. *Mol. Syst. Biol.* **2010**, *6*. [CrossRef] [PubMed]

40. Niu, Y.; Zhu, X.; Li, J.; Hirst, G. Analysis of Polarity Information in Medical Text. *AMIA Ann. Symp. Proc.* **2005**, *2005*, 570–574.

41. Tsai, R.T.-H.; Wu, S.-H.; Chou, W.-C.; Lin, C.; He, D.; Hsiang, J.; Sung, T.-Y.; Hsu, W.-L. Various criteria in the evaluation of biomedical named entity recognition. *BMC Bioinform.* **2006**, *7*. [CrossRef] [PubMed]

42. Kim, J.-D.; Ohta, T.; Tsuruoka, Y.; Tateisi, Y. Introduction to the bio-entity recognition task at JNLPBA. In Proceedings of the International Workshop on Natural Language Processing in Biomedicine and its Applications (JNLPBA-04), Geneva, Switzerland, 28–29 August 2004; pp. 70–75.

43. Tsuruoka, Y.; Tateishi, Y.; Kim, J.D.; Ohta, T.; McNaught, J.; Ananiadou, S.; Tsujii, J.I. Developing a robust part-of-speech tagger for biomedical text. In *Advances in Informatics*, Proceedings of the 10th Panhellenic Conference on Informatics, PCI 2005, Volas, Greece, 11–13 November 2005; Bozanis, P., Houstis, E.N., Eds.; Lecture Notes in Computer Science. Springer: Berlin/Heidelberg, Germany, 2005; Volume 3746, pp. 382–392.

44. Aha, D.W.; Bankert, R.L. A comparative evaluation of sequential feature selection algorithms. In *Learning from Data: Artificial Intelligence and Statistics V*; Fisher, D., Lenz, H.-J., Eds.; Springer: New York, NY, USA, 1995; pp. 199–206.

45. Guyon, I.; Elisseeff, A. An introduction to variable and feature selection. *J. Mach. Learn. Res.* **2003**, *3*, 1157–1182.

46. Klinger, R.; Friedrich, C.M. Feature Subset Selection in Conditional Random Fields for Named Entity Recognition. In Proceedings of the International Conference RANLP 2009, Borovets, Bulgaria, 14–16 September 2009.

47. Brody, S.; Diakopoulos, N. Cooooooooooooooooolllllllllllllll!!!!!!!!!!!!!!: Using word lengthening to detect sentiment in microblogs. In Proceedings of the Conference on Empirical Methods in Natural Language Processing, Edinburgh, UK, 27–29 July 2011.

48. Wang, C.-K.; Singh, O.; Dai, H.-J.; Jonnagaddala, J.; Jue, T.R.; Iqbal, U.; Su, E.C.-Y.; Abdul, S.S.; Li, J.Y.-C. NTTMUNSW system for adverse drug reactions extraction in Twitter data. In Proceedings of the Social Media Mining Shared Task Workshop at the Pacific Symposium on Biocomputing, Big Island, HI, USA, 4–8 January 2016.

49. Lai, S.; Liu, K.; Xu, L.; Zhao, J. How to Generate a Good Word Embedding? 2015. arXiv:1507.05523.

50. Galar, M.; Fernandez, A.; Barrenechea, E.; Bustince, H.; Herrera, F. A review on ensembles for the class imbalance problem: Bagging-, boosting-, and hybrid-based approaches. In *IEEE Transactions on Systems, Man, and Cybernetics, Part C: Applications and Reviews*; IEEE: New York, NY, USA, 2012; Volume 42, pp. 463–484.

51. Jonnagaddala, J.; Dai, H.-J.; Ray, P.; Liaw, S.-T. A preliminary study on automatic identification of patient smoking status in unstructured electronic health records. *ACL-IJCNLP* **2015**, *2015*, 147–151.

52. Jonnagaddala, J.; Jue, T.R.; Dai, H.-J. Binary classification of Twitter posts for adverse drug reactions. In Proceedings of the Social Media Mining Shared Task Workshop at the Pacific Symposium on Biocomputing, Big Island, HI, USA, 4–8 January 2016.

11

A Comparative Study on Weighted Central Moment and Its Application in 2D Shape Retrieval

Xin Shu [1,2,3,*], Qianni Zhang [3], Jinlong Shi [1] and Yunsong Qi [1]

[1] School of Computer Science & Engineering, Jiangsu University of Science & Technology, Zhenjiang 212003, China; jlshifudan@gmail.com (J.S.); mailqys@163.com (Y.Q.)
[2] School of Internet of Things Engineering, Jiangnan University, Wuxi 214122, China
[3] School of Electronic Engineering and Computer Science, Queen Mary University of London, London E1 4NS, UK; qianni.zhang@qmul.ac.uk
[*] Correspondence: shuxin@just.edu.cn

Academic Editor: Willy Susilo

Abstract: Moment invariants have been extensively studied and widely used in object recognition. The pioneering investigation of moment invariants in pattern recognition was due to Hu, where a set of moment invariants for similarity transformation were developed using the theory of algebraic invariants. This paper details a comparative analysis on several modifications of the original Hu moment invariants which are used to describe and retrieve two-dimensional (2D) shapes with a single closed contour. The main contribution of this paper is that we propose several different weighting functions to calculate the central moment according to human visual processing. The comparative results are detailed through experimental analysis. The results suggest that the moment invariants improved by weighting functions can get a better retrieval performance than the original one does.

Keywords: Hu moments; moment invariants; weighting function; weighted central moment

---

1. Introduction

Shape is a significant visual clue for human perception. Using the shape of an object for object recognition and image retrieval is a hot topic in computer vision [1]. Moment invariants have been extensively studied and widely used in shape recognition and identification since they were first proposed by Hu [2]. Since then, many other kinds of moments have been proposed in the literature, including Zernike moments [3–5], Legendre moments [6,7], Fourier-Mellin moments [8–10], *etc.* [2]. Zernike moments and Legendre moments are both proposed by Teague [11]. Zernike moments are used in pattern recognition applications as invariant descriptors of the image shape. The Zernike moment descriptor has desirable properties such as rotation and scale invariance, robustness to noise, expression efficiency and fast computation. Legendre moments use Legendre polynomials as basis functions. These polynomials are orthogonal and cause Legendre moments to extract independent features within the image, with no information redundancy. Though Legendre moments have good retrieval properties, they are not invariant to linear operation and rotation. The Fourier-Mellin moment is one of the complex moments and it was proposed by Sheng and Shen [12]; it can be transformed to rotation and translation invariants. It attains good results in shape recognition. These various moment invariants have been successfully utilized as pattern features in a number of applications including character recognition [13,14], aircraft recognition [15], object identification and discrimination [16,17], content-based image retrieval [18], two-dimensional (2D) flow fields analysis [19], *etc.* [20–22].

It is known that Hu's moment invariants are area moment invariants, which means that they are computed over all pixels including the shape boundary and its associated interior part. All pixels are usually taken as identically important in computing these moment invariants, which may not be in accordance with human perception. Generally, there are two ways to specify a 2D shape. One is to specify a shape with the whole region occupied by the object. Another way is to define a shape by only specifying its boundary. Based on the concept of shape representation through boundaries, Chen [17] introduced the curve moment invariants, which are reformulations of Hu's moments, and they are a set of invariants devised in such a way as to be evaluated only with the object boundary pixels. Though this modification reduces computation, the shape information is reduced to a certain extent as well. In order to increase the ability of noise tolerance, Balslev [21] introduced a spatial weighting function to Hu's central moment. Their weighting technique emphasized heavy weights to the areas near the center-of-mass for noise tolerance. As far a 2D non-rigid shape with a single closed contour is concerned, the centroid of the object may be outside of the region of the object. Balslev's method is not suitable for such cases.

In this work, we present several novel weighting functions into the central moment formula from a completely different perspective for 2D non-rigid shape retrieval. We have a completely different starting point from [23]. The specific weighting techniques will be discussed in detail in Section 3.

The paper is organized as follows. Section 2 of this paper provides the basic idea of traditional Hu's moments. Section 3 explains our weighting functions for the central moment according to human perception. Section 4 analyzes the experimental results and presents a discussion. Finally, the conclusion is given in Section 5.

2. Traditional Geometric Moment Invariants

In this section, we briefly review Hu's invariant moments. The 2D traditional geometric moments of order $p + q$ of a density distribution $f(x, y)$ are defined as

$$m_{pq} = \int_{-\infty}^{\infty} \int_{-\infty}^{\infty} x^p y^q f(x, y) dx dy \qquad p, q = 0, 1, 2, \ldots \tag{1}$$

When the geometric moments m_{pq} in Equation (1) are referred to the object centroid (x_c, y_c), they become the central moments, and are given by

$$\mu_{pq} = \int_{-\infty}^{\infty} \int_{-\infty}^{\infty} (x - x_c)^p (y - y_c)^q f(x, y) dx dy \tag{2}$$

where $x_c = m_{10}/m_{00}$ and $y_c = m_{01}/m_{00}$.

For a digital image represented in a 2D array, Equations (1) and (2) are given as Equations (3) and (4), respectively,

$$m_{pq} = \sum_{x=1}^{M} \sum_{y=1}^{N} x^p y^q f(x, y), \qquad p, q = 0, 1, 2, \ldots \tag{3}$$

$$\mu_{pq} = \sum_{x=1}^{M} \sum_{y=1}^{N} (x - x_c)^p (y - y_c)^q f(x, y) \tag{4}$$

where M and N are the horizontal and vertical dimensions, respectively, and $f(x, y)$ is the intensity at point (x, y) in the image.

The normalized central moments of an image are given by

$$\eta_{pq} = \frac{\mu_{pq}}{\mu_{00}^{\gamma}} \tag{5}$$

where $\gamma = \dfrac{p + q}{2} + 1, p + q = 2, 3, \cdots$. These moments are invariant to both translation and scale of the image.

Hu defines a set of seven moment invariants of orders of three or less, which are invariant to object scale, translation and rotation. In terms of the central moments, the seven moments are given as:

$$\phi_1 = \eta_{20} + \eta_{02} \tag{6}$$

$$\phi_2 = (\eta_{20} - \eta_{02})^2 + 4\eta_{11}^2 \tag{7}$$

$$\phi_3 = (\eta_{30} - 3\eta_{12})^2 + (3\eta_{12} - \eta_{03})^2 \tag{8}$$

$$\phi_4 = (\eta_{30} + \eta_{12})^2 + (\eta_{21} + \eta_{03})^2 \tag{9}$$

$$\phi_5 = (\eta_{30} - 3\eta_{12})(\eta_{30} + \eta_{12})[(\eta_{30} + \eta_{12})^2 - 3(\eta_{21} + \eta_{03})^2] \\ +(3\eta_{21} - \eta_{21})(\eta_{21} + \eta_{03})[3(\eta_{30} + \eta_{12})^2 - (\eta_{21} + \eta_{03})^2] \tag{10}$$

$$\phi_6 = (\eta_{20} - \eta_{02})[(\eta_{30} + \eta_{12})^2 - (\eta_{21} + \eta_{03})^2] \\ +4\eta_{11}(\eta_{30} + \eta_{12})(\eta_{21} + \eta_{03}) \tag{11}$$

$$\phi_7 = (3\eta_{21} - \eta_{03})(\eta_{30} + \eta_{12})[(\eta_{30} + \eta_{12})^2 - (\eta_{21} + \eta_{03})^2] \\ +(3\eta_{12} - \eta_{30})(\eta_{21} + \eta_{03})[3(\eta_{30} + \eta_{12})^2 - (\eta_{21} + \eta_{03})^2] \tag{12}$$

3. Several Weighting Functions

3.1. Boundary Weighting Function

Let us discuss the issue of shape recognition from another angle. For a 2D non-rigid shape with a single closed contour, as illustrated in Figure 1, an object's shape is mainly discriminated by its boundary pixels according to the characteristics of human visual perception. In other words, the boundary part of the object makes a greater contribution for distinguishing the object's shape than the central part of the object does [24,25].

Figure 1. Object and its contour.

Based on this fact, we propose a kind of boundary-weighted central moment in this paper. In the process of the central moment being calculated, pixels closer to the object boundary should be assigned larger weights and inner pixels farther away from the object boundary should be assigned smaller weights. According to this idea, Equation (4) should be modified as follows

$$\mu_{pq} = \sum_{x=1}^{M} \sum_{y=1}^{N} (x - x_c)^p (y - y_c)^q f(x,y)\delta(x,y) \tag{13}$$

where $\delta(x,y)$ is a weighting function which should emphasis the weights of those pixels closer to the object boundary. Both the linear and nonlinear functions are considered in our work.

If the linear weighting function is concerned, $\delta(x,y)$ can be set simply as Equation (14):

$$\delta(x,y) = \frac{1}{d(x,y)} \tag{14}$$

If the nonlinear weighting function is concerned, $\delta(x, y)$ can be set simply as the Gauss function in Equation (15)

$$\delta(x, y) = \frac{1}{\sigma\sqrt{2\pi}} e^{\frac{-(d(x,y) - \mu)^2}{2\sigma^2}} \tag{15}$$

$$d(x, y) = \min(\|(x, y), (x_i, y_i)\|), \forall (x_i, y_i) \in BPs \tag{16}$$

where $\|*\|$ denotes some sort of distance metric (Euclidean distance is used in this paper), BPs is a set of pixels that is located on the shape boundary, $d(x, y)$ is the minimum distance between BPs and a pixel (x, y) which belongs to the inner region of the shape. Parameters μ and σ are the mean and the standard deviation with its variance σ^2, and μ is set to 0 in the experiments.

Both Equations (14) and (15) contain the information that the pixels at different locations in a shape have different contributions. Those pixels closer to the shape boundary enjoy larger weight values, and on the contrary, those inner pixels farther away from the shape boundary enjoy smaller weight values. Let us take Equation (14) as an example. If inner pixel (x, y) is close to the object boundary, the distance $d(x, y)$ between it and the BPs will get a small value, and the weight function $\delta(x, y)$ will get a large value. Equation (15) has a similar effect as well.

3.2. Balance Weighting Function

Chen [17] proposed to compute moment invariants based on shape boundary pixels only and neglected the pixels within the region. In other words, the weights of pixels on the boundary are set to 1 while the weights of pixels within the region are set to 0. Thus, the computing cost is reduced, and the contribution of the interior region disappears as well. In order to achieve the balance, we propose a general linear rational weighting function as in Equation (17)

$$\delta(x, y) = \frac{p \times (d_{\max}(x, y) - d(x, y))}{p \times d_{\max}(x, y) - (2p - 1) \times d(x, y)} \tag{17}$$

where $d(x, y)$ is same as in Section 3.1, and $d_{\max}(x, y)$ is the maximum such distance in the object. Additionally, p is an adjustable parameter. If p is prone to 0, the moments converge with the boundary moments; if p is prone to 1, the moments converge with the traditional geometric moments. This weighting function balances the traditional geometric moments and boundary moments.

3.3. Central Weighting Function

In order to enhance the noise tolerance, Balslev [23] proposed a spatial function so that the regions near the center-of-mass are given higher weights. This central weighting function is given as follows

$$\delta(x, y) = \frac{1}{1 + \alpha^2 \left((x - x_0)^2 + (y - y_0)^2 \right)} \tag{18}$$

where α is an adjustable parameter, (x_0, y_0) is the center-of-mass. The typical range for α is $0 < \alpha < 10/R_G$, where R_G is the radius of gyration, $R_G = \sqrt{(\mu_{20} + \mu_{02})/\mu_{00}}$. Balsley's weighting function emphasizes the pixels that are close to the center-of-mass and weakens the pixels that are close to the boundary.

4. Experimental Study

4.1. Data Set and Distance Measure

We will give the details of the comparative study of the retrieval performance of variant-modified Hu moment invariants based on different weighted central moment approaches in 2D non-rigid shapes with single closed contours. We use the common performance measures, i.e., average precision and recall of the retrieval, as the evaluation measures (also called PVR curve). For each query, the precision of the retrieval at each level of the recall is obtained. The resulting precision of the retrieval is the average precision of all the query retrievals. Most publicly obtained benchmark shape databases, including Kimia's shape dataset and the MPEG-7 dataset, will be considered in the following comparative experiments, respectively. Kimia's shape dataset has 18 classes, each consisting of each 12 images. The MPEG7 dataset has 70 classes, each consisting of 20 images.

For the sake of simplicity, we defined seven invariants from Hu's moment invariants, based on the different weighted central moment as the features of the shape region. The dissimilarities (distances), defined in Equation (19), between the shapes are measured by the Euclidean distance.

$$Dist(Q, T) = \sqrt{\sum_{i=1}^{7} (\phi_i^q - \phi_i^t)^2} \tag{19}$$

where Q and T denote the query image and target image, respectively.

4.2. Comparative Study on the Different Weighting Approaches

In this section, the average precision and recall curves of queries using the original Hu moments [2], boundary moments [17], centroid weighted moments [23] and proposed weighted moments in the two different shape datasets are shown in Figures 2 and 3 respectively.

In order to obtain good performance, the parameters are hand-picked. In Kimia's shape database, parameter σ for the non-linear weighting function is set as 0.05, parameter p for the balance weighting function is set as 0.01, and parameter α for the central weighting function is set as $4/R_G$. In the MPEG-7 shape database, parameter σ for the non-linear weighting function is set as 0.05, parameter p for the balance weighting function is set as 0.02, and parameter α for the central weighting function is set as $3/R_G$. There are no parameters for the other weighting functions.

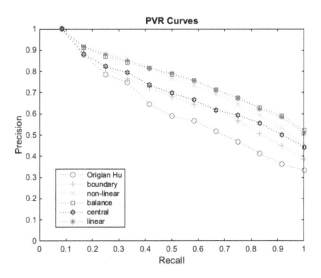

Figure 2. Average retrieval precision-recall curves on Kimia's shape database.

It is clear from the average precision and recall curves that the modified Hu moment invariants based on the linear weighting function, non-linear weighting function, balance weighting function and central weighting function can get better retrieval results compared with the original Hu moment invariants and the boundary moment invariants. In addition, the boundary moments outperform the original Hu moments, but underperform when compared to the improved Hu moments based on other weighting functions. Thus, the weighting scheme for the central moments defined in this paper is effective in identifying different 2D shapes.

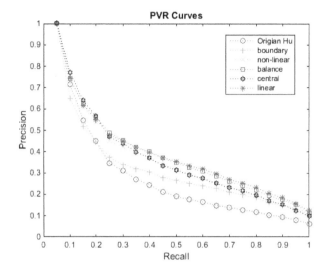

Figure 3. Average retrieval precision-recall curves on MPEG-7 shape database.

The bull's-eye test is selected as another evaluation criterion in the experiments as well. In the bull's-eye test, each shape is used as a test query. Retrieval is considered correct if it is in the same class as the query. Figures 4 and 5 show the bull's-eye test results on Kimia's shape datasets and MPEG-7 shape datasets, respectively. All of the improved approaches can get a better retrieval performance compared with the original Hu invariant moments, especially the two improved Hu moments based on central moments with the balance weighting function and linear weighting function.

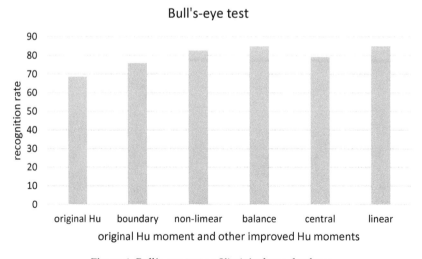

Figure 4. Bull's-eye test on Kimia's shape database.

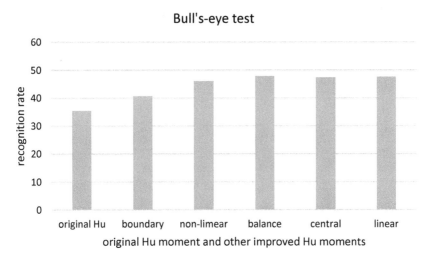

Figure 5. Bull's-eye test on MPEG-7 shape database.

4.3. Comparative Study of the Parameters

Several weighted central moment approaches have been presented in Section 3. From Equations (15), (17) and (18), it is clear that the nonlinear weighting function has two parameters that should be carefully set (μ is set to 0 in all experiments), and that both the balance weighting function and central weighting function have one parameter that should be carefully set as well. It is necessary to discuss the influence of different parameters on the retrieval performance. Figures 6–8 show the details of the influence of different parameters on the retrieval performance on Kimia's and the MPEG-7 shape database. As for parameters μ and p, they should be set around 0.03 so that the performances are optimized. Additionally, parameter α should be set around $3/R_G$ so that the performances are optimized.

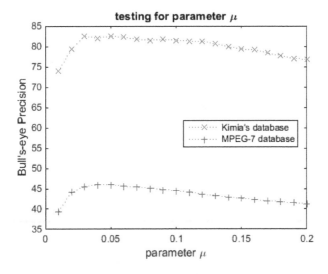

Figure 6. Bull's-eye test with different values for parameter μ in Equation (15).

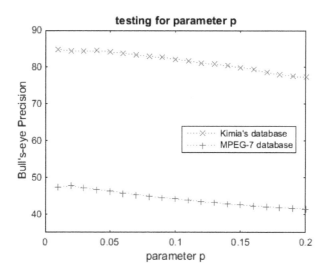

Figure 7. Bull's-eye test with different values for parameter p in Equation (17).

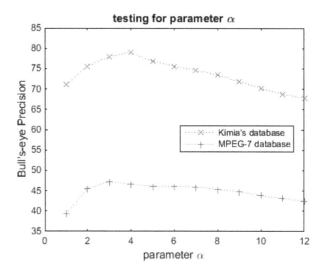

Figure 8. Bull's-eye test with different values for parameter α in Equation (18).

4.4. Comparative Study of Different Distance Metrics

The distance metric is very important for shape similarity measurements. As the moment invariants extracted from the images are vectors, Euclidean distance is used to measure the distance between two shapes in the above experiments for simplicity. Besides Euclidean distance, there are some other commonly used distance metrics including the Cityblock distance, Mahalanobis distance, Correlation distance, Chebychev distance and Cosine distance. Figures 9 and 10 express the comparison results of these different distance metrics used for the similarity measurement of the modified Hu moment invariants with the linear weighting function on Kimia's and the MPEG-7 shape database, respectively. From Figure 9, it is clear that Euclidean distance gets a better retrieval performance than the other distance metrics, followed by Cityblock distance and others. As illustrated in Figure 10, Mahalanobis distance obtains the best retrieval performance while it gets inferior results in Figure 9. Mahalanobis distance is not robust enough. Euclidean distance gets the second-best performance in Figure 10, followed by Cityblock distance and others. From Figures 9 and 10 Euclidean distance gets favorable results in both shape databases.

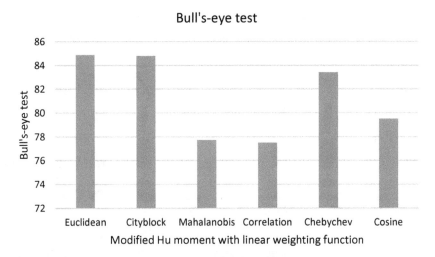

Figure 9. Bull's-eye test on Kimia's shape database.

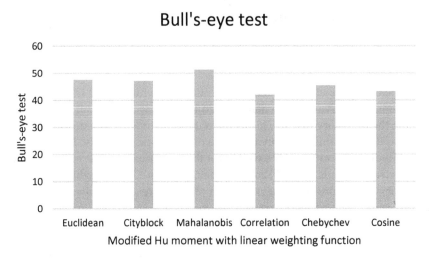

Figure 10. Bull's-eye test on MPEG-7 shape database.

4.5. Retrieval Illustration

Table 1 lists the retrieval results with 10 query images from Kimia's shape database. The left column shows query shapes and the right rows show the first 11 ranked nearest neighbors for each query shape, respectively. The returned images that do not belong to the query types are marked with a blue background in the table grids.

Table 1. Some query results from Kimia's shape database.

4.6. Discussion

We have tested the original Hu invariant moments and other improved Hu moments in the above sections. The original Hu invariant moments assign identical weights to all of the pixels within an object, including the boundary pixels. This leads to their relatively low performance. For reducing the computations, Ref. [17] considers only the pixels on the shape boundary. Thus, the weights of the pixels on the contour are set to 1, and the weights of the inner pixels are set to 0. Compared with the original Hu invariant moments, Ref. [17] achieved better results. Other weighting approaches take all the pixels of an object into consideration and assign different weights to different pixels according to some rules. This brings us more robust results. The central weighting function assigns larger weights to pixels close to the center-of-mass and this gives favorable results. However, this approach may be disabled when the center-of-mass of an object is located outside of the object boundary. According to human perception, the boundary weighting approaches (Equations (14) and (15)) emphasize the region near the object boundary and allocate heavy weights to the pixels close to the object boundary. This modification makes the performance more robust. The balance weighting method shares the merits of both the central weighting function and the boundary weighting function. If parameter p is selected carefully, a better performance will be obtained. In addition, compared with other weighting functions, the weighting function of Equation (14) does not need any parameters and can obtain respectable results.

5. Conclusions

In this paper, we elaborate on several weighting functions for calculating the central moment from the perspective of different angles. With the experiments, it is shown that the weighting functions applied in the calculation of central moments are able to considerably increase the performance, compared with the original Hu moments, in 2D shape retrievals. The results also show that different pixels in an object have different contributions for object identification. Future work can try to introduce the weighting method to other kinds of moments and apply them to other image-related applications, such as character recognition.

Acknowledgments: The authors wish also to thank the reviewers for their helpful and constructive comments. This work is partly supported by National Natural Science Foundation of China (Grant Nos. 61373055, 61471182), Natural Science Foundation of Jiangsu Province of China (Grant No. BK20130473), Postdoctoral Scientific Research Foundation of Jiangsu Province (Grant No. 1402068C), Natural Science Foundation of Jiangsu Higher Education Institutions of China (Grant No. 13KJB5200003, 14KJB520009) and Innovation Funds of Industry-Academy-Research Cooperation of Jiangsu Province (Grant No. BY2013066-03).

Author Contributions: Xin Shu and Qianni Zhang designed the experiments; Xin Shu and Jinlong Shi performed the experiments; Yunsong Qi analyzed the data; Xin Shu wrote the paper.

Conflicts of Interest: The authors declare no conflict of interest.

References

1. Zhang, D.; Lu, G. Review of shape representation and description techniques. *Pattern Recognit.* **2004**, *37*, 1–19. [CrossRef]

2. Hu, M.K. Visual pattern recognition by moment invariants. *IRE Trans. Inform. Theory* **1962**, *8*, 179–187.

3. Kim, W.Y.; Kim, Y.S. A region-based shape descriptor using Zernike moments. *Signal Process. Image Commun.* **2000**, *16*, 95–102. [CrossRef]

4. Chong, C.W.; Raveendran, P.; Mukundan, R. Translation invariants of Zernike moments. *Pattern Recognit.* **2003**, *36*, 1765–1773. [CrossRef]

5. Belkasim, S.; Hassan, E.; Obeidi, T. Explicit invariance of Cartesian Zernike moments. *Pattern Recognit. Lett.* **2007**, *28*, 1969–1980. [CrossRef]

6. Hosny, K.M. Exact Legendre moments computation for gray level images. *Pattern Recognit.* **2007**, *40*, 3597–3605. [CrossRef]

7. Fu, B.; Zhou, J.Z.; Li, Y.H.; Zhang, G.J.; Wang, C. Image analysis by modified Legendre moments. *Pattern Recognit.* **2007**, *40*, 691–704. [CrossRef]

8. Chao, K.; Mandyam, D.S. Invariant character recognition with Zernike and orthogonal Fourier-Mellin moments. *Pattern Recognit.* **2002**, *35*, 143–154.

9. Derrode, S.; Ghorbel, F. Robust and efficient Fourier-Mellin transform approximations for gray-level image reconstruction and complete invariant description. *Comput. Vis. Image Underst.* **2001**, *83*, 57–78. [CrossRef]

10. Zhang, H.; Shu, H.Z.; Haigron, P.; Luo, L.M.; Li, B.S. Construction of a complete set of orthogonal Fourier-Mellin moment invariants for pattern recognition applications. *Image Vis. Comput.* **2010**, *28*, 38–44. [CrossRef]

11. Teague, M. Image analysis via the general theory of moments. *J. Opt. Soc. Am.* **1980**, *70*, 920–930. [CrossRef]

12. Sheng, Y.L.; Shen, L.X. Orthogonal Fourier-Mellin moments for invariant pattern recognition. *J. Opt. Soc. Am.* **1994**, *11*, 1748–1757. [CrossRef]

13. Flusser, J.; Suk, T. Affine moment invariants: A new tool for character recognition. *Pattern Recognit. Lett.* **1994**, *15*, 433–436. [CrossRef]

14. Chim, Y.C.; Kassim, A.A.; Ibrahim, Y. Character recognition using statistical moments. *Image Vis. Comput.* **1999**, *17*, 299–307. [CrossRef]

15. Zhang, F.; Liu, S.; Wang, D.; Guan, W. Aircraft recognition in infrared image using wavelet moment invariants. *Image Vis. Comput.* **2009**, *27*, 313–318. [CrossRef]

16. Sluzek, A. Identification and inspection of 2-D objects using new moments-based shape descriptors. *Pattern Recognit. Lett.* **1995**, *16*, 687–697. [CrossRef]

17. Chen, C.C. Improved moment invariants for shape discrimination. *Pattern Recognit.* **1993**, *26*, 683–686. [CrossRef]

18. Cheng, S.C. Content-based image retrieval using moments-preserving edge detection. *Image Vis. Comput.* **2003**, *21*, 809–826. [CrossRef]

19. Schlemmer, M.; Heringer, M.; Morr, F.; Hotz, I.; Bertram, M.-H.; Garth, C.; Kollmann, W.; Hamann, B.; Hagen, H. Moment invariants for the analysis of 2D flow fields. *IEEE Trans. Vis. Comput. Graph.* **2007**, *13*, 1743–1750. [CrossRef] [PubMed]

20. Zhu, Y.; De Silva, L.C.; Ko, C.C. Using moment invariants and HMM in facial expression recognition. *Pattern Recognit. Lett.* **2002**, *23*, 83–91. [CrossRef]

21. Zhang, Y.; Wang, S.; Sun, P.; Phillips, P. Pathological brain detection based on wavelet entropy and Hu moment invariants. *Bio-Med. Mater. Eng.* **2015**, *26*, 1283–1290. [CrossRef] [PubMed]

22. Wang, S.; Pan, H.; Zhang, C.; Tian, Y. RGB-D image based detection of stairs, pedestrian crosswalks and traffic signs. *J. Vis. Commun. Image Represent.* **2014**, *25*, 263–272. [CrossRef]

23. Balslev, I.; Døring, K.; Eriksen, R.D. Weighted Central Moments in Pattern Recognition. *Pattern Recognit. Lett.* **2000**, *21*, 381–384. [CrossRef]

24. Nasreddine, K.; Benzinou, A.; Fablet, R. Variational shape matching for shape classification and retrieval. *Pattern Recognit. Lett.* **2010**, *31*, 1650–1657. [CrossRef]

25. Direkoglu, C.; Nixon, M.S. Shape classification via image-based multiscale description. *Pattern Recognit.* **2011**, *44*, 2134–2146. [CrossRef]

12

A Framework for Measuring Security as a System Property in Cyberphysical Systems

Janusz Zalewski [1,*], Ingrid A. Buckley [1], Bogdan Czejdo [2], Steven Drager [3], Andrew J. Kornecki [4] and Nary Subramanian [5]

[1]   Department of Software Engineering, Florida Gulf Coast University, Ft. Myers, FL 33965, USA; zalewski@fgcu.edu (J.Z.); ibuckley@fgcu.edu (I.A.B.)

[2]   Department of Math & Computer Science, Fayetteville State University, Fayetteville, NC 28301, USA; bczejdo@uncfsu.edu

[3]   Air Force Research Laboratory, Rome, NY 13441, USA; steven.drager@us.af.mil

[4]   Department of Electrical, Computer, Software, and Systems Engineering, Embry-Riddle Aeronautical University, Daytona Beach, FL 32114, USA; kornecka@erau.edu

[5]   Department of Computer Science, University of Texas at Tyler, Tyler, TX 75799, USA; nsubramanian@uttyler.edu

*   Correspondence: zalewski@fgcu.edu

Academic Editor: Eduardo B. Fernandez

Abstract: This paper addresses the challenge of measuring security, understood as a system property, of cyberphysical systems, in the category of similar properties, such as safety and reliability. First, it attempts to define precisely what security, as a system property, really is. Then, an application context is presented, in terms of an attack surface in cyberphysical systems. Contemporary approaches related to the principles of measuring software properties are also discussed, with emphasis on building models. These concepts are illustrated in several case studies, based on previous work of the authors, to conduct experimental security measurements.

Keywords: computer security; information security; security assessment; software metrics

1. Introduction

Measuring security, in general, and that of cyberphysical systems, in particular, is a difficult task for a number of reasons including primarily: vagueness of the concept of security itself, and inadequate knowledge of the principles of measurement. Despite multiple publications on the subject, there are no valuable or verified methods that would move the discipline forward. The conjecture of this paper is that measuring security as a system property has to be addressed in a broader context. Useful questions to define precisely what is meant by security as a property, include: What does security really mean in terms of the system? What are the implications for computer security, system security, information security and data security? To define what is meant by the cyberphysical system, a model of the system helps to realize the technical ramifications of design and through simulation answer questions, which determine what is being protected and made secure.

Probably the most important aspect of measuring security is the description of the measurement process itself. What is actually meant by a measurement? Understanding the measurement process is not necessarily the strongest side of security studies or practices. However, the real issue might be how to distinguish between the concepts of metrics and measures.

Accordingly, the objective of the paper is to clarify the concepts and illustrate their meaning through use in several case studies based on previous work of the authors. The paper is structured as follows. Section 2 outlines and advocates one view of security as a system property, Section 3 provides an overview of essential architectures and features of cyberphysical systems, with respect to measuring security, Section 4 presents a discussion of fundamental concepts of measurement theory, and Section 5 discusses five different case studies. The article ends with a conclusion in Section 6.

2. Security as a System Property

In a review of measuring security, there have been numerous publications in the last decade on security assessment, including books [1,2], research and engineering papers [3,4], government reports [5–7], and Internet sources [8,9], all of them discussing security metrics. However, the vast majority of the references deal with metrics at the management level and have very little to do with measurement in a scientific sense of the term, as developed in measurement theory [10].

What is meant by security and its metrics in these publications is primarily adherence to policy and standards, whether established in industry standards [11–13] or internal to the company [14,15], leading to the assessment of how security policies are executed, for example, by implementing respective processes and auditing them. As one paper defines it [16], security metrics mean "the measurement of the effectiveness of the organization's security efforts over time." While this method of security assessment is beneficial and productive, means to measure security as a property of a computing system or software are not particularly well developed and documented.

Focus on the quantitative assessment of operational aspects of security has become more popular in recent years. A thorough survey was published in 2009 [17], covering quantitative representation and analysis of operational security since 1981, and addressing the question whether "security can correctly be represented with quantitative information?" The major finding of this study was that "there exists significant work for quantified security, but there is little solid evidence that the methods represent security in operational settings."

What is of specific interest in the current paper is not security at the enterprise or the organization level, but rather how security as a computer system property or software property can contribute to protecting information and other resources during system's operation. In this regard, security can be viewed as one specific aspect of system's dependability, the other two aspects being safety and reliability, with one of the earliest papers addressing this issue published over twenty years ago [18].

One has to remember, however, that security and safety, with reliability in between, are two sides of the same coin, mutually complementary aspects of dependability, as illustrated in Figures 1 and 2. According to the International Electrotechnical Commission (IEC) [19], safety is defined as "freedom from unacceptable risk to the outside from the functional and physical units considered" whereas security is defined as "freedom from unacceptable risk to the physical units considered from the outside." Translating this into the language used in the current paper:

- Safety is concerned when a failure leads to severe consequences (high risk) for the operational environment;
- Security is concerned when a failure to protect assets (a breach) leads to severe consequences (high risk) for the system itself (and potentially to its operational environment).

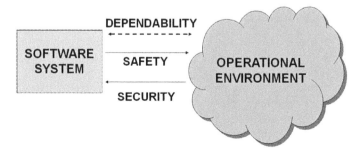

Figure 1. Relationship between safety and security with the environment.

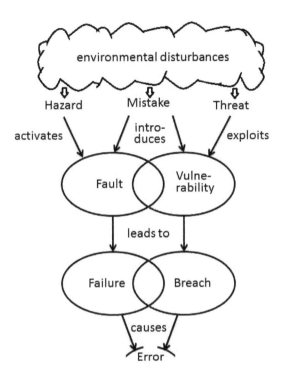

Figure 2. Impact and relationships of hazards and threats.

Looking at definitions of security in established standard glossaries, such as [20] or [21], it becomes immediately clear that in none of these documents is security defined as a system property. For example, one of several definitions in [21] reads as follows: "Protection of information and data so that unauthorized persons or systems cannot read or modify them and authorized persons or systems are not denied access to them" and a corresponding one in [22]: "A condition that results from the establishment and maintenance of protective measures that enable an enterprise to perform its mission or critical functions despite risks posed by threats to its use of information systems."

Both of these definitions make sense, but not for our purposes, because they both refer to security as a state, as opposed to ability. System state is a discrete entity and can be described, by analogy to a program state, by all its variables and their values at any given time. This implies that a state can change upon applying appropriate inputs, and respective outputs can also be associated with the change of state.

A definition of security as a system property must imply a continuum and an assumption that one can measure it. In this regard, just like for several other properties [20,21], the definition should include a phrase "the extent to which" or "the degree to which". Consequently, we propose adopting the definition of security from [21], to read as follows: "The extent to which information and data are protected so that unauthorized persons or systems cannot read or modify them and authorized persons or systems are not denied access to them."

What is additionally important and captured well in [21] is the fact that the secure system must be not only protected against threats but also accessible to those authorized to use it.

Having the definition in place, one needs to figure how to assess "the extent" or "the degree" to which the conditions spelled out in the definition are met. The community has adopted several ways to do it. One view, which gained especially wide popularity, is called the C-I-A triad, where the acronym comes from the first letters of, what are called, Confidentiality, Integrity, and Availability properties [23]. The assessment of the degree to which a system is secure can be based on meeting the three criteria of the C-I-A triad.

3. Cyberphysical Systems

Cyberphysical systems have their roots in embedded computer systems, which in turn evolved from control systems, long before digital computer control was conceived [24]. The essential structure of a simple control system is widely known, but for completeness is shown in Figure 3. It consists of a controller and a controlled object (commonly termed a plant). The sensor installed on a plant delivers a measurement signal to the controller, which on this basis, and a prescribed plan (setpoint), takes a decision value of a control signal to apply to an object via an actuator, to counteract potential variations in a controlled (measured) variable caused by disturbances.

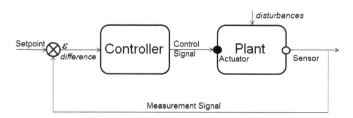

Figure 3. Illustration of a control system influenced by disturbances.

A typical example of this sort of control system, which we are all familiar with, either from our homes, offices or cars, is a temperature controller, otherwise known as a thermostat. Historically, the oldest known device, which applies this type of control principle, is the Ktesibios water clock (third century B.C. [25]), stabilizing the water level in a tank to let it flow at constant rate, out to another tank at the lower level, to mark the passage of time.

With the development of digital technologies, control systems became miniaturized and directly embedded into plants, that is, controlled objects. At the same time, they were expanded to include operator (user) interface, and their parameter values, such as a setpoint, evolved into more sophisticated data sets, soon to reach the size of true databases. This expanded embedded control system's structure is shown in Figure 4.

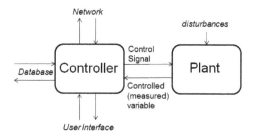

Figure 4. Illustration of interactions in a modern control system.

Once it became possible and desirable to implement a network connectivity feature in embedded controllers, a new breed of systems called cyberphysical systems came into being, which are in fact old embedded control systems enhanced by connectivity mechanisms. This is reflected in Figure 4 by a network interface.

Thus, for the purpose of this paper, a cyberphysical system can be defined as a computing system with access to physical measurement and control instruments as well as with connectivity to the Internet. As shown in Figure 4, in addition to a physical process (a plant) and network interfaces, user and database interfaces are also present.

Taking the analogy from control engineering, one would only keep interfaces relevant to security during the system's operation and, as a result, derive a model of an embedded controller (or more broadly, a cyberphysical system) subject to security threats as shown in Figure 5.

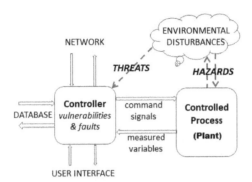

Figure 5. Illustration of basic terms and an attack surface.

Figure 5 shows that multiple controller interfaces to the process, the operator, the network, and the database, are all subject to security threats, forming the *attack surface*. More importantly, to take the analogy further, just like control theory assumes that the controlled process (a plant) is subject to disturbances, security theory, if one is developed for this model, could assume that known or unknown threats play the role of disturbances to the controller, via its all interfaces.

In this model, vulnerabilities affecting the controller are understood as a "weakness of an asset or group of assets that can be exploited by one or more threats" [26] or as a "weakness in an information system, system security procedures, internal controls, or implementation that could be exploited by a threat source" [22], while a threat can be defined as "a state of the system or system environment which can lead to adverse effects" [20]. Consequently, the disturbances in Figure 5 are an abstraction incorporating all threats relevant to security and play a role in assessing security.

With this complexity of controller interactions, when designing a Controller one has to take into account the Controller's internal state, which may be a cause of significant disruptions to the Controlled Process, when a Controller fails. This is the subject of fault tolerance.

Technically, in safety engineering, external disruptions are representing hazards and in the model from Figure 5 can be viewed as affecting the Controlled Process, as specific disturbances. Formally, a hazard is "an intrinsic property or condition that has the potential to cause harm or damage" [21]. To assure dependability, the Controller has to be designed to deal with safety hazards, but they are not always easy to capture and are especially difficult to account for in the case of hardware or software faults.

Pairing this understanding of safety related concepts of Hazards and Faults with security related concepts of Threats and Vulnerabilities, one arrives at the aggregated model suitable for security modeling, as shown in Figure 6, which matches, from a different perspective, the model of Figure 2.

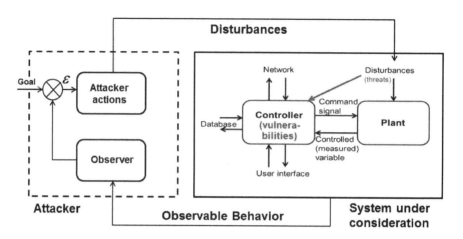

Figure 6. Modern cyberphysical system: disturbances and attacks.

4. Principles of Measurement

With measures we often take things for granted, especially if it concerns such "trivial" quantities as length (distance) and weight (mass), but it has not always been so. As legend has it, it was Henry I, the King of England, who decreed in the first half of the XII-th century that a yard shall be "the distance from the tip of the King's nose to the end of his outstretched thumb", proclaiming what is believed to be the first standard of measuring length [27]. It appears that at the current stage of understanding how to measure security as a system property, we are at the point comparable to the early days of attempting to measure length. All methods we have are as vague as the one applied by Henry I in defining the unit of length. This section is devoted to clarification of the basic concepts of measurement and how they can be applied to building a model of security as a system property that could be used to measure security.

4.1. Hermann von Helmholtz's Concept of Measurement

Although there are several concepts of measurement, they all seem to converge to the idea formulated in the 19-th century by Herman von Helmholtz, in his groundbreaking work "Zählen und Messen" [28], in which Helmholtz says: "The special relation which can exist between the attributes of two objects and which is designated by us by the name equality is characterized by [...] Axiom I: If two magnitudes are equal to a third, they are equal to each other."

This statement, which may seem trivial from today's perspective, actually is very constructive and quite distinctly sets the stage for conducting measurements in a way that it determines the following:

- a property (called an attribute by Helmholtz) of an object to be measured;
- a standard, that is, in Helmholtz' words, the third magnitude, to which others are compared;
- implying an existence of a procedure used to make the comparisons between magnitudes.

This procedure is further characterized by von Helmholtz in the same work, as follows: "The procedure by which we put the two objects under proper conditions in order to observe the stated result and to be able to establish its occurrence or its non-occurrence, we shall designate as the method of comparison."

Defining measurement procedures as a method of comparison, von Helmholtz gives several examples of physical quantities that can be measured, by comparison with a standard, including distance, time, brightness, pitch of tone, and weight, measured with the use of scales, for which he explains the measurement principle further: " ... the bodies the weights of which we compare can consist of the most different materials and can be of different form and volume. The weight which we call equal is only an attribute of these bodies discriminated by abstraction."

To summarize, the contribution of von Helmholtz was to make a clear distinction between three factors necessary for a measurement to make sense: (1) a property to be measured; (2) a standard against which comparisons are made; and (3) a procedure to determine how to make the comparisons. In modern terms, the standard can be viewed as a metric, and the measurement procedure relates to a measure, that is, the measuring instrument.

The contribution of von Helmholtz is significant, in terms of the logic of measurement and the associated theory. However, without questioning his work, newer theories treat the measurement processes as statistical in nature. The principal assumption of the statistical approach to measurements is that due to the inherent uncertainties in the measurement process, the result of a measurement always consists of two numbers: the value of the measured quantity and the estimation of the measurement uncertainty with which this value has been obtained (error).

4.2. Lessons from Measurements in Physics

To help realize the challenge of measuring system properties, one can look closer at the extreme of measuring strictly physical properties (quantities). In addition to length, mentioned above, among physical properties we are most familiar with are time and mass.

The current definition of a second, a metric (unit) of time, involves atomic radiation and reads as follows [29]: "the duration of 9 192 631 770 periods of the radiation corresponding to the transition between the two hyperfine levels of the ground state of the cesium 133 atom." It must be noticed that this definition, just like the one of a unit of length, evolved historically from much less precise definitions and understanding of respective quantities. A historical background can be found in [29].

The metric of mass (its unit), a kilogram, is currently the only physical unit that officially remains defined based on a physical artifact, a prototype stored in the International Bureau of Weights and Measures. However, there is a substantial push towards defining it more precisely, using the number of atoms in a silicon 28 crystal [30]. Developing this new definition has yet to be fully successful, but (in the context of considering the definition of security) it is worth mentioning, why this is so: "The measurement uncertainty is 1.5 higher than that targeted for a kilogram redefinition [...]. The measurement accuracy seems to be limited by the working apparatuses." Clearly, any measurement of security must involve the use of measuring devices and assessment of their accuracy.

It may be further argued that security is not a physical property and cannot be measured directly, so considering such measurements would make little sense. In physics, however, there are quantities, which do not measure directly certain properties of matter. One such example is temperature, which is essentially a quantity corresponding to and measuring kinetic energy.

It is clear from these lessons that several points have to be taken into consideration, if one is to develop scientifically based security measurements:

- The process of designing a validated metric of security may take years, if not decades;
- Any measures of security must be treated as (physical or mental) measurement devices (instruments), to which regular statistical measurement theory applies;
- Security is likely to be measured only indirectly, possibly via its inherent components.

Following the observation from [31], for the assessment of a value of a system property, where there is no science or theory developed, one could try conducting measurement experiments. Nevertheless, if experimental assessment of a system property quantitatively is impossible, one can apply simulation. As Glimm and Sharp, for example, point out [32]: "It is an old saw that science has three pillars: theory, experiment, and simulation." This principle is broadly applied in physics, the mother of modern sciences, but it has also been adopted in various ways in computing [33].

However, before any theory, experiment or simulation is developed, putting all of the cards on the table is necessary by developing an initial model of the phenomena whose properties are to be measured. This is the critical first step to conduct the measurement. The authors' previous work involved building all three types of models: Theory, Experiment, and Simulation, with respective examples in [34] on rough sets *vs.* Bayesian Belief Networks (BBN's), [35] on software tools assessment, and [36] on threat modeling.

With respect to theoretical approaches, a combination of basic concepts of BBN's and rough sets are shown to enhance the process of reasoning under uncertainty in the case of missing values of certain properties of a cyberphysical system [34]. Rough set is a formal approximation of a conventional set, in terms of a pair of sets, which define the lower and upper bounds of the original set. The rough sets theory helps make BBN's more valuable in the case of the occasional lack of evidence. On the other hand, when supportive theory has not yet been developed, what is left is experimental measurements. To assess the quality of software tools for real-time software development, four metrics and their respective measures were established in [35]: functionality, usability, efficiency, and traceability, and experiments conducted on a specially designed testbed to assess the tools' quality. In [36], in turn, simulation studies on a remote robotic device have proven to be a valuable aid to the early detection and prevention of potentially serious flaws in the core of a cyberphysical system with the functionality applicable for software-intensive aviation system.

4.3. Defining the Measurement Process

Summarizing the considerations of this section, the critical elements in measurements of any property are the following:

1. Clearly identify the *property* to be measured. It is at this point where building a model of the phenomenon is necessary. We use the term "property", which corresponds to von Helmholtz' "attribute", although in measurement theory [37], it is called measurand.
2. Establish a *metric* to quantitatively characterize the property. Ideally, this would be a unit of measurement, but for vaguely defined properties it can be just a standard against which measurements are applied, or a scale against which the property can be evaluated.
3. Develop a *measure*, which would apply the metric to related objects under investigation. Ideally, this is just a measuring instrument, but for vaguely defined metrics it can be a formula or any other mental device to apply a metric and make comparisons. One important characteristic of a measure should be its linearity, that is, any two identical changes in the property value should be reflected as two identical changes in the measure.
4. Design the *measurement process* to deliver results. An important part of this process is calibration of the measuring device [37], an activity almost never thought of in soft sciences. Another crucial component of this process is the collection and availability of data.
5. Make sure that each instance of a measurement delivers a *result* composed of the value of the measurement and the estimate of its accuracy (an error). Alternatively, and consistently with current views in measurement theory, it could be a range of values designating one value as the "measured quantity value" [37].

So, knowing all of this, the question is, are we able to develop a model for security measurement? The model should embrace all important factors regarding this phenomenon.

Thus far, we have determined the model for security assessment for one particular class of systems, cyberphysical systems, and defined security as a term. What is necessary in the next step is developing the measurement process (with metrics and measures) for measuring security in the proposed context. This is, of course, an open question and a tremendous challenge.

4.4. Guidelines for Applying the Process

The model of Figures 5 and 6 forms the basis for building a case study for security assessment, by analyzing threats and vulnerabilities. In this paper, because of the need for a more quantitative approach, a strongly quantitative method is advocated, based on assessing the vulnerabilities as per the Common Vulnerability Scoring System (CVSS) [38].

The following items have to be addressed: a *metric*, which for CVSS is a continuous numerical scale; a *measure*, which for CVSS is a set of integrated formulas; and the *measurement process*, which in this case relies on applying the measures to continuously collected data. With these assumptions, the data can be obtained by online checking of the subject entity (embedded device, server, cyberphysical system, *etc.*, for which security is being measured) for known vulnerabilities, as per the Common Vulnerability Exposure (CVE) database [39]. Calculating the *security score* based on the CVSS can then be accomplished. Several authors have proposed use of CVE/CVSS data [40] for security measurement purposes, although without theoretical underpinning.

The unpredictable nature of threats remains a challenge. Even if one can design countermeasures for existing threats and assess those, there is high likelihood that new, unknown, threats will eventually appear, so one has to design the security system for the unknown, as well as include this type of unpredictability in the computational model for security assessment. The lack of sufficient information for calculating security values suggests building the model based on one of the theories which deal with uncertainty, for example, Bayesian belief networks or rough sets. The next section presents five case studies that illustrate, from various perspectives, how potential measurement processes can be designed.

5. Case Studies

5.1. Case Study #1: Using Markov Chains

The security model assumed here takes into account availability, as a dominating security component of the C-I-A triad [23]. This case study presents aspects of evaluating security in a cyberphysical system, based on availability assessment with Markov chains. The essential assumption in the approach and the proposed model is that a security breach may cause degradation of the service and ultimately a failure. The security model concentrates on the system's interaction with the environment via a communication channel. It is based on a previous publication [41].

5.1.1. Methodology: Markov Model

The essential assumption in the approach and the model proposed in this case study is that a security breach is not a binary event (full or no security) but that it usually causes degradation of system services and may lead to a failure. Under this assumption, a cyberphysical system working in a 24/7 regime, at any given point in time will be in one of the following states: (1) the normal state; (2) the failure state; or (3) one of the possible intermediate degraded states, depending on the violation of security and the system's ability to detect and recover from those violations.

Due to the dynamic state transition observed here, we consider a Markov model which typically includes the state with all elements operating and a set of intermediate states representing partially failed conditions, leading to the state in which the system is unable to perform its function. The model may include failure transition paths, as well as repair transition paths. The corresponding failure and repair rates between states can be derived from system analysis. The Markov model equations describe the situation where the transition path between two states reduces the probability of the state it is departing, and increases the probability of the state it is entering, at a specified rate.

A Markov chain may be constructed to model the changes of the system state depending on the probability of certain security vulnerabilities and probabilities that the system can be restored back to the regular state. The transition paths and the probability of transition between the various states define the system equations whose solution represents the time-history of the system. In a regular Markov model, the state is directly visible to the observer, and therefore the state transition probabilities are the only parameters.

In the system where deviations from the regular state are due to potential external attacks, we can identify the attack's effects and their probabilities (e.g., for a communication system, percentage of messages corrupted, lost, incorrectly inserted, *etc.*). In turn, the system in such a degraded state can return to the regular state due to application of a mitigation mechanism or fail (also with assumed rate). Even after failure, we can consider a system that can be repaired assuming a certain repair rate. Such a model is useful to quantify how a specific vulnerability, expressed in terms of the probability of potential attacks, affects the system and what is the effective reliability and availability of the system. Respective simulations can give a basis for understanding how effective each mitigation method needs to be in order to ensure that the system meets or exceeds its required level of security.

5.1.2. Cooperative Adaptive Cruise Control

The Cooperative Adaptive Cruise Control (CACC) system selected as the case study [42,43] is a cyberphysical system for automobiles which automatically monitors and adjusts a vehicle's speed according to the traffic conditions in its immediate vicinity.

In the CACC, as shown in Figure 7, to effect a change in the vehicle's speed, the system issues commands to the throttle device as well as to the brake pedal. The CAAC, in addition to receiving the necessary data it needs from sensors on the vehicle, communicates via a wireless network connection with other vehicles in the vicinity (Other CACC Systems) and with a centralized SMDC (Street Monitoring Data Center). These external interfaces have the highest risk of malicious attack. Security violation can result from external connection, *i.e.*, by incorrect data from SMDC or from unauthorized external communication imitating other CACC equipped vehicle.

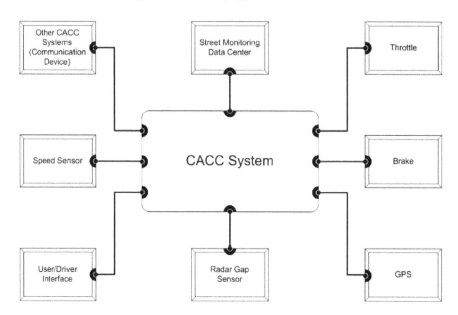

Figure 7. Context diagram of the CACC design.

The specific vulnerabilities fall into four categories:

- Message Introduction: an untrue SMDC or Other CACC message is injected.
- Message Deletion: SMDC or Other CACC System message is not received by CACC.
- Message Corruption: the contents of an SMDC or Other CACC message are altered before being received by the CACC.
- Message Flooding: multiple frequent SMDC or Other CACC System messages are received causing the CACC to choke and not perform its required tasks within the deadlines.

To enhance the level of security, changes have been made to the original CACC architectural model by adding authentication and secure communication components. The level of security added will determine the probability with which the state transitions will occur. The probability for detection and recovery increases when the overall reliability of the system increases.

For the presented example, the following assumptions and simplifications were made:

- It is assumed that only one security breach can occur at any given time.
- Only one message channel is modeled. To model both the SMDC and the Other CACC channels simultaneously, more states and associated transitions would be required.
- It is assumed that an undetected or unsuccessfully handled security breach leads to a system failure even though the system may not physically fail.

Relex/Winchill [44] reliability analysis software was used to assess the reliability of the Markov model in Figure 8. Each edge in the state machine has the probability that this transition will occur.

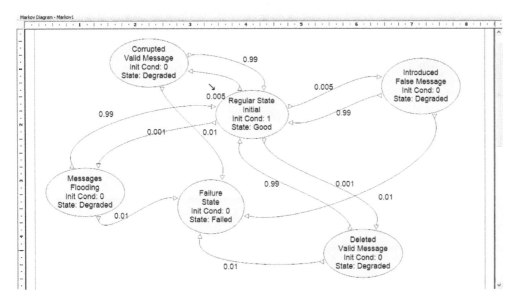

Figure 8. Markov model of the CACC system (no repairs). Init Cond: is 1 (true) for the initial state and 0 (false) for non-initial state (it is just a notation of the used tool).

5.1.3. Experimental Results

In this example, the probability of security breaches, *i.e.*, of corruption of a valid message, an injection of a false message, having a message deleted, or getting a flood of false messages, as well as the related attack detection, recovery and the failure probabilities were assumed (Table 1). Case 1 represents low and Case 2 high attack rates.

Table 1. Probabilities of transitions.

Probability	Assigned Values
Corrupted Valid Message	Case 1: 0.005/Case 2: 0.05
Introduced False Message	Case 1: 0.005/Case 2: 0.05
Deleted Valid Message	Case 1: 0.001/Case 2: 0.01
Message Flooding	Case 1: 0.001/Case 2: 0.01
Return to Regular (security mitigation works)	0.99/0.9/0.5
Failing Return to Regular (security mitigation fails)	0.01/0.1/0.5
Return from Fail to Regular (repair rate)	0 (no repair)/0.5/0.9

In the initial Markov model, the failure state was modeled as a terminal state. However, availability of the system could be increased by adding the possibility of a repair. In the CACC system, the monitor process is able to reset the system, if it detects a failure. This would be equivalent to a transition from the failure state back to the normal state.

The updated Markov model is shown in Figure 9. The repair rate of the system is a parameter one would like to explore. Two cases, one with repair rate 0.5 and other with 0.9 were simulated.

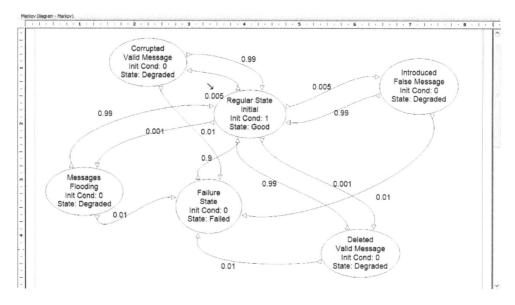

Figure 9. CACC Markov model showing repair from the failure state.

The baseline model (Figure 8) does not incorporate a transition from the failure state to the normal state, which corresponds to there being no possibility of repair after it has failed. The resulting reliability is 93.0531% with mean availability of 98.9873%. Since the first time to failure is estimated to be 83.33 h, we can deduce that in such a scenario our system meets the expectations imposed on security. Even though 83.33 h may seem like a low value, one must remember that this is counted for a car, which has been reset and restarted (a car is rarely supposed to run 80 h without a stop).

The results are summarized in Table 2 for two scenarios (low and high attack rate).

It is shown that the addition of repair increases the availability. A higher repair rate results in only a marginal increase in the system availability. For a system with higher attack rate (Case 2), when only half of the attacks are mitigated, introducing 0.9 probability of repair increases availability by 8.56%. Similarly, when up to 90% of the attacks are mitigated, the availability is increased 1.65%. We may infer that not much effort needs be expended in designing a system with a repair capability. For higher attack rates, more value may be obtained in increasing the detection and recovery rates for the specific attacks, *i.e.*, security mitigation rather than expending resources on system repair.

The results in Table 2 show a high correlation between security and availability. Six scenarios (with only three data points) are shown. A linear regression allows computation of the slope and intersection and predicted values show only marginal prediction error. Due to a marginally minimal set of data, the regression holds only in the very near vicinity of the values of the independent variables. However, the results are promising in that the security can be assessed if only the availability of the system, the attack rate frequency, and the repair status and its probability are known.

The presented case study suggests viewing the attacks and related security breaches as a system failure, thus allowing one to reason about security by modeling availability with the existing tools. In general, a probability increase of successful attack detection and mitigation/recovery would result in a decrease in system performance because more effort, and hence execution time, is needed. A tradeoff, therefore, needs to be made, since performance is always an important consideration. For the defined probabilities of attack and the specified probabilities of detecting and handling the attack effects, a

Markov model allows estimation of the system availability, providing valuable information on the level of security to be applied and to determine system's sensitivity to security breaches.

Table 2. Simulation results.

Availability	Security	Correlation	Slope	Intercept	Predicted Security	Prediction Error (%)
case 1: low attack rate/no repair						
97.7408	50	0.9999996	39.324	−3793.510	50.005	0.010%
98.7572	90	-	39.324	−3793.510	89.973	−0.030%
98.9873	99	-	39.324	−3793.510	99.022	0.022%
case1: low attack rate/0.5 repair probability						
98.3877	50	0.9999998	80.005	−7821.549	50.003	0.007%
98.8874	90	-	80.005	−7821.549	89.982	−0.020%
99.0003	99	-	80.005	−7821.549	99.015	0.015%
case1: low attack rate/0.9 repair probability						
98.5872	50	0.9999998	117.478	−11531.829	50.003	0.007%
98.9275	90	-	117.478	−11531.829	89.981	−0.021%
99.0044	99	-	117.478	−11531.829	99.015	0.015%
case 2: high attack rate/no repair						
80.4847	50	0.9999546	4.822	−338.064	50.052	0.104%
88.7127	90	-	4.822	−338.064	89.730	−0.301%
90.6804	99	-	4.822	−338.064	99.218	0.220%
case 2: high attack rate/0.5 repair probability						
85.7505	50	0.9999823	9.736	−784.806	50.032	0.064%
89.8385	90	-	9.736	−784.806	89.831	−0.187%
90.7943	99	-	9.736	−784.806	99.137	0.138%
case 2: high attack rate/0.9 repair probability						
87.3755	50	0.9999877	14.214	−1191.917	50.027	0.053%
90.1779	90	-	14.214	−1191.917	89.859	−0.156%
90.829	99	-	14.214	−1191.917	99.114	0.115%

5.1.4. Summary of the Measurement Process

In summary, the following steps of security assessment are identified using the above method, consistent with the outline of security measurement (Section 4.3). Given the attack surface is defined within the framework of a cyberphysical system (Figures 4–6), respective steps include: (1) security model restricted to the availability component of the C-I-A triad; (2) metric defined on a probabilistic scale [0,1]; (3) measure defined by the Markov chain computational formula; (4) the measurement process determined by simulation; and (5) accuracy defined statistically as a prediction error.

5.2. Case Study #2: Threat Modeling

This case study analyzes the application of threat modeling to assess quantitative security of a cyberphysical system using an example from the automotive domain: Inter Vehicle Communication (IVC). Threats are modeled using the Threat Modeling Tool [45], generating the Analysis Report from which they are mapped to vulnerabilities, which in terms of DREAD characteristics lead to risk assessment. The description of this case study is loosely based on an earlier publication [46].

5.2.1. Outline of Threat Modeling

The modeling of threats in computer systems has been used at least since the beginning of this century, and involves a number of techniques. The essential process has been described in [45] and discussed in practice [47], and includes the following five steps: (1) Understand the Adversary's View; (2) Create a System Model; (3) Determine and Investigate the Threats; (4) Mitigate the Threats; and (5) Validate the Mitigations.

In this work, we are only interested in selecting the right model of the system (Step 2) and determining and investigating the threats (Step 3), since this is sufficient for security assessment. The model of a cyberphysical system assumed, as presented in Figures 3–6 (for a generic system and a case study, respectively), maps very nicely onto the thread modeling process discussed in [45,47], which uses data flow diagrams. Principles of creating data flow diagrams correspond nearly identically to our representation of cyberphysical systems and do not need additional discussion.

Regarding Step 3, the traditional way of determining and investigating threats is split into three phases: (1) Identifying/defining threats using the STRIDE method; (2) Using threat trees to assess vulnerabilities; and (3) Characterizing risks associated with vulnerabilities using the DREAD method, where STRIDE, which stands for Spoofing, Tampering, Repudiation, Information disclosure, Denial of service, and Elevation of privilege, and DREAD, which stands for Damage potential, Reproducibility, Exploitability, Affected users, and Discoverability, are relatively well described techniques of dealing with threats and corresponding risks [45,47].

While STRIDE, attack trees, and DREAD are common in general security analysis, in the case of cyberphysical or embedded systems, there are no well-known examples of the application of these techniques for practical security analysis. A thorough literature study for IVC systems revealed only a couple of examples [48,49].

5.2.2. Inter Vehicle Communication (IVC)

Aijaz *et al.* [48] developed the most complete list of vulnerabilities for IVCs, which correspond partially to and overlap with the CACC system, discussed in Section 5.1. They distinguish four groups of applications that cover the attack surface and form respective subtrees in the global attack tree structure. This includes: car-to-car, car-to-infrastructure, car-to-home, and router-based applications. For the first two groups, which are the only ones of interest in the current project, the following two subtrees, with corresponding leaves are listed:

- for car-to-car traffic: either disseminate false messages by generating new message, replaying existing message, and modifying a message, or—disturb the system;
- for car-to-infrastructure applications: either disseminate false messages (in seven different ways), or disturb the system by paralyzing onboard or roadside units, or by affecting the communication channel.

More recently, Vestlund [49] presented a thorough analysis of threats for IVC, but technically used fault tree analysis (FTA) rather than attack trees, defining the difference as follows: "attack trees describe the attacker's possible method of attack, while FTA describes the system's vulnerabilities and failure events." The analysis is both broader than that in [48], because it includes additional groups of applications, and deeper, since it goes into the behaviors at the level internal to a vehicle, including its Electronic Control Units (ECUs) and their interconnection via a message bus, such as Controller Area Network (CAN).

A relatively large number of cases for fault/attack trees have been built by the author [49], but regarding the message communication in IVC, only the following threat classes are important:

- communication denial
- modified communication data
- intercepted communication data
- falsified communication.

Both studies, [48,49] validate the selection of the CACC model and its respective functionalities, as described in Section 5.1. Following this model, to verify the usefulness of threat modeling for establishing state transition probabilities for the Markov chain (strictly, the Discrete Time Markov Chain—DTMC), an actual example of a message exchange system over the CAN network has been set up. It includes two CAN nodes communicating over the CAN bus, with additional Internet connectivity for both nodes. The arrangement, which imitates part of the functionality of a larger CACC system, is shown implemented in the Microsoft Threat Modeling Tool [45] in Figure 10. The vulnerabilities exist at the inter-node boundaries, where CAN frames are passing between nodes, and where status and command messages are subjected to interference.

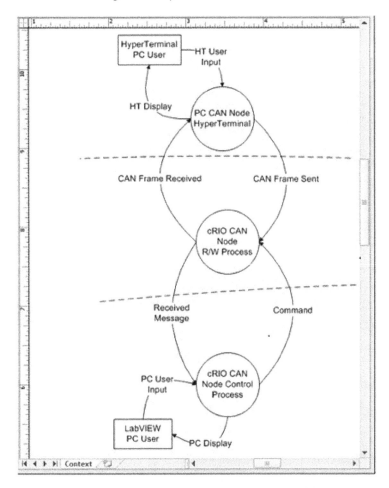

Figure 10. Representation of a CAN example in the modeling tool.

5.2.3. Experimental Results

One specific report of interest, which the tool generates, leading to quantitative analysis, is the Threat Model Analysis Report shown, in part, in Figure 11. It connects system components with threat types. With this information on hand, one can extract the parts, which affect communication, and use a DREAD related technique similar to that proposed in [47] to assign numerical values to specific vulnerabilities, which can then be normalized to probabilities. For example, Discoverability, w_d, Reproducibility, w_r, and Exploitability, w_e, would denote the likelihood of threats, and Affected users, au, and Damage potential, dp—their severity, leading to a numerical risk assessment, according to the following formula:

$$risk = (w_d + w_r + w_e) * (au + dp)$$

where *au* and *dp* are expressed in financial terms. The intermediate step from STRIDE, as generated by the tool (threat types in Figure 11), to DREAD involves mapping from the threats onto vulnerabilities. Once this is done, assigning values of likelihoods, in the simplest case, can rely on counting the relative frequency of occurrence of threats.

Threat Model Analysis Report:	
Element Name	Threat Type
CAN Frame Received	Tampering
CAN Frame Received	InformationDisclosure
CAN Frame Received	DenialOfService
CAN Frame Sent	Tampering
CAN Frame Sent	InformationDisclosure
CAN Frame Sent	DenialOfService
Command	Tampering
Command	InformationDisclosure
Command	DenialOfService
HT Display	Tampering
HT Display	InformationDisclosure
HT Display	DenialOfService
HT User Input	Tampering
HT User Input	InformationDisclosure
HT User Input	DenialOfService
PC Display	Tampering
PC Display	InformationDisclosure
PC Display	DenialOfService
PC User Input	Tampering
PC User Input	InformationDisclosure
PC User Input	DenialOfService
Received Message	Tampering
Received Message	InformationDisclosure
Received Message	DenialOfService
Hyper Terminal PC User	Spoofing
Hyper Terminal PC User	Repudiation
LabVIEW PC User	Spoofing
LabVIEW PC User	Repudiation
cRIO CAN Node R/W Process	Spoofing
cRIO CAN Node R/W Process	Tampering
cRIO CAN Node R/W Process	Repudiation
cRIO CAN Node R/W Process	InformationDisclosure
cRIO CAN Node R/W Process	DenialOfService
cRIO CAN Node R/W Process	ElevationOfPrivilege
cRIO CAN Node Control Process	Spoofing
cRIO CAN Node Control Process	Tampering
cRIO CAN Node Control Process	Repudiation
cRIO CAN Node Control Process	InformationDisclosure
cRIO CAN Node Control Process	DenialOfService
cRIO CAN Node Control Process	ElevationOfPrivilege
PC CAN Node Hyper Terminal	Spoofing
PC CAN Node Hyper Terminal	Tampering
PC CAN Node Hyper Terminal	Repudiation
PC CAN Node Hyper Terminal	InformationDisclosure
PC CAN Node Hyper Terminal	DenialOfService
PC CAN Node Hyper Terminal	ElevationOfPrivilege

Figure 11. Example of an analysis in the modeling tool.

However, this method of quantitatively assessing the risk and corresponding probabilities of security breaches is still vague and requires a significant amount of well-informed judgment in the assessment process to get to numerical values. An alternative approach, based on assessing the vulnerabilities as per the Common Vulnerability Scoring System (CVSS) [38], is more promising since it has specific formulas to calculate risk. Both these methods, however, have been developed for analyzing security of Internet based applications and are not specific to cyberphysical systems, mostly because of a lack of publicly available data for such systems. This situation may change with the recent establishment of a disclosure framework for industrial control systems [50]. Additional work is needed to include the completion of a more extensive IVC model, and involvement of other types of cyberphysical systems, such as SCADA, RFID or time triggered applications.

5.2.4. Summary of the Measurement Process

Threat modeling is not commonly used in cyberphysical systems but this case study proves that the method can be effective, if the attack surface is precisely defined, as in the case of IVC, making the model theoretically valid. The mapping of this method into five steps of security measurement, as outlined in Section 4.3, may look as follows: (1) security property is evaluated by security risk assessment, built around five DREAD characteristics (Discoverability, Reproducibility and Exploitability determining the likelihoods of threats, and Affected users and Damage potential determining the severity of threats); (2) a usually discrete scale, on which risk is assessed, forms the metric; (3) the measure is the risk assessment formula, traditionally understood as the weighted sum of the products of severity of threat (or magnitude of the potential loss) and its likelihood (probability that the loss will occur), for all factors involved, forming the computational procedure construed according to threat modeling principles; (4) the measurement process is defined by the measure and the use of a modeling tool for computations; (5) errors may be introduced in several steps during this process and require separate error analysis, which has not been done in this research.

5.3. Case Study #3: Fault Injection in Time-Triggered Systems

This case study analyzes the application of the fault injection method to assess quantitatively security of a system with Time-Triggered Protocol (TTP), in an automotive application (brake-by-wire system). The security model makes use of a vulnerability as the primary feature to evaluate security, and then applies simulation to uncover security breaches by fault injection. It shows how to assess the extent security is violated by fault injection, thus showing how vulnerable the system is as a whole. It is based on earlier publications [51,52].

5.3.1. Fault Injection Method [52]

Fault injection techniques have been developed by academia and industry for system dependability evaluation identifying fault effects and improving system fault robustness (see [53,54] and references therein).

The fault injection campaign is composed of fault injection experiments related to specific system resources, fault classes, their triggering time and location. In fault injection experiments, we have to specify not only the fault load but also workload in accordance with the analysis goal, e.g., checking fault susceptibility, error detection mechanisms, integrity/security violation, *etc*. An important issue is to trace fault effect propagation from its source via physical effects (failure) to application level impacts (errors). In this process, we can check the effectiveness of various error detectors. They may relate to low level hardware mechanisms (e.g., segmentation faults, access violation, invalid opcode, parity error—signaled as system exceptions, watchdog timer alarms, *etc.*) or microkernel mechanisms (alarms related to detected deadline misses, abnormal termination of a system call, exceptions).

Dealing with security problems relying on Denial of Service (DoS) attacks, we should select appropriate fault models directly (e.g., transmission flooding, simulated attacks), or indirectly (simulating internal system errors which can be attributed to external violations). In this process, an important issue is to identify objects susceptible to threats (e.g., access ports), sensitive information within the system and possible paths of accessing or modifying it [55]. We should also take into account the problem of security compromises as a consequence of other faults in the system (e.g., transient disturbances) and checking if they do not increase the probability of security threats, data leakage, open access paths to sensitive data, reveal passwords, create side channels for attacks, *etc*.

Beyond the classical error detection mechanisms available in commercial systems (invalid opcode, access violation, memory parity, *etc.*) we may include special software assertions checking program control flow, *etc.* Moreover, these mechanisms can be supported with on-line monitoring of event or performance logs provided by the system or applications. These logs characterize normal operations so many security DoS attacks may disturb the image of logs (operational profile) and facilitate their detection or threat prediction.

One important problem in security of cyberphysical systems is the definition of their vulnerabilities, which can affect the controller. In order to define them, one first needs to differentiate a cyberphysical system from a traditional computing system. Among typical characteristics of cyberphysical systems, one can find [56]: multiple interacting nodes, incorporation into control systems operating without human intervention, purpose other than general computing and communications, natural or engineered contexts.

Figure 12 shows an example high-level model that takes into account the above system features. This model consists of the following main subsystems, consistent with those presented in Figures 5 and 6: Plant (the controlled process), Controller (main computing device issuing control commands to the Plant), and Observer (implicit, not shown, used to measure plant's response via its output variables).

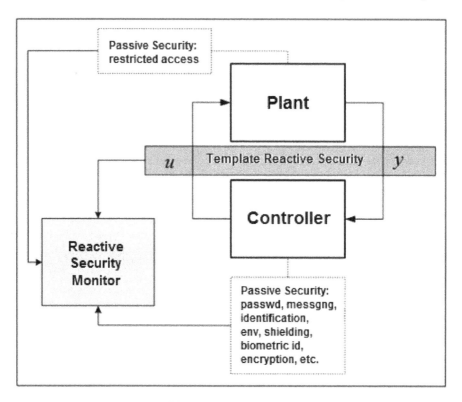

Figure 12. System view of the security monitoring in a cyberphysical system.

The Plant inputs are Controller outputs and environment disturbances (non-malicious and malicious). The malicious disturbances can be modeled as security threats and they affect mainly a controller or plant operation. In modern embedded systems, the controller often interfaces with a network (real-time and non-real-time), database, and a user. These interfaces are not shown in Figure 12 but are implicitly included in the controller.

Security threat models are mostly concerned with network, database and user interfaces because a breach in those can reduce confidentiality, integrity and availability of exchanged information in a cyberphysical system. In this project, we are mainly concerned with network interface security threats.

Specifically, in our modeling approach, after [41], we consider: introduction of spurious network messages, message deletion, message corruption, message flooding.

5.3.2. Brake-by-Wire System [51]

To analyze the behavior of time-triggered systems under various faults, an anti-lock braking system (ABS) in a Brake-by-Wire version was chosen as an example. For simulations, a 4-node TTTech development cluster with a disturbance node [57] was used in conjunction with Matlab's Simulink and Real-Time Workshop [58]. The basic models of anti-lock braking systems were transformed to improve performance under various faults. Models of an ABS system on a single wheel (QVM—Quarter Vehicle Model) and of an entire car (FVM—Four-wheel Vehicle Model) were used in the simulations but to simplify the presentation only single wheel models are described in this paper.

An ABS system serves to prevent the wheel lock. The ability of a vehicle to lock the brakes is related to the fact that the static coefficient of friction between tires and the road surface is much greater than the dynamic coefficient of friction. That is, when the part of the tire in contact with the road is moving relative to the road, it takes less force to continue moving. This results in the wheel lock and increased stopping time and distance traveled by the vehicle between the time of brake application and the end of the vehicle's movement. Preventing the wheel lock is accomplished by appropriately regulating the application of the vehicle's brakes.

In a typical ABS system (Figure 13), there are several major components. These are speed sensors, brake (pedal) position sensors, brake line valves to relieve pressure, and the real-time controller. When the operator of a vehicle attempts to apply the brakes, the wheel-speed sensors detect the deceleration of the wheels. If the deceleration on a wheel is too large, the ABS controller forces the appropriate valves to relieve pressure on that wheel's brake. This decreases the brake-force on that wheel, and decreases the deceleration of the wheel. This is crucial as great deceleration typically leads to wheel-lock. Two preexisting Simulink ABS models were considered in this work: QVM and FVM [51,52].

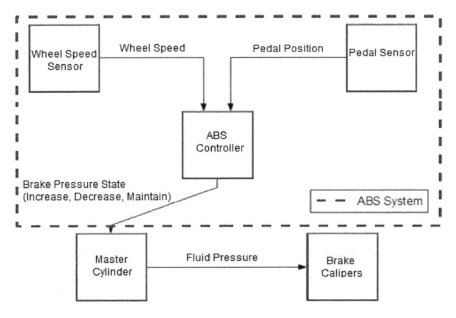

Figure 13. Illustration of an ABS system operation (brake-by-wire).

5.3.3. Simulation and Quantitative Analysis

The main emphasis of experiments was to measure the impact of disturbing various components on the simulated system with the presence of specific faults. For illustration of the encountered behavior related to security measurement, all in a 4-node TTTech development cluster [57], let us consider a disturbance scenario where the pedal sensor runs on a separate node (Node D), while the remaining three nodes (Nodes A, B and C) redundantly calculate the brake force. The wheel speed monitor runs on one of the brake force calculating nodes. Similarly, the brake model runs on another node containing the brake force calculation.

Simulation models were tested under individual node disturbance (fault injection) scenarios to simulate component failures. The nodes of the cluster communicated via a dual-channel bus, to which each node is connected, over TTP protocol. The fault injection scenarios specified a particular schedule for the disturbance node to "communicate" on the bus. Essentially, the disturbance node was set to send a high (jamming) signal on the bus at specific time periods for specific lengths of time so as to prevent a specific node from being able to send its messages. In all experiments in the disturbance scenario, execution began between rounds 1100 and 1400 and lasted 3000 rounds.

Different fault models were selected for this and other distributed QVM/FVM simulations. These fault models define the disruption of the communication of individual nodes via the TTTech disturbance node, to simulate component disruption in a manner similar to that which may be observed in a real ABS.

Sample results of the simulation are illustrated in Figure 14. The first cycle shows the ideal characteristics with no disturbance during this time of the simulation. The second cycle shows the ideal characteristics even though disturbance scenario was executed at round 1100; the second cycle simulation ran to completion with no changes. However, the decline of the wheel speed in the third cycle became linear which was incorrect. For such simulations some techniques for multifactor measurements of system vulnerability were developed. In general, the vulnerability to be measured is the range of modification (degeneration) of the ideal time characteristic of the cyberphysical system under various faults. We analyzed various metrics to quantitatively evaluate this characteristic.

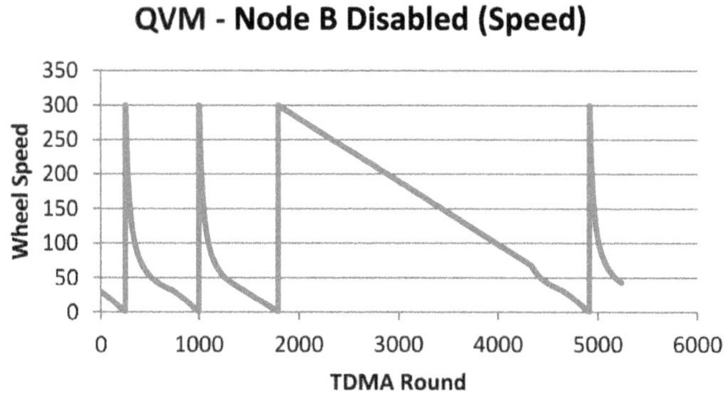

QVM - Node B Disabled (Speed)

Figure 14. Results of disabling Node B of QVM. TDMA stands for Time Division Multiple Access method of multiple nodes to the bus, while TDMA Round is a duration of a single experiment.

We considered both simple and complex metrics. The simple metrics is based on comparing so-called critical points in the ideal time characteristics (ideal, that is, without faults) and the critical points in characteristics obtained under fault. The critical points are related to critical functionality of the controlled device. An example of a critical point in our ABS system was to identify the complete stop time (time for a vehicle to reach speed zero). We could express the corresponding metric as a value between 0 and 1 computed by dividing the ideal duration of the time to stop, t_d, and the time to stop under the fault, t_f.

In the simulation from Figure 14, the second cycle finished unchanged giving the vulnerability metric $(1 - t_d/t_f) = 0$ (perfect) for the cycle that already started when the fault was generated. However, for the next cycle where the ideal time to stop, t_d, was around 800, the delayed time to stop, t_f, because of the fault, was around 3000. That gave us the vulnerability metrics equal to value of $(1 - 800/3000) = 73\%$, which practically represents the failure of the system.

A more complex metric is based on comparing complete ideal characteristics and the actual characteristics obtained under fault. For this ABS system, we could express the complex metric also as a value between 0 and 1 but computed by dividing the area below the ideal characteristic and the characteristic under the fault. In our example, the second cycle finished unchanged giving complex vulnerability metric also 0 (perfect) for the cycle that already started when the fault was generated. For the next cycle, the complex metric can be calculated by comparing the areas under both curves.

In summary, for cyclic systems modelled by cyclic simulations, we have to distinguish between modification of ideal characteristics by a fault generated during the current cycle and for the next one. Calculation of simple or complex time characteristics (metrics) can be done and is generally related to a specific model of cyberphysical systems and its functionality. For example, for some devices not the time to stop but reduction of the speed to half might be critical. As a result the vulnerability (and, at the same time, security) measurement is relative to such metrics.

In addition, for cyberphysical systems exhibiting cyclic behavior, the aggregate metrics can be introduced. The aggregate metrics involve counting/averaging across multiple cycles, e.g., taking into account missing or significantly modified spikes. This metric accounts for the loss of functionality in the system for a longer time. Our simulation studies show that, in addition to detecting anomalous time-triggered system behavior related to malicious attacks of network messages in a TTP-based system, it is also possible to calculate a numerical value of the degree of security violations.

5.3.4. Summary of the Measurement Process

The Brake-by-Wire model fits well into a cyberphysical system framework, with its process (sensors and actuators) and network interfaces to represent the attack surface. With this, respective steps in security assessment using fault injection can be mapped onto those from Section 4.3, as follows: (1) The primary feature (attribute), which determines security implications is vulnerability; (2) The metric involves the departure (distance) from the intended behavior and is mapped on the continuous scale for the interval [0,1]; (3) The measure is a related computational formula defined for a particular fault injection method; (4) The measurement process is defined by injecting faults into a pre-built Simulink model (based on differential equations) and observing effects in terms of departure from the standard (prescribed) behavior; (5) Accuracy of the measurement is governed by the error of the simulation process, which includes building the model itself, that may introduce a systematic error.

5.4. Case Study #4. Non-Functional Requirements

This case study examines the application of non-functional requirements (NFR) method to assess quantitatively security of a SCADA system. SCADA stands for Supervisory Control And Data Acquisition and has been heavily used for the last 40+ years in distributed process control of larger plants. It consists of a master unit that controls the working of the entire system by reading sensors and activating actuators throughout a distributed plant. The process for converting non-functional requirements to a quantitative assessment of security is outlined in this section, based on a related earlier publication [59].

5.4.1. Outline of the NFR Approach [59]

The NFR Approach is a goal-oriented method that can be applied to determine the extent to which objectives are achieved by a design—here the objectives are defined as achieving security for a cyberphysical system. NFR considers properties of a system such as reliability, maintainability, flexibility, scalability, *etc.*, and could equally well consider functional objectives. The NFR uses a well-defined ontology for this purpose that includes NFR softgoals, operationalizing softgoals, claim softgoals, contributions, and propagation rules; each of these elements is described briefly below [59]. Furthermore, since strictly quantitative assessment of soft or vaguely defined properties is difficult, the NFR Approach uses the concept of satisficing, a term borrowed from economics, which indicates satisfaction within limits instead of absolute satisfaction of the goal.

NFR softgoals represent NFRs and their decompositions. Elements that have physical equivalents (process or product elements) are represented by operationalizing softgoals and their decompositions. Each softgoal is named using the convention: *Type [Topic1, Topic2 ...]*, where *Type* is the name of the softgoal and *Topic* (could be zero or more) is the context where the softgoal is used. Topic is optional for a softgoal; for a claim softgoal, which is a softgoal capturing a design decision, the name may be the justification itself. Softgoals may be decomposed into other softgoals in two ways: in an AND-contribution satisficing all child softgoals is essential to satisfice the parent; in an OR-contribution satisficing one child softgoal is sufficient to satisfice the parent.

Contributions (MAKE, HELP, HURT, and BREAK) are usually made by operationalizing softgoals to NFR softgoals. Reasons for these contributions are captured by claim softgoals and, in this case, there is a contribution between a claim softgoal and the contribution being justified. Each of the four types of contributions has a specific semantic significance: MAKE contribution refers to a strongly positive degree of satisficing of objectives by artifacts (could be design decisions), HELP contribution refers to a positive degree of satisficing, HURT contribution refers to a negative degree of satisficing, and BREAK contribution refers to a strongly negative degree of satisficing.

Propagation rules propagate labels from a child softgoal to its parent across decompositions, from operationalizing softgoals to NFR softgoals across contributions, and from claim softgoals to contributions; propagation rules aid in the rationalization process of the NFR Approach.

There are four iterative steps for applying the NFR Approach for evaluating security:

1. Decompose NFR security.
2. Decompose the architecture of the system into its constituent operationalizing softgoals.
3. Determine the contributions made by the operationalizing softgoals to the NFR softgoals.
4. Evaluate the overall security by applying the propagation rules and observing the labels propagated to the softgoals.

5.4.2. SCADA Installation

The NFR Approach is applied to assess safety and security of control system in oil pipelines, where these two properties are critically important. The system architecture for an oil pipeline SCADA system is shown in Figure 15. A typical oil-pipeline control system has several Remote Terminal Units (RTU's) that are connected to field instruments that measure physical quantities such as pressure, temperature, or rate of flow of the oil in the pipeline. The field instruments also contain actuators that can affect the state of oil flow such as changing the rate of flow or the pressure. The RTUs communicate with a central master station using communication links such as Ethernet, satellite, cable, cellular, or fiber optic transmission media. The central Master Station gets the complete operational view of the entire system that allows planners to take appropriate actions based on business needs.

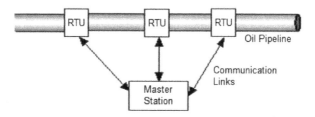

Figure 15. Typical oil pipeline control system.

The system analyzed for safety and security properties is the SCADA system at the Center for Petroleum Security Research (CPSR) at UT Tyler. The architecture of the CPSR is shown in Figure 16.

The system consists of an Allen-Bradley Control Logix (Rockwell Automation, Inc., Milwaukee, WI, USA) that serves as the master and RS Logix 500 units (also from Rockwell) serving as RTUs. The latter controls field equipment such as valves, meters, and sensors.

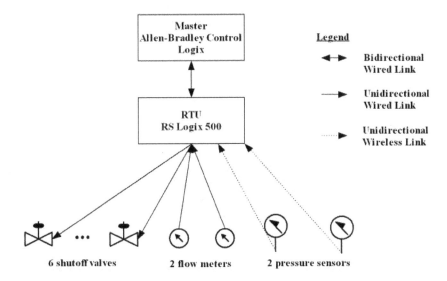

Figure 16. CPSR system architecture.

Security requirements include the following: only authorized personnel control the system, all events are logged for audit, and encrypted data are used for wireless transmissions. The NFR approach is used to evaluate the security of this cyberphysical system, which is addressed in the following section.

5.4.3. Applying the NFR Approach

The Softgoal Interdependency Graph (SIG) for this cyberphysical system is shown in Figure 17. The upper part shows the decomposition of security requirements, while the lower part shows the decomposition of the architecture of CPSR, the example cyberphysical system. The arrows between them show the contributions made by architectural (design) elements to requirements. Justifications for these contributions are captured by the claim softgoals.

NFR security for the system is represented by the softgoal Security [CPS] which is AND-decomposed into softgoals Access Control [Personnel], Audit Log [Events], and Encryption [Wireless], which refer to, respectively, the activities of access control, logging events for audit, and wireless encryption, all three of which help improve security and, therefore, the AND-decomposition of the NFR security.

Wireless encryption can be unidirectional or bidirectional, so softgoal Encryption [Wireless] is OR-decomposed into two NFR softgoals: Encryption [Wireless, RTUtoMaster] and Encryption [Wireless, MastertoRTU], representing the two directions in which wireless encryption can be done (either from RTU to Master or from Master to RTU). The final step in the application of the NFR Approach is to apply the propagation rules, the details of which have been presented in an earlier paper [59].

One of the major benefits of the NFR Approach is that quantitative evaluation of properties is possible. The first step for quantitative analysis is to map qualitative aspects of the SIG into quantitative aspects as shown in Figure 18.

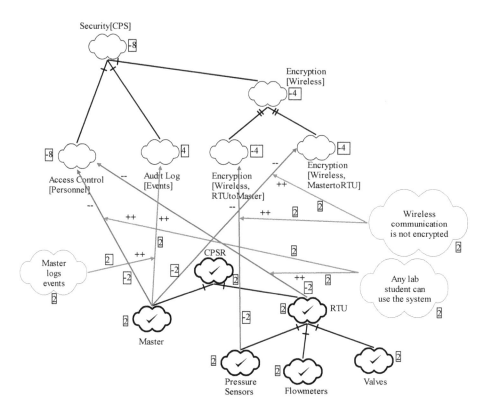

Figure 17. SIG for evaluating security of the cyberphysical system and phase 1 in the NFR approach.

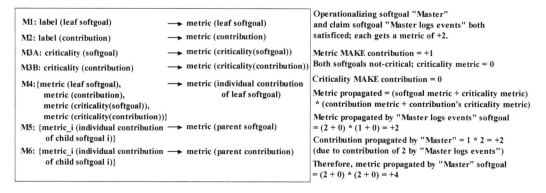

Figure 18. Mapping qualitative aspects of SIG to a quantitative evaluation scheme (**left**) and example of single-value quantitative scheme calculation (**right**).

First, as per M1, the label for the leaf softgoals is converted to a corresponding metric; thus, a satisfied leaf softgoal (it could be an operationalizing softgoal, an NFR or a claim softgoal) is converted to a corresponding metric and a denied softgoal is converted to its corresponding metric. Then, as per M2, each contribution (MAKE, HELP, HURT, BREAK) is converted to a corresponding quantitative representation. If either softgoals or contributions have associated criticalities, then we generated metrics for these criticalities (M3A and M3B).

Then, by M4, the quadruple of <leaf softgoal metric, leaf softgoal criticality metric, contribution metric, and contribution criticality metric> is converted into a metric representing the individual contribution of the leaf softgoal to its parent (which could be a softgoal or a contribution). By mapping rule M5, the collection of all individual contributions from child softgoals is converted into a metric for the parent softgoal.

Likewise, by mapping rule M6, the collection of all individual contributions from child softgoals is converted into a metric for the parent contribution. These metrics are then propagated recursively up the SIG, with each newly evaluated softgoal as the next leaf softgoal. The metrics propagated are indicated inside rectangles in Figure 17.

Any quantitative scheme that satisfies this mapping can be used to calculate safety and security metrics. Example calculations using the single-value scheme are shown in Figure 18 (right). Applying this scheme, we get a metric of -8 for security; details are given in [59]. However, we have the complete rationale for these metrics and more importantly we know how to improve (or even reduce) a desired metric. Also, the SIG maintains the historical record of decisions. Since the metrics trace back to the requirements of the system, we can quickly (re-)calculate the impact of changed requirements on these metrics. Besides deterministic quantitative scheme, the NFR Approach permits probabilistic, fuzzy logic, and other schemes to be used for deriving metrics.

5.4.4. Summary of the Measurement Process

The initial step is to make sure that SCADA fits into the model of a cyberphysical system of Section 3, which it does perfectly with its measurement/control interfaces and network interfaces, defining the attack surface. The following steps summarize how the security assessment process using the NFR approach, as described in details above, follows the security measurement guidelines of Section 4.3. It turns out that the NFR approach fits very naturally into Steps (1)–(5) of the guidelines, namely: (1) security decomposition into individual factors (softgoals) forms a valid model as a basis for assessment; (2) the degrees of satisficing, from strongly positive to strongly negative, form the metric for comparisons; (3) combinations of individual contributions of softgoals constitute an NFR measure; (4) application of propagation rules across the SIG defines the measurement process; and (5) due to the discrete nature of a metric, which is integer, a minimum error in an estimate is determined by the distance between two consecutive values of the metric.

5.5. Case Study #5: Security Patterns

This case study analyzes the application of security patterns to assess quantitatively the security of a cyberphysical system using an example of web services. This is in line with the pervasive nature of the Internet of Things (IoT), which poses new challenges to the developers of cyberphysical systems. This section is based on earlier publications [60,61]. In subsequent subsections, we describe an approach to measuring security with security patterns indirectly, using the following features: complexity, usability, ease of implementation and efficiency of the pattern.

5.5.1. Overview of Security Patterns

A pattern is a recurring combination of meaningful units that occurs in some context and which embody expert experience and good design practices within the field. Patterns provide a systematic approach to building systems that possess non-functional properties such as security, safety or reliability. The use of patterns is fairly new to software development, however, their use and application have provided significant benefits to the quality of software systems [62,63].

Security patterns, in particular, provide a solution to a security problem within a given context. The Pattern Oriented Software Architecture (POSA) template [64] defines a systematic way to describe patterns. It consists of a number of units, each describing one aspect of a pattern, and is designed to capture the experience of professionals that have solved common problems.

The previous work by one of the co-authors [61], and summarized elsewhere [63], introduces two comprehensive methodologies for integrating security properties during system development with the use of security patterns. In these approaches, a specific security problem is mapped to a given security policy which is realized with the use of a security pattern as a solution. The security pattern describes the countermeasures and defenses that should be implemented to handle a particular security problem. In other words, these approaches inform how to develop a system from inception through to implementation stage that meticulously considers security at each stage.

In essence, each security requirement is tested and compared to the actual results obtained on a set of defined threats that the system is supposed to protect against. Figure 19 shows a secure software lifecycle, indicating where security can be applied (white arrows) and where to audit for compliance with security principles and policies (dark arrows). A security test case is an implementation that realizes a security requirement and, when it is executed, we can determine if the expected result of the security requirement is the same as to the actual result obtained from the test case.

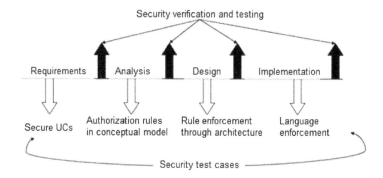

Figure 19. Overview of security verification over the life cycle.

Moreover, software testing tools such as Eclipse, JUnit and Maven allow for detail unit, component, system level testing [65], and test coverage for each security test case to further allow for verification of the expected security requirements. These tools provide useful information that includes: the time it takes for a threat to be handled and the type of failure that occurs if the threat is not mitigated as expected. These test results can be easily measured quantitatively based on the implementation of a particular method that implements security and one that does not. Coverage is an important factor that is measurable; and with the use of tools it is easier to determine what percentage of a system passes or fails for each security test case.

Other system properties that affect security directly, such as safety and reliability, can be easily integrated and evaluated using patterns. Work in [60,61] provides several hybrid patterns for integrating security and reliability during system development. In general, security patterns provide a versatile yet effective means of integrating security at a granular level throughout the entire system development cycle that can be measured at each stage.

5.5.2. Example of Web Services

Unhandled faults and vulnerabilities in software development can have catastrophic consequences. When a fault manifests itself and is not contained, it can result in a failure, which indicates that the system is not following the specifications. A policy can avoid or handle a failure or a threat. A pattern realizes the policy that can handle the fault and vulnerability. By enumerating all the faults and vulnerabilities starting at the requirements stage and having appropriate patterns to handle them, one can build secure and reliable systems.

Security and reliability aspects in a computer system are expressed differently at different architectural layers (levels) and stages of the software development process. Case in point, web services are widely used in the software units of cyberphysical systems with the adoption of the Service-Oriented Architecture (SOA) and the Cloud Architecture. Assessing the level of security and reliability in such services may not always be straightforward. Typically, vendors are not forthcoming in sharing the security countermeasures and defenses they utilize in their web services. Figure 20 illustrates a solution that integrates both security and reliability properties in a web service [61]. The solution utilizes a role-based access control defense, which ensures that only authorized users can access a service. This protects the confidentiality and integrity of the web service.

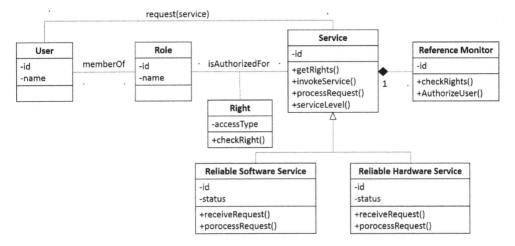

Figure 20. Class diagram for the Secure Reliability Pattern.

Figure 20 shows a class diagram for the Secure Reliability pattern that implements authorization for each user that wishes to access a service. It also guarantees reliability by ensuring that the service has redundancy, so that if it fails, it is immediately replaced by another service that will carry out the exact same operation. As shown in Figure 20, every user is a member of a role, and each role has specific rights associated with it. The service entity implements a strategy pattern, which chooses a software or hardware service, depending on the needs of the application. The reference monitor enforces the authorized use of the service. One approach to assess a web service is with the use of security and reliability certificates [60] as outlined in the next sub-section.

The security defenses, such as authorization via RBAC (Role Based Access Control), which are implemented using the pattern described above can be assessed using our security assessment approach and, based on the weighted average, we can determine whether or not the security pattern will be feasible and meet the expected security needs.

5.5.3. Security and Reliability Certificates Checking

Assessing security and reliability properties can be achieved with the use of machine-readable certificates. Let us consider the following example (Figure 21), given an enhanced SOA infrastructure composed of the following main parties [60]:

1. Client (*c*)—the entity that needs to select or integrate a remote service based on its reliability and security requirements. Here, the Client is a user who would be authorized by the reference monitor defense depicted in Figure 20.
2. Service provider (*sp*)—the entity implementing remote services accessed by *c*.
3. Certification Authority (*CA*)—an entity trusted by one or more users to assign certificates.
4. Evaluation Body (*EB*)—an independent, trusted component carrying out monitoring activities. EB is trusted by both *c* and *sp* to correctly check the certificate validity on the basis of the monitoring rules and metrics.
5. Service Discovery (*UDDI*)—a registry of services enhanced with the support for security and reliability certificates. Universal Description, Discovery, and Integration (*UDDI*) is an XML-based standard for describing, publishing, and finding web services. It is a specification for a distributed registry of web services that is a platform-independent, open framework.

The service invocation process enhanced with certification [60] is composed of two main stages, illustrated in Figure 21. First (Steps 1–2), *CA* grants a reliability certificate to a service provider, *sp*, based on a service implementation and a security and reliability pattern. Then (Steps 3–9), upon receiving the certificate for the service, *s*, *sp* publishes the certificate together with the service interface in a service registry. Next, the client, *c*, searches the registry and compares the certificates of the available services. Once the client has chosen a certificate, it will ask the trusted component, *EB*, to confirm its validity. *EB* checks that the monitoring rules hold and returns a result to *c*. If the result is positive, *c* proceeds to call the service. The SOA paradigm supports runtime selection and composition of services, which makes it difficult to guarantee *a priori* the security and reliability of a process instance.

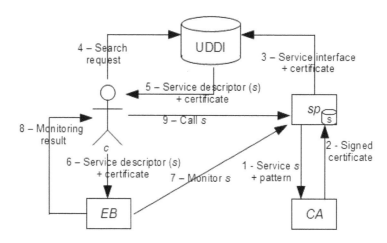

Figure 21. An SOA enhanced with security and reliability certification.

The technique described above is based on machine-readable certificates that use reliability and security patterns to conduct *a posteriori* evaluation of web services. When an assessment of the security pattern using our security pattern assessment approach is completed, the weighted average is then used to determine whether or not a security pattern is certifiable. Pattern properties are assessed using the following features:

1. Complexity: The feature which refers to the number of security defenses that the pattern provides. For example, one pattern may only provide monitoring while another may conduct monitoring, authentication and authorization of users.
2. Usability: The feature which refers the ease with which the user can apply the pattern to solve a problem.
3. Ease of Implementation: This feature ties back to the template used to describe a security pattern. Some patterns do not provide enough relevant information to be useful to the user. Here, ease of implementation is measured by how comprehensive the security pattern description is.
4. Efficiency: This feature is measured using the degree of the side effects and consequences that is introduced by implementing the security pattern.

Each of the four features described above is evaluated using the following scale: Low—has a value weight of 1; Medium—has a value weight of 3; High—has a value weight of 5. Each of these four properties may be given a different weight, for example, usability is subjective and may not carry the same weight as efficiency or complexity.

Figure 21 illustrates the assessment process via interactions within the SOA enhanced with security and reliability certificates [60]. The primary interaction that realizes security is with the use of a reference monitor pattern and reliability patterns which satisfy the four security properties described above. The reference monitor pattern is written as outlined in the POSA template [62,63]. This pattern is widely accepted and utilized as an effective security control that directly satisfies security properties 2 and 3. Additionally, the reference monitor utilized in Figure 21 affords three pertinent security controls—that is, monitoring, authorization and authentication—and is further enhanced with reliability. Reliability here is realized in the form of redundancy patterns to ensure that, if any of the security controls fail, a backup is immediately invoked to seamlessly carry out the required security functionality, thereby satisfying properties 1 and 4.

There are many degrees to which redundancy can be implemented in the certificates described in Figure 21, whether by N-modular, dual-modular redundancy, triple-modular redundancy or N-Version programming [65]. Similarly, additional security controls can be added to the reference monitor such as a secure communication channel to further increase the security of the enhanced SOA certificates, however this decision must be made by the developer, to decide what degree of security and reliability is feasible depending on the nature of system being designed. Depending on the exact implementation of security and reliability, their value can be assessed using the scale of low, medium, or high within each of the four security features and an appropriate corresponding ranking value (1–5) can be determined to assess the degree of security that is achieved with the use of these certificates. Thus, the security and reliability patterns offer effective and systematic solution toward achieving increased security and reliability in cyberphysical systems that are measureable.

5.5.4. Outline of the Measurement Process

The SOA architecture and related patterns fall within the framework of a cyberphysical system at the higher level through the concept of Internet of Things (IoT), which allows access to low-level measurement and control devices via networks and related protocols that resemble an attack surface. To assess information security in this arrangement, a pattern can be evaluated according to the measurement process outlined in Section 4.3, as follows: (1) the property is split into four characteristics, including complexity, usability, ease of implementation, and efficiency; (2) a metric is defined as non-numerical scale of at least three levels (High, Medium, and Low); (3) a measure is defined by a formula composed of a linear combination of the assessment of all four features characterizing security patterns; (4) the measurement process follows principles of collecting data on patterns from industry and government sources and via expert interviews, and then applying the measure; (5) the accuracy of the measurement involves the concept of trustworthiness and is the subject of current research.

6. Conclusions

This paper discussed issues relevant to measuring security as a system property in cyberphysical systems. After introducing a definition of security as a property, placed in the context of cyberphysical systems, principles of measurement were presented, based on the modern view of measurement theory. It relies on defining the attack surface, first, then decomposing security into constituent features (attributes). This is followed by defining a metric as a scale, and a measure, which is a computational formula to evaluate security on the scale. The measurement process involves application of respective techniques using the measure to find a quantitative or qualitative estimate of security, and determine the accuracy or trustworthiness of the result.

Within this framework, five case studies taking diverse approaches to security assessment and measurement are discussed, based on, respectively: Markov chains, threat modeling, fault injection, non-functional requirements, and security patterns. Each approach is applied to a corresponding example of a cyberphysical system, and attempts to quantify the results in respective experiments.

In this view, results of this work can be summarized as follows:

- Markov chains are an effective tool for modeling degradation of services due to security threats, and allow for an efficient assessment of security in cases when probabilities of state transitions can be reasonably determined;

- threat modeling is useful in investigating system behavior at boundaries forming an attack surface, and—given the tool support—results in analysis of possibilities, which can negatively affect security, thus facilitating use of respective methods for quantitative evaluation of risks;
- fault injection allows introducing deliberate disturbances to a cyberphysical system by distorting messages or message flow in the system; experiments with time-triggered protocol revealed that it is possible to quantify the extent of damage caused by security lapses;
- non-functional requirements approach adds to the spectrum of quantitative evaluation methods the ability to evaluate designs; this capability is crucial in the development of cyberphysical systems, since it enables Design for Security, rather than security assessment as an afterthought;
- security patterns by their very nature allow developing preventive security measures and their quantitative assessment; it makes them a very important tool for software designers, who may not be experts in security.

Each of the case studies presented here uses some security defense, such as: monitoring, failure or threat detection and various countermeasures to mitigate those threats and failures. However, not all defenses are equally effective. It is therefore imperative that the defenses, which are utilized in cyberphysical systems, actually work well. This gives rise to an important question: how can these defenses be evaluated and their effectiveness measured?

At present, there is no way to determine if a system is more or less secure when one adds or subtracts a particular application. Current approaches to evaluating security are policy based, assuring that certain procedures have been followed. However, this does not tell us if one design is more "secure" than another or if adding or subtracting a component strengthens or weakens the system.

Given that system developers are not typically experts in security, it makes sense to place greater emphasis on these aspects, and the presented techniques may serve as useful solutions to this problem. Security patterns, in particular, can be integrated in every stage of the software development life cycle as a defense mechanism, to ensure that the implementation is sound and that it will effectively protect the cyberphysical system from attacks.

Overall, the authors believe that this research is a step forward towards clarification of what is needed to assess and measure security as a system property. As they say "there is no one size that fits all", the presented case studies shed some light on the subject by addressing the issue from a variety of viewpoints. It is also clear that there is a need to create a better database to keep track of the security problems we encounter, since way too often the problems are not being disclosed for a variety of business or political reasons. While addressing most of these issues and finding answers to similar questions are still the subject of intense research, this paper provides some uniformity in treating the area of security measurement and can serve as a framework for further studies.

Acknowledgments: Janusz Zalewski acknowledges the 2015 Air Force Summer Faculty Fellowship at Rome Labs. Part of this project was funded under a grant SBAHQ-10-I-0250 from the U.S. Small Business Administration (SBA). SBA's funding should not be construed as an endorsement of any products, opinions or services. Thanks are due to Dawid Trawczynski for educating the authors about fault injection methods. Eduardo Fernandez is gratefully acknowledged for his role in straightening the authors' understanding of security patterns.

Author Contributions: All authors made significant contributions to the paper. Janusz Zalewski conceived the concept, oversaw the development of case studies, and led the writing process. Ingrid Buckley conceived and designed the security patterns; Bogdan Czejdo contributed to evaluation of time-triggered systems; Steven Drager contributed to threat modeling; Andrew Kornecki was instrumental in conducting the availability case study; Nary Subramanian proposed and applied the NFR approach. All authors have read and approved the final manuscript.

Conflicts of Interest: The authors declare no conflict of interest. Cleared for public release on 29 February 2016: Reference No. 88ABW-2016-0922. Any opinions, findings and conclusions or recommendations expressed in this material are those of the author(s) and do not necessarily reflect the views of AFRL.

References

1. Herrmann, D.S. *Complete Guide to Security and Privacy Metrics: Measuring Regulatory Compliance, Operational Resilience and ROI*; Auerbach Publications: London, UK, 2011.
2. Brotby, W.K.; Hinson, G. *Pragmatic Security Metrics: Applying Metametrics to Information Security*; CRC Press: Boca Raton, FL, USA, 2013.
3. Atzeni, A.; Lioy, A. Why to Adopt a Security Metric? A Brief Survey. In *Quality of Protection: Security Measurements and Metrics*; Gollmann, D., Massacci, F., Yautsiukhin, A., Eds.; Springer: New York, NY, USA, 2006; pp. 1–12.
4. Bayuk, J.; Mostashari, A. Measuring Systems Security. *Syst. Eng.* **2013**, *16*, 1–14. [CrossRef]
5. *Performance Measurement Guide for Information Security*; National Institute of Standards and Technology: Gaithersburg, MD, USA, 2008.
6. Jansen, W. *Directions in Security Metrics Research*; National Institute of Standards and Technology: Gaithersburg, MD, USA, 2009.
7. Barabanov, R.; Kowalski, S.; Yngström, L. *Information Security Metrics: State of the Art*; Swedish Civil Contingencies Agency: Stockholm, Sweden, 2011.
8. A Community Website for Security Practitioners. Available online: http://www.securitymetrics.org (accessed on 7 June 2016).
9. Hinson, G. Seven Myths about Security Metric. Available online: http://www.noticebored.com/html/metrics.html (accessed on 7 June 2016).
10. Laird, L.M.; Brennan, M.C. *Software Measurement and Estimation: A Practical Approach*; John Wiley & Sons: Hoboken, NJ, USA, 2006.
11. *Department of Defense Trusted Computer Systems Evaluation Criteria*; DoD 5200.28-STD; Department of Defense: Washington, DC, USA, 1985.
12. *Common Criteria for Information Technology Security Evaluation, Parts 1–3*. Documents No. CCMB-2012-09-001, 002 and 003. Available online: http://www.commoncriteriaportal.org/cc/ (accessed on 7 June 2016).
13. ISO/IEC. *ISO/IEC 15408 Information Technology—Security Techniques—Evaluation Criteria for IT Security—Part 1: Introduction and General Models*; ISO/IEC: Geneva, Switzerland, 2009.
14. Bartol, N.; Bates, B.; Goertzel, K.M.; Winograd, T. *Measuring Cyber Security and Information Assurance*; Information Assurance Technology Analysis Center (IATAC): Herndon, VA, USA, 2009.
15. *Software Security Assessment Tools Review*; Booz Allen Hamilton: McLean, VA, USA, 2009.
16. Chapin, D.A.; Akridge, S. How Can Security Be Measured? *Inf. Syst. Control J.* **2005**, *2*, 43–47.
17. Verendel, V. Quantified Security Is a Weak Hypothesis. In Proceedings of the NSPW'09, New Security Paradigms Workshop, Oxford, UK, 8–11 September 2009; ACM: New York, NY, USA, 2009; pp. 37–50.
18. Littlewood, B.; Brocklehurst, S.; Fenton, N.; Mellor, P.; Page, S.; Wright, D.; Dobson, J.; McDermid, J.; Gollmann, D. Towards Operational Measures of Computer Security. *J. Comput. Secur.* **1993**, *2*, 211–229. [CrossRef]
19. International Electrotechnical Commission (IEC). *Electropedia: The World's Online Electrotechnical Vocabulary*; IEC: Geneva, Switzerland; Available online: http://www.electropedia.org/ (accessed on 7 June 2016).
20. ISO/IEC/IEEE. *2476-2010 Systems and Software Engineering—Vocabulary*; ISO/IEC: Geneva, Switzerland, 2011. [CrossRef]
21. *IEEE Software and Systems Engineering Vocabulary*. Available online: http://computer.org/sevocab (accessed on 7 June 2016).
22. *National Information Assurance (IA) Glossary*; Available online: https://www.ncsc.gov/nittf/docs/CNSSI-4009_National_Information_Assurance.pdf (accessed on 7 June 2016).
23. *Standards for Security Categorization of Federal Information and Information Systems*; National Institute of Standards and Technology: Gaithersburg, MD, USA, 2004.
24. Zalewski, J. Real-Time Software Architectures and Design Patterns: Fundamental Concepts and Their Consequences. *Ann. Rev. Control* **2001**, *25*, 133–146. [CrossRef]
25. Mayr, O. *Zur Frühgeschichte der technischen Regelungen*; Oldenburg Verlag: München, Germany, 1969; (English translation: *The Origin of Feedback Control*; MIT Press: Cambridge, MA, USA, 1970).
26. ISO/IEC. *27005-2011 Information Technology—Security Techniques—Information Security Risk Management*; International Organization for Standardization: Geneva, Switzerland, 2011.

27. National Physical Laboratory. *History of Length Measurement*; Teddington: Middlesex, UK; Available online: http://www.npl.co.uk/educate-explore/posters/history-of-length-measurement/ (accessed on 8 June 2016).

28. Von Helmholtz, H. Zählen und Messen: Erkentnisstheoretisch betrachtet. In *Philosophische Aufsätze: Eduard Zeller zu seinem fünfzigjährigen Doctorjubiläum gewidmet*; Fues Verlag: Leipzig, Germany, 1887; pp. 17–52, (English translation: *Counting and Measuring*; Van Nostrand: New York, NY, USA, 1980).

29. *Definitions of the SI Base Units*; National Institute of Standards and Technology: Gaithersburg, MD, USA. Available online: http://physics.nist.gov/cuu/Units/current.html (accessed on 8 June 2016).

30. Andreas, B.; Azuma, Y.; Bartl, G.; Becker, P.; Bettin, H.; Borys, M.; Busch, I.; Fuchs, P.; Fujii, K.; Fujimoto, H. Counting the Atoms in a 28Si Crystal for a New Kilogram Definition. *Metrologia* **2011**, *48*, S1–S13. [CrossRef]

31. Evans, D.; Stolfo, S. The Science of Security. *IEEE Secur. Priv.* **2011**, *9*, 16–17. [CrossRef]

32. Glimm, J.; Sharp, D.H. Complex Fluid Mixing Flows: Simulation *vs.* Theory *vs.* Experiment. *SIAM News* **2006**, *39*, 12.

33. Longman, R.W. On the Interaction Between Theory, Experiments, and Simulation in Developing Practical Learning Control Algorithms. *Intern. J. Appl. Math. Comput. Sci.* **2003**, *13*, 101–111.

34. Zalewski, J.; Kornecki, A.J.; Wierzchon, S. Reasoning under Uncertainty with Bayesian Belief Networks Enhanced with Rough Sets. *Int. J. Comput.* **2013**, *12*, 135–146.

35. Kornecki, A.J.; Zalewski, J. Experimental Evaluation of Software Development Tools for Safety-Critical Real-Time Systems. *Innov. Syst. Softw. Eng. A NASA J.* **2005**, *1*, 176–188. [CrossRef]

36. Baquero, A.; Kornecki, A.J.; Zalewski, J. Threat Modeling for Aviation Computer Security. *CrossTalk J. Def. Softw. Eng.* **2015**, *28*, 21–27.

37. *International Vocabulary of Metrology—Basic and General Concepts and Associated Terms (VIM)*, 3rd ed.; Report JCGM 200:2012; BIPM Joint Committee for Guides in Metrology: Sèvres, France, 2012.

38. Mell, P., Scarfone, K., Romanosky, S., Eds.; *CVSS—A Complete Guide to the Common Vulnerability Scoring System*; Version 2.0.; National Institute of Standards and Technology: Gaithersburg, MD, USA, 2007; Available online: http://www.first.org/cvss/cvss-guide (accessed on 8 June 2016).

39. *National Vulnerability Database*; Version 2.2. National Institute of Standards and Technology: Gaithersburg, MD, USA. Available online: http://nvd.nist.gov/ (accessed on 8 June 2016).

40. Wang, J.A.; Wang, H.; Guo, M.; Xia, M. Security Metrics for Software Systems. In Proceedings of the ACM-SE '09, 47th Annual Southeast Regional Conference, Clemson, SC, USA, 19–21 March 2009. Article No. 47.

41. Kornecki, A.J.; Zalewski, J.; Stevenson, W. Availability Assessment of Embedded Systems with Security Vulnerabilities. In Proceedings of the SEW-34, 2011 IEEE Software Engineering Workshop, Limerick, Ireland, 20–21 June 2011; pp. 42–47.

42. Cooperative Adaptive Cruise Control (CSE491–602 Class Projects), 2006. Available online: http://www.cse.msu.edu/~chengb/RE-491/Projects/cacc_msu-ford.pdf (accessed on 8 June 2016).

43. Stevenson, W. *Evaluating the Impact of Adding Security to Safety Critical Real-Time Systems*; Graduate Research Project, Embry-Riddle Aeronautical University: Daytona Beach, FL, USA, 2010.

44. *Relex/Windchill Reliability Prediction Tool*; PTC Product Development Company: Needham, MA, USA; Available online: http://www.ptc.com/products/relex/reliability-prediction (accessed on 8 June 2016).

45. Swiderski, F.; Snyder, W. *Threat Modeling*; Microsoft Press: Redmond, DC, USA, 2004.

46. Zalewski, J.; Drager, S.; McKeever, W.; Kornecki, A. Threat Modeling for Security Assessment in Cyberphysical Systems. In Proceedings of the CSIIRW 2013, 8th Annual Cyber Security and Information Intelligence Workshop, Oak Ridge, FL, USA, 8–10 January 2013. Article No. 10.

47. Ingalsbe, J.A.; Kunimatsu, L.; Baten, T.; Mead, N.R. Threat Modeling: Diving into the Deep End. *IEEE Softw.* **2008**, *25*, 28–34. [CrossRef]

48. Aijaz, A.; Bochow, B.; Dötzer, F.; Festag, A.; Gerlach, M.; Kroh, R.; Leinmüller, T. Attacks on Inter Vehicle Communication Systems—An Analysis. In Proceedings of the WIT2006, 3rd International Workshop on Intelligent Transportation, Hamburg, Germany, 14–15 March 2006; pp. 189–194.

49. Vestlund, C. Threat Analysis on Vehicle Computer Systems. Master's Thesis, Linköping University, Linköping, Sweden, 2010.

50. Common Industrial Control System Vulnerability Disclosure Framework, 2012. Available online: http://www.us-cert.gov/ (accessed on 8 June 2016).

51. Czejdo, B.; Zalewski, J.; Trawczynski, D.; Baszun, M. Designing Safety-Critical Embedded Systems with Time-Triggered Architecture. *Technol. Railw. Transp. (TTN—Technika Transportu Szynowego, Poland)* **2013**, *19*, 2265–2276.

52. Trawczynski, D.; Zalewski, J.; Sosnowski, J. Design of Reactive Security Mechanisms in Time-Triggered Embedded Systems. *SAE Intern. J. Passeng. Cars Electron. Electr. Syst.* **2014**, *7*, 527–535. [CrossRef]

53. Arlat, J.; Crouzet, Y.; Karlsson, J.; Folkesson, P. Comparison of Physical and Software-Implemented Fault Injection Techniques. *IEEE Trans. Comput.* **2003**, *52*, 1115–1133. [CrossRef]

54. Trawczynski, D. Dependability Evaluation and Enhancement in Real-Time Embedded Systems. Ph.D. Thesis, Warsaw University of Technology, Warsaw, Poland, 2009.

55. Rothbart, K.; Neffe, U.; Steger, C.; Weiss, R. High Level Fault Injection for Attack Simulation in Smart Cards. In Proceedings of the ATS 2004, 13th IEEE Asian Test Symposium, Kenting, Taiwan, 15–17 November 2004; pp. 118–121.

56. Computer Science and Telecommunications Board. *Embedded Everywhere: A Research Agenda for Networked Systems of Embedded Computers*; National Research Council: Washington, DC, USA, 2001.

57. TTTechComputertechnik AG. *TTP-Powernode—Development Board*. Product Description. Available online: http://www.tttech.com/products/ttp-product-line/ttp-powernode (accessed on 8 June 2016).

58. MathWorks. *Simulink*. Product Description. Available online: http://www.mathworks.com/products/simulink/ (accessed on 8 June 2016).

59. Subramanian, N.; Zalewski, J. Quantitative Assessment of Safety and Security of System Architectures for Cyberphysical Systems Using the NFR Approach. *IEEE Syst. J.* **2016**, *10*, 397–409. [CrossRef]

60. Buckley, I.A.; Fernandez, E.B.; Anisetti, M.; Ardagna, C.A.; Sadjadi, M.; Damiani, E. Towards Pattern-based Reliability Certification of Services. In Proceedings of the DOA-SVI'11, 1st International Symposium on Secure Virtual Infrastructures, Hersonissos, Greece, 17–21 October 2011; Lecture Notes in Computer Science 7045, Part II. Springer: Berlin/Heidelberg, Germany, 2011; pp. 558–574.

61. Buckley, I.A.; Fernandez, E.B. Patterns Combing Reliability and Security. In Proceedings of the Third International Conference on Pervasive Patterns and Applications, Rome, Italy, 25–30 September 2011.

62. Schmidt, D.; Stal, M.; Rohnert, H.; Buschmann, F. Pattern-Oriented Software Architecture. In *Patterns for Concurrent and Networked Objects*; John Wiley & Sons: New York, NY, USA, 2000; Volume 2.

63. Fernandez, E.B. *Security Patterns in Practice: Designing Secure Architectures Using Software*; John Wiley & Sons: New York, NY, USA, 2013.

64. Buschmann, F.; Meunier, R.; Rohnert, H.; Sommerlad, P.; Stal, M. *Pattern-Oriented Software Architecture: A System of Patterns*; John Wiley & Sons: New York, NY, USA, 1996; Volume 1.

65. Buckley, I.A.; Fernandez, E.B. Enumerating software failures to build dependable distributed applications. In Proceedings of the HASE 2011, 13th IEEE International Symposium on High Assurance Systems Engineering, Boca Raton, FL, USA, 10–12 November 2011; pp. 120–123.

Permissions

All chapters in this book were first published in Information, by MDPI; hereby published with permission under the Creative Commons Attribution License or equivalent. Every chapter published in this book has been scrutinized by our experts. Their significance has been extensively debated. The topics covered herein carry significant findings which will fuel the growth of the discipline. They may even be implemented as practical applications or may be referred to as a beginning point for another development.

The contributors of this book come from diverse backgrounds, making this book a truly international effort. This book will bring forth new frontiers with its revolutionizing research information and detailed analysis of the nascent developments around the world.

We would like to thank all the contributing authors for lending their expertise to make the book truly unique. They have played a crucial role in the development of this book. Without their invaluable contributions this book wouldn't have been possible. They have made vital efforts to compile up to date information on the varied aspects of this subject to make this book a valuable addition to the collection of many professionals and students.

This book was conceptualized with the vision of imparting up-to-date information and advanced data in this field. To ensure the same, a matchless editorial board was set up. Every individual on the board went through rigorous rounds of assessment to prove their worth. After which they invested a large part of their time researching and compiling the most relevant data for our readers.

The editorial board has been involved in producing this book since its inception. They have spent rigorous hours researching and exploring the diverse topics which have resulted in the successful publishing of this book. They have passed on their knowledge of decades through this book. To expedite this challenging task, the publisher supported the team at every step. A small team of assistant editors was also appointed to further simplify the editing procedure and attain best results for the readers.

Apart from the editorial board, the designing team has also invested a significant amount of their time in understanding the subject and creating the most relevant covers. They scrutinized every image to scout for the most suitable representation of the subject and create an appropriate cover for the book.

The publishing team has been an ardent support to the editorial, designing and production team. Their endless efforts to recruit the best for this project, has resulted in the accomplishment of this book. They are a veteran in the field of academics and their pool of knowledge is as vast as their experience in printing. Their expertise and guidance has proved useful at every step. Their uncompromising quality standards have made this book an exceptional effort. Their encouragement from time to time has been an inspiration for everyone.

The publisher and the editorial board hope that this book will prove to be a valuable piece of knowledge for researchers, students, practitioners and scholars across the globe.

51. Czejdo, B.; Zalewski, J.; Trawczynski, D.; Baszun, M. Designing Safety-Critical Embedded Systems with Time-Triggered Architecture. *Technol. Railw. Transp. (TTN—Technika Transportu Szynowego, Poland)* **2013**, *19*, 2265–2276.
52. Trawczynski, D.; Zalewski, J.; Sosnowski, J. Design of Reactive Security Mechanisms in Time-Triggered Embedded Systems. *SAE Intern. J. Passeng. Cars Electron. Electr. Syst.* **2014**, *7*, 527–535. [CrossRef]
53. Arlat, J.; Crouzet, Y.; Karlsson, J.; Folkesson, P. Comparison of Physical and Software-Implemented Fault Injection Techniques. *IEEE Trans. Comput.* **2003**, *52*, 1115–1133. [CrossRef]
54. Trawczynski, D. Dependability Evaluation and Enhancement in Real-Time Embedded Systems. Ph.D. Thesis, Warsaw University of Technology, Warsaw, Poland, 2009.
55. Rothbart, K.; Neffe, U.; Steger, C.; Weiss, R. High Level Fault Injection for Attack Simulation in Smart Cards. In Proceedings of the ATS 2004, 13th IEEE Asian Test Symposium, Kenting, Taiwan, 15–17 November 2004; pp. 118–121.
56. Computer Science and Telecommunications Board. *Embedded Everywhere: A Research Agenda for Networked Systems of Embedded Computers*; National Research Council: Washington, DC, USA, 2001.
57. TTTechComputertechnik AG. *TTP-Powernode—Development Board*. Product Description. Available online: http://www.tttech.com/products/ttp-product-line/ttp-powernode (accessed on 8 June 2016).
58. MathWorks. *Simulink*. Product Description. Available online: http://www.mathworks.com/products/simulink/ (accessed on 8 June 2016).
59. Subramanian, N.; Zalewski, J. Quantitative Assessment of Safety and Security of System Architectures for Cyberphysical Systems Using the NFR Approach. *IEEE Syst. J.* **2016**, *10*, 397–409. [CrossRef]
60. Buckley, I.A.; Fernandez, E.B.; Anisetti, M.; Ardagna, C.A.; Sadjadi, M.; Damiani, E. Towards Pattern-based Reliability Certification of Services. In Proceedings of the DOA-SVI'11, 1st International Symposium on Secure Virtual Infrastructures, Hersonissos, Greece, 17–21 October 2011; Lecture Notes in Computer Science 7045, Part II. Springer: Berlin/Heidelberg, Germany, 2011; pp. 558–574.
61. Buckley, I.A.; Fernandez, E.B. Patterns Combing Reliability and Security. In Proceedings of the Third International Conference on Pervasive Patterns and Applications, Rome, Italy, 25–30 September 2011.
62. Schmidt, D.; Stal, M.; Rohnert, H.; Buschmann, F. Pattern-Oriented Software Architecture. In *Patterns for Concurrent and Networked Objects*; John Wiley & Sons: New York, NY, USA, 2000; Volume 2.
63. Fernandez, E.B. *Security Patterns in Practice: Designing Secure Architectures Using Software*; John Wiley & Sons: New York, NY, USA, 2013.
64. Buschmann, F.; Meunier, R.; Rohnert, H.; Sommerlad, P.; Stal, M. *Pattern-Oriented Software Architecture: A System of Patterns*; John Wiley & Sons: New York, NY, USA, 1996; Volume 1.
65. Buckley, I.A.; Fernandez, E.B. Enumerating software failures to build dependable distributed applications. In Proceedings of the HASE 2011, 13th IEEE International Symposium on High Assurance Systems Engineering, Boca Raton, FL, USA, 10–12 November 2011; pp. 120–123.

Permissions

All chapters in this book were first published in Information, by MDPI; hereby published with permission under the Creative Commons Attribution License or equivalent. Every chapter published in this book has been scrutinized by our experts. Their significance has been extensively debated. The topics covered herein carry significant findings which will fuel the growth of the discipline. They may even be implemented as practical applications or may be referred to as a beginning point for another development.

The contributors of this book come from diverse backgrounds, making this book a truly international effort. This book will bring forth new frontiers with its revolutionizing research information and detailed analysis of the nascent developments around the world.

We would like to thank all the contributing authors for lending their expertise to make the book truly unique. They have played a crucial role in the development of this book. Without their invaluable contributions this book wouldn't have been possible. They have made vital efforts to compile up to date information on the varied aspects of this subject to make this book a valuable addition to the collection of many professionals and students.

This book was conceptualized with the vision of imparting up-to-date information and advanced data in this field. To ensure the same, a matchless editorial board was set up. Every individual on the board went through rigorous rounds of assessment to prove their worth. After which they invested a large part of their time researching and compiling the most relevant data for our readers.

The editorial board has been involved in producing this book since its inception. They have spent rigorous hours researching and exploring the diverse topics which have resulted in the successful publishing of this book. They have passed on their knowledge of decades through this book. To expedite this challenging task, the publisher supported the team at every step. A small team of assistant editors was also appointed to further simplify the editing procedure and attain best results for the readers.

Apart from the editorial board, the designing team has also invested a significant amount of their time in understanding the subject and creating the most relevant covers. They scrutinized every image to scout for the most suitable representation of the subject and create an appropriate cover for the book.

The publishing team has been an ardent support to the editorial, designing and production team. Their endless efforts to recruit the best for this project, has resulted in the accomplishment of this book. They are a veteran in the field of academics and their pool of knowledge is as vast as their experience in printing. Their expertise and guidance has proved useful at every step. Their uncompromising quality standards have made this book an exceptional effort. Their encouragement from time to time has been an inspiration for everyone.

The publisher and the editorial board hope that this book will prove to be a valuable piece of knowledge for researchers, students, practitioners and scholars across the globe.

Hong-Jie Dai
Department of Computer Science & Information Engineering, National Taitung University, Taitung 95092, Taiwan
Interdisciplinary Program of Green and Information Technology, National Taitung University, Taitung 95092, Taiwan

Musa Touray
Graduate Institute of Biomedical Informatics, Taipei Medical University, Taipei 11031, Taiwan

Jitendra Jonnagaddala
School of Public Health and Community Medicine, UNSW Australia, Sydney, NSW 2052, Australia
Prince of Wales Clinical School, UNSW Australia, Sydney, NSW 2052, Australia

Shabbir Syed-Abdul
Graduate Institute of Biomedical Informatics, Taipei Medical University, Taipei 11031, Taiwan
International Center for Health Information Technology, Taipei Medical University, Taipei 11031, Taiwan

Xin Shu
School of Computer Science & Engineering, Jiangsu University of Science & Technology, Zhenjiang 2102003, China
School of Internet of Things Engineering, Jiangnan University, Wuxi 214122, China
School of Electronic Engineering and Computer Science, Queen Mary University of London, London E1 4NS, UK

Qianni Zhang
School of Electronic Engineering and Computer Science, Queen Mary University of London, London E1 4NS, UK

Jinlong Shi and Yunsong Qi
School of Computer Science & Engineering, Jiangsu University of Science & Technology, Zhenjiang 212003, China

Janusz Zalewski and Ingrid A. Buckley
Department of Software Engineering, Florida Gulf Coast University, Ft. Myers, FL 33965, USA

Bogdan Czejdo
Department of Math & Computer Science, Fayetteville State University, Fayetteville, NC 28301, USA

Steven Drager
Air Force Research Laboratory, Rome, NY 13441, USA

Andrew J. Kornecki
Department of Electrical, Computer, Software, and Systems Engineering, Embry-Riddle Aeronautical University, Daytona Beach, FL 32114, USA

Nary Subramanian
Department of Computer Science, University of Texas at Tyler, Tyler, TX 75799, USA

List of Contributors

Jia Yu
Graduate School of Advanced Technology and Science, Tokushima University, Tokushima 770-8501, Japan
Communication Engineering Research Center (CERC), Shenzhen Graduate School, Harbin Institute of Technology, Shenzhen 518055, China

Shinsuke Konaka and Masatake Akutagawa
Graduate School of Advanced Technology and Science, Tokushima University, Tokushima 770-8501, Japan

Qinyu Zhang
Communication Engineering Research Center (CERC), Shenzhen Graduate School, Harbin Institute of Technology, Shenzhen 518055, China

Jeng-Fung Chen and Shih-Kuei Lo
Department of Industrial Engineering and Systems Management, Feng Chia University, Taichung 40724, Taiwan

Quang Hung Do
Department of Electrical and Electronic Engineering, Faculty of Information Technology, University of Transport Technology, Hanoi 100000, Vietnam

Udesh Oruthota, Furqan Ahmed and Olav Tirkkonen
Department of Communications & Networking, Aalto University, P.O. Box 13000 FI-00076 AALTO, Espoo, Finland

Bo Tian and Jingti Han
School of Information Management & Engineering, Shanghai University of Finance and Economics, Shanghai 200433, China

Kecheng Liu
Informatics Research Center, University of Reading, Reading RG6 6UD, UK

Feng Zhang and Yuetong Xu
College of Geography and Environment, Shandong Normal University, Jinan, 250014, China

Anhtuan Le and Kok Keong Chai
School of Electroic Engineering and Computer Science, Queen Mary University of London, London E1 4NS, UK

Jonathan Loo and Mahdi Aiash
School of Science and Technology, Middlesex University, London NW4 4BT, UK

Kaori Fujinami
Department of Computer and Information Sciences, Tokyo University of Agriculture and Technology, 2-24-16 Naka-cho Koganei, Tokyo 184-8588, Japan

Suman Saha and Satya P. Ghrera
Department of Computer Science and Engineering, Jaypee University of Information Technology, Waknaghat, Solan 173215, India

Xinpeng Zhang
School of Computer Science and Engineering, University of Electronic Science and Technology of China, Chengdu 611731, China
Logistic Information Center, Joint Logistics Department, Chengdu Military Region, Chengdu 610015, China

Chunxiang Xu and Xiaojun Zhang
School of Computer Science and Engineering, University of Electronic Science and Technology of China, Chengdu 611731, China

Taizong Gu, Zhi Geng and Guoping Liu
Logistic Information Center, Joint Logistics Department, Chengdu Military Region, Chengdu 610015, China

Index

A

Accelerometer, 98-99, 101-104, 117-118, 120

Activity Recognition, 98-99, 106, 117-120

Additive White Gaussian Noise (awgn), 31

Adverse Drug Reactions, 153, 169, 171-172

Artificial Neural Network (ann) Model, 18

B

Beta Distribution, 46-47, 50, 55-56, 58, 63

Big Data Supporting, 137, 139

Bpel (business Process Execution Language), 67

Business-to-consumer E-commerce, 46, 66

C

Channel Quality Indicator (cqi), 29

Closed-loop Feedback, 46, 55, 63

Closed-loop Feedback Computation Model, 46, 63

Cloud Storage, 137-145, 149-152

Cnc Millingmachine, 23

Community Detection, 121-123, 126-130, 132-136

Complex Network, 121-127, 129-130, 132-133

Computer Security, 66, 152, 185, 215-216

Coordinated Multiple Points, 1

Coordinated Multipoint (comp), 1

Cross-entropy (ce), 1-2

Cutting Vibration, 18-19

Cyberphysical Systems, 185, 188, 192, 198, 201-202, 204-205, 209-210, 213-214, 216-217

D

Decision Tree, 18, 20

Device Localization, 98, 100, 103, 108, 119

Downlink Miso Transmission, 28

Downlink Multi-cell System, 30

Dynamic Integrity Verification, 137, 139

Dynamical Reputation, 46-47, 54, 59-60, 63

E

Energy Efficiency, 1-2, 8-9, 14-16, 79, 94-96

F

Fault Injection Method, 201, 205

Feature Engineering, 153-154, 160, 169

Feature Selection, 98-99, 105, 108-109, 117-118, 120, 153-155, 160, 163-165, 169, 171

G

Geospatial Entity, 67

Geospatially Constrained Workflow Modeling, 67

H

Hermann Von Helmholtz's Concept of Measurement, 190

Heterogeneous Networks, 1, 16

Hetnets, 1-2, 16

Hu Moments, 173, 177-179

I

Information Security, 185, 213, 215

Intelligent Systems, 98

Inter Vehicle Communication (ivc), 197-198

Internal Threats, 79-82, 94-96

L

Local Trust Evaluation, 46

Local Trust Rating, 46

Locality Sensitive Hashing, 121-122, 124-126, 130, 133, 135

Long-term Evolution-advanced (lte-a), 1

M

Machine Learning, 27, 98, 100, 105, 108, 120, 134, 159, 168-169

Machine Tools, 18-20, 25

Machine Type Communications (mtc), 28

Measuring Security, 185-186, 192, 209, 213

Metalworking Sectors, 18

Metric Space, 121-122, 124-128, 133-134

Microelectromechanical Systems (mems), 98

Mobile Communication Systems, 1-2, 28

Moment Invariants, 173-175, 177-178, 183

N
Named Entity Recognition, 153-154, 170-171
Natural Language Processing, 153-154, 169-172

O
On-body Smartphone Localization, 98, 102
Opportunistic Sensing, 98

P
Privacy-preserving, 137-139, 142-145, 147, 149, 151-152

Q
Quality of Service (qos), 28

R
Radio Resource Management (rrm), 1-2, 33
Reputation Computation, 46, 53, 64, 66
Routing Protocol for Low Power and Lossy Network (rpl), 79
Rpl-based Network Topology, 79, 96

S
Security Assessment, 185-186, 192-193, 197-198, 205, 208-209, 211, 213-216
Signal-to-noise Plus Interference Ratios (sinrs), 28

Sinr Variability, 28, 30, 33-34, 38, 41
Social Media, 135, 153-155, 165, 168-172
Software Metrics, 185
Specification-based Ids, 79-85, 94, 96
Support Vector Machine, 18, 20, 27, 108-109, 169
System Model, 2-3, 30, 198
System Property, 185-187, 191, 213-214

T
Time-triggered Protocol (ttp), 201
Twitter Posts, 153-154, 158-159, 161, 164, 168, 172

U
Ultra-reliable Communication, 28, 44
Ultra-reliable Communications (urc), 28
Ultra-reliable Link Adaptation, 28
User Revocation, 137-139, 141, 151-152

W
Wearable Computing, 98
Weighted Central Moment, 173, 175, 177, 179
Weighting Function, 173-175, 177-178, 181-182
Word Embedding, 153, 167, 170, 172